Platform Engineering and Security

Security and compliance integration in software development lifecycle using platform engineering

Kuldeep Singh Tomar

Govindarajan Vishnuchithan

bpb

www.bpbonline.com

First Edition 2026

Copyright © BPB Publications, India

ISBN: 978-93-65892-406

LIMITS OF LIABILITY AND DISCLAIMER OF WARRANTY

To View Complete
BPB Publications Catalogue
Scan the QR Code:

Dedicated to

My beloved parents
Late Shri Bhagwan Singh Tomar and Late Smt Munni Devi
and
my wife Seema
and my sons Adiya and Aniket

- Kuldeep Singh Tomar

My beloved parents
Late Shri Vishnuchithan G and Smt Andal Nachiyar V
and
my wife Saranya
and my son Abhinav

- Govindarajan Vishnuchithan

About the Authors

- **Kuldeep Singh Tomar** is a cybersecurity leader and strategist with over 20 years of IT experience, currently heading the information security function at Games24x7, one of the largest online gaming companies in India. He is responsible for developing and executing the organization's cybersecurity strategy, vision, and programs, ensuring the protection and compliance of information assets and technologies across multiple platforms and products.

  His core competencies include cyber and cloud security, DevSecOps, business continuity, and regulatory compliance, as well as team leadership, project management, innovation, and education. He has successfully delivered multiple IT automation and security projects, working with interdisciplinary teams and partnering with business leadership. He has a passion for learning and sharing knowledge, and he has been a guest faculty at the Indian Law Institute, teaching computer security and cyber law. He holds a bachelor's and master's degree in computer science with various IT, cyber, and cloud-related certifications, such as ISO 42001 LA, CCSK, CIPP, CIPM, CISA, TOGAF, PMP, and CFA.

- **Govindarajan Vishnuchithan** heads platform engineering at RamSoft, where he leads DevOps, IT, FinOps, and information security functions, driving innovation, scalability, and operational excellence across the organization. A hands-on technologist and strategic leader, he combines deep technical acumen with a transformative vision to build and scale high-performing engineering teams.

  With over 20 years of experience in product development, Govindarajan has spearheaded large-scale cloud and platform transformations with a strong focus on automation, security, and developer empowerment. His expertise spans Kubernetes, observability, cloud cost optimization, and DevSecOps, enabling engineering cultures that are automation-first, self-service-oriented, and security-aware. Known for his pragmatic approach and passion for simplification, he continuously challenges the status quo while nurturing engineering excellence.

  A lifelong unlearner and systems thinker, Govindarajan brings the same curiosity and analytical rigor to his personal pursuits. Beyond work, he enjoys traveling to under-explored destinations and uncovering hidden gems. A keen investor, he loves analyzing stocks, not just for financial performance but to understand the invisible business dynamics shaping industries.

About the Reviewers

❖ **Naga Venkata P Janapareddy** is a distinguished leader in the IT industry with over 18 years of unparalleled experience. He is recognized as one of the foremost experts in Oracle DBA and Oracle EBS technologies, as well as a cloud solution architect. Renowned for his strategic vision and technical acumen, he excels in deploying and managing cutting-edge Oracle solutions that drive enterprise success. Over the years, he has partnered with customers, the engineering team, and product and program managers to build roadmaps, launch plans for database migrations, build scalable support structures, and recommend end-to-end security mechanisms while advocating for the customers and influencing product and service specifications within the roadmaps.

❖ **Hrushikesh Deshmukh** is a seasoned cloud and DevOps solutions architect with a distinguished career spanning industry leaders such as Apple Inc., Amazon, Fidelity Investments, Capital One, Teradata, Comcast, T-Mobile, AT&T, Fannie Mae, and others. With deep expertise in cloud migration strategies, infrastructure automation, CI/CD pipelines, containerization, and security best practices, he has been instrumental in driving cutting-edge digital transformations for global enterprises.

Recognized as a strategic cloud leader, innovative solutions architect, and technical visionary, he brings extensive experience in operational excellence, cross-functional leadership, and customer engagement. His ability to develop effective proposals, manage stakeholder relationships, and implement scalable cloud solutions has made him a trusted expert in the field. Passionate about advancing cloud technologies, he actively contributes to the tech community through research, publications, and speaking engagements at global conferences.

Acknowledgements

There are a few people I want to thank for the continued and ongoing support they have given me during the writing of this book. First and foremost, I would like to thank my wife for continuously supporting me in writing the book. I could have never completed this book without her support.

I am grateful to the course and the companies I have worked with (Play Games24x7 and Oracle India), which gave me support throughout the learning of DevSecOps and platform engineering.

Thank you for all the hidden support provided. I gratefully acknowledge Rajat Bansal (CTO, Games24x7), and Edie Edwards Gilmore (Sr. VP, Oracle US) for their encouragement and extended support. I would also like to thank my co-author, Govindarajan Vishnuchithan, and ex-colleague Sanjay Singh for sharing their views and multiple discussions on platform engineering.

I am deeply grateful to the team at BPB Publications for their generous support, which included providing the significant time needed to complete this book. Their willingness to accommodate the complexities of the dynamic field of platform engineering allowed for comprehensive coverage without creating an overly voluminous work.

- Kuldeep Singh Tomar

I would like to express my heartfelt gratitude to all those who have supported and encouraged me throughout the journey of writing this book. Foremost, I owe immense thanks to my wife for her unwavering support and patience; this book would not have been possible without her and my son.

I am also thankful to the organizations I have been part of, HP, Standard Chartered GBS, PlayGames24x7, and RamSoft, for providing a foundation that fostered my learning in DevSecOps and platform engineering. I especially appreciate the often-unseen support that made this endeavor achievable. My sincere thanks go to Vijay Ramanathan (CEO, RamSoft) and Siva Ramanathan (CTO, RamSoft) for their encouragement and ongoing support.

I would like to extend my appreciation to my co-author, Kuldeep Singh Tomar, and to my mentor, Sanjay Singh, for their insightful discussions and valuable perspectives on platform engineering.

I would also like to take a moment to remember my father, who passed away during the writing of this book. His values, advice, and knowledge continue to guide me. This book is a tribute to his memory and will always be a blessing and a reminder of him.

Lastly, I am deeply grateful to the team at BPB Publications for their generous and accommodating support. Their understanding of the ever-evolving nature of platform engineering enabled the creation of a work that is both comprehensive and focused.

- Govindarajan Vishnuchithan

Preface

This book covers platform engineering as a secure software delivery platform. Platform engineering is an emerging trend intended to modernize enterprise software delivery, particularly for digital transformation. Platform engineering is focused on enhancing developer productivity by reducing the complexity and uncertainty of modern software.

In the last few years, complex microservice architectures, technologies like Kubernetes, and approaches like **infrastructure as code** (**IaC**) have become an industry standard. Even simple tasks now require developers to have an end-to-end understanding of their toolchain, vastly increasing their load and leading to inefficiencies in their operations.

This book is divided into 11 chapters. The purpose of this book is to understand the methodologies to help individuals and organizations prepare for DevOps and platform journeys. This book is going to describe the building blocks of platform engineering.

The initial few chapters of this book will cover the core pillars of platform engineering and everything as code. Later chapters will cover designing and building toolchains and workflows that enable self-service capabilities for software engineering organizations in the cloud-native era, which is also referred to as the internal developer platform, covering the operational necessities of the entire lifecycle of an application. Knowledge gained from this book will help to gain an understanding of enabling organizations for their DevOps journey and reducing inefficiency in this system, codification of security and policy requirements, removing toils from the system, and building a platform as needed by the organization.

Chapter 1: Concepts of Platform Engineering – The first chapter lays the base for current challenges in DevOps practices and the journey from existing DevOps, security, and compliance practices in self-service to a developer and more automated manner as everything as code. This chapter will also talk about a few case studies and why organizations have started moving away from the current DevOps model. Readers will learn about the past practices and the evolution of platform engineering.

Chapter 2: Platform Culture and Product Mindset – This chapter will cover the shift from DevOps or traditional approach. Platform engineering has to adopt the product mindset for the development of the platform. The platform team cannot solve all developer problems while starting to build the platform. They have to use a product approach to start with a **minimum viable product** (**MVP**) and keep adding new features. This chapter will help the readers to learn the approach and methodology to start building a platform.

Chapter 3: Building Blocks and Architecture – This chapter will cover the pillars of platform engineering. Platform engineering is the discipline of designing and building toolchains and workflows that enable self-service capabilities for software engineering teams. These tools and workflows comprise an internal developer platform, which is often referred to as just a platform. In its simplest form, the platform may be seen as two components, a frontend comprising one or more end-user interfaces and a backend that provides the necessary infrastructure, services, and tooling automation to the frontend, therefore, enabling end users to use these capabilities in a self-service manner for better productivity, accelerated product development, and consistent security and governance policy control.

Chapter 4: Build Infrastructure with Security and Compliance - This chapter will cover how stitching and automation include provisioning basic infrastructure resources like virtual private clouds, identity and access management roles, and load balancers to complex resources like Kubernetes clusters, complete environments, by using IaC and GitOps practices to provision infrastructure. Security teams define a security framework and a baseline security posture for all the components, services, and infrastructure that the entire organization uses. The security baseline policies include single sign-on and role-based access controls, network security, **Open Policy Agent (OPA)** for implementing granular compliance and security policies at the resource level, image scanning for vulnerabilities, runtime container security, CIS benchmark tests, etc.

Chapter 5: Platform and DevSecOps – This chapter will cover how platform engineering eases the burden of DevOps by providing an internal development platform that serves as a golden path for developers, and an internal developer platform can simplify the practice of DevSecOps. DevSecOps requires a shift (also known as shift left) in culture, process, and tools across development, security, and operations teams to make security a shared responsibility. From testing for security vulnerabilities to building business-driven security services, everyone is accountable for building security into the DevOps **continuous integration and continuous delivery (CI/CD)** workflow. By ensuring security is an integral part of the entire development lifecycle, DevOps teams can deliver secure applications with speed and quality and prevent future vulnerabilities. Dev teams have a centralized view of vulnerabilities, and they can plan to resolve vulnerabilities as part of their release plan.

Chapter 6: Platform Engineering and Containerization - This will cover how platform engineers are tasked with ensuring high availability and fault tolerance for applications, which often involves setting up redundant systems, implementing failover strategies, and orchestrating seamless transitions in case of failures. The open-source container orchestration platform has swiftly risen to prominence as a powerful solution that directly addresses the challenges faced by platform engineers. Kubernetes steps in as a unifying force, providing a standardized platform for deploying, managing, and scaling applications, irrespective of their underlying intricacies. By encapsulating applications in containers, Kubernetes abstracts away the specifics, enabling platform engineers to treat every application consistently.

Chapter 7: Embed Security and Compliance in Platform – This chapter will cover how platform engineering goes beyond application-level security to focus on securing the entire platform, including the underlying infrastructure and tools that host and manage applications. We will look at embedding security and compliance early, focusing on applications, utilizing specialized tools, such as **Static Application Security Testing (SAST)** and **Dynamic Application Security Testing (DAST)**, and incorporating security policies into the application code.

Chapter 8: Self-service for Developers – This chapter will cover how platform teams build shared tools and services to help development teams develop, deploy, and operate cloud infrastructure on a self-service basis. This includes cloud infrastructure, container orchestration platforms, databases, networking, monitoring, code repositories, and deployment pipelines. By providing developers with infrastructure and tools to deploy and operate their applications efficiently, platform engineers enable developers to focus on building great software.

Chapter 9: Productization and Collaboration – This chapter will cover how platform engineering teams are the backbone of the tech ecosystem within a company, often interacting with various departments, including development, operations, product, security, and more. Engineers must understand and cater to different technical needs and grasp the broader business context. Ultimately, effective collaboration is not just about processes and practices; it is also about culture. Fostering a culture of respect, understanding, and mutual support can go a long way in improving collaboration. This does not happen overnight, but investing in it can pay significant dividends in the long run.

Chapter 10: Data Lake and Observability – This chapter will cover how observability tools allow developers to efficiently monitor the performance of applications in production and testing environments, troubleshoot cloud services, and make informed decisions on how to improve their applications. In platform engineering architecture, observability is a key aspect to achieve the key metrics, such as MTTD, MTTR, and you can only achieve it when you have a data lake to keep all the required data and have a governance model for real-time issue and anomaly detection, auto-discovery and integrations across different control planes and environments, accurate alerting, tracing, logging, and monitoring, tagging, labeling, and data-model governance, and observability as code.

Chapter 11: Future Trends of Platform Engineering – This chapter will cover emerging technologies and trends, such as serverless computing and edge computing, which will continue to shape the future of platform engineering. AI and machine learning are going to transform platform engineering by helping teams automate and optimize many aspects of software development, including testing and monitoring. This will lead to faster development cycles and improved efficiency. The future of platform engineering is exciting, with emerging technologies like AI and ML set to play an even more significant role in platform engineering. As businesses continue to undergo digital transformation, platform engineering will remain a key enabler of success.

Code Bundle and Coloured Images

Please follow the link to download the
Code Bundle and the *Coloured Images* of the book:

https://rebrand.ly/90d1ff

The code bundle for the book is also hosted on GitHub at
https://github.com/bpbpublications/Platform-Engineering-and-Security.
In case there's an update to the code, it will be updated on the existing GitHub repository.

We have code bundles from our rich catalogue of books and videos available at
https://github.com/bpbpublications. Check them out!

Errata

We take immense pride in our work at BPB Publications and follow best practices to ensure the accuracy of our content to provide with an indulging reading experience to our subscribers. Our readers are our mirrors, and we use their inputs to reflect and improve upon human errors, if any, that may have occurred during the publishing processes involved. To let us maintain the quality and help us reach out to any readers who might be having difficulties due to any unforeseen errors, please write to us at: errata@bpbonline.com

Your support, suggestions and feedbacks are highly appreciated by the BPB Publications' Family.

At www.bpbonline.com, you can also read a collection of free technical articles, sign up for a range of free newsletters, and receive exclusive discounts and offers on BPB books and eBooks. You can check our social media handles below:

Instagram

Facebook

Linkedin

YouTube

Get in touch with us at: business@bpbonline.com for more details.

Piracy

If you come across any illegal copies of our works in any form on the internet, we would be grateful if you would provide us with the location address or website name. Please contact us at business@bpbonline.com with a link to the material.

If you are interested in becoming an author

If there is a topic that you have expertise in, and you are interested in either writing or contributing to a book, please visit www.bpbonline.com. We have worked with thousands of developers and tech professionals, just like you, to help them share their insights with the global tech community. You can make a general application, apply for a specific hot topic that we are recruiting an author for, or submit your own idea.

Reviews

Please leave a review. Once you have read and used this book, why not leave a review on the site that you purchased it from? Potential readers can then see and use your unbiased opinion to make purchase decisions. We at BPB can understand what you think about our products, and our authors can see your feedback on their book. Thank you!

For more information about BPB, please visit www.bpbonline.com.

Join our Discord space

Join our Discord workspace for latest updates, offers, tech happenings around the world, new releases, and sessions with the authors:

https://discord.bpbonline.com

Table of Contents

CHAPTER 1
Concepts of Platform Engineering

Introduction

This chapter will cover the background and history of DevOps, security, and compliance practices concerning self-service by developers and the development of platform engineering across the industry. Platform engineering enables software development teams to deliver faster and error-free software. This helps companies with development and user experience. In this chapter, we will explain the different definitions of platform engineering and its high-level architecture. This chapter will also explain the importance of codifying everything.

Structure

The chapter covers the following topics:

- Platform engineering and history
- Challenges in DevOps practices
- Codification of everything
- Platform adoption case studies

Objectives

At the end of this chapter, you will understand the background and history of platform engineering and its adoption and evolution by market leaders. This chapter will also cover some case studies on adopting platform engineering globally and by market leaders.

Platform engineering and history

DevOps is a term coined by *Patrick Debois,* a technologist. This inspired many companies to do multiple daily deployments, which means quick delivery. Everyone who understands DevOps knows what it takes from tooling, culture, trust, and refined working methods. It changed the way time is spent, how communication happens, how team members feel ownership of their work, and how teams focus on organizational velocity instead of local and sequential processes.

Organizations had started building **internal developer platforms** (IDP) and integrating tools that were easier for developers to use independently of Ops. However, an established discipline did not exist until 2019, when a group started the first platform engineering meetup in Berlin. During the first meeting, some engineers were frustrated with DevOps adoption at their organizations.

The DevOps team has helped some software development teams increase productivity and efficiency. However, it has become a bottleneck for many other companies due to inefficient adoption.

You build it, you run it. DevOps helped some software teams boost productivity and efficiency, but it was harrowing for everyone else.

For many organizations, including digital native businesses, challenges included the growing complexity of cloud-native technologies and architectures, and a rapid release cycle. Development teams burn out trying to ship code fast under an increasingly high cognitive load. Ops teams were engaged in tickets from developers and overwhelmed by their DevOps setups. **Dev + Ops (DevOps)** was frustrated and did not help with productivity increase; something needed to change.

Evan Bottcher, in 2018, gave a name to the platform these organizations were building. He defined this digital platform (IDP) as *a building block of self-service APIs, tools, services, knowledge, and support*. The idea is that platforms are and should be treated as products for organizations and a foundation of platform engineering.

In August 2022, many people started talking about how DevOps is dead and started hailing platform engineering.

Other participating organizations have also started coming up with a **reference architecture**. *McKinsey & Company* has also developed a reference architecture that companies can use irrespective of their cloud service providers, **Amazon Web Services (AWS)**, **Google Cloud Platform (GCP)**, or Microsoft Azure.

Tip: **A reference architecture is a generic architecture that identifies and outlines the system. It provides the foundation and outlines generic elements, relationships, principles, and guidelines required for architecture.**

The following reference architecture helped organizations to adopt the platform development faster with the required five main planes:

- **Developer control plane**: Configuration and main interaction layer for the developers and other teams.

- **Integration and delivery plane**: Used for building and storing images, creating applications with infrastructure configurations.

- **Resource plane**: Here, actual infrastructure exists, such as clusters, database, storage, etc.

- **Monitoring and logging plane**: Provide real-time metrics and logs for application, infrastructure, and audit.

- **Security plane**: It helps to manage identity, secrets, and sensitive information.

Refer to the following figure:

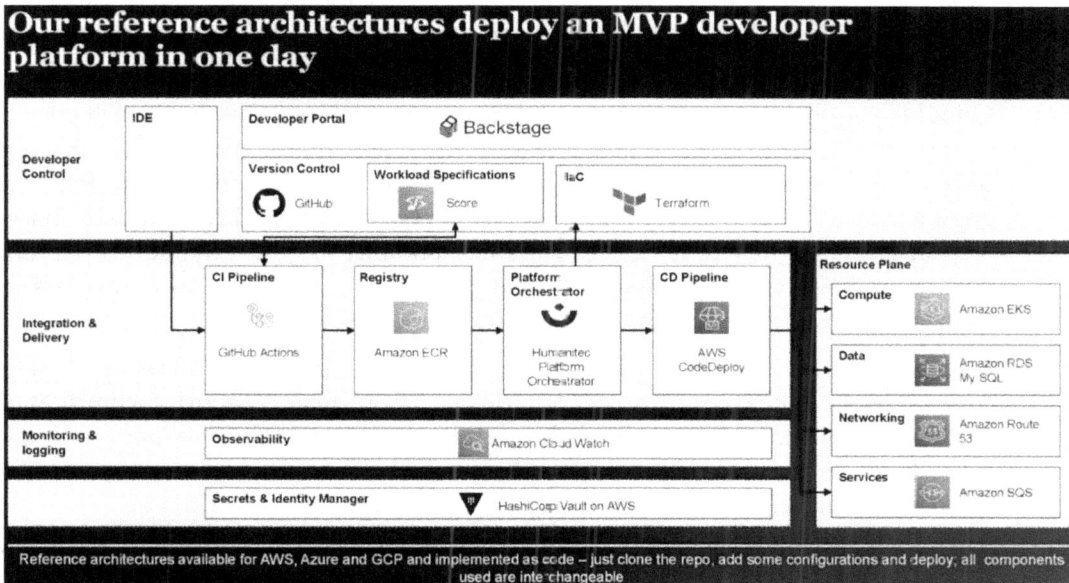

Figure 1.1: *Platform engineering reference architecture by McKinsey & Company*

Source: *https://www.youtube.com/watch?v=RD5krNEGspg*

Platform engineering

Platform engineering is a new branch that includes designing and building toolchains and workflows that enable self-service capabilities as a developer experience for software engineering teams. These tools and workflows comprise an IDP, which is often referred to as just the **developer platform**. An IDP team aims to increase developer productivity, facilitate frequent releases, improve application stability, lower information security and compliance risks, and reduce costs.

Platform engineering is the new technology that can help deliver applications and the pace at which they produce business value as customer experience.

The DevOps model introduces a cognitive load on the developers expected to handle pipeline deployment and successfully run the services they develop. This causes slower onboarding, reduced productivity, and operational fatigue, resulting in poor developer experience and increasing feature lead time for the organization.

Some of the industry leaders' views on platform engineering:

- **Gartner**: Platform engineering is the latest technology approach that can accelerate the delivery of applications using self-service by the development teams (Dev experience) and the pace at which they produce business value (customer experience).

  IDP improves developer experience and productivity by providing self-service capabilities with automated infrastructure provisioning and operations. This trend is increasing because it promises to optimize the developer experience and accelerate product teams' delivery of business value.

- **Google**: As per Google, platform engineering practice helps build self-service infrastructure and hide the complexity within an organization, unify different utility tools, and accelerate developer experience and productivity. Platform engineering's practice aims to mitigate the cognitive overload caused by a shared responsibility model and help companies enhance day-to-day developer and customer experience. The Google Cloud team is one of the pioneers in working with the Humanitec team for the quick adoption of IDP.

- **Microsoft**: As per Microsoft, platform engineering is a practice built using DevOps principles that helps to improve each development team's security, compliance, costs, and time-to-business value through improved developer experiences and self-service within a secure, governed framework. The software development life cycle has changed drastically in the last two decades.

  We have seen the world moving from 2-tier (client-server architecture) to n-tier distributed architecture, and now to a microservice-based architecture. Multiple teams work on their assigned microservice, and the release cycle is rapid. Building and deploying cloud-native applications is much more complex than the 2-tier architecture applications.

- **Atlassian**: As per Atlassian, *platform engineering teams create capabilities that product teams can use with little overhead and effort. Platform teams help minimize the resources and cognitive load of the Product Teams. Platform teams can help a better customer and developer experience by enabling them to develop/release faster without dependency on*

DevOps, IT, or Infosec teams. These teams spend their time on helpful contributions rather than toils (operational work).

According to *Martin Fowler* and *Evan Bottcher, an IDP is a foundation of self-service APIs, tools, services, knowledge, and support arranged as a compelling internal product that integrates with required tools. This helps them to provision infrastructure quickly and build and deploy their release with all the required guardrails (quality, security, testing, and compliance) built into the tool. With reduced coordination, autonomous delivery teams can use the platform to deliver product features faster.*

Attributes of platforms

For a successful IDP, there are some key attributes:

- **The platform itself is a product**: It has a product life cycle. Rather than working on operational tasks, the platform team started developing the internal product to help developers use the platform as a **self-service platform (SSP)** rather than raising a ticket with the DevOps team.

- **Developer experience**: The development team is a customer of the *platform team*; their goal is to provide a platform to help them build and deploy their code faster without thinking about other concerns.

- **Developer onboarding**: Another objective for the *platform team* is to onboard developers quickly on the IDP. The developer shall be productive on his first day of joining.

- **Prescriptive paved way**: It is a set of recommended and supported development **production paths** and **practices** that are a way to develop and use internal platforms. **Paved paths** in an IDP are designed to help developers through critical requirements and standards without sacrificing quick release. The following is the list of the prescriptive paved way:
  - Boilerplate source code
  - A quick-start tutorial
  - **Infrastructure as code (IaC)** template
  - Dependency management
  - CI/CD pipeline template
  - Kubernetes configuration (YAML)
  - Policy guardrails
  - Logging and monitoring (observability)
  - Cloud infrastructure as code template
  - Cost visibility to the management
  - Reference documentation

The following figure explains the flow of application development and deployment with golden paths adopted by development teams and enforced by platform engineering:

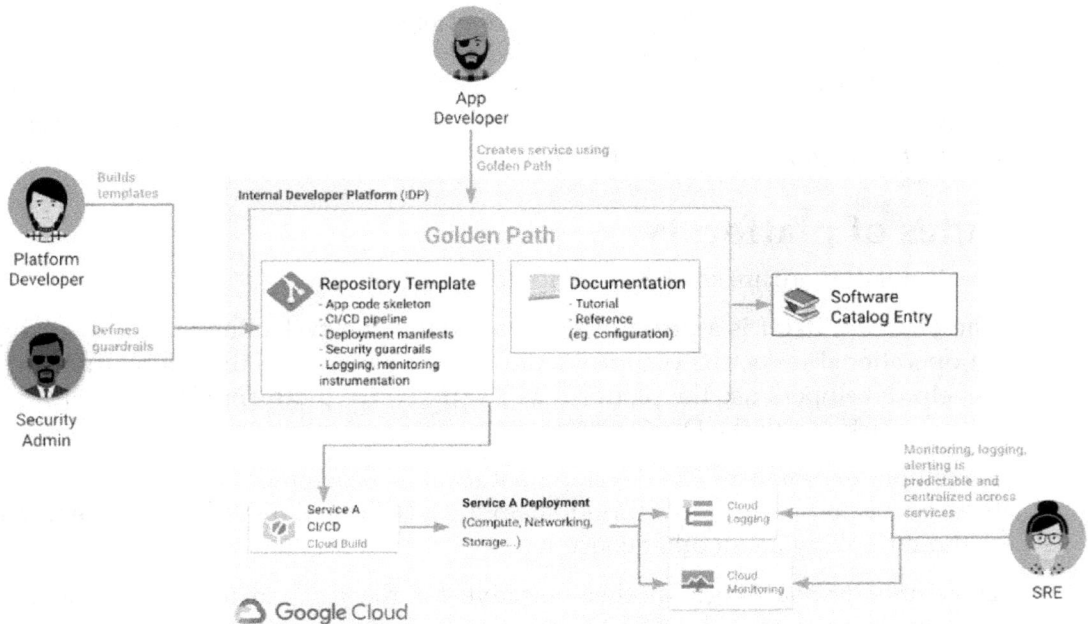

***Figure 1.2:** Platform engineering with Golden Path*

***Source:** https://cloud.google.com/blog/products/application-development/*
golden-paths-for-engineering-execution-consistency

- **Composability**: Platforms can combine or connect different components or elements to create an integrated platform.

- **Extensibility**: The platform team can continue adding new functionality or modifying existing functionality.

- **Secure by design**: Secure by design principles shall be integrated during the design and build phase of a product's development lifecycle to reduce the number of vulnerabilities before the product's release. Products should be secure by default, secure configurations should be enabled by default, and required security features such as multi-factor authentication, logging, and **single sign-on** (**SSO**) should be available at no additional cost.

- **Secure at runtime**: This is the process of protecting workloads, software systems, and applications from security vulnerabilities during their execution in the production environment. It means that runtime security measures are implemented and monitored while the application runs, ensuring that all critical data and processes are secure.

Guiding principles

The following are the guiding principles:

- Standard opinionated and prescribed way
- A more superficial facade to complex cross-cutting concerns to reduce cognitive load
- Internal developer portal for performing self-service and centralized visibility
- Seamless developer journey for the path to production
- Transparent abstraction over organizational structures and processes
- Open for permissible extensions and customizations

Challenges in DevOps practices

Moving from the waterfall model to the agile way of working, DevOps has helped with faster software delivery. However, adopting cloud computing and containerization requires better integration and productization in the form of a **platform**. There are specific challenges in DevOps practices that have led to the development and adoption of platform engineering.

Monolithic to microservices

Many organizations have a complex monolithic architecture, and it is not easy for them to move from legacy technology. However, at the same time, companies need digital transformation. Sticking to complex monolithic architecture limits the company's prospects. If they start moving to a newer microservices architecture, it will enable faster development and innovation. Transitioning to microservices from monolithic does not come without challenges, the most significant being the increased complexity and drastic changes in the current architecture.

The organization should have the required automated configuration management, automation baselines, and **continuous integration and continuous delivery (CI/CD)**.

Change management

Change is essential for the growth of an organization. However, it is not easy for many people who have been doing something in a particular manner to resist changes. DevOps implementation, therefore, should not be an enforced decision for the people. This is a cultural change, and DevOps shall be adopted as the company's culture. This change shall be driven by expert practitioners or consultants to establish the right DevOps culture. It could begin with an existing small product set and adopt DevOps practices. Such small projects could help people learn, experiment, and overcome some of the technical challenges of DevOps. Once this becomes part of the organization's culture, it is easier to integrate with all the products and projects.

Tools adoption and integration with existing ecosystem

Automating everything is impossible, and you need tools to harness DevOps effectively; teams face challenges in selecting various tools for development, testing, and deployment, and working in an integrated platform. There is a learning curve for each tool, too.

The tools selection process also posed a considerable challenge to the teams as they needed to meet security requirements and integrate easily with their infrastructure. There is also **adequate training for developers on new tools** so that productivity is not compromised for the users. The ultimate idea is to automate many things and reduce the manual touchpoints. So, if teams have standard interfaces and need not worry about working on new tools, they can quickly adopt them.

Data-driven using DevOps metrics

The saying goes, *Whatever you cannot measure, you cannot improve*. Therefore, determining the metrics that are the most relevant and valuable for a particular organization is crucial. It is also one of the top challenges in business transformation because a wide range of metrics is available as **DevOps Research and Assessment (DORA)** matrices to measure the effectiveness and efficiency of a DevOps process:

- Deployment frequency
- Lead time for changes
- Mean time to recover from failures
- Defect escape rate

Organizations could adopt a data-driven approach to identify and track DORA metrics[1]. It can involve using tools and platforms for analytics to collect and visualize data on various metrics of the DevOps process. It can help organizations find the right metrics and identify the patterns and trends in their data. It will also help them to focus on areas where they may be able to improve their processes. It also helps to identify the bottlenecks or other issues. Data and metrics are the way to make transitions and improvements.

Secure DevOps

Secure DevOps means security needs are built in and adequately integrated throughout development. It is very different from the traditional approaches, where security is a barrier to the rapid development and deployment of code. Organizations adopting a continuous delivery model, where code changes are made and deployed frequently, cannot work in a traditional model where security is an afterthought and has a lengthy review and sign-off process.

---

1 DORA provides a standard set of DevOps metrics used for evaluating process performance and maturity, which are called DORA metrics.

Organizations could use the DevSecOps approach to integrate security into code integration, build, and deployment processes. DevSecOps integrates security into the DevOps at each stage. It involves collaborating with security, Dev, and operations teams to build and deploy compliant and secure systems with required security guardrails continuously and fully automated.

To adopt and implement the DevSecOps approach, organizations must adopt required security scanning tools, such as **Static Application Security Testing (SAST), Software Composition Analysis (SCA)**, automated testing, and **Dynamic Application Security Testing (DAST)**, to identify the security issues early in the development cycle and fix them too. This cycle starts from day one when the developer begins doing thread modeling, developing code, or building with security tools.

Cross-functional teams and collaboration

Organizations have cross-functional teams in a DevOps environment. These team members should have the necessary skills and knowledge to collaborate effectively and deliver products. Building and establishing a team with the needed skills can be very challenging. DevOps team members need diverse skills and expertise, including development, operations, security, and testing. They need to have knowledge and experience in end-to-end development and operational tasks.

However, finding a person with all the required skills is challenging and time-consuming. Many organizations find it very difficult and prefer to hire and train people. DevOps teams can create a culture of ownership and collaboration within the organization.

According to *Lewis Stevens,* Sr Cloud DevOps and Infra Engineer in one of the prominent organizations, *the main challenge in DevOps is the developers or the operations teams finding it difficult to work on each other's repositories.*

So, collaborating with cross-functional teams is the best way to solve these issues.

DevOps Center of Excellence

Center of Excellence (COE) ensures that the teams successfully implement and adopt secure DevOps practices. COE comprises team members with the required skill set and helps the organization build the required practices and processes.

COE effectively supports and facilitates the development, build, and deployment processes across the organization in a standard manner. COE must collaborate and coordinate with multiple teams and functions across the organization and may need to juggle different priorities and demands. However, COE contains a set of experts to remove these challenges.

One way to solve this DevOps challenge is to start adopting a collaborative and consultative approach to the build COE model. COE works closely across the teams, understands their requirements, and provides guidance and support as needed. The COE team can help the organization quickly adopt and mature the DevOps practice.

Cost optimization

Most organizations have started moving to the public cloud for digital transformation. However, this leads to another challenge: organizations must ensure that DevOps environments have budget allocations and keep track of costs to align with the organization's needs.

With a wide range of tools and cloud services used by the DevOps teams, it can be very challenging to determine which areas are most important and should be prioritized.

Companies could engage required stakeholders in budgeting to overcome this DevOps challenge. They also establish clear policies and procedures for reviewing costs and allocating resources. Development and deployment teams must ensure that resources are used effectively to support their product's development and deployment processes.

Cost optimization is a crucial goal for all organizations. Development and DevOps teams need to ensure that the provisioned infrastructure is sized correctly per capacity planning and that these resources are scalable in case of a requirement.

Solving these challenges

DevOps culture was a big help to organizations where the release cycle is rapid. Their business is dependent upon quick feature release. However, the challenges mentioned above persist after adopting DevOps. Organizations have started moving to IDP to solve the above challenges. IDP is a collection of tooling built by platform engineers and used by developers for build and deployment. IDP is often a heterogeneous tool chain stitched together to minimize cognitive load for developers without abstracting away significant meaning.

There is no fixed set of tools to build the platform. It can be categorized as follows:

- **Code development: Integrated development environments (IDEs)** like VS Code, Eclipse, and JetBrains.
- **Version control systems (VCS)**: Bitbucket, GitHub, GitLab, etc.
- **Containers**: Docker, Kubernetes, databases, storage, compute, transit, etc.
- **Container registries**: Docker Hub, ECR, etc.
- **Observability**: Datadog, Grafana, Sumo Logic, etc.
- **Vulnerability scanners**: ZAP, Burp, Nessus, etc.
- **CI tools**: CircleCI, GitHub Action, and Bitbucket.
- **GitOps tools**: Argo CD.
- **IaC**: Terraform, Ansible, and Pulumi.
- **Platform Orchestrators**: Humanitec, Shipa.
- **Internal developer portals**: Configure8 or Backstage.

Most organizations already use these tools at different code development and deployment stages, but not as a platform with usability, scalability, and guardrail limitations.

IDP can help to provide interfaces such as **application programming interface** (**API**), **command-line interface** (**CLI**), and integration with **customer experience** (**CX**) tools to execute self-serve actions. The primary benefit of self-serve actions is not to consume the developer's time for repetitive, time-consuming work (toils) and wiring components together in code while increasing productivity, consistency, and reliability. Here are some of the benefits of using IDP:

- **Microservice architecture**: Microservices development includes providing a boilerplate code for a new service, deploying, reverting, upgrading a package version, etc.

- **Provisioning of dev stack**: Allow teams to create a developer's stack and terminate after their work is done. They do not need an Infra/DevOps team to create a development or test environment. A newly created environment has all the required guardrails and associated costs visible to the development team.

- **Cloud resources**: The team has resource provisioning, modification, and access request capabilities available.

- **Data engineering**: Running an Airflow **directed acyclic graph** (**DAG**), creating a remote Jupyter scaffolding notebook, pre-processing data, etc.

- **Scalability and performance**: Allow the team to update auto-scaling groups, pod counts, etc.

Codification of everything

It is easy for machines to understand the code. It is easy for developers to maintain the code. This code can be kept in VCS for versioning. You can quickly make changes and deploy. In a disaster, you have a code backup and can reconstruct everything.

Everything as code (**XaC**) is not a technology but a practice of treating all components of the system as code. Companies can store configuration and source code in a repository and maintain a **software development life cycle** (**SDLC**) for all components. It allows companies to store configurations from bottom to top, such as communication switches, bare metal servers, operating systems, build configurations, application properties, and deployment configurations, as tracked code that can be recreated at the click of a button. This means all teams, including architects, developers, Infra, QA, and Infosec, must focus on codification and best practices.

Currently, no company or intelligent bit of code makes XaC a reality. XaC is a philosophy; it is as simple as expressing the application in as many parts as possible, and the team can codify the infrastructure. A few examples are as follows:

- If you want to create a new infrastructure, you have a standard code available to provision this infrastructure.

- You need to build and deploy your application. You need a pipeline; this pipeline service is available as code to launch it anywhere.

- You need monitoring services for your deployed application to observe any performance or downtime. Monitoring and observability services are available as code to deploy along with your application deployment.

The code defining your infrastructure and services should be treated like your team's application code. It should be checked into VCS, and the code shall be reviewed, tested, and open for regular modification by the team working on this code. This code is available and understood by cross-teams as well.

We can compare this with cloud computing systems over the last decade. The earliest versions of DevOps teams focused purely on quickly launching and configuring a single system to work. As they have migrated applications to the cloud, companies have shifted their approach from relatively large monolithic services to microservices. Now, they do not need big servers to host their services; instead, they can quickly deploy their services to small servers and horizontally scale their servers. Application or system configuration moved from just configuring a single server to configuring services comprising interconnected multiple logical servers and scaling them quickly.

These practices include using code to configure as much as possible and storing that code in **version control systems (VCS)**, VCS, just like any other code, known as GitOps. People's first reaction after hearing GitOps is that it is an alternative to DevOps, but it is essential to understand that they do not work in opposition; rather, they complement each other.

Initial GitOps implementations have one identified flaw: the code and configuration files are logically distinct. To a certain extent, this made sense because the required tools similarly work with configuration and code. Today, that is no longer the case, and many teams practice the configuration for the infrastructure. It can be part of the same repositories and known as XaC.

Before going deep into XaC, it is crucial to understand the challenges that prompted a paradigm shift in automation. Manual processes:

- Introduced inconsistencies

- Delayed deployments

- Posed challenges in maintaining a standardized client experience

The demand for speed, reliability, security, and precision has led to the evolution of more automated solutions, leading to DevOps and, subsequently, XaC.

XaC is a new trend in the IT world. Teams can code to define and manage resources of all types, including infrastructure, application security requirements, and CI/CD processes across the software delivery pipeline. IaC focuses on managing servers, cloud infrastructure, and other resources with code; XaC takes a broader, code-centric approach to IT and Dev operations. Let us discuss how.

We have already said that XaC is not technology but philosophy.

Infrastructure as code

Think about creating thousands of servers manually or through some scripts. You need to select configuration or complex code into the script for each different type of server for various purposes (app servers, DB servers, mid-tier servers, caching servers). It is not scalable, leads to inconsistency or errors, and requires many person-hours to complete the job.

A pioneer in IaC technology is HashiCorp, known for Terraform. Adopting IaC ensures that the servers and services your application creates or maintains are defined by the code they run. IaC is the foundation of the XaC philosophy. IaC enables the provisioning and management of infrastructure through machine-readable script files (YAML, JSON), leading to unprecedented levels of automation and scalability. This approach not only accelerates the deployment of resources but also ensures repeatability and consistency, mitigating the risks associated with manual interventions. You can use IaC for on-prem or cloud deployment.

Configuration as code

For IaC, **configuration as code** (**CaC**) is the natural choice. Instead of simply defining the cloud resources your application needs, you also actively configure them in the code. CaC is pivotal in standardizing and automating the configuration management process.

Organizations consistently manage and implement performance and security for their IT environments by codifying the configuration. It streamlines the configuration process and enhances the security posture by reducing misconfigurations and drifts.

Security as code

Security is the biggest concern in the new digital era. Security is no longer an afterthought process. It needs to be baked in different stages of the development life cycle.

Security as code (**SaC**) is an approach that integrates practices seamlessly into the development lifecycle. Defining and maintaining security policies as code to ensure security is an integral part of the development and deployment process, and not an afterthought:

- Organizations can automate security checks through a continuous scan
- Vulnerability assessments
- Compliance monitoring

SaC and DevSecOps aim to integrate security into the development lifecycle, but differ in their focus. SaC emphasizes treating security **policies as code** (**PaC**), enabling automation of security checks and compliance monitoring within the development process. On the other hand, DevSecOps is a philosophy promoting collaboration and shared responsibility among development, operations, and security teams throughout the entire development pipeline. SaC is a specific practice within the larger DevSecOps framework, concentrating on code-centric automation (SAST, SCA, and DAST scans) for security measures. Now, security teams' focus is more on maintaining security checks and gates through the declarative code for different environments (Dev, QA, and Prod) and not making changes manually to various environments.

Pipelines as code

In the digital era, teams do not need to build and deploy code manually. Pipelines are the heart of the CI/CD process. However, maintaining pipelines requires expertise from another stream of knowledge. As your number of builds and deployments increases, pipelines are choked, and development becomes slow.

PoC is a software development concept that has recently gained momentum. The team has started moving the entire software delivery pipeline as code. Teams can define pipeline stages, steps, tasks, and configurations as code. Before this, software development pipelines were determined using custom scripting languages. Now, pipeline as code can include everything the application needs as code.

Adopting a CI/CD pipeline is a common benefit of DevOps adoption. Instead of manually deploying code to servers, your continuous build and deployment pipeline pushes that code to the selected environment as soon as developers merge their code. PaC also configures those pipelines within the code repository, just like the infrastructure and configuration code.

One of the significant advantages of DevOps is adopting a CI/CD pipeline. As developers merge code, your constant deployment pipeline delivers that code to the appropriate environment, removing the need for manual server deployment.

Additionally, teams can version control and collaborate by treating the pipeline configuration as code. It ensures a seamless and reproducible workflow.

Policy as code

Policies are regulations that can be standardized and applied to various systems. In a fast-paced environment, the compliance team cannot create a policy as a document and maintain multiple versions of the same document. It is difficult for the development team to understand and follow the policies written by the compliance team.

Consider PaC, a system of guidelines that specify guardrails for noncompliance or violations. The compliance team can write and implement policy, and developers will not have to update the app or infrastructure or worry about it breaking or being altered by policy implementation and changes. It implies that teams can modify the policy's coding without modifying the app's coding. PaC differs from SaC as this is more like a superset involving policies confined to security and other organizational and industry standards, frameworks, and regulatory requirements.

However, as said previously, XaC is not a technology but a philosophy where organizations can codify their **computing environment** and **data analytics** as code.

Environments as code

Almost all cloud service providers, including Google Cloud Platform's Compute Engine, such as Google Cloud Deployment Manager and Amazon's EC2, use the CloudFormation template to create computing environments as code.

Scripting engines allow teams to create computing environments in a machine-readable script, facilitating the automated deployment and configuration of resources. It reduces the dependency on the manual creation of resources and enables faster deployment and delivery of products, irrespective of the selected cloud service provider.

Dev setup as code

It is essential for any product team member to join in, and the Dev setup is done quickly with a standard Dev setup.

However, the Dev setup is often more personal, which leads to configuration drift. Even if two developers on the same team work on the same technology, they have the same Dev setup. It leads to *it is working on my machine, not yours*. It often leads to slower onboarding.

Organizations can bring standardization by codifying the development setup for a given technology team. However, they have the freedom to explore and innovate new technologies. The environment should be composable and disposable.

Documentation as code

It is now that developers are maintaining their documents in wikis and shared folders. Teams have started moving away from static pages. Such practices led to stale documents.

Code is continuously modified throughout SDLC, and all documents created outside of code repositories are not keeping pace with the rate of code changes being updated. A better way to avoid this drift is to maintain the documentation related to the code base as part of the same repository.

The documentation is standard across multiple code repositories, or generic documentation can be maintained in a standalone repository where the documentation can be edited like any other code and undergo pull requests and merges. A pipeline can perform validation, and document conversion can happen as part of the pipeline steps. It can be published to documentation sites or shared folders, etc.

Data analytics as code

Data analytics is the key to any organization. They must look at the current business trends, user behavior, and forecasting. Data science teams are an integral part of any organization. Machine learning and data pipelines can be translated into code. Data scientists can transfer data analytics components from one project to another using data pipelines as code.

Diagram as code

It is essential for all teams to create and manage the architecture diagrams. They must manage the architecture diagram for all the components and their solutions.

Diagramming is the most complex and non-standardized part of documentation. By codifying the diagrams, we can achieve standardization and take them through the process of CI/CD to keep them up-to-date.

Architecture diagrams can be maintained as code. Codifying the diagram helps assess design-level indicators and drift continuously as part of continuous integration.

Threat modeling as code

Security and risk teams often use threat modeling to identify the application's security risks. They can use different frameworks, such as the MITRE ATT&CK framework, to determine the risk.

This exercise is often repetitive, and threat modeling should also be codified to bring standardization. It helps the teams to continuously assess threat level indicators as part of SDLC, just like we do for application code. These risks are codified, and threat profiles can be created with the help of threat modeling as code.

Monitoring as code

Observability and monitoring are the most critical aspects of the SDLC. While developing code or fixing any issue, you need to look at the monitoring tools to troubleshoot any problem. You need observability tools to monitor or observe any performance issues with the application.

Monitoring as code refers to codifying and automating monitoring systems' configuration, deployment, and maintenance. It treats monitoring infrastructure, alerting rules, and dashboards as code, allowing for version control, collaboration, and automation throughout the monitoring lifecycle. Now, the teams can declaratively define their monitoring configurations, version control the same, and automate and apply guardrails. Tools like *Terraform, Ansible, K8s operators, Grizzly*, etc., can be used to achieve MaC.

Tip: **The preceding list of services as code is incomplete. All IT, Dev, and security operations can be extended with the help of codification. Adopting code at every stage of the software development lifecycle can help with automation and high-quality software delivery with fewer manual touchpoints.**

There are many reasons why technical teams started adopting an XaC approach:

- **Consistency and standardization**: As part of SDLC, teams work in a range of environments. Teams managing these environments can employ uniform configurations. Apart from uniform configurations, with the help of XaC, teams can prevent any configuration drift while setting up cloud resources, access control policies, CI/CD tools, or infrastructure in a unified manner. It led to standardized processes for software delivery.

- **Version control**: One of the significant advantages of XaC is that the team finds it more straightforward to define their configurations using a vendor-neutral code with the help of available tools. It is easy to manage different vendors' configurations with the help of code. Another significant advantage is the easier tracking of changes and rollbacks. It allows them to experiment and roll back in case any experiment fails.

- **Idempotency**: Idempotency is a key principle that enables platform engineers to build robust, reliable, and self-service platforms. It is the ability of an operation to be executed multiple times without changing the result beyond the initial application. Tools like Terraform and Ansible are designed with idempotency in mind. You can apply the same configuration multiple times, and the tool will only make changes if necessary to reach the desired state.

- **Interoperability**: One goal of every company is to avoid vendor lock-in and interoperability of their applications. After companies moved their applications into the cloud, one of the significant worries was vendor lock-in due to the use of native services provided and the cost associated with them. So, all companies want to keep their services vendor-neutral with the help of open-source or vendor-neutral tools and technologies.

- **Automation**: All IT operations, including managing operating systems, network setups, and pipelines for all the IT components, can be extended to include XaC. Teams can codify everything from the beginning to the end of the software development lifecycle. It leads to automation and faster delivery of high-quality products. Although automation is not a new buzzword, companies use automation for infrastructure creation, application deployment, using scripting, and build and deployment tools. The evolution of DevOps culture and new tools such as Terraform, Ansible, Chef, and pipeline software help automate and deliver software quickly.

- **Scalability**: In today's world, you can get everything at the click of a button. You can search, select, and order your desired items using your mobile or web application.

However, this leads to many transactions per second for all applications, and the scalability and performance of applications are key for all businesses. Teams can leverage duplicate configuration files and tools across large-scale settings, and XaC can assist teams in scaling operations. It also improves standardization across IT systems and procedures and lowers the possibility of human errors.

- **Auditability**: One significant aspect of all applications and compliance or regulatory requirements is logging all activities and auditing all code files. Engineers and administrators can automatically review and compare configuration resources with previous versions. Auditors can also visit and review any changes in line with the change management process. They have all the configuration and code change logs available for validation. Verifying the setup with this method is more efficient than examining each resource separately.

- **On-demand infrastructure**: One of the significant advantages of IaC is that infrastructure can be deployed whenever needed. This is also known as on-demand infrastructure. One can also dynamically create and remove environments with the help of DevOps pipelines. These pipelines can incorporate all the required security, cost, quality guardrails, and approval workflow. It helps the management team review required matrices and identify the critical issues for improvement.

- **Highly repeatable**: One of the significant challenges for the IT industry is retaining people. No person likes to keep doing repetitive and monotonous jobs. XaC eliminates the need for IT professionals to complete all the jobs manually. It not only increases morale and employee satisfaction but also saves a significant amount of time. Engineers can use the same time to learn, work on innovative tasks, and concentrate on higher-value work.

- **Eliminating human error risks**: XaC eliminates the manual touchpoints. It is evident that when everything is specified in code, there is no need to worry about an engineer forgetting to perform something or making an accidental error. The compliance team can also relax knowing everything is peer-reviewed, predictable, and consistent.

- **Security integration in the DevOps process**: Continuous security integration ensures the development lifecycle using *DevSecOps*, a significant advantage of XaC. Infrastructure and security rules are codified by XaC. It makes applying security controls consistently across environments and versioned configurations possible. It leads to a security-first, collaborative culture. It enables DevOps services workflows with proactive risk mitigation, quick reactions to threats, and adequate security documentation.

Suppose you can implement XaC correctly. In that case, it enables teams to set rules, quality, and security gates and then defer decision-making to the systems with the help of machine-readable configurations. It makes problem-solving and application development more accessible, allowing more individuals to participate in creating better-end products.

We can compare how the development world has moved from a **monolithic** to a **microservice world** and how it helps to reduce the release cycle. Refer to the following table:

Monolithic	Microservices
The cost of change is very high	The cost of change is low
Changes represent failure (need a good change management process)	Changes are quick
Reduce the opportunity to fail	Maximize the speed of improvement
Deliver in large batches, test at the end	Deliver small changes, test continuously
GUI or manual configuration changes	Configuration as code

Table 1.1: Monolithic vs. microservices

Platform adoption case studies

DevOps started as a buzzword around one and a half decades ago and tried to solve the problem of the waterfall model in an agile way. However, the DevOps model was quite challenging. Platform engineering has attempted to solve challenges, and some of the leading players in the industry have adopted and are working actively on platform engineering. Here are a few case studies for these major players.

Google Cloud

Google Cloud is integrating with Humanitec, a Platform Orchestrator. The Platform Orchestrator performs as follows:

- Integrates with the CI/CD pipeline to perform all the jobs initiated by the team in a self-service manner.
- After developers push their code changes, it reads the configurations to identify the resources required to run the application code.
- It provisions the identification resources by integrating with drivers that handle the actual interactions with infrastructure and services.
- The Platform Orchestrator generates the necessary configurations and executes deployments based on the configurations.

Google Cloud as a service provider and reference architecture implementation by Humanitec is available at the following URL: **https://humanitec.com/reference-architectures/gcp**.

Organizations can use the reference architecture code in the GitHub repo and implement the IDP. Refer to the following figure:

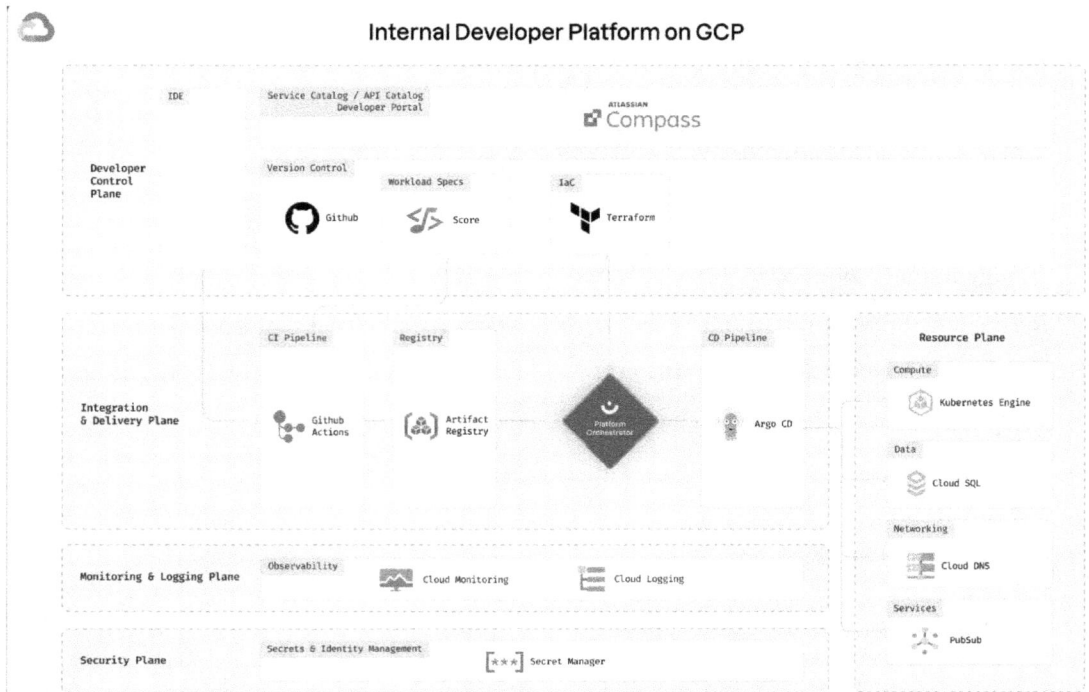

Figure 1.3: Humanitec reference architecture using Google Cloud Platform

Source: *https://github.com/humanitec-architecture/reference-architecture-gcp*

Building an IDP is not straightforward and has specific challenges. The Humanitec team has created a set of reference architectures for different cloud service providers based on hundreds of real-world setups. The reference architectures described in the code provide a reference code to build your own IDP quickly, along with customization capabilities to ensure your platform meets the unique needs of your users.

Microsoft platform engineering

Microsoft is one of the pioneers in adopting new technologies and best practices for its SDLC processes. Microsoft has started using platform engineering to improve the **developer experience (DevEx)** and increase product teams' delivery of **customer value (CustEx)**.

Gartner launched a survey and found that around 80 percent of engineering organizations will have a team dedicated to building a platform for them by 2026. These teams focus on creating an IDP, which is a Platform Orchestrator to help development teams and enhance customer experience.

Irrespective of the domain, sales lifecycle (Microsoft Dynamics, Salesforce), service fulfillment (ServiceNow), and communications (Twilio), platforms having a large user base are designed to achieve an immense scale and reduce the time it takes to deliver business value and experience.

Over the past two decades, the software development life cycle has changed dramatically. Code building and deploying distributed, cloud-native applications is a bit more complex than the classic client-server apps. Application builds and deployment interfaces with many tools to facilitate seamless collaboration across increasingly globally distributed and time-shifted teams. Open-source tools and libraries have become essential to every project.

Developers are overwhelmed by the complexity of these tools and services and are starting to face constant interruptions. They are expected to become experts in nearly everything, with a context of switching between these tools. This has impacted their cognitive load and ability to focus. We observe that:

- On a good day, most developers only spend approximately 1.5 hours coding.
- Developers use an average of 16 or more tools per day.
- It takes 23 minutes to regain focus after context-switching.

This leads to developers being exhausted very soon. It is incredibly inefficient for their organizations. Organizations want their developers to be more productive. They must also ensure their software is secure, compliant, and meets customer quality expectations. Customer experience is critical for all businesses. Businesses need to launch new services and features very quickly. It is tough using the legacy process-based and manual way of working.

The organization needs to focus on optimizing the software development lifecycle. It can only be achieved through developer experience and by adopting the practice of platform engineering. Developers can use the IDP to complete their tasks quickly without having dependencies on quality, DevOps, or Infosec teams. They can self-serve utilizing a platform to launch new infrastructure, build and deploy their code, and test automatically through testing automation.

Microsoft's platform engineering team has evolved the DevOps practice to improve team collaboration, security, quality, compliance, costs, and time-to-business value with self-service developer experiences within required security guardrails within a governed framework. The team focuses on maturing the platform for the Dev experience for faster delivery.

Microsoft has a team of developers who build tools and services for other developers. The internal and external teams of Microsoft have a culture that is like thinking of internal teams as the first customers. Over the past many months, Microsoft's own platform engineering team has brought a focus on the end-to-end developer experience and a product mindset. The platform has the power to eliminate toil throughout the software development lifecycle. It has helped to simplify operations for Dev teams at a large-scale. As software companies like Microsoft grow more prominent than ever before, there is also a need to drive consistency across their organization to build better business agility and enhance customer experience.

Developer experience

At Microsoft, **developer experience (DevEx)** is always at the core of any new development. The teams' focus is always on reducing cognitive load, increasing how quickly developers can be productive, and improving how efficiently they can build feedback loops into the system. It has helped significantly improve products and processes.

The platform engineering team at Microsoft makes sure of the following guidelines for IDP development:

- Developers are the primary customers when building an IDP, but they collaborate with other critical stakeholders.

- Organizations must prioritize the *paved path* sections that should be created first and ensure each path includes approaches to streamline onboarding, moderation, and advocacy for internal use.

- Matrices are essential to measure the platform's effectiveness and help the team retain talent. Matrices are critical for measuring speed, quality, ease of use, and whether internal customers are satisfied with the platform. The platform has helped them to build and deploy their code quickly.

- The development team cannot wait for other teams to react when dependencies are marked to them. Delivering self-service within guardrails can empower development teams to make decisions with required guardrails and gates. The stakeholders have established and agreed to these guardrails and gates. It allows developers to work independently while appropriately managing security, quality, compliance, operations, standards, and costs.

- There is no exception to IDP product and adoption motions. Teams can start with the *right template* to bootstrap the development process. Controls and governance through automated policy, security scanning, and testing throughout the project lifecycle. Quality, security, and compliance are shifted left into the developer experience, which can ensure that code and infrastructure will stay right.

- Prioritize automation without any manual touchpoints. What team chooses to automate first will depend on the organization and the developers' requirements. It is critical to plan and prioritize to meet the organization's needs; there is more than one starting point for tasks.

- One of the critical requirements for any organization is to eliminate sprawl and waste. These problems are significant and need to be corrected early in development. As the organization scales, duplicative efforts are discovered because one team does not know about the other team's work. Technical sprawl and waste can be reduced by improving the discovery and association of resources. Having a static inventory can help track these items significantly in the case of the cloud, where teams have multiple regions and associated resources managed by various teams.

- You can introduce the workflows for required governance and dev experience. Unified portals are the way forward for development, but this may or may not be the best approach. Meeting developers where they are in their workflows, in the code editors and code collaboration tools they use day-to-day, is critical for building up a platform engineering practice.

Developer happiness and customer experience

It is of utmost importance for teams to have the right tools, services, and systems support for efficient ways of working at scale. It helps them to achieve their goals without compromising quality, privacy, security, or compliance. Developers can apply their more creative aspects of collaboration and product making.

Developers who build quality products feel more purposeful and satisfied than ever before. Platform engineering helps them to achieve their goals.

To learn more about platform engineering by Microsoft, refer to the following links:

https://learn.microsoft.com/en-us/platform-engineering/

https://devblogs.microsoft.com/engineering-at-microsoft/building-paved-paths-the-journey-to-platform-engineering/

Platform engineering at Netflix

Netflix is one of the pioneer companies in achieving microservice architecture. They have found that this traditional approach is becoming complex and fragmented as the platform tooling grows. They needed to unify developer experiences and help them achieve the required quality and security across the company's SDLC.

To achieve the required features in SDLC, Netflix has created the **Platform Experiences and Design** (**PXD**) team. The PXD team at Netflix decided to build a platform. The Netflix platform console is a unified portal for all the engineers who must develop and deploy software. It consolidates many services and requires tools into a single, easy-to-use interface. It has made developers' lives easy and let them focus on their core jobs, i.e., writing code and providing services.

To achieve the required developer experience, Netflix has interviewed many developers and used the following feedback to build a platform:

- **Working on multiple tools**: Developers must work on too many tools daily, challenging learning, adapting, developing, delivering, and managing multiple services and software. It is not unusual for a developer to use VCS tools such as GitHub or Bitbucket to review poll requests, security tools (SAST, SCA, and DAST) for continuous scanning by deployment pipelines, pipeline tools (Jenkins, GitLab, CircleCI) to check on their build processes and observability tool for any kind of failure or performance issues, etc., throughout the SDLC. This process continues for multiple builds during the day. It has created dissatisfaction in the developer community, where they must spend lots of time learning and adopting new tools rather than writing code for their services.

- **Platform to help**: Product owners have created tools and documentation for developers. Many developers do not know about the existence of some of the tools. Developers will not immediately know how many tools and documents their teams use. It might create a dependency on tribal knowledge passed from old team members to new team members. Conversely, a developer who stays with the organization longer might not know about new tools added.

- **Context switching between tools**: In daily life, developers need to use multiple tools and services and switch between them contextually. Approximately one developer does this context switching 20 times a day. It can lead to inefficiencies and errors, as the developer might forget and not be an expert in some of the tools.

It was apparent to the platform team that developers will benefit from a single view where they assess the status of their services and a launch point to discover and reach the tools necessary to create and manage their services.

Netflix's team first evaluated available open-source and proprietary tools that could solve the problem. They have evaluated and selected the tools required by developers and service providers. The team concluded that Backstage was the tool that best suited their requirements and developer experience.

Backstage, created by Spotify and is an open-source developer portal, could help the team due to the following reasons:

- o Backstage's loose coupling between the UI (frontend) and backend services would allow the team to integrate their existing backend solutions easily.

- o Backstage UI technologies aligned with the team's expertise.

- o The Backstage available plugin is lightweight and unobtrusive.

- o It is easy to integrate and manage.

While developing the platform console, the initial goal was to create an MVP that focused on a unified experience with a single dashboard to view and access the state of their project. The existing tools within the console also need to be linked. The plan is to build a platform where all the organization's tools are fully managed.

In designing and developing these plugins, the team's approach was not simply to lift and shift but to rethink and create value for the teams. The platform team at Netflix has introduced the concept of collections to view and access the status of a fleet of services:

- o A unified platform console can help unify the Netflix engineering experience by providing a dashboard to view the access and status of services.

- o The team built the platform by providing a single console for existing and new workflows, leading to developers' quick adoption of the platform.

o   They also enriched the console with new functionality, hoping users would develop new routines, become accustomed to the platform console, and organically add it to their toolchair.

o   Platform development and adoption do not depend on consolidating functionalities. The platform provides a single console for existing and new workflows for the developers to succeed.

It has helped adopt the platform at Netflix and is one of the most producive teams in feature releases (customer experience).

Conclusion

Platform engineering practice helps organizations to build self-service infrastructure, integrating required toolsets and hiding the complexities.

Platform engineering has tried to solve the DevOps challenges to help unify scattered tools and accelerate developer productivity as a self-service platform. Platform engineering aims to mitigate the cognitive overload caused by a shared responsibility model and improve developer experience. Organizations can leap forward in terms of DevOps maturity if platform engineering is adopted in the right way. XaC should be the first guiding principle, followed by automate everything. Most importantly, platform engineering should be built as a product, not as an initiative to integrate and orchestrate different tools.

Readers must have a good understanding of DevOps challenges, the history of platform engineering, and XaC, which inspired industry leaders' development and adoption of platform engineering.

Companies have the freedom to curate their DevOps toolset based on their specific needs and preferences. Here is a breakdown of common categories and popular options:

Developers leverage a comprehensive set cf tools throughout the SDLC. For code development, they utilize IDEs like VS Code, Eclipse, and JetBrains. VCS such as Bitbucket, GitHub, and GitLab manage code changes. Containers (Docker, Kubernetes) and their registries (Docker Hub, ECR) are crucial for packaging and deployment. Observability tools (Datadog, Grafana) ensure application health, while vulnerability scanners (ZAP, Burp) maintain security. CI tools (CircleCI, GitHub Action) automate builds, and GitOps tools (Argo CD) facilitate continuous delivery. IaC is handled with Terraform, Ansible, and Pulumi. Finally, Platform Orchestrators (Humanitec, Shipa) and Internal Developer Portals (Configure8, Backstage) streamline overall operations and developer experience.

In the next chapter, readers will learn the building blocks and architecture of platform engineering. They will learn about reference architecture, and they can adopt it as a baseline architecture. Besides this, they will go through the six pillars of platform engineering and the importance of these core pillars in platform development. Readers will read about product mindset for the development of the platform. They will also understand the importance of starting with a **minimum viable product** (**MVP**) and keep adding new features.

Multiple choice questions

1. **What is the full form of IDP?**

    a. Internal design platform

    b. Internal data platform

    c. Internal developer platform

    d. Internal device platform

2. **What are the major challenges in DevOps way of working?**

    a. Microservices, change management, tools adoption, security

    b. Automation, dependency on Ops

    c. Large team, too much work

    d. Skill set, hiring

3. **What is security as code?**

    a. Companies do not need a security team now

    b. They do not need security tools and use code for security

    c. Integration of security and policies in SDLC

    d. This is just a DevSecOps practice

Answers

1. a

2. a

3. c

Join our Discord space

Join our Discord workspace for latest updates, offers, tech happenings around the world, new releases, and sessions with the authors:

https://discord.bpbonline.com

CHAPTER 2
Platform Culture and Product Mindset

Introduction

Platform engineering is a complete shift from DevOps or a traditional approach. Platform engineering must adopt the product mindset for the development of the platform. The platform team cannot solve all developer problems while building the platform. They must use a product approach, start with a **minimum viable product (MVP)**, and keep adding new features.

Structure

This chapter covers the following topics:

- Culture shift
- Product approach
- Minimum viable platform
- Industry case study

Objectives

By the end of this chapter, you will understand the importance of culture shift for platform engineering success. Most organizations started embracing DevOps, continuous improvement, and agile methodologies, facilitating rapid, iterative platform development. Prioritizing an MVP enables faster market validation and feedback-driven enhancements. A lean product approach ensures efficient resource utilization and focuses on delivering core functionalities early on. By empowering developers and optimizing their workflows, platform engineering teams can accelerate innovation and achieve greater agility in response to market demands.

Culture shift

Platform engineering is a new buzzword for most companies. This aims to solve most of the problems for developers and remove any friction between the dev and Ops teams. However, the platform engineering initiatives are not kicking off in the expected manner and are failing. Most of the companies do not struggle due to a lack of skills or a lack of tools required to build an IDP, but fail due to culture and process. There are some compelling reasons for the failure of platform engineering initiatives:

- Most of the top-level executives feel that platform engineering is just an automation and integration of tools like DevSecOps. The platform engineering team is not able to communicate the real benefits in business language.

- Developers are very much tied to existing infrastructure, and changing to a new way of working is difficult for them. The platform engineering team is more focused on building rather than understanding the developers' issues.

- Transition from the current toolset to the platform where most of the things are abstracted, developers may not feel comfortable when the platform engineering team is building the abstraction layers for them.

So, platform engineering success is not just based upon technological implementations but greatly depends on cultural shifts within organizations.

Platform engineering's growing importance

It is important to remember that platform engineering builds upon the foundations laid by DevOps. Platform engineering addresses DevOps shortcomings and adapts to the increasing complexity of cloud-native development. It is about creating a paved path for developers, enabling them to focus on building and delivering value quickly and safely. The following are the key changes driven by platform engineering:

- **Collaboration**: Although the primary purpose of bringing DevOps culture was to break the silos between Dev, Ops, and security teams, they have still drawn boundaries around their work. They are more focused on their break rather than collaborating. Platform engineering mandates collaboration where they cannot develop a feature without bringing the dev and security teams in confidence.

- **Automation**: Platform engineering emphasizes building automation for repetitive tasks, reducing errors, and providing platforms in a self-service manner, so developers are more focused on innovation and feature development. This approach needs everything to be coded and automated wherever possible.

- **Self-service**: The DevOps team has access to the complete infrastructure, and they have centralized control. The platform engineering approach empowers developers with self-service capabilities, allowing them to provision resources and deploy applications without worrying about guardrails, which are built in by default.

Before platform engineering started buzzing into the industry, there was a rise in DevOps from the traditional way of software delivery. The following were the reasons for the rise of DevOps:

- Continuous integration and continuous deployment/delivery
- DevOps builds a culture of collaboration and communication between the dev and operations teams
- Agility to absorb new feature requirements
- Fault tolerance and recovery
- Continuous feedback

This allows teams to deliver software faster. This also allows integration of tools such as Jenkins (2.497), Git (2.48), Docker (27.5), Kubernetes (1.32), etc., into DevOps practices. However, it also leads to some challenges:

- There was no centralization of DevOps practices within the same company. One good example is the adoption of DevOps in a different way in the same company. There might be different toolsets used by different teams in the same company.
- DevOps teams focus more on automation rather than solving the real challenge for the development teams.
- Cloud adoption leads to an increase in cost. No or minimal guardrails for security and cost, with the assumption of security by default, led to security and cost issues.

A fast-paced digital transformation required improvements in current DevOps practices and the adoption of a new practice and culture for the organization.

Platform engineering as next-gen to DevOps

Resolving the preceding challenges required a new approach to build a centralized tool for:

- Abstracted system to help in scalability and resilience
- Allow standardization by using standard templates
- Layered architecture with standard toolset integrated into the platform

- Stability and reliability as integrated features

- Adding required security and compliance

Platform engineering combines software engineering, infrastructure management, and operations to build and maintain a suitable platform. The platform engineering teams focus on:

- Creating flexible technology stacks

- Leverage cloud infrastructure and containerization

Team collaboration and relationships

With the pace of releases where some companies can move thousands of changes to production, it is nearly impossible to bridge the gap between development and operations teams. Platform engineering can foster collaboration and streamline the processes between different teams. Platform engineering helps to develop collaboration and knowledge sharing across software developers, infrastructure, and operational teams. The infrastructure team helps to provide a standardized development environment, centralized management, and observability with security as a common layer across all other services.

Tools and technologies

One of the core features of platform engineering is to provide a standard toolset to all the teams. Platform engineering relies on tools such as Kubernetes for container orchestration, Terraform for infrastructure provisioning, and Prometheus for monitoring and observability. The primary reason for integrating these tools with platforms is to build scalable and resilient platforms.

Approach for platform engineering

The organization shall focus on some of the key aspects of platform engineering success:

- Strong culture of collaboration

- Focus on automation and everything as code

- Selection of the right tools and technologies

- Cloud-first approach

- Continuous learning and training for the platform engineering team

- Feedback loop to learn developers' pain points and resolve them

- Fostering a culture of experimentation and innovation

These aspects lay the stone for a strong foundation of platform engineering's success in the organization.

Advantages of platform engineering

All organizations and top management in the organization seek a return on their investment. They need solid reasons to keep investing in platform engineering. The following figure shows the key advantages for any organization to bring efficiency and growth:

| Improved Agility | High Availability | Scalability and Efficiency | Bring Innovation | Quick to Market demand |

Figure 2.1: Platform engineering advantages to the organizations

Product approach

There are many different variations or terms used for the internal platforms, including:

- Internal developer platform
- Engineering platform
- Platform engineering
- Developer enablement
- Digital platform
- Infrastructure platform
- DevOps platform

As per *Evan Bottcher, A digital platform is the foundation of self-service APIs, tools, services, knowledge, and support, which are arranged as a compelling internal product. Autonomous delivery teams can make use of the platform to deliver product features at a higher pace, with reduced coordination.*

Internal developers help organizations to:

- Better developer experience
- Reduce cognitive loads on developers
- Make the path to production easy
- Security and compliance are integrated
- Required tools and technologies are integrated

So, as per the definition by *Bottcher*, a digital platform, e.g., an IDP, is developed for an organization; it is a compelling internal product that enables the users of the platform (developers) to reduce their cognitive load and helps organizations to reduce time to market. Platform as a product only happens when you apply a product mindset to your internal platform.

Organizations are under constant pressure to release features fast, so organizations' performance also depends on:

- Software delivery performance
- Operational performance

So, this pressure boils down to the engineering teams. The engineering team must take care of time to market, feedback loop, system availability, system performance, risks, regulatory compliance, scalability, and costs to make management and customers happy. Refer to the following figure:

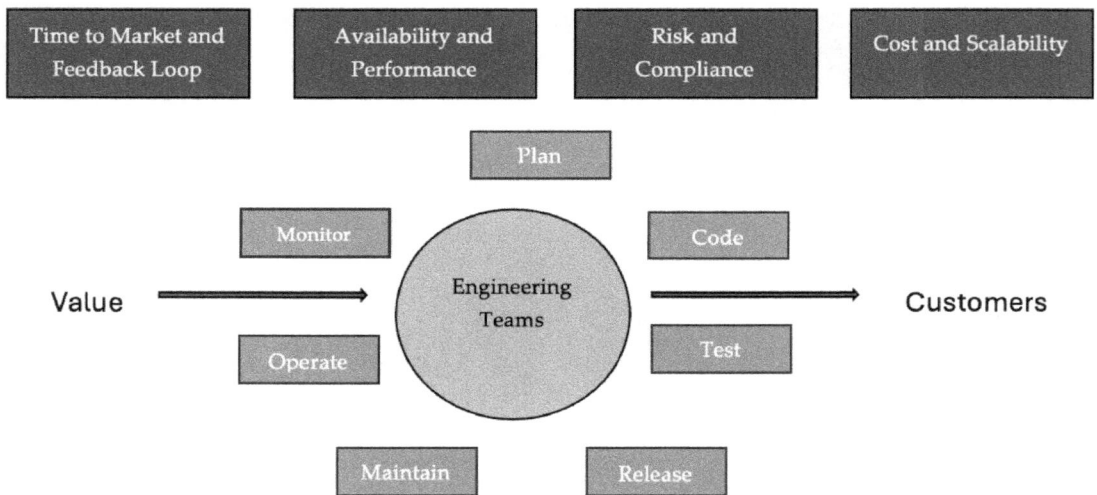

Figure 2.2: Cognitive load on the engineering team to deliver the value (features) to the customers

The platform is a product that builds a curated experience for engineering teams. The platform is a set of innovative tools and concepts for structuring the engineering requirement as a bundle of self-service APIs, tools, and support. In the following example, all software development cycle processes are moved and integrated into a platform where developers have integrated toolsets and services to complete their jobs. They need not worry about security and compliance as separate tasks. Tools and services integrated into the platform can take care of these requirements with required guardrails to remind developers of any mistakes.

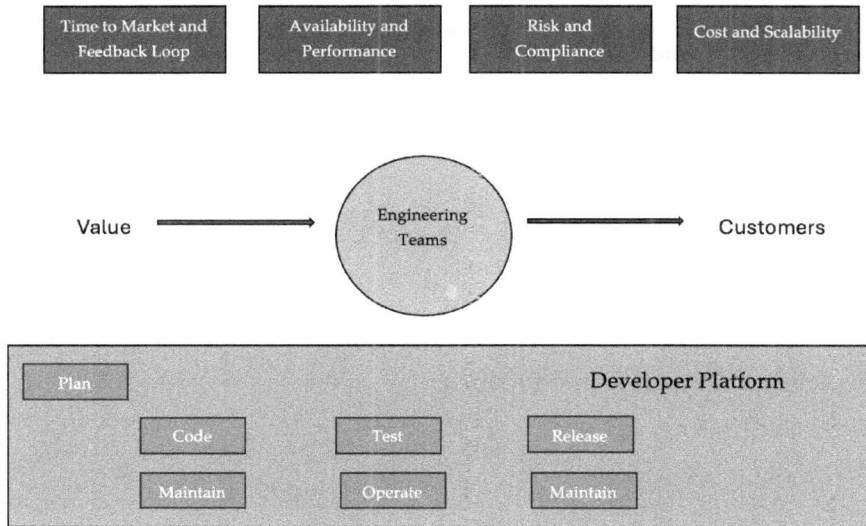

Figure 2.3: Developer platform helps the engineering team to deliver the value (features) to the customers

Internal platform as a product

Organizations, when they start building the IDP, have certain doubts about the success of these initiatives, which is not a small change in the way of working of the organization, but needs a very well-defined strategy to build the platform. Some of the queries from the key stakeholders:

- How do we foresee the benefits of the platform that we are building?

- How do we measure productivity and user developer experience?

- What is the MVP? Shall we build it initially?

- Shall we work on better reliability or faster delivery?

- How is the platform going to support the company's mission and strategy?

- Are our competitors building the same?

In answer to the preceding questions and to avoid the failure of the IDP, the platform shall be treated as a product (reliable, usable, and fit for purpose):

- The platform shall not be forced on the developers and shall be used voluntarily.

- The platform teams shall advocate for their platform product and market it to the internal teams:

  o   Its usage and benefits.

  o   The platform shall be carefully designed and curated. It shall be designed with users in mind, mainly focusing on the developer's experience.

- The platform is quick and cheap to start using with quick start guides, documentation, and sample codes.

- The platform is secure and compliant by default.

- The platform shall simplify day-to-day tasks for the users and must help users to achieve their goals.

- The platform evolves to take advantage of the latest tools and technologies.

Platform as a product shall also consider the five key pillars of platform capabilities:

- Delivery infrastructure

- APIs and architectural remediation

- Self-service data

- Experimental infrastructure

- Customer touchpoint technologies

In IDP as a product, there are certain challenges for the product team related to:

- **Customers**: There are no external customers for the product team. Your customers are technical teams, so you need to speak in their language in technical terms to get their buy-in.

- **Product**: One of the prerequisites for the product is that it shall not be forced on the users. However, in the case of an internal platform, this may not be optional for the users. Sometimes, it is hard to define the product features as some of them are intrinsic and default.

- **Outcomes**: Internal product outcomes are not very direct. Product managers may not be able to define ROI or delayed returns for some of the crucial features required.

Key principles and goals of platform team

It is important to look at some of the key principles and main goals for a platform engineering team:

- The foremost job for the platform engineering team is to take initiative and build an IDP.

- The platform team should adopt a productization approach and provide value to developers as customers.

- They need to remove pain points for developers, such as removing cognitive load and providing a good developer experience.

- The product manager assigned to the team helps the team build tight feedback loops with key stakeholders.

Key features of IDP

A well-designed IDP provides the following features:

- **Standardization**: It drives the standardization across all workflows and configurations.
- **Everything as a code**: It automates away redundant tasks, for example, such as on-call or ticket Ops.
- **CI/CD workflows**: It has features for continuous integration, deployment, infra orchestration, security, access management, and workload life cycle management.
- **Security and compliance**: It ensures security and compliance across all golden paths.
- **Cost management**: It provides the required templates and visibility to manage the cost.
- **Observability**: It provides the required alerts, monitoring, and tracing capability.

Forming the platform team

To build a platform as a product, it is essential to start forming a team as follows:

- **Head of platform engineering**: This is a managing role, but can be a very technical, it requires a hands-on person playing this role. This role is responsible for allocating required resources such as headcount and budget. This role also manages North Star Metrics, **key performance indicators (KPIs)**, and **objectives and key results (OKRs)**. This is the most powerful role in the team that understands and manages the priorities of all stakeholder groups.
- **Product manager**: Internal platform product manager skills are different from product managers delivering or building market-driven products. Here, consumers of the product are technical teams, and product managers need to be well-versed in technical terms and the language spoken by the developers. They must have hands-on experience with multiple skills such as infrastructure, cloud, security, risks, and compliance. They need to keep upgrading the latest tools and technologies to evolve their product.
- **Designer**: This is another key profile from the ideation to the building stage of the internal platform. Key aspects of the internal platform are self-service and development experience, which require a good UI/UX for the developer.
- **DevEx platform engineers**: They are the ones who may be part of application development teams delegated with responsibilities to build platforms. They understand the developer's pain points and general developer experience struggles. They ensure the developer's workflow is integrated into the platform.
- **Infrastructure platform engineers**: They are delegates of the infrastructure and operations teams. They make sure that IDP acts as an interface that facilitates the

consumption of resources and infrastructure by developers in a compliant and standardized way.

Other key teams that are part of the platform engineering team to build a platform as a product:

- **Security teams**: They are responsible for security governance and security features to be incorporated into the platform. They should take the security-by-design approach. The platform team needs to reach out to them for any security considerations and get their approval, such as **role-based access control (RBAC)** and networking.

- **Compliance and legal**: They share their compliance requirements with the platform team and design and implement them across the IDP.

- **Enterprise architects**: The platform team should understand and support the strategy for technology transformations or the future state of the architecture.

- **Solution architects**: Platform team should work closely with solution architects to understand workflows to be integrated to support standard application architectures designed by the solution architects.

- **Infrastructure and operations teams**: They can focus on operational efficiency rather than resolving tickets by optimizing the current infrastructure performance or adding new tools. They can ask platform teams to integrate the required tools to be consumed by the developers.

- **Developers**: They have self-service portals available. They can now self-serve to run their applications without a dependency on the infrastructure and operations team.

- **Executives**: They are the sponsors of the project.

All stakeholders work together, along with the platform product manager, to build the platform.

The stakeholders form the team with the product manager and are designed to start the productization of the platform, as shown in the figure:

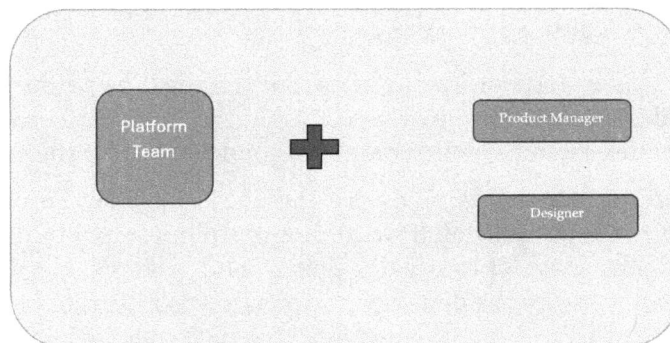

Figure 2.4: IDP, initial team

It is a wrong perception that the platform team is the next-gen version of DevOps, and this team is moved to the platform team to create and manage the platform. The platform team consists of developers, Ops team members, and security and compliance team members to support product managers in building and maintaining the platform. Refer to the following figure:

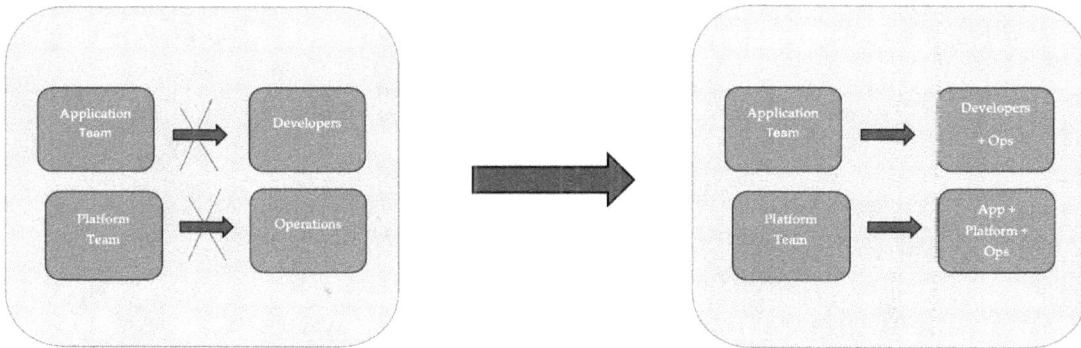

Figure 2.5: The IDP team is not a DevOps team

A continuous process of building and monitoring

This is a continuous process for building the internal platform as a product. The product manager shall avoid the *loudest voice in the room* and keep working on the overall quality of the platform. The choice of building new features or integration must be data-driven. Analysis is key, and the product manager must pull out the regular metrics to support their decision, such as:

- **Adoption metrics**: We need to determine the number of teams or users who have adopted the internal platform's services and features since their launch. They should be more focused on frequently used or critical features required.

- **Use case coverage and variation metrics**: Identify the most frequently used developer use cases.

- **Technical performance metrics**: The key reason for building a platform is to support developers in building their software faster. Platform performance and scalability are key reasons for adopting the platform by developers.

Developing an IDP as a product is a continuous process that involves constant learning, building, and measuring the effectiveness of features as described in the following figure:

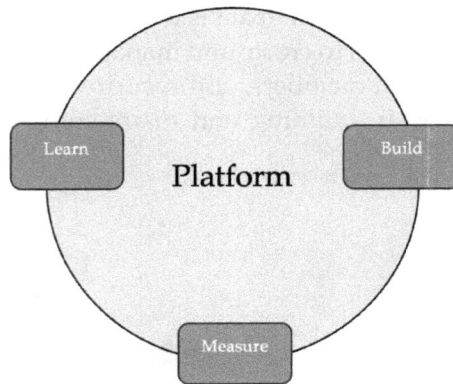

Figure 2.6: IDP development continuous process

IDP Backstage product case study for Spotify

Spotify recognized that developer productivity and satisfaction are crucial for innovation and delivering value to external customers. Spotify has developed Backstage, an IDP that prioritizes the needs of its internal developer customers:

- **Backstage: A customer-centric approach**

  Spotify's platform team takes a customer-centric approach to developing and evolving Backstage. They actively seek to understand the challenges and needs of their developers through various methods:

  o **Identifying developer needs**:

    - **Surveys**: Regularly surveyed developers to gather feedback on their pain points, priorities, and desired features. Questions like *What are your biggest challenges when building and deploying new services?* provide valuable insights.

    - **Interviews**: Conducted in-depth interviews with developers across different teams to understand their specific workflows, tools, and pain points. Asking developers to *walk through their typical day* can reveal valuable information about their needs.

    - **Developer forums and feedback channels**: Established dedicated communication channels where developers can openly share their thoughts, suggestions, and feedback on the platform.

    - **Usage data analysis**: Analyzed how developers interact with Backstage to identify areas for improvement, popular features, and opportunities for new functionalities.

  o **Defining a clear value proposition**: Based on the insights gathered, Spotify's platform team has defined a clear value proposition for Backstage:

- Backstage is a developer portal that provides a unified and streamlined experience for building, managing, and operating all software at Spotify.

- This value proposition acts as a guiding principle for the platform's development and ensures that it remains focused on delivering value to its internal customers.

- **Backstage's product features**

  Backstage offers a comprehensive suite of features designed to address the specific needs of Spotify's developers, much like a consumer-facing product would cater to its users:

  o **Software catalog**: A centralized repository of all software components within Spotify's ecosystem, including microservices, libraries, and data pipelines. This catalog allows developers to easily discover, understand, and reuse existing components, fostering collaboration and reducing redundant effort. It is akin to Spotify's music catalog for its listeners.

  o **Tech docs**: A unified platform for all technical documentation, ensuring that information is up-to-date, easily accessible, and searchable. This feature streamlines knowledge sharing and reduces the time developers spend searching for information.

  o **Plugins**: Backstage's extensible architecture allows developers to build and integrate their own tools and services into the platform. This customization empowers teams to tailor Backstage to their specific workflows and preferences.

  o **Unified search**: A robust search engine that enables developers to quickly find the information they need, whether it is code, documentation, or specific tools.

- **Continuous iteration and improvement**

  Spotify emphasizes continuous iteration and improvement of Backstage, ensuring that it remains a valuable and evolving resource for its developers:

  o **Feedback loops**: Strong feedback loops are established to actively solicit and incorporate feedback from developers, allowing the platform team to prioritize new features and address pain points effectively.

  o **Open-source community**: By open-sourcing Backstage, Spotify has fostered a vibrant community of contributors who help improve and extend the platform's functionality.

  o **Data-driven decisions**: The platform team leverages usage data and metrics to track the effectiveness of Backstage and make informed decisions about its future development.

By embracing a product mindset, Spotify has created an IDP that empowers its developers, accelerates software delivery, and ultimately contributes to the company's overall success. Backstage serves as a compelling example of how platform teams can effectively cater to the needs of their internal customers, fostering a culture of innovation and efficiency within their organizations.

Minimum viable platform

Many of the internal platform projects are not successful because platform teams do not have the right process and expertise to deliver the desired value to the users (developers). Most of the organizations are not able to:

- Align the stakeholders with the platform engineering initiative. There is already too much pressure on development teams to spare time for new initiatives.

- Quickly develop and prove the value to the stakeholders, and slowly lose the momentum. Most of the team wants to develop most of the features for developers and accommodate all the use cases where you need the MVP framework, which removes all of these issues.

By creating an efficient and KPI-driven team with an MVP defined to build the internal developer platform, the team can quickly prove the IDP's value to the key stakeholders. With a productization approach, teams can also build a clear roadmap to iterate on the future state of the platform as well.

MVP allows the team to take simpler use cases to make progress faster and easier to prove value and get the required resources and support necessary to expand. It helps to pass a few hurdles and get the feedback faster. This helps remove users' pain points and encourages adoption.

Focus on building a platform

Platform engineering is a new buzzword, and platform engineering teams are tempted to build a platform quickly:

- Build an engineering-centric self-service portal for the developers.

- As part of the self-service portal, providing an information service catalog to users that provides a view of services, infrastructure, and architecture.

- Provide a feature-rich platform for quick adoption.

Building MVP

This is important to identify and build the most important features first. The following are the key steps that will guide you to start building a MVP for your organization:

1. Identify your team that will drive this effort. This team shall be skilled in container or cloud migration.

2. Define your use cases, which are very simple to build the simplest version of the platform.

3. Develop, integrate tools, simplify, and repeat this process like a product release, considering the users' feedback.

4. Demo the platform to the key stakeholders to help you with adoption and expansion.

Reference the four-step process to build an MVP for your platform. Refer to the following figure:

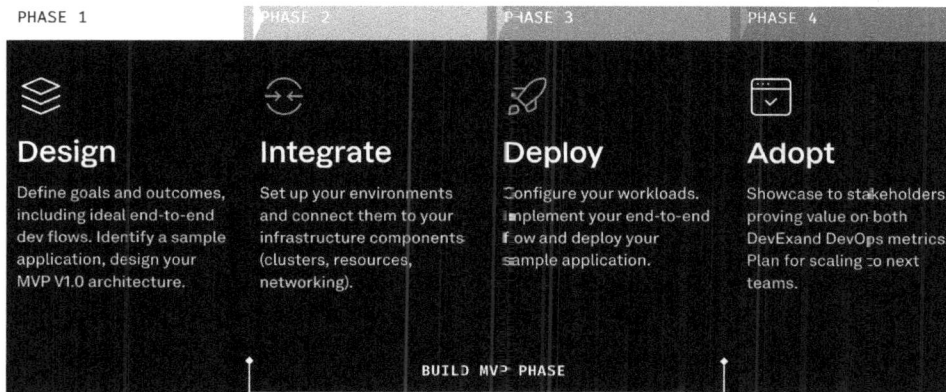

Figure 2.7: *Minimum viable platform in just four phases by Humanitec*

Source: *https://humanitec.com/minimum-viable-platform-mvp*

Four phases of MVP framework

Platform teams can use an MVP to showcase their skills and platform capabilities to get additional investment and extension to the current development. This will lead to the development of a full-scale IDP. This whole process is outcome-focused and metrics-driven. These outcomes are mapped with the business objectives and goals.

Let us discuss the four phases of the MVP framework:

1. **Phase 1: Discovery**

   Initiation or discovery is the most important project of any of the key projects. If you miss or mess up anything in this phase, there will be a high chance of failure in later cycles. In this phase, get the buy-in of your key stakeholders to align the outcome of this project with the broader business objectives and scope it correctly. Be sure to document the following:

   • Desired outcomes mapped with the MVP

   • Business goals that are aligned with the platform engineering initiative

- Success criteria of MVP
- Paint the points of the developers and user stories to cover these pain points
- Pain points of the Ops and the Infra team to be resolved by IDP
- System and developer metrics to be tracked by the IDP

There are some key considerations and metrics to compare before and after the rollout of IDP:

- Time to write the first program and be able to first PR by the developer
- Total tickets received by the Infra and Ops team to resolve in a week or a month
- The Infra team can build the infra using IaC

Your further phase in MVP depends on the MVP discovery phase, so teams need to be very careful in this phase.

2. **Phase 2: Integration**

   In *Phase 1*, teams have documented outcomes and success criteria of MVP; this phase allows the team to start setting up the organization with a platform orchestrator, assigning all admin and other roles along with integrating a cloud service provider and Kubernetes clusters.

   This phase allows you to create all the resources required to deploy the first application.

3. **Phase 3: Deployment**

   After resource creation, the platform team can setup resource definitions and rules to allow developers to consume infrastructure. In this phase, teams can define values and secrets and setup CI/CD pipelines.

4. **Phase 4: Preparation for adoption**

   You demo the solution to all stakeholders. This gives visibility to move further and helps stakeholders to measure the ROI. The platform head and product manager can create and present the complete roadmap for the IDP.

Create MVP for IDP

The platform team has been formed, and they have discovered the business goals and success criteria and are now ready to begin with a minimal viable portal. The MVP is a small subset of all tasks performed by the developers, and serves real developer needs. These use cases can be tested and iterated on. The MVP and each subsequent step are prepared in an agile manner using quick sprints. Once the MVP is ready, the platform team can add more developer workflows and grow the functionality of the portal. This will keep on growing until the platform team is ready for the general availability of the platform as a product.

You can define your user stories for the MVP sprint-wise. Refer to the following figure:

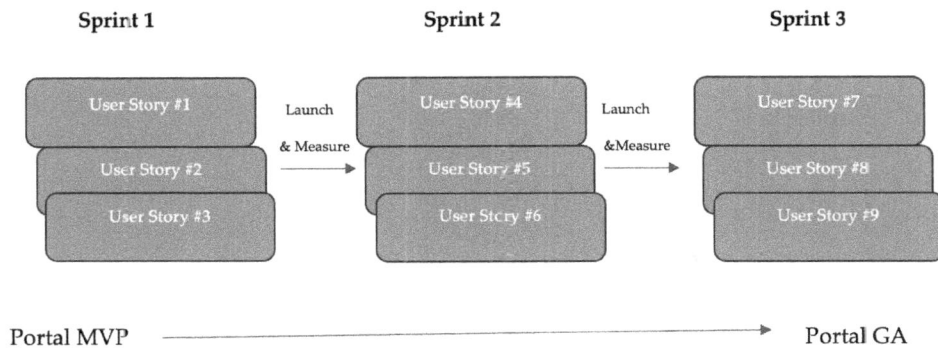

Figure 2.8: *MVP sprint-wise user stories and incremental deliveries for the final product (GA)*

For MVP, you need to pick and choose the key features from all requirements consolidated for the platform for day-to-day routines:

- **Plan your day**:
    o   Manage PRs review
    o   See my Jira tickets
    o   My on-call shifts
    o   Manager's initiatives
    o   Prioritize security issues

- **During development:**
    o   Find the API documentation
    o   Find service data
    o   Add IaC to the service
    o   Create a new service
    o   Manage configurations
    o   Force merge code
    o   Deploy the dev environment
    o   Manage secrets

- **Ship features:**
    o   Build the code
    o   Promote the code
    o   Deploy the code
    o   Toggle feature flags

- o   Manage canary
- o   Run migrations

- **Operate productions:**
  - o   Rollback
  - o   Restart service
  - o   Monitor service health
  - o   Report an incident
  - o   Temp permissions to DB
  - o   Find outage RCA
  - o   Troubleshoot outages

We can plan to achieve everything in our roadmap, which covers the entire end-to-end developer journey in SDLC and everything needed by them for their routine work. They do not need to switch to different tools to do their job; they have everything in one place. However, developing this platform needs a long-term approach and a product mindset, but MVP lets you develop incrementally and provide everything required by developers.

For example, we can create an initial MVP to deploy a few demo applications to give confidence to the developers and senior stakeholders to get their buy-in to build a full-fledged platform:

- Developers finding service data
- Creating new services
- Deploying a developer environment, such as creating a developer stack and running it
- Continuous delivery to the production environment
- Allow rollback of service

This will allow developers to quickly search software catalogs and build and deploy services in a self-service manner. This is a good start to create the MVP and gain the confidence of key stakeholders to further build the platform as a product. This MVP will provide a developer experience:

- They do not need to context switch as they have the required tools and developer environment available in a single tab.

- Golden Path integrated into the platform.

- They are allowed to create infrastructure and workload, ready to deploy. This is abstracted and just needs them to click a few buttons.

- Developers need not be experts in tools and technologies integrated into the platform.

- They do not need to raise a ticket with IT-Ops or DevOps for infrastructure or dependent services.

Stories to be picked for the MVP

To select user stories to be picked up for the MVP, the following are criteria to look for:

- Solve the key challenges that are in high demand
- Not very complex and easy to implement
- Must be of high value

Refer to the following figure:

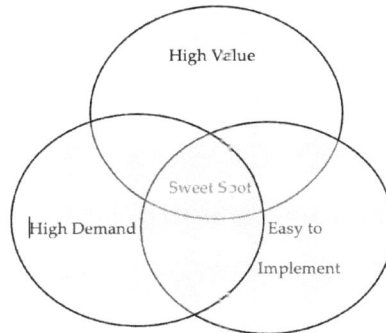

Figure 2.9: Choose the right MVP

In addition, we need to consider a few more things:

- The problem severity with the current way of working is to be automated
- The potential impact on developers using a self-service portal
- Defined success metrics

These user stories can be mapped with subsequent sprints to deliver the product features. Refer to the following figure:

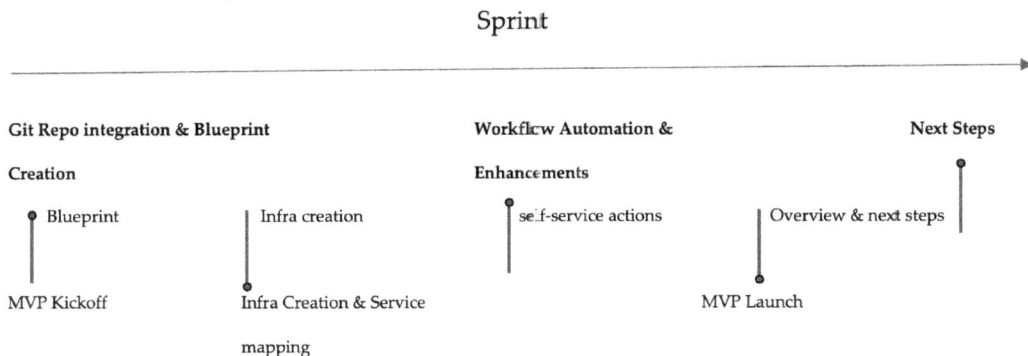

Figure 2.10: Sprint-wise MVP mapping

A case study of MVP for IDP

While many MVP examples focus on customer-facing products, the concept is equally valuable for internal tools like developer platforms. This is a hypothetical case study of an MVP for an internal developer platform:

- **Company**: A mid-sized gaming company with a growing engineering team.
- **Challenge**: Developers waste significant time on manual tasks like environment setup, deployments, and infrastructure provisioning. This slows down development and reduces developer satisfaction.
- **Solution**: Build an IDP to automate these tasks and provide a self-service experience for developers.

The following is the MVP approach:

1. **Identify core needs**:
   a. Focus on the most time-consuming and frustrating tasks for developers.
   b. Conduct surveys and interviews to gather specific pain points.
   c. **Example**: Determine the time spent on setting up a new development environment.

2. **Prioritize essential features**:
   a. Choose the features that will deliver the most value with the least effort.
   b. **Example**:
      i. Self-service environment creation with pre-configured tools and dependencies.
      ii. Automated deployment pipeline with basic CI/CD.
      iii. Simple dashboard to track deployments and resource usage.

3. **Build a basic platform**:
   a. Use existing tools and services where possible to minimize development time.
   b. **Example**:
      i. Leverage a cloud provider's managed services (e.g., AWS CloudFormation, Azure DevOps) for infrastructure provisioning and CI/CD.
      ii. Use open-source tools for basic dashboards and monitoring.

4. **Deploy to a pilot group**:
   a. Start with a small group of developers to get early feedback and iterate on the platform.
   b. Gather feedback through surveys, interviews, and usage data.

5. **Iterate and expand:**

   a. Based on feedback, prioritize new features and improvements.

   b. Gradually expand the platform to more teams and use cases.

Example MVP features:

- **Self-service environment creation**: Developers can spin up new environments with a single click, pre-configured with the necessary tools and dependencies.

- **Automated deployment pipeline**: Code changes are automatically built, tested, and deployed to various environments.

- **Basic monitoring and logging**: Developers can track the status of their deployments and view basic logs.

This case study demonstrates how an MVP approach can be used to build a successful internal developer platform. By starting small and focusing on core values, organizations can quickly deliver a valuable tool to their developers and lay the foundation for a more comprehensive platform in the future.

Industry case studies

In this section, we will go through some industry case studies:

- **Uswitch: Platform as a product model**

  Uswitch is one of the group brands of RUV and operates the UK's leading home services price comparison site **www.uswitch.com**. Initially, their engineering strategy was primarily around team autonomy and distributed across their different services, such as energy providers or mobile companies. However, this leads to cognitive load for different teams. They must spend a lot of time managing infrastructure services provided by their cloud service provider, AWS.

  This led them to alternate solutions and develop an IDP to build and manage as a product, shown as follows:

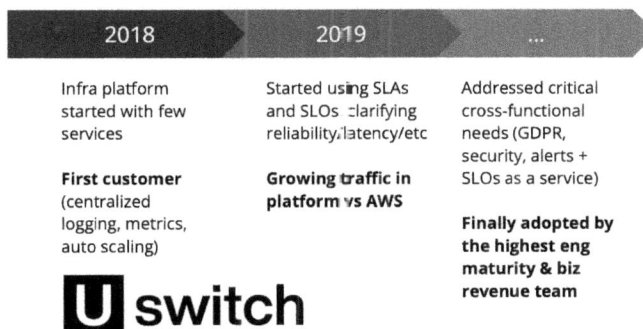

Figure 2.11: Uswitch case study to build a platform

Source: https://platformengineering.org

The IDP solution is designed and built using Kubernetes. This provides a self-service portal to the company, reduces developers' cognitive load, and allows them to focus more on building services rather than on infrastructure, security, or cost. This allows them to focus on the company's foundational software engineering principles:

o   Autonomy

o   Self-service infrastructure

o   Minimal coordination

- **Netflix is a pioneer in IDP adoption**

Netflix embraced platform engineering to empower its developers and achieve remarkable business outcomes.

Netflix's explosive growth from a DVD rental service to a global streaming giant presented significant challenges for its engineering team. Their initial monolithic architecture struggled to keep up with the increasing demands of millions of users and a rapidly expanding content library. They faced the following challenges faced by them:

o   **Increase developer velocity**: Enable developers to build and deploy features quickly and independently.

o   **Improve operational efficiency**: Reduce the overhead of managing a complex and growing infrastructure.

o   **Enhance reliability and scalability**: Ensure the platform can handle massive traffic loads and remain resilient to failures.

Netflix adopted a platform engineering approach to address these challenges. They built an internal developer platform, known as dispatch, to provide developers with a self-service, automated, and standardized environment for building, deploying, and managing applications. They have adopted a productization approach to building their IDP dispatch.

The following are the key features of dispatch:

o   **Self-service capabilities**: Developers can provision infrastructure, deploy applications, and manage resources on demand, without relying on a separate operations team.

o   **Automated workflows**: Dispatch automates many common tasks, such as building, testing, and deploying code, freeing developers to focus on writing code.

o   **Standardized tools and processes**: Dispatch provides a standardized set of tools and processes for building and deploying applications, ensuring consistency and reducing errors.

o **Microservices architecture**: Dispatch supports a microservices architecture, allowing developers to build and deploy small, independent services that can be scaled and updated independently.

o **Comprehensive monitoring and observability**: Dispatch provides tools for monitoring application performance, identifying bottlenecks, and troubleshooting issues.

Netflix's journey provides a compelling case study for organizations looking to embrace platform engineering. By adopting a similar approach, companies can empower their developers, accelerate software delivery, and achieve greater business agility.

Conclusion

The chapter gave a good overview of platform engineering and focused on the shift from traditional DevOps to a product-centric approach. It emphasized cultural changes, including collaboration, automation, and self-service, to enable faster, more efficient software delivery. The key concept is treating the internal development platform as a product, with a focus on user experience (developers) and continuous improvement.

This chapter outlined the structure of a platform team, its key principles, and the importance of building an MVP to address developers' pain points and achieve early success. It also included a case study of Uswitch, highlighting the benefits of adopting a platform as a product model. This chapter provided a comprehensive overview of platform engineering's core principles and practical steps for successful implementation. The next chapter will cover the building blocks and the seven core pillars of platform engineering.

Multiple choice questions

1. **Which of the following is not a key cultural shift driven by platform engineering**?

   a. Collaboration

   b. Automation

   c. Centralization

   d. Self-service

2. **What is the primary goal of an MVP in platform engineering?**

   a. To build a feature-rich platform from the outset.

   b. To demonstrate the value of the platform to stakeholders quickly.

   c. To replace all existing DevOps tools and practices.

   d. To create a complex platform that addresses all possible use cases.

3. **Which of the following roles plays a crucial part in understanding and addressing the technical needs of developers using the platform?**

   a. Head of platform engineering

   b. Product manager

   c. DevEx platform engineer

   d. Infrastructure platform engineer

4. **Which phase of the MVP framework involves identifying pain points and defining success criteria?**

   a. Discovery

   b. Integration

   c. Deployment

   d. Preparation for adoption

5. **What is the core concept behind treating the IDP as a product?**

   a. Focusing primarily on the needs of the platform team.

   b. Prioritizing features based on the loudest voices.

   c. Building a platform that developers are forced to use.

   d. Adopting a user-centric approach and focusing on developer experience.

Answers

1. c
2. b
3. c
4. a
5. d

References

1. https://thenewstack.io/a-shortcut-to-building-an-enterprise-grade-developer-platform/

2. https://www.getport.io/blog/internal-developer-portal-how-do-i-get-started#

3. https://humanitec.com/blog/how-to-build-a-minimum-viable-platform-mvp

4. https://humanitec.com/blog/the-four-phases-to-minimum-viable-platform-mvp

CHAPTER 3
Building Blocks and Architecture

Introduction

This chapter of the book will cover the basic building blocks and platform engineering. It will also explore the seven core pillars of platform engineering and provide details of the **Please Help Yourself** (**PHY**) created by the authors as one of the implementations for one of the companies.

Structure

The chapter covers the following topics:

- Building blocks
- Seven pillars of platform engineering
- Platform architecture
- Platform reference architecture

Objectives

At the end of this chapter, you will understand the building blocks and the seven core pillars of platform engineering. This will help readers to create or design a *platform architecture* specific to their organization's needs.

Building blocks

In *Chapter 1, Concepts of Platform Engineering*, we had an overview of platform engineering. It is a transition of IT operations from data centers to the public cloud. **Amazon Web Services** (**AWS**) is the leader in providing cloud platforms to the world. Organizations had started moving their applications from on-prem or data centers to the public cloud. It has helped them to adopt agile methodology and start doing faster releases. Organizations started moving from monolithic to microservices-based architecture.

This shifted the application development process and the needed changes in people, processes, and technologies. This required largely static, dedicated servers in a private data center with a large service capacity available on demand from different cloud service providers. This also led to some challenges in managing the cloud operations:

- Infrastructure
- Security
- Networking
- Applications

So, the flexibility given by the cloud has helped many companies scale up and grow faster. Companies can run multiple features, build and deploy them during the day. Companies like *Amazon* and *Airbnb* do 125 thousand deployments during a single day. This could not be done using manual processes. Companies have started with the following:

- Changes from manual infrastructure creation and provisioning using **infrastructure as code** (**IaC**).
- There is no single username and password to protect, but the management of sensitive data is based on identity at all layers.
- Service identity is a new parameter for networking, access, and connections.
- Workload-based management of applications, deployment.

Consistency and standardization are critical goals for any organization that must do many deployments in a single day. This can only be achieved by building a platform with all the automation and built-in guardrails. The team has established the best practices for developers to utilize cloud services. These best practices are codified into workflows created in the platform.

A platform is a single place for integration for all teams, including operations, security, and compliance, to ensure that best practices are baked into the system. Other essential requirements are monitoring, reporting, and auditing the system. To achieve these core requirements, a single platform of all components is needed that is well-designed and integrated into the system. It included:

- Persona-based access
- Unified experience layer
- **Continuous integration and continuous deployment** (**CI/CD**) integrations

- Centralized access management
- Unified security across all layers

A PHY platform architecture was created to help their organization. Let us explore it:

- This view was created to help an organization move from its current DevOps practice to platform engineering:

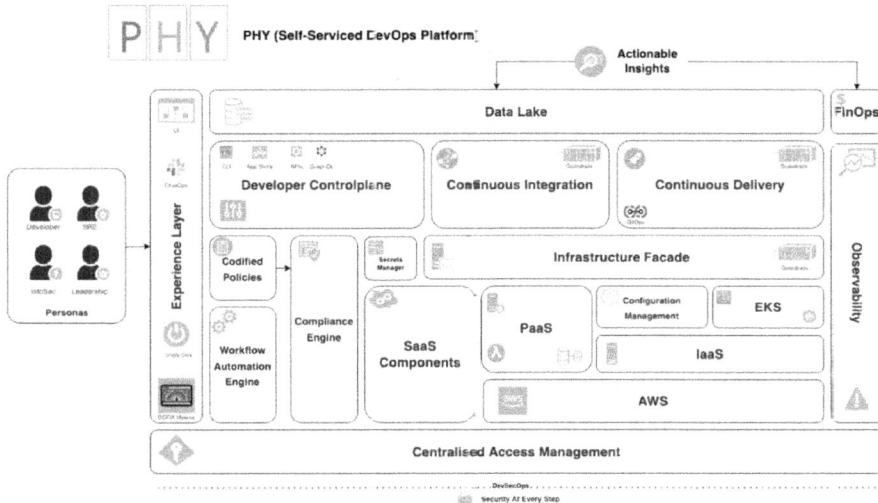

Figure 3.1: Platform engineering, self-service platform

- This architectural view is tool agnostic detailed view:

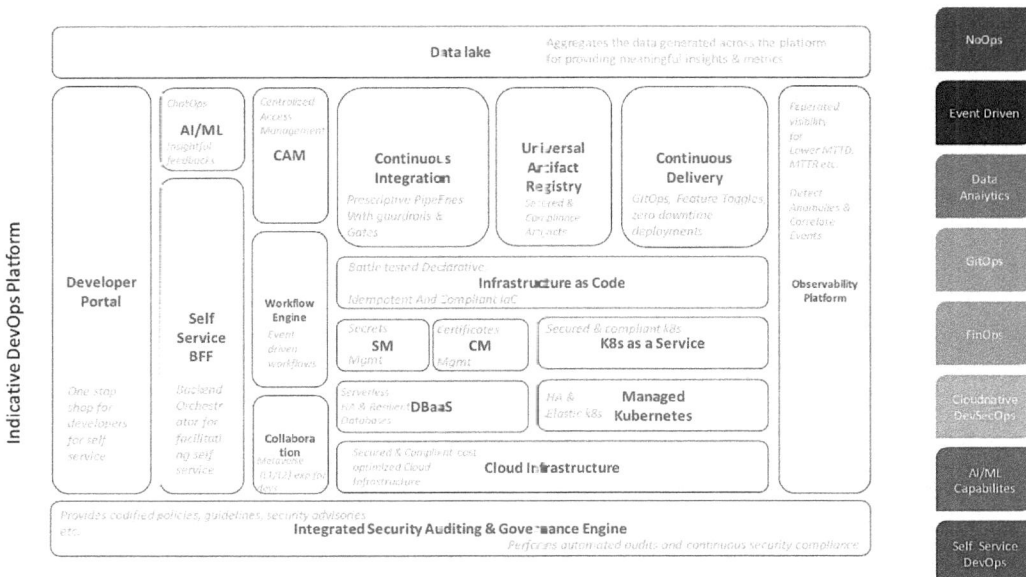

Figure 3.2: A tool-agnostic detailed view showing various comments under PHY

- This is another view created with some industry-leading tools:

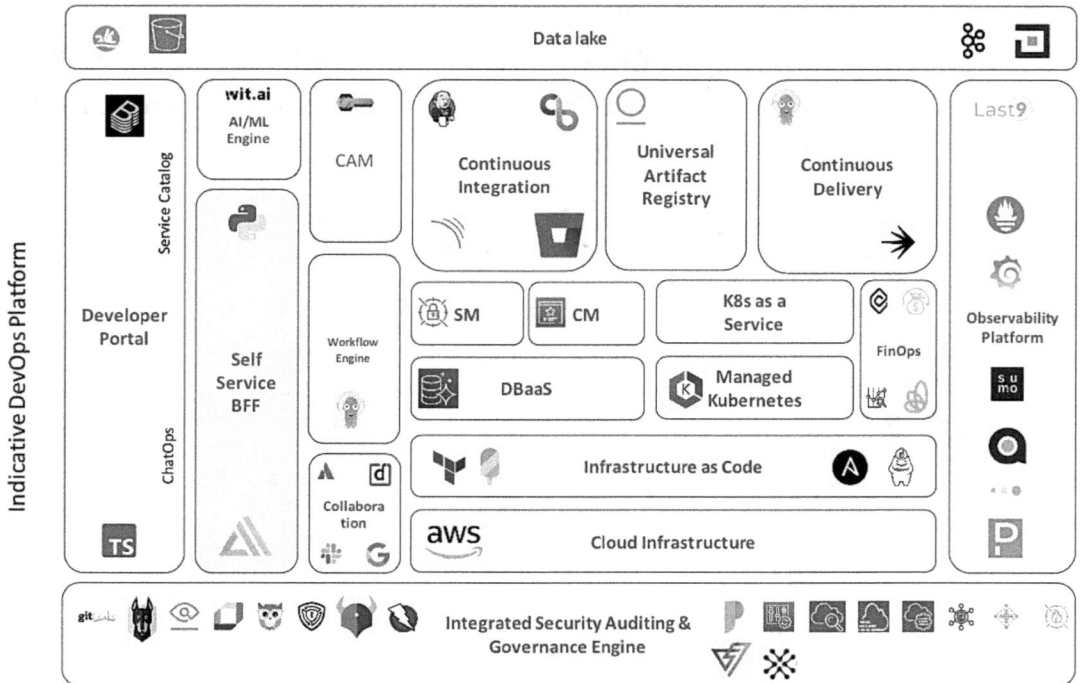

Figure 3.3: An indicative view using industry-standard tools for PHY

Cloud-native application architecture

Today, applications have shifted toward cloud-native, which Kubernetes and containers support. Understanding the system architecture and the different layers of architecture management is essential.

There is a growing complexity in all cloud-native applications due to the large number of APIs used in microservice-based architecture. This leads to a need for different layers to abstract and manage this complexity. Similar to the line of network layers to abstract and manage the complexity, the cloud-native and container management is divided into three different planes:

- **Data plane:** Houses and transports applications and data traffic.

- **Control plane:** Configures rules for the data plane.

- **Management plane:** Sets guardrails for the data and control planes.

The following figure gives an explanation by F5 (NGINX) for these planes:

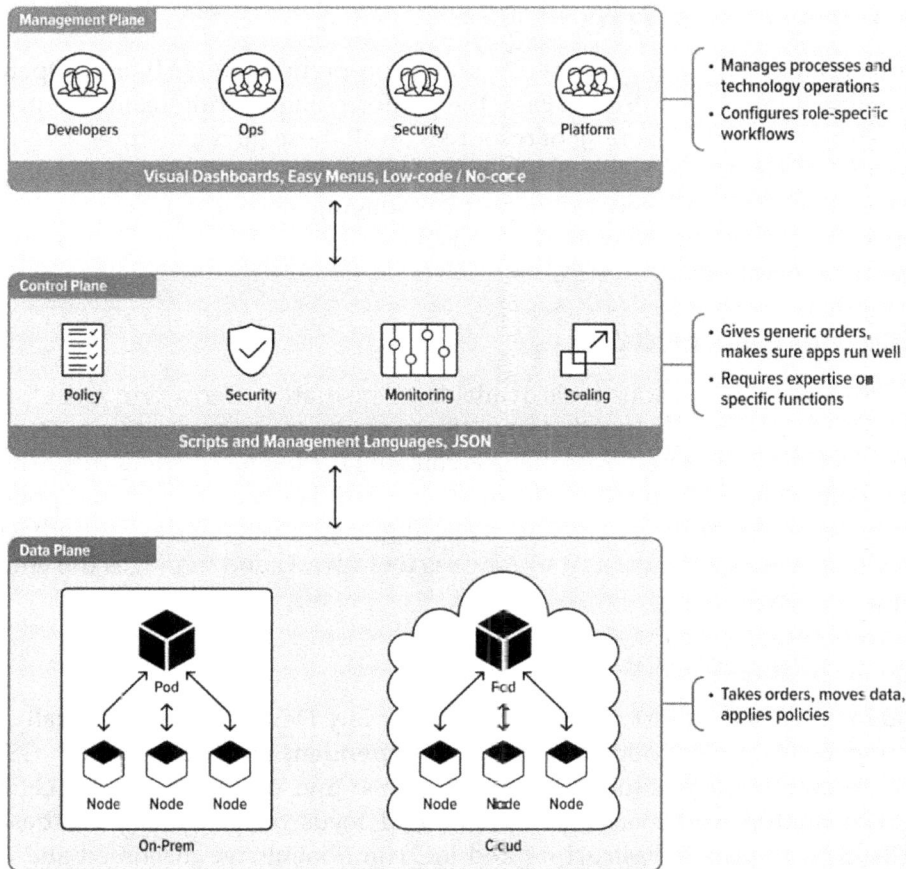

Figure 3.4: Control, data, and management plane by F5

The data plane is the layer for implementing policies and **service-level agreements (SLAs)** for the working and behavior of an application. It can take the required instructions from other planes and do retries, keepalives, and horizontal scaling to meet the application SLA. The data plane controls the data flow through applications and application behavior at the pod level.

The control plane's components make decisions at the cluster level for all the pods and detect and respond to cluster events, such as starting up a new pod when an existing one fails or becomes unresponsive. It is like the traffic cop enforcing the rules of the road for data movement around in the data plane.

The management plane allows different teams to manage the application policy, governance, and behavior. In this plane, the development team can add required guardrails to ensure that users do not make errors that cause the system to go down. These guardrails allow teams and organizations to operate systems efficiently and deploy code quickly and with considerably less risk.

Cloud infrastructure

Suppose an organization uses any hyper scaler, on-prem (like VMWare, OpenStack, etc.), or a combination of both. In that case, the platform engineering team is expected to consistently support the provisioning of resources on all those infrastructures, irrespective of the type of infrastructure being dealt with. Hence, the platform engineering team is expected to have the required expertise in managing and administering the cloud infrastructure used by the organization. Choosing an IaC tool or tools that consider all those aspects is imperative.

Infrastructure as code

IaC can be achieved using various tools available in the market. Terraform and OpenTofu top the list. Ansible is a de facto tool that sometimes automates configuration management and provisioning infrastructure. Cross plane is catching up and has a bright future because it uses Kubernetes's reconciliation loop to ensure no drift between the defined policy and the state of the infrastructure. If someone is starting from scratch today, our advice is to explore the Crossplane approach, as it minimizes tool sprawl and manages the entire IaC in a cloud-native way.

Database as a service

Managing databases is the most challenging task for any DevOps team. Generally, using managed services from the cloud provider or **independent software vendors (ISVs)** is advisable. This will mainly reduce the cognitive load and operations in managing the databases. The platform engineering teams should focus on providing **database as a service (DBaaS)** using the infrastructure and IaC components we discussed and choose the right managed services for DB administration, which will work behind the scenes for the development teams. Development teams are expected to share their **recovery time objective (RTO)**, **recovery point objective (RPO)**, and throughput requirements depending on the type of databases.

Managed Kubernetes

Managed Kubernetes refers to a service offered by cloud providers or other companies that handles the underlying infrastructure and management of a Kubernetes cluster for you. It allows you to reap the benefits of Kubernetes without dealing with the complexities of setting it up and maintaining it yourself. Platform engineering should leverage this service or build automation around **Kubernetes (K8s)** management and administration if they are expected to provide K8s as a service on top of on-prem or private cloud infrastructure.

The platform team can choose one or all of the following approaches depending on their needs:

- A few centralized clusters
- Separate clusters for each team and environment

The second option is about providing K8s provisioning as a service. A self-serve pipeline or workflow can help the requesting development team get the cluster based on their requirements.

A centralized cluster will reduce the operation overhead and bring in economies of scale, standardization, etc., but it has many limitations, which are as follows:

- The blast radius is quite large as these clusters may be the potential single point of failure.
- Enforcing proper isolation and access controls becomes crucial to prevent security breaches.
- Different teams might have specific requirements for their deployments.
- A central cluster may not provide the flexibility to cater to these diverse needs.
- Sharing a central cluster can slow down individual teams.

The platform engineering team is expected to choose the approach that would make sense to their customers (development teams).

FinOps

While the infrastructure is getting provisioned, providing cost visibility to the requestors is pretty helpful. The leadership would like to have visibility around cost usage across the fleet of resources. The platform engineering team must ensure that certain hygiene, like standardized tagging and enforcement, is in place. In the case of K8s, proper labeling should be enforced. A compliance engine like Kyverno can help the platform team enforce the proper labeling being followed in the workload manifests before and after workloads are deployed into Kubernetes. Services like AWS Config can be used to enforce tagging on AWS resources. It is better to follow the shift left approach by ensuring your IaC tools, like Terraform or OpenTofu modules, are enforcing the tagging standards. IaC compliance tools can also help in enforcing tagging standards.

The platform team should provide visibility around cost using an internal developer portal. They may need to federate expenses from multiple sources and centralize the visibility. Again, different personas may expect different levels of visibility, such as the leadership, which may like to see the overall cost. The application owner may want to see the **Total Cost of Ownership (TCO)** of their application.

Certificate manager and secrets manager

Managing certificates and secrets is an operation-intensive task. Platform engineering teams should use services provided by the cloud providers to meet these requirements. AWS provides **AWS Certificate Manager (ACM)**, AWS **Secrets Manager (SM)**, and AWS SSM Parameter Store, services that can be used to store secrets. The other hyperscalers provide similar services. Automatic renewal of certificates and rotation of secrets should be possible using these managed services. Also, these services integrate well with their hyperscaler's ecosystem, which reduces the cognitive load on the platform engineering team.

Workflow engine

The workflow engine can be different from the CI server. Some organizations prefer to use CI as the workflow engine, however, this approach is not recommended. The CI server is meant for developers to carry out their development workflows related to **software development life cycle (SDLC)**, such as CI or CD. Keeping your workflow engine different from CI will keep CI decluttered and provide the required isolation.

Developers see their pipeline executions on CI servers while the workflow engine executes their workflows around SDLC, which is more of a state machine with pipeline-like functionality. Tools like Argo Events and Argo Workflows fit the bill. Some companies have adopted tools like Humanitec, and some even have gone ahead with a different setup of the same CI services. It is up to the teams to decide what their workflow engine should be.

Self-service Backend for Frontend

The self-service backend for the front layer is more of a facade layer that can provide the backend component so that any client can talk to the platform. It can also orchestrate across multiple toolchains behind the scenes. Therefore, this layer is critical to maintaining a tool-agnostic platform experience for your developers.

Universal artifact registry

An organization needs an internal, reliable repository to download invulnerable packages sourced from public repositories but scanned and certified for use. Application artifacts like war, DLL, etc., should also be stored in an internal registry. Container images, Helm charts, Operators, Linux packages (Debian, Yum, etc.), MacOS (brew tap), Chocolatey (Windows), Maven, Gradle, Nuget, NPM, etc., should be downloaded only from the internal repository.

The internal repository might have a virtual repository integrated with external public sources. The public repositories may sometimes go down, leading to deployment failures. A robust internal repository is critical for platform engineering teams to provide a seamless experience to their developers.

Data lake

All generated data within the platform are federated into a data lake setup on top of an object store. Apache DevLake can provide some of the metrics development teams may be interested in. DefectDojo can be a good vulnerability dashboard for the InfoSec team to monitor vulnerabilities across the organization. It will also help the platform engineering team ensure the action items are assigned to the correct owners and remediations are tracked. Data logistics can be facilitated using services like Kafka, Kinesis, etc.

Observability

Metrics, logs, events, and traces (**MELT**) should be federated into a unified observability stack so that the development teams can correlate these inputs and derive better outcomes. The platform engineering team should leverage managed services as much as possible to ensure their observability stack is robust, performant, and highly available.

A fully managed incident platform should be part of this observability stack to handle notifications and alerts without much delay. **Mean time to acknowledge** (**MTTA**), **mean time between failures** (**MTBF**), **mean time to resolve/restore** (**MTTR**), etc., are greatly influenced by the robustness of the observability stack.

Centralized access management

Access management is the most operation-centric activity in any organization, and the most draining activity for any platform engineer if they are supposed to take care of access control. The following figure illustrates a sample implementation of centralized access management:

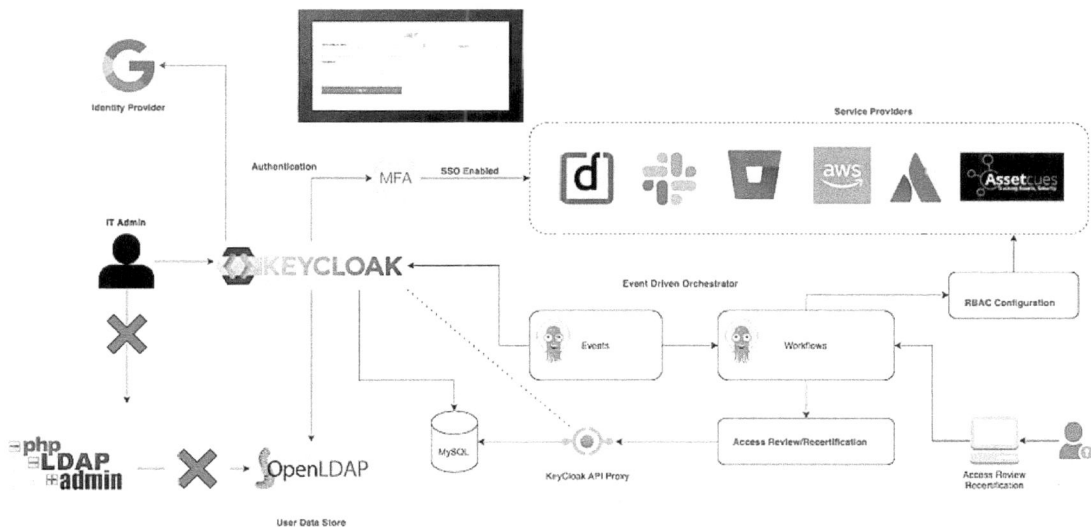

Figure 3.5: Centralized access management workflow solution

The platform engineering team can choose a sophisticated service like Okta or implement their own workflows and integrations on top of Keycloak. Our platform was implemented with Keycloak as the orchestrator. the following is the sequence flow diagram that depicts the workflow:

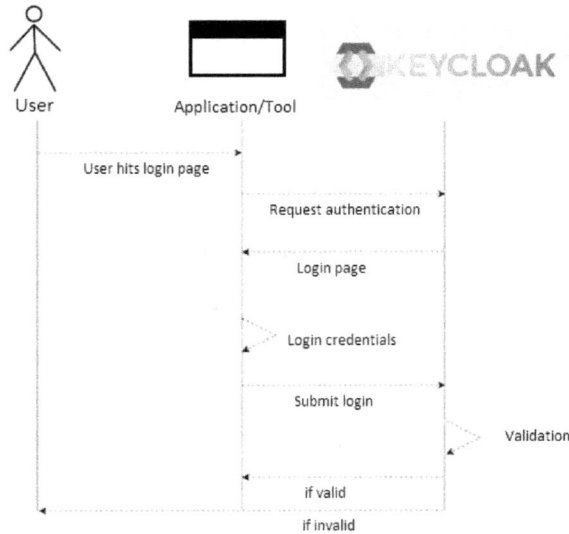

Figure 3.6: Centralized access management sequence workflow

Seven pillars of platform engineering

The internal developer platform is a developer platform and is built by developers.

This platform should not be designed in a vacuum. It can only help the developers if they participate in building it (developer experience). Building and maintaining a platform involves continuous discussions and buy-in from developers and business stakeholders.

Most of the organization must follow the prescribed seven pillars of platform engineering, which are:

- Provisioning
- Pipeline (**version control systems (VCS)**, CI/CD)
- Security
- Connectivity
- Orchestration
- Observability
- Analytics

Let us take a look at each one by one.

Provisioning

Infrastructure provisioning in platform engineering automates the setup of compute, storage, and networking resources to accelerate developer productivity. It ensures consistent, scalable environments through IaC, enabling rapid, reliable deployments, modules, and images.

Creating standardized infrastructure workflows necessitates platform teams to decompose their infrastructure into:

- **Reusable**: In addition to machine images, IT enterprises are adopting a strategy of modularizing their infrastructure code to create frequently utilized components into reusable modules. This practice is crucial because a fundamental component of software development is to avoid unnecessary repetition, a principle applicable to infrastructure code. They are typically overseen through VCS and interface with external entities like service catalogs or testing frameworks.

- **Immutable**: Immutable infrastructure, widely adopted in modern IT, streamlines troubleshooting, enhances reliability, and fortifies security. Immutability entails deleting and recreating infrastructure for any alterations, minimizing server patching and configuration changes.

  It ensures that each service iteration launches from a new, thoroughly tested, and current instance. Many organizations implement immutability through tools like Terraform, CloudFormation, or Pulumi (IaC), enabling the construction and reconstruction of extensive infrastructure via configuration code modifications. Some also employ golden image pipelines, which focus on generating and continuously deploying standardized machine images validated for security and policy compliance. It helps developers to use infrastructure modules and golden image pipelines without any inner workings of the infrastructure. It is repeatable, scalable, and predictable, and enforces best practices.

Platform engineering has provisioning of modules and images as a core pillar with the following workflow:

1. A developer commits code to VCS and runs the pipeline.

2. The CI/CD platform submits a request to your internal developer platform for validation (AuthN and AuthZ).

3. If validation is successful, the pipeline triggers test, build, scanning, and deployment tasks.

4. CI/CD workflow is used to build modules, artifacts, images, and other infrastructure components for the developers. Developers do not need to know the internal workings of these flows.

5. Any success or failure message and metadata are passed to the CI/CD platform with audit trails.

The infrastructure components, such as modules, artifacts, and image configurations, are stored and gradually deployed in different environments (dev, stage, and prod). The following figure shows a provisioning workflow:

CI/CD Workflow

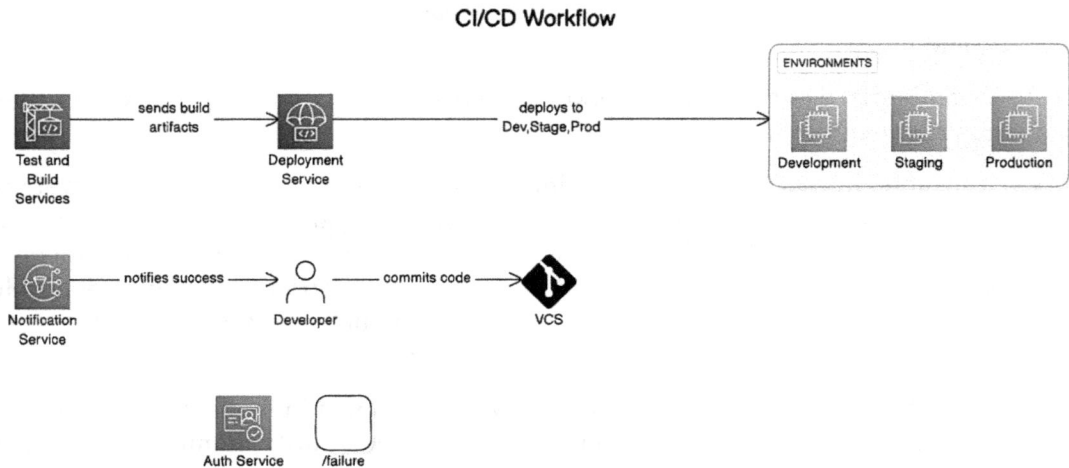

Figure 3.7: Provisioning workflow

Policy as code

Agile development practices have transformed infrastructure provisioning from solely an operational concern to a critical aspect of faster application delivery expectations. Today, quicker and more efficient provisioning is a pivotal factor of business success, with its significance tied to advancing organizational strategies and fulfilling customer experience rather than solely managing operational costs.

As we transition to an application-delivery-focused approach, we must adapt workflows and procedures accordingly. Traditionally, operational staff managed provisioning through ticket-based workflows, encompassing tasks such as access validation, approvals, security checks, and cost assessments. Additionally, these processes underwent rigorous auditing to ensure compliance and adherence to control standards. As platform engineering evolves to support self-service infrastructure provisioning, embedding security and compliance into the provisioning process becomes essential, driving the adoption of policy as code as a core practice. Refer to the following list:

- It enables developers and other platform end users to make provisions via a self-service workflow.

- It means that a new set of codified security controls and guardrails must be implemented to satisfy compliance and control practices.

- Most companies have started adopting the cloud for cloud-native applications, and these security controls and guardrails are implemented by policy as code.

- Policy as code uses programmable rules and conditions for software and infrastructure deployment and uses policy engines that codify best practices, compliance requirements, security rules, and cost controls.

- It helps shift controls to the left during infrastructure provisioning. It is owned by the platform engineering team, which ensures that policies are correctly mapped to identified risks and mitigated by implementing required controls.

The following figure depicts a policy as code workflow:

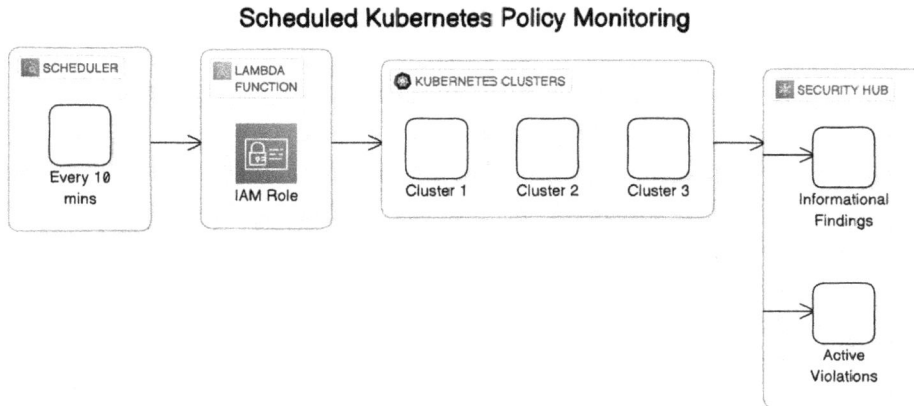

Figure 3.8: Policy as code workflow

CI/CD and version control systems pipeline

A critical initial phase for any platform team is integrating and restructuring the software delivery pipeline. It involves a close review and assessment of the organization's existing VCS and CI/CD pipelines for better control and self-service by developers. It helps them release software and features faster.

Many organizations employ multiple VCS and CI/CD solutions at varying stages of maturity, which can be semi-configurable or fully configurable and automated. Given the evolving nature of these platforms, it is advisable to adopt a component-based API platform or catalog model. This approach ensures future extensibility without sacrificing functionality or frequent refactoring.

In a cloud-native model, infrastructure and configuration are managed as code; therefore, a VCS is required for this core function. Using a VCS and managing code provides the following benefits:

- Uniformity and standardization
- Agility and speed
- Scalability and flexibility
- Configuration as a form of documentation
- Repetition and collaboration
- Disaster recovery

- Troubleshooting capabilities and traceability
- Adherence to compliance and security

A typical VCS and CI/CD workflow in platform engineering looks like this:

1. The developer commits the code to the VCS.

2. The task is automatically submitted to the pipeline.

3. The CI/CD platform submits a request to the internal developer platform for validation (AuthN and AuthZ).

4. If validation is successful, the pipeline triggers tasks (e.g., test, build, deploy).

5. The output and artifacts are shared within platform components or external systems for further processing.

6. Security systems may be involved in post-run tasks, such as de-provisioning access credentials.

The following figure depicts a CI/CD workflow with security validation embedded as part of the workflow:

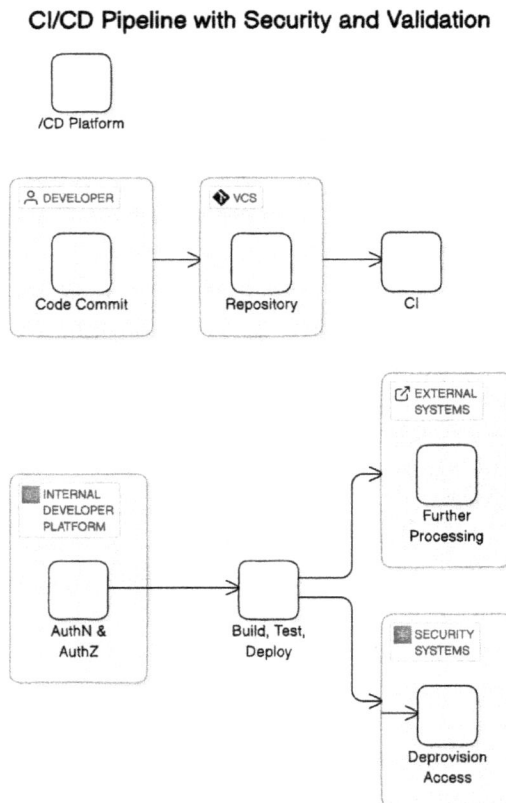

CI/CD Pipeline with Security and Validation

Figure 3.9: CI/CD and VCS pipeline

As platform teams select and evolve their VCS and CI/CD solutions, they must consider what this transformation means for existing or legacy provisioning practices, security, and compliance. Teams should assume that building new platforms will affect existing practices, and they should work to identify, collaborate, and coordinate change within the business.

Security

As part of the different teams in the organization, various team members may have different security challenges, such as:

- The leadership team has the accountability to manage the business risks and ensure that the security and compliance requirements of their system and applications are met.

- The security team has the primary responsibility to add the required guardrails to safeguard the assets.

- Development needs to ensure that best practices are followed and required security features are built into the system.

Very often, we can see the following requests coming from different teams:

- Account creation

- Credentials setup

- Accessing API keys

- Infrastructure provisioning

In the *Provisioning* section, we have seen that we can use version control and continuous integration for infrastructure provisioning using code. However, we shall also consider security as our primary concern. Many organizations have adopted DevSecOps to enforce security and policy guardrails, but this is hindered by team silos and too many tools adopted to take care of different security requirements. Platform engineering can help consolidate diversified tools and teams into a unified platform. The platform engineering team needs to ensure that the integration of these tools is effective and data-driven.

One of the critical aspects of the *Security* pillar is to codify security governance. Apart from the effective working of tools, security by default, policies, and regulations are directly embedded into templated development and deployment processes. This not only enforces compliance but also minimizes human error. Another significant aspect of codification is that it creates consistency and auditability. The platform enforces the recording of every action, change, and decision and compares it with enforced security policies.

The following figure shows the reference model for security capabilities in the internal developer platform by Gartner:

Reference Model for Security Capabilities in Internal Developer Platforms

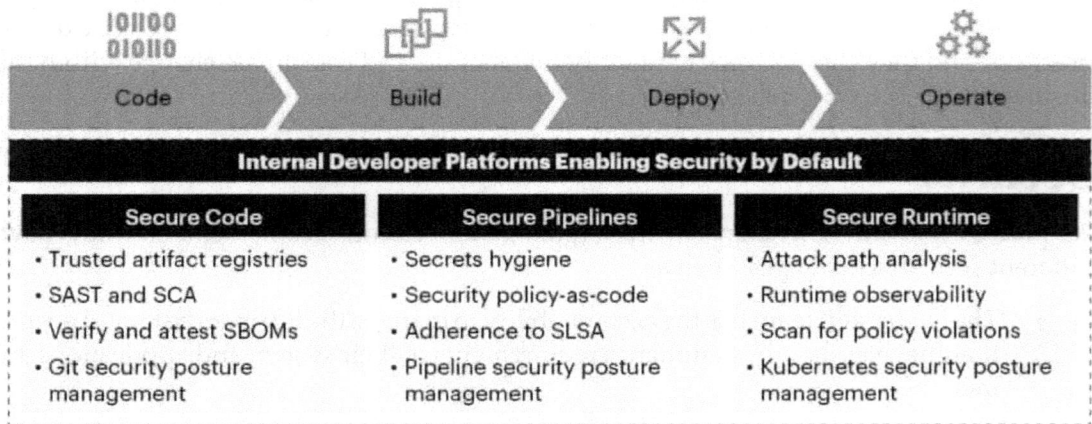

Secure Code	Secure Pipelines	Secure Runtime
• Trusted artifact registries	• Secrets hygiene	• Attack path analysis
• SAST and SCA	• Security policy-as-code	• Runtime observability
• Verify and attest SBOMs	• Adherence to SLSA	• Scan for policy violations
• Git security posture management	• Pipeline security posture management	• Kubernetes security posture management

Figure 3.10: Reference model for security capabilities in IdP

Platform security teams are structured to help the platform engineering team in the following manner:

- **Manage access**: The security team needs to ensure the effective working of **identity and access management (IAM)**, **privileged access management (PAM)**, Zero Trust, and internal access.

- **Developer tooling for security**: Ensuring developers build secure services. During SDLC, the developer has tools available for encryption services, secrets management, authentication, identity, etc.

- **Security operations**: Vulnerability management, security reviews, risk assessments, and more. The platform security team can develop and automate, which helps the security team scale with a small number.

Manage access

In cloud native architecture, humans, applications, and services all present an identity that can be authenticated and validated against a central source. A multi-tenant secrets management, encryption platform, and **identity provider (IdP)** can serve your organization's security needs.

Identity provider

Establishing strong, unified identity is foundational to platform security, ensuring that all users, services, and applications are authenticated and authorized through a single trusted identity provider with embedded IAM controls and a deny-by-default access model. Here are a few key considerations:

- All humans, applications, and services must have a well-defined form of identity and be validated against a single trusted IdP.

- Identity systems must support cross-platforms and multiple runtimes.

- IAM controls are embedded.

- Humans, machines, and services shall have valid identities for AuthN and AuthZ.

- Once verified, access is brokered through deny-by-default policies to minimize impact in the event of a breach.

- AuthZ review shall have an audit process and, ideally, granted just in time:

  - Audit trails are routinely reviewed to identify excessively broad or unutilized privileges for threat detection.

  - Past audit data provides non-repudiation.

  - Compliance with data storage requirements.

Secrets management and encryption

Once identity is successful for any human system, it needs access in an automated way:

- Retrieving a secret (a credential, password, key, etc.)

- Brokering access to a secure target

- Managing secure data (encryption, decryption, hashing, masking, etc.)

All secrets in a secrets management system should be:

- Centralized

- Encrypted in transit and at rest

- Limited in the scoped role and access policy

- Dynamically generated, when possible

- Time-bound (i.e., defined **time-to-live** (TTL))

- Fully auditable

Secure remote access (human to machine)

Although most systems are supposed to be immutable and do not allow any changes by humans, many times, you need secure remote access for troubleshooting purposes. The secure system access control is illustrated as follows:

System Access Control

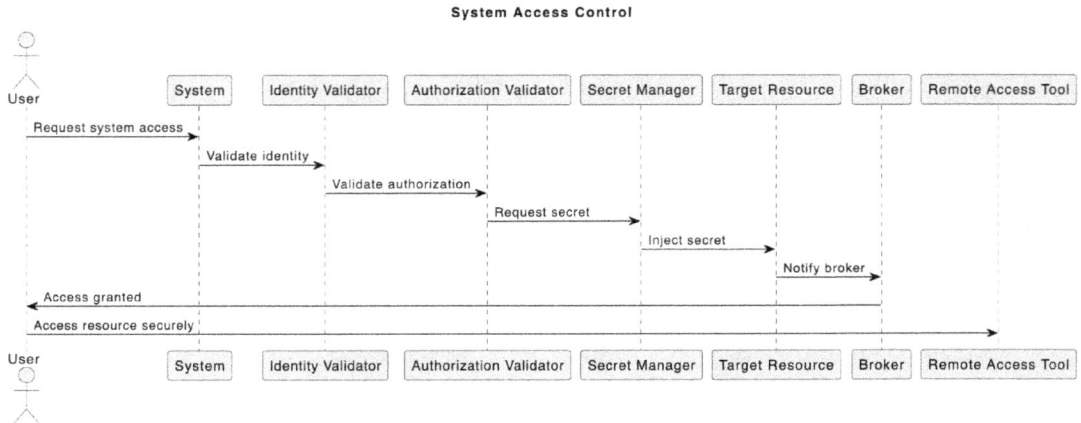

Figure 3.11: Secure system access control

A remote infrastructure access workflow for a human user typically follows these steps:

1. A user initiates a system access request.

2. The user's human identity undergoes validation against the trusted identity broker.

3. Upon successful authentication, authorization is verified for the target system.

4. The platform requests a secret (either static or short-lived) for the target system.

5. The platform injects the obtained secret into the corresponding target resource.

6. A response is transmitted back to the identity broker by the platform.

7. The platform proceeds to grant end-user access.

8. The user securely accesses the target resource via a contemporary, secure remote access tool.

Developer tooling for security

Adopting security in the DevOps process helps organizations embed security at every SDLC stage. Essential security requirements are:

- Start embedding the security from the initiation and planning stage. Security is task zero and shall be the top priority of the development process.

- The primary objective is to secure all stages:

  o Planning | Threat modeling

  o Development | Scanning tools

  o Build | Secure and compliant supply chain

  o Deployment | Code and artifacts are scanned

  o Runtime | Monitoring the application for any vulnerability

- Security tools are integrated into the platform to scan and fix vulnerabilities:
  - o **Static Application Security Testing (SAST)**
  - o **Software Composition Analysis (SCA)**
  - o **Dynamic Application Security Testing (DAST)**
  - o **Runtime application self-protection (RASP)**
- Security policies are incorporated into application code, making them an integral part of the development and deployment process.

Security operations

Platform engineering helps organizations to make sure that security is built into all operations in the following manner:

- IaC allows platform engineers to define and manage infrastructure in code, which helps to ensure that security is baked in from the start.

- Platform engineering can implement secure secret management solutions to protect sensitive data, such as passwords and API keys.

- Platform engineering can automate vulnerability scanning and remediation processes, helping teams to identify and fix security vulnerabilities more quickly and efficiently.

- Platform engineering can centralize and standardize security controls and configurations, making it easier for teams to manage compliance across the organization.

- Platform engineering can provide teams with access to secure tools and infrastructure, helping them to develop and deploy more secure software.

Platform engineering and security intersect at the core of creating and maintaining secure and robust platforms for deploying applications and services. It involves designing, implementing, and managing platforms with built-in security measures to safeguard against threats and vulnerabilities throughout the software development lifecycle.

Connectivity

Networking connectivity is the most under-discussed pillar of platform engineering, with many legacy networks and hardware still in use at many enterprises. For network-related configurations, ticket-driven processes were expected to support routine tasks:

- Creating DNS entries
- Opening firewall ports
- Managing network ACLs
- Updating traffic routing rules

It caused days-to-weeks-long delays in simple application delivery tasks, even when the preceding infrastructure management was fully automated. In addition, these simple updates are often manual, error-prone, and not conducive to dynamic, highly fluctuating cloud environments.

Networking remains one of the challenges in bridging these gaps. Development teams can be isolated from infrastructure teams, and they do not always understand the basics of networks (IP addresses, VLANs, BGP, etc). However, networking remains crucial to connecting the applications and data, whether those reside in LANs, WANs, datacentres, **software as a service (SaaS)** applications, or cloud services.

The process of integrating networking with platform engineering may be daunting, but let us take a look at ways it can happen.

Unifying the silos

A common complaint in IT organizations is that security, infrastructure, and applications teams operate in silos without understanding each other's needs. The same challenge can be found in **line of businesses (LoBs)**, which created the challenge of shadow IT. An LoB might develop an app without knowing what other teams or partners use. For the organization's goals, this is not always the best approach. The following figure depicts a siloed environment:

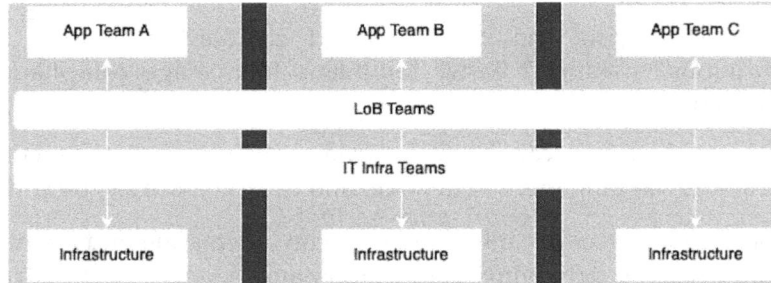

Figure 3.12: LoB app teams working in silos

It needs careful consideration and strategies alongside the provisioning pillar since connectivity allows apps to exchange data and is part of the infrastructure and application architectures.

Building common infrastructure services

One way to tear down the silos is to build a standardized set of infrastructure that everyone can share. Developers need an interface to provision, configure, and manage infrastructure without complexity.

It can remove some infrastructure complexity from the app, LoB, or DevOps teams. We can integrate a ticketing system with platform engineering for self-service by developers and auditing requirements by the security and compliance team. Refer to the following figure:

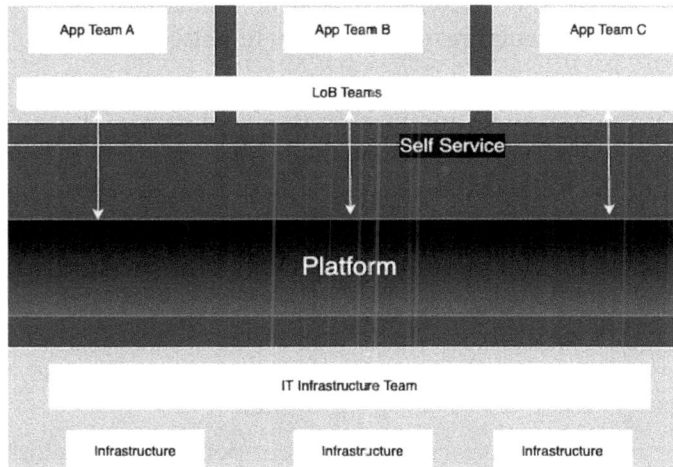

Figure 3.13: LoB app teams using self-service platform

Integrating networking self-service into platform engineering is a shift from a human-focused approach to a machine-first approach. Let us take a look at the differences between these two approaches:

Human-focused approach	Machine first approach
CLI will continue to dominate network interfaces.	APIs (REST) will become the primary interface.
A network is unique and special.	Networks should be treated like all infrastructure.
Network discovery, maps, and blinky lights are critical to manage.	Repeatable, automated processes to create and deploy devices and services that are critical to managing networks.
IT OSS systems perform all fulfillment activities.	The network provides an API that abstracts network-specific configurations from SOM and OSS platforms.
Users expect higher bandwidth and no downtime.	Users expect on-demand, innovative services at the speed of cloud.
Inventory is not very accurate.	We store inventory and assets in federated sources.
Maintenance is performed in the middle of the night with humans to avoid outages.	We thoroughly test in the lab and automate to ensure we can run changes 24/7.

Table 3.1: Human versus machine-focused approach

Platform teams are bringing networking functions, software, and appliances into their infrastructure to adapt networking to modern dynamic environments as code configurations. It brings the automated speed, reliability, and version-controlled traceability benefits of infrastructure, such as code, to networking.

Organizations adopting microservices architectures swiftly recognize the benefits of software-driven service discovery and service mesh solutions. These solutions establish an architecture where services are autonomously discovered and linked, governed by centralized policies within a Zero Trust network. Permissions determine whether services can connect, and if not explicitly permitted, the default is the secure denial of service-to-service connections. In this model, service-based identity is pivotal in adhering to established security frameworks. The workflow used by application teams for network connectivity is as follows:

- A centralized registry to discover, connect, and secure services across any region, runtime platform, and cloud service provider.

- Support for multiple interfaces for different personas and workflows (GUI, API, CLI, SDK).

- Health checks for all services.

- Multiple segmentation.

- Layer 4 and Layer 7 traffic management.

- Implementation of security best practices such as defense-in-depth and deny-by-default.

- Integration with trusted identity providers with single sign-on and delegated RBAC.

- Audit logging.

- Enterprise support based on an SLA.

- Infrastructure as code, runbooks.

So, networking is one of the most essential pillars of platform engineering and needs to be carefully designed and integrated. For developers, it needs to be fully abstracted and made available as an easy option to configure.

Orchestration

Container orchestration is another essential pillar of platform engineering. Container orchestration is about managing the container life cycle and the containerization of multiple environments. The container life cycle follows the build-deploy-run phases of traditional software development, with some steps that differ based on the container orchestration tool (Kubernetes, HashiCorp Nomad) being used. One of the most popular container orchestration tools is Kubernetes, which is widely used and helps organizations enable engineers to:

- Manage when and how containers start and stop.
- Schedule and coordinate component activities.
- Monitor container health, distribute updates, and perform failovers and recovery procedures.

Modern orchestration tools use declarative programming (YAML) to ease container deployments and management. The declarative approach lets engineers define the desired outcome without feeding the tool with step-by-step details of how to do it.

Container orchestration automates and manages tasks across the container life cycle. Workload orchestrators like Kubernetes and HashiCorp Nomad provide many benefits over traditional technologies. The level of effort may vary to achieve the following benefits:

- Provisioning and deployment
- Resource allocation
- Configuration and scheduling
- Redundancy and availability
- Health monitoring
- Regular updates
- Scaling for containers (upscale or downscale)
- Moving containers between nodes
- Load balancing
- Traffic routing
- Securing container interactions

It leads to the following benefits for the organizations:

- **Increased productivity**: Container orchestration tools automate the deployment of applications by CI/CD process and reduce errors, helping development teams focus on application development.
- **Faster deployments**: Container orchestration tools make deploying containers more user-friendly. It can be scaled faster to handle the large traffic loads.
- **Reduced costs**: Use fewer resources or optimal capacity to reduce the cost.
- **Stronger security**: It helps to build the required security guard rails and policies to be enforced as admission controllers.
- **Scalability with ease**: Container orchestration tools enable users to scale applications with a single command.
- **Quick discovery and troubleshooting**: Container orchestration platforms can detect issues like infrastructure failures and auto-recover or auto-scale, help high availability, and increase the uptime of your application.

Like other pillars of the platform, the primary objective is to standardize workflows, and an orchestrator serves as a prevalent method through which modern platform teams consolidate deployment workflows, thereby eliminating ticket-driven processes.

When choosing an orchestrator, it is essential to ensure that it is flexible enough to handle future additions to your environments and heterogeneous workflows. It is also crucial that the orchestrator can handle multitenancy and easily federate across multiple on-premises data centers and multi-cloud environments.

It is important to note that not all systems can be containerized or shifted to a modern orchestrator, such as vendor-provided monolithic appliances or applications, so platform teams need to identify opportunities for other teams to optimize engagement and automation for orchestrators as per the tenets of the different platform pillars.

Container orchestration dramatically reduces the complexity of application deployment. It helps reduce the cost of deploying, managing, and scaling so the dev team can focus on creating applications that deliver value to your customers and your business.

Observability and analytics

Fundamentally, observability is about recording, organizing, and visualizing data. We cannot get the actual value of observability by just keeping this data in the system. Site reliability engineering, DevOps, or other teams determine what data to generate, collect, aggregate, summarize, and analyze to gain meaningful and actionable insights.

In cloud environments, observability enables teams to track availability, performance, cost, usage, and security across a changing cloud infrastructure. Once a project has been deployed, it must be managed and maintained across multiple cloud providers.

Observability plays a crucial role in maintaining the stability of the application infrastructure by establishing alerts for critical events. Additionally, it leverages logs and analysis tools to provide insight into application behavior, track errors, and facilitate more effective issue troubleshooting. Lastly, implementing tracing systems that can monitor the flow of requests across different microservices and components aids in identifying performance bottlenecks, understanding latency issues, and optimizing system behavior.

In platform engineering, observability helps monitor and analyze the performance of the platform itself and the applications running on it. It involves:

- **Log management**: Involves collecting, storing, and analyzing logs from various platform components. We must use the right tools to build log monitoring capabilities to continuously monitor the application behavior and system performance.

- **Telemetry**: This encompasses gathering metrics and events from the platform to understand its health and performance. Telemetry data is a must to have to detect any anomalies and troubleshoot.

- **Tracing**: This involves tracking the journey of requests through the various services and components of the platform, which is essential for identifying bottlenecks and performance issues.

It emphasizes platform engineers' need to integrate observability into every environment from the outset. When provisioning resources, it is crucial that observability data is readily available to all stakeholders. It entails integrating and correlating data from various sources, including logs and events, to expedite troubleshooting processes. The following are some of the aspects that highlight the need for observability-based approach in platform engineering.

- **Automated systems**: With automation becoming the backbone of modern operations, understanding the inner workings of these automated processes is crucial. Observability allows you to ensure that your automated systems are running as intended, identify inefficiencies, and optimize performance.

- **Complexity**: Modern applications are intricate ecosystems, and managing their performance can be challenging, given their distributed and diverse nature.

- **Need for speed**: In today's 24/7 world, downtime is costly, and businesses must identify and resolve issues rapidly to meet customer expectations.

- **Proactive performance**: Observability is not just about fixing issues; it is about foreseeing them. It empowers businesses to stay ahead, pinpoint bottlenecks, and optimize their systems.

- **Self-services**: In the era of self-service platforms, end users require seamless experiences. Observability ensures all the application functionalities are available and meet the user's expectations.

Subsequently, these teams adopt and develop observability solutions. Observability solutions leverage metrics, traces, and logs as data types to gain insights into and debug systems. Enterprises require unified observability across the entire stack, encompassing cloud infrastructure, runtime orchestration platforms like Kubernetes or Nomad, cloud-managed services such as Azure Managed Databases, and business applications. This unified approach aids teams in comprehending the interdependencies of cloud services and components.

Integrating observability solutions into your infrastructure code offers numerous benefits. Developers gain a deeper understanding of how their systems function and the reliability of their applications. Teams can swiftly troubleshoot issues and trace them to their root cause. The organization can make data-driven decisions to enhance the system, optimize performance, and improve the user experience.

Enterprise-level observability requires:

- Accurate alerting, tracing, logging, and monitoring

- Real-time issue and anomaly detection

- Auto-discovery and integrations across different control planes and environments
- Tagging, labeling, and data-model governance
- Observability as code
- Scalability and performance for multi-cloud and hybrid deployments
- Security, privacy, and RBACs for self-service visualization, configuration, and reporting

Observability is not a mere tool for platform engineering. It is a thought that defines how we understand, manage, and optimize platforms. Software development is evolving, and those using next-gen observability will be able to build high-performing, scalable, and user-centric platforms that create the best software.

Platform architecture

Platform engineering became popular in software companies because it helped developers focus less on infrastructure and more on application development.

The goal of any platform is to abstract the tooling so that the developers can use a UI or the exposed APIs to get the infrastructure ready. It is a goal of a solid internal developer platform, so, the more it overlaps with the developer's comfort zone, the better the architecture and the more influential the platform.

When it comes to the internal developer platform, there are three main goals:

- **Improved developer experience**: The platform must reduce the cognitive load on the developer and eliminate repetitive manual work for both the platform team and the developer.
- **Standardize the regular tasks**: Many workflows in the software delivery cycles can be standardized, for e.g., security, compliance, monitoring, and many other supporting infrastructures.
- **Self-service capability**: Self-service capability is possibly the most critical aspect of an internal developer platform. The goal is to reduce turnaround times so that developers can get the required infrastructure for application development.

In its simplest form, the platform may be seen as two components:

- **Frontend**: It provides one or more end-user interfaces for the developers to interact with IdP and for self-service. The platform engineering team works on integrating tools and services supported by the platform. Developers leverage these capabilities autonomously to enhance productivity, expedite product development, and ensure consistent security and governance policy adherence.
- **Backend**: It provides the necessary infrastructure, services, and tooling automation. The platform team keeps working on developing the platform as a product. While the platform team focuses on developing the platform as a product,

their responsibilities include ensuring the continuous release of new features, integrating new services and tools, and establishing necessary security guardrails for security governance. It ensures the platform remains innovative, adaptable, and secure, meeting the organization's and its stakeholders' evolving needs.

The following figure depicts a platform architecture setup showing various components and personas:

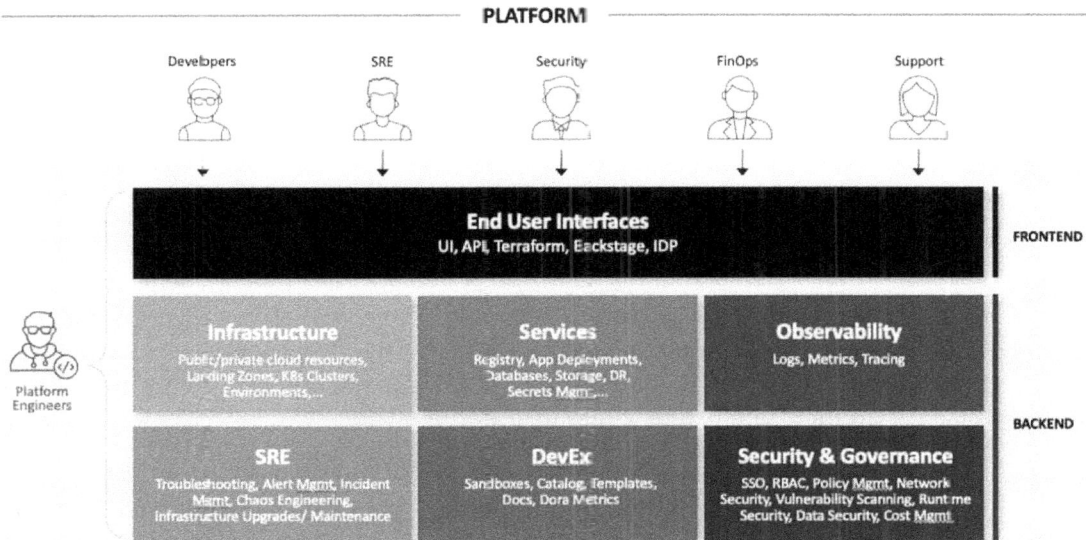

Figure 3.14: Platform architecture

It could entail defining infrastructure resources through declarative specifications for specific teams stored in a Git repository. Through GitOps, these infrastructure resources are automatically provisioned and managed, streamlining the deployment and management processes. GitOps helps with configuration, and the code for the infrastructure and applications is stored in a Git repository. Changes to the system's desired state are made through **pull requests** (**PRs**) and are applied to the dev, stage, and prod environments automatically through CI/CD pipelines. This approach enables versioning, auditability, and collaboration while ensuring that the production environment always reflects the desired state defined in the Git repository.

The backend comprises infrastructure automation (IaC), application services (CI/CD), developer-experience tools, SRE tools and frameworks, and security and governance policy-management tools. Platform teams often augment this backend by introducing an extra layer of automation on top of these infrastructure components, services, and tools. This enhancement enables seamless accessibility through various frontends. Each of the significant components of a platform's backend is described as follows:

- **Infrastructure**: This component facilitates the automation needed to provision and orchestrate both public and private cloud resources. This automation spans from provisioning fundamental infrastructure resources like virtual private clouds and identity and access management roles to more complex resources such as Kubernetes clusters and entire environments. Platform teams frequently employ IaC and GitOps practices to automate these processes.

- **Services**: Every application team uses various tools and services in software development that are not part of the main application, such as container registry, CI/CD pipelines, and Vault for secret management to services like messaging, caching, data backup, etc.

  Platform teams automate these services and offer them to application teams through user-friendly interfaces for streamlined onboarding and integration processes. This approach minimizes repetitive tasks and cognitive burdens on the application teams, allowing them to concentrate on core application development and expedite product delivery.

- **Observability**: Observability encompasses the process of gathering data from operational systems, which serves multiple purposes, such as troubleshooting and issue resolution, analyzing resource utilization for performance enhancement, gathering metrics for capacity planning, and constructing systems to identify potential problems before they manifest.

  Logging, metrics, and tracing form the foundational components of the observability stack. Platform teams commonly employ open-source and commercial solutions and often implement additional automation to integrate with diverse applications for data collection seamlessly. This data is then provided to developers and SRE/Ops teams for analysis and troubleshooting.

- **SRE**: In addition to observability tools, SRE and operations teams leverage various other tools and technologies to oversee and maintain large-scale application infrastructure. These may encompass automation for managing and operating infrastructure, service reliability, incident tracking, alert management tools, customized troubleshooting utilities, and self-healing capabilities.

  Platform teams often establish standardization by adopting a mix of open-source and commercial products for specific tooling requirements, making them accessible to SRE teams. Additionally, platform teams may develop bespoke solutions tailored to their infrastructure and application needs, particularly for tasks like fleet management, advanced debugging, and self-healing functionalities.

- **Developer experience**: Developers are often forced to work on repetitive things when developing a new service or an application. Large organizations have internal application teams, product teams, and business teams, where there is often little sharing of code and tools and work is done in silos. These automations include creating boilerplate code templates for new or existing services, creating dev, stage, prod environments, etc.

Besides this, developers also need to keep a catalog of services they own, what resources they use, services' health, change management, and access to the latest logs. Platform teams build and integrate these capabilities into the platform. Developers can access these services through a unified developer portal. Some of the well-known developer portals, such as Backstage (**https://Backstage.io/**), Port (**https://www.getport.io/**), and Atlassian Compass (**https://www.atlassian.com/software/compass**), provide the capabilities for automating repetitive tasks.

- **Security and governance**: The main task of InfoSec teams is to:

  o   Define a security framework.

  o   Security posture baselining for all the software components, services, and infrastructure.

  o   Enforce all the security policies and practices across the systems in line with the security baseline posture. It also needs continuous compliance with the baseline to detect any drift and required remediation for any security and compliance violations.

The security baseline policies include:

- Authentication through SSO

- Authorization through RBAC

- Identity and rule-based network security

- Continuous compliance tools such as **Open Policy Agent** (**OPA**), Kyverno for implementing granular compliance and security policies at the resource level

- Vulnerability management through image scanning

- Runtime container security using agents

- Use of benchmarking tools such as CIS

Cost-control policies are also very essential in every organization. Platform teams must build checks, provide visibility, and apply cost-control policies automatically at each application development, deployment, and infrastructure management stage.

Platform reference architecture

A group of volunteers at **https://platformengineering.org/** hosted a set of platform reference architectures and allowed participant organizations to create and modify reference architectures. These reference architecture Google slides are hosted at:

https://docs.google.com/presentation/d/1yAfFSjiA0bAFukgu5p1DRMvvGGE1fF4Khv Zbb7gn2I/edit#slide=id.g2a0a50cf76a_0_527

Users may use the reference architecture created for any *cloud service providers* and make their own version of the platform architecture.

We have worked on the AWS Cloud and used the reference architecture created for the **internal developer platform on AWS Cloud**, shown as follows:

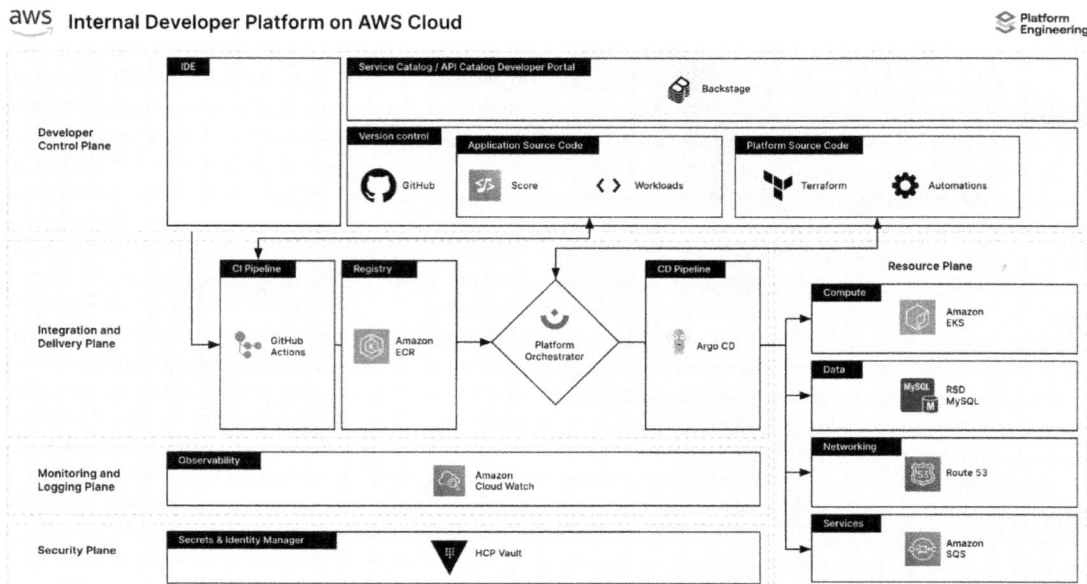

Figure 3.15: Reference platform architecture of IdP on AWS Cloud

The reference architecture created for IDP on AWS Cloud uses most AWS cloud-native services, but these services can be replaced by other equivalent industry-standard tools or services. In reference architecture, the internal developer platform contains four layers:

- **Developer control plane**: It contains a service catalog or API catalog developer portal to access services through a self-service portal or any other frontend tool integrated with backend API for developers to do their tasks. It also contains a VCS to store infrastructure and application code.

- **Integration and delivery plane**: This layer contains the CI pipeline, image registry, orchestrator, and workflow tool to automate the tasks. This layer is essential for task workflow and doing the backend job.

- **Monitoring and logging plane**: It is the observability layer and records all the logs and metrics. The observability layer in platform engineering serves as a vital component for monitoring and analyzing the performance and behavior of the platform's infrastructure and applications. This layer encompasses various tools and practices to collect, analyze, and have visibility to gain a detailed insight into the platform's health, performance, and usage patterns.

- **Security plane**: The security layer in platform engineering is a fundamental component responsible for safeguarding the platform, its infrastructure, and the applications running on it from potential threats, vulnerabilities, and unauthorized access. This layer incorporates various tools, practices, and measures designed to enforce security policies, mitigate risks, and ensure compliance with regulatory requirements.

- **Resource plane**: The resource layer in platform engineering refers to the foundational components and infrastructure resources that support the operation and functionality of the platform. This layer provides the necessary computing, networking, storage, and other resources required to deploy, manage, and run applications and services within the platform environment.

The architectural perspective is grounded in a reference architecture, with each component layer explained in detail in the *Building blocks* section. Refer to the following figure:

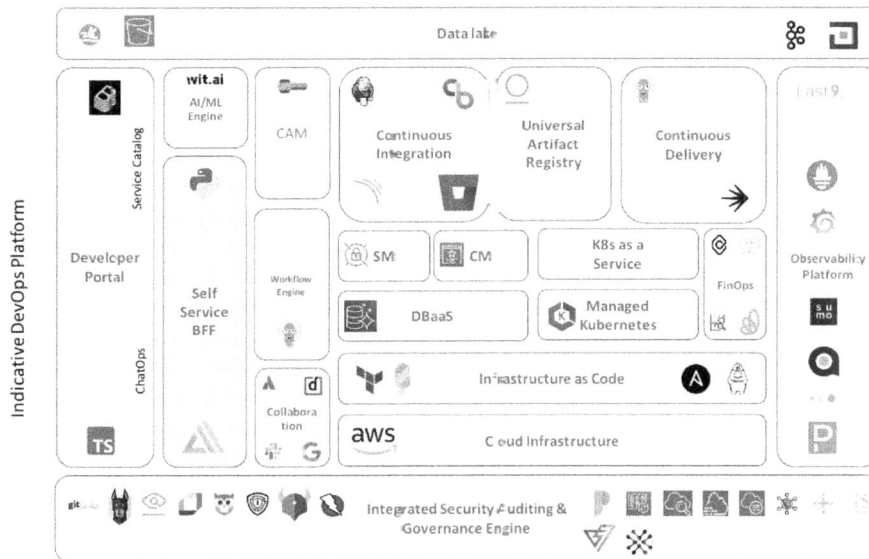

Figure 3.16: Platform architecture view

Platform engineering practice helps organizations build self-service infrastructure, integrate required toolsets, and hide complexities.

Platform engineering has tried to solve the DevOps challenges to help unify scattered tools and accelerate developer productivity as a self-service platform. Platform engineering aims to mitigate the cognitive overload caused by a shared responsibility model and improve developer experience. Organizations can leap forward regarding DevOps maturity if platform engineering is adopted correctly. **Everything as code (XaC)** should be the first guiding principle, followed by *automate everything*. Most importantly, platform engineering should be built as a product, not as an initiative to integrate and orchestrate different tools.

Readers must understand DevOps challenges, the history of platform engineering, and XaC, which inspired industry leaders' development and adoption of platform engineering.

Conclusion

There is no one-size-fits-all approach while building the platform engineering competency in the organization. Organizations are at different maturity states of their DevOps journey, depending on the organization's specific requirements and priorities for platform development. The platform is not just a frontend, backend, or self-service capability. There are different teams and personas (developers, IT team, security, SRE, etc.). Platform teams must possess a comprehensive grasp of user personas and service requirements, ensuring that the platform effectively delivers optimal value to all internal users.

The building blocks and architecture of platform engineering encompass various components and layers that work together to provide a robust and scalable platform for deploying and managing applications and services. Overall, the architecture of platform engineering is designed to provide a scalable, resilient, and agile foundation for developing and operating modern, cloud-native applications and services. It emphasizes modularity, automation, observability, security, and developer experience to enable rapid innovation and value delivery to end users. Multiple reference architectures are available to tweak and modify the organization's needs.

The next chapter will cover how to automate the provisioning of resources with required security guardrails and policies implemented by default.

Multiple choice questions

1. **How many deployments are done by AWS and Airbnb in a day?**

    a. 100

    b. 1000

    c. 10000

    d. More than 100000

2. **What is managed Kubernetes?**

    a. Self-hosted and managed Kubernetes

    b. Developer managed Kubernetes

    c. Kubernetes service offered by cloud providers

    d. It does not exist

3. **Workflow engines are the same as CI/CD pipeline.**

    a. True

    b. False

4. **Observability stacks need the following for correlation:**

    a. Logs only

    b. Logs, events, metrics

c. Logs, events, traces

d. Metrics, logs, events, and traces

5. **How many core pillars are there of platform engineering?**

   a. 2

   b. 6

   c. 4

   d. 7

6. **Policy as code means:**

   a. Developer can use any programming language to enforce policies.

   b. Developer needs specific policy engine and programming language for it.

7. **Platforms inject the required security and compliance policies into SDLC.**

   a. True

   b. False

8. **Internal developer platform can only be created using Kubernetes.**

   a. True

   b. False

9. **Organizations have to follow the platform engineering reference architecture.**

   a. No, they can tweak and modify as per the organization's needs.

   b. They need to stick to reference architecture.

   c. They need to take permission from the respective cloud provider.

   d. They do not need any reference architecture.

Answers

1. d

2. c

3. b

4. d

5. c

6. b

7. a

8. b

9. a

Join our Discord space

Join our Discord workspace for latest updates, offers, tech happenings around the world, new releases, and sessions with the authors:

https://discord.bpbonline.com

CHAPTER 4

Build Infrastructure with Security and Compliance

Introduction

This chapter of the book will cover the application of **everything as code** in infrastructure and the required security and policy governance. This chapter will explore **infrastructure as code** (**IaC**) and the application of security and policies across all phases of the **secure software development life cycle** (**SSDLC**), achieved with the help of platform engineering. This helps developer teams to develop faster without any dependencies. All security attributes and checks are built in as part of platform engineering.

Structure

The chapter covers the following topics:

- Infrastructure as code
- Security policies and benchmarking
- Policy as code

Objectives

By the end of this chapter, you will understand how to codify your **infrastructure as code** (**IaC**), **security as code** (**SaC**), and **policies as code** (**PaC**). This will automate the provisioning of resources with required security guardrails and policies implemented by default.

Overview of platform engineering

Platform engineering is the practice of designing, building, and maintaining the foundational infrastructure that helps in software development.

Platform engineering has its roots in DevOps. It helps software engineering teams create infrastructure management components (servers, networks, databases, APIs, and other development tools) to manage the software development process effectively.

Consider a scenario in which your application has many microservices, and each microservice is running on a different tech stack. Besides this, each services have a different scale. Now, if you need to create a large infrastructure for multiple services in a manual way or through script automation, it will take several hours or days to complete this activity. Also, if we must do this activity regularly as per the demand of resources, you need many people to do this task.

Here, IaC is going to help you manage large-scale, distributed systems, cloud-native applications, and microservices-based architecture. You are going to get rid of manual processes that were more error-prone and could not be scaled, much less standardized.

IaC can help teams to deliver changes continuously, quickly, and reliably in a highly scalable infrastructure. This book describes various principles, practices, and patterns for achieving this. There are a few fundamental best practices:

- Achieving complete automation by defining everything as code. The following are some examples of everything as code:
  - o **Virtual servers**: Instead of manually configuring **virtual machines** (**VMs**) through a **graphical user interface** (**GUI**), IaC tools like Terraform or AWS CloudFormation use code to **define** and **create VMs**. This ensures consistency, reproducibility, and version control for your server infrastructure.
  - o **Hardware devices**: The configuration and management of hardware devices can be automated through code. Tools like Ansible or Puppet can be used to define and enforce configurations, update firmware, and manage network devices.
  - o **Application deployments**: Deployment pipelines automate the process of building, testing, and deploying applications. Tools like Jenkins, GitLab CI/CD, or Azure DevOps use code to define the steps in the pipeline, ensuring consistent and reliable deployments.
  - o **Delivery pipelines**: Entire delivery pipelines, including infrastructure provisioning, application deployment, and testing, can be defined and managed through code. This enables **continuous integration and continuous delivery** (**CI/CD**) practices.
  - o **Platform services**: Cloud platforms like AWS, Azure, and GCP offer a wide range of services that can be managed through code. This includes databases,

message queues, storage services, and more. IaC tools allow you to define and provision these services in a consistent and repeatable manner.

o **Tests**: Automated tests are essential for ensuring the quality and reliability of software systems. Testing frameworks and tools allow you to write code to define and execute tests, ensuring that your applications and infrastructure function as expected.

• Implement continuous integration and delivery as a work-in-progress, ensuring rapid feedback and reduced risks. This needs implementation of:

o Source code management and versioning

o Pipelines with required testing integration and guardrails setup

Use a modular approach by building small, independent pieces that can be easily modified or replaced. This requires tooling and policy automation integrated with IDP.

Infrastructure as code

IaC is a basic building block of platform engineering and can be achieved using several tools in the market. Some of the well-known tools, such as Terraform, OpenTofu, Pulumi, and Ansible, are widely used for automated configuration management and provisioning infrastructure. Cross plane is another tool that is promising and uses Kubernetes's reconciliation loop to ensure no drift between the defined policy and the state of the infrastructure. If someone is starting from scratch and building a cloud-native application, they can explore the cross plane tool, as this reduces the number of tools and manages the entire IaC in a cloud-native way.

Before infrastructure as code, infrastructure provisioning and management were through clicking in a **user interface** (**UI**), running commands using CLI, running batch scripts, or using configuration management tools that were not designed considering cloud infrastructure. Each of these methods has some shortcomings; for example, manual interactions through GUI or **command-line interfaces** (**CLI**) can introduce unpredictability and inconsistencies, making it challenging to achieve repeatable and reliable results. There are some manual inputs required, which lead to human errors. Configuration management tools and automation scripts are mostly imperative (procedural) and will not be able to manage infrastructure declaratively. Modern-day IaC tool now uses the full software development lifecycle, such as planning, design, code development, and build.

Brief history of IaC

While DevOps has been around for just over a decade, IaC is a core part of it. While it seems that IaC is a new development after DevOps, it is not true. IaC has been around since the 1970s as configuration management. When we hear the term IaC, we usually think about modern tools like Chef, Ansible, or Terraform.

We can see the IaC journey with the help of the following figure:

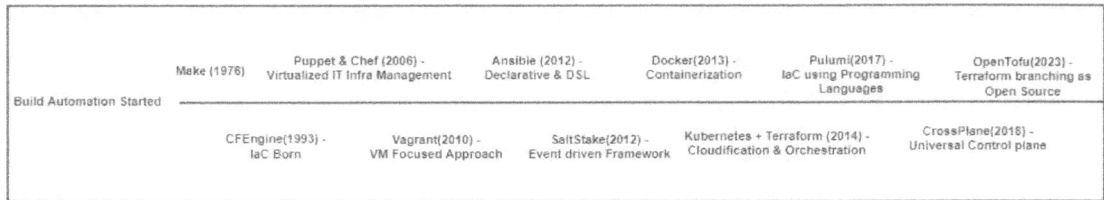

| Build Automation Started | Make (1976) | Puppet & Chef (2006) - Virtualized IT Infra Management | Ansible (2012) - Declarative & DSL | Docker(2013) - Containerization | Pulumi(2017) - IaC using Programming Languages | OpenTofu(2023) - Terraform branching as Open Source |
| | CFEngine(1993) - IaC Born | Vagrant(2010) - VM Focused Approach | SaltStake(2012) - Event driven Framework | Kubernetes + Terraform (2014) - Cloudification & Orchestration | CrossPlane(2018) - Universal Control plane | |

Figure 4.1: IaC journey and history

We are going to cover these tools and the history of IaC tools as follows:

- **Make (building and configuration management, 1976)**: Make is a build automation and configuration management tool that has been around since the early days of Unix. Make is a utility that automates the process of building, compiling, and linking software projects. It was originally designed to simplify the build process for large C programs, but it has since become a widely used tool for managing builds and configurations in various environments. All *nix lovers must have used the **make** utility at some point in time for their work:

  o   Dependency tracking

  o   Rule-based building

  o   Makefiles that contain the build rules and dependencies for your project

- **CFEngine (the beginning of modern IaC, 1993)**: CFEngine is an early open-source configuration management tool that was released in 1993. CFEngine was developed by *Mark Burgess* for his research in theoretical physics. He was supposed to maintain several Unix workstations that were running different versions of Unix, each with its own set of issues, which required a lot of time-consuming manual scripting and user support.

  o   **Declarative configuration**: CFEngine uses a simple, readable syntax (like YAML) to define the desired state for hosts.

  o   **Agent-based**: Each host runs an agent that connects back to the CFEngine master server to receive configuration updates and report on its current state.

  o   **State-based**: CFEngine ensures that each host's configuration is in the desired state by comparing the reported state with the desired state.

  o   **Declarative**: Mark found a way to differentiate between these platforms using a **domain-specific language** (**DSL**). The declarative style of configuration management helped to ease the configuration management process for a long time.

  o   **Desired state**: State-based configuration describes the desired end state, like ensuring the package **nginx** is installed and the service **nginx** is running.

o **Idempotent**: CFEngine will only make changes if the system is not already in the desired state. Running the same configuration multiple times has the same effect as running it once.

o **Automatic correction**: If the system deviates from the desired state (e.g., someone manually removes the **nginx** package), CFEngine will automatically detect and rectify the issue.

State-based IaC tool is different from imperative configuration tools:

o **Procedural**: We create a sequence of commands as a script to execute, like **download nginx package, install nginx package, start nginx service**.

o **Not inherently idempotent**: Running the same script multiple times might lead to errors or unintended consequences (e.g., reinstalling the package).

o **No automatic correction**: If something changes outside the script's execution, it will not be automatically fixed. You need to make changes to the script to handle these exceptions.

- **Puppet and Chef (2006)**: Puppet and Chef revolutionized the management of IT infrastructure in virtualized environments. These tools streamline the provisioning and configuration process, offering a centralized approach to managing system resources across many servers. Their declarative languages allow administrators to define the desired state of the infrastructure, reducing manual errors and ensuring consistency. The following is the list of key differentiators for Puppet and Chef:

  o **Automation**: Automation is a key aspect of both Puppet and Chef. They enable the automation of deployment tasks, software installations, and updates, saving time and effort for IT teams.

  o **Compliance and security**: Puppet and Chef play a crucial role in ensuring compliance and security. They provide mechanisms to enforce security policies and regulatory requirements, automating the process of checking and maintaining server configurations.

  o **Scalability and efficiency**: Overall, Puppet and Chef have become essential tools for modern IT operations, offering powerful capabilities for managing and automating large-scale infrastructure with efficiency and reliability.

- **Vagrant (VM-focused approach, 2010)**: Vagrant was once a preferred IaC tool for building complete development environments. It simplifies the creation, management, and provisioning of virtualized environments. It enables teams to replicate development, testing environments effortlessly, ensuring consistency across the software development lifecycle. Vagrant automates the setup and configuration of complex environments and seamlessly integrates with popular virtualization platforms and cloud providers. Its user-friendly interface and extensive plugin ecosystem make Vagrant an essential tool for modern software development, offering agility, scalability, and reproducibility in infrastructure deployment. Vagrant uses **Vagrantfile** for declaratively defining the desired state.

- **Ansible (2012)**: In 2012, Ansible was introduced, which uses a declarative, domain-specific language. It was like **Puppet** and **CFEngine**. However, Ansible is unique in that it is agentless, meaning it does not require a component installed or running on the managed machine. Rather than using an agent, it creates a temporary SSH connection to the machine. Initially, it was thought that managing resources and state for an application, rather than an entire machine, was necessary. The current era of configuration management tools focuses on configuring machines and operating systems, which fall under the category of configuration management and can be used in the codification of Infrastructure.

- **SaltStack (2012)**: Salt, built on the Python programming language, is an event-driven automation tool and framework designed to simplify the deployment, configuration, and management of complex IT systems. The team can automate routine infrastructure using SaltStack, ensuring that all components operate in a consistent state. Its versatile nature makes it suitable for various applications, including configuration management, which involves:

  o OS deployment management and configuration.

  o Servers, virtual machines, containers, databases, web servers, and network devices management.

  o Consistent configuration and preventing configuration drift from baseline or best practices.

- **Docker (2013)**: It is the next generation of configuration management with logical progression. Virtualization and cloud services led to the adoption of container technologies. The introduction of Docker in 2013 led to a significant surge in complexity, resulting in the creation of more advanced solutions and architectures, but also generating new issues in terms of scalability. This development occurred at around the same time that the idea of constructing applications as a set of microservices rather than monolithic systems began to gain traction, a design approach that Docker is well-equipped to handle.

- **Kubernetes and Terraform (2014)**: Terraform and Kubernetes were launched in 2014. Terraform also provides comprehensive infrastructure configuration management with a domain-specific language like its predecessor. However, Terraform was primarily designed for managing diverse and complex IT operational workflows in a declarative manner. Terraform has a large community, and with the growth of the cloud, Terraform became the first choice as an IaC tool.

To create a deployment to manage your workloads in Kubernetes, the following is a Kubernetes deployment configuration file. It defines a deployment named **nginx-deployment** that will create three replicas of a pod running the **nginx: 1.14.2** image. Refer to the following code:

```
apiVersion: apps/v1
kind: Deployment
metadata:
  name: nginx-deployment
  labels:
    app: nginx
spec:
  replicas: 3
  selector:
    matchLabels:
      app: nginx
  template:
    metadata:
      labels:
        app: nginx
    spec:
      containers:
      - name: nginx
        image: nginx:1.14.2
        ports:
        - containerPort: 80
```

Code 4.1: Create a deployment for the workload

To use this deployment:

1. **Save**: Save this configuration to a file (e.g., **nginx-deployment.yaml**).

2. **Apply**: Use the **kubectl apply** command to create the deployment:

   Bash prompt:

   kubectl apply -f nginx-deployment.yaml

   This will create the deployment and the associated pods in your Kubernetes cluster. You can then access the NGINX web server running in the pods.

3. **Create pods**: When you apply this configuration to a Kubernetes cluster, the deployment controller will create three pods.

4. **Manage replicas**: The deployment controller ensures that three replicas of the pod are always running. If a pod fails, the controller will automatically create a new one.

5. **Updates**: If you update the deployment (e.g., change the image version), the deployment controller will gradually roll out the update by creating new pods with the updated configuration and terminating old ones.

The following Terraform configuration will create a **t2.medium** EC2 instance in the **ap-south-1** region using the specified AMI in AWS. The following configurations have three blocks as **required_providers**, providers, and resources. For resource configuration in resource block, you specify:

o   **Amazon Machine Image (AMI)**: AMI ID to use for the instance. It is essentially a template that contains the software configuration (operating system, application software, and other settings) required to launch an instance, which is a virtual server in the cloud.

o   **Instance_type**: Sets the instance type, which determines the hardware configuration (e.g., CPU, memory) of the instance (**t2.medium**).

o   **Tags**: Assigns tags to the instance for identification and organization. Here, a tag with the key name and value. An example instance is added, shown as follows:

```
terraform {
required_providers {
aws={
source = "hashicorp/aws"
version="~>4.16"
}
}
required_version=">1.2.0"
}
provider "aws" {
region="ap-south-1"
}
Resource "aws_instance" "app_server" {
    ami = "ami-232024e2"
    instance_type = "t2.medium"
    Tags=  {
          Name="ExampleInstance"
    }
}
```

Code 4.2: Create an AWS ec2 instance using terraform code

How to use this code:

1.   **Save the code**: Save this code as a **.tf** file (e.g., **main.tf**).

2.   **Initialize Terraform**: Run **terraform init** in the directory where you saved the file. This will download the necessary AWS provider plugins.

3. **Plan the changes**: Execute `terraform plan` to see what Terraform will create.

4. **Apply the changes**: Run `terraform apply` to create the EC2 instance in your AWS account.

This Terraform configuration will create a **t2.medium** EC2 instance in the **ap-south-1** region using the specified AMI:

- **Pulumi (2017)**: Most of the software engineers were more comfortable in programming languages rather than using DSLs they are unfamiliar with, and increasingly found themselves in situations where a programming language would be more expressive, such as loops and logical conditions, where Terraform is not very expressive. Pulumi is an emerging tool that approaches infrastructure management using a choice of programming language rather than a DSL.

The following Python script provides a basic example of using Pulumi to create and configure AWS resources rather than using declarative language:

```python
import pulumi
import pulumi_aws as aws
group = aws.ec2.SecurityGroup(
    "web-sg",
    description="Enable HTTP access",
    ingress=[
        {
            "protocol": "tcp",
            "from_port": 80,
            "to_port": 80,
            "cidr_blocks": ["0.0.0.0/0"],}
    ],
}
server = aws.ec2.Instance(
    "web-server",
    ami="ami-0319ef1a70c93d5c8",
    instance_type="t2.micro",
    vpc_security_group_ids=[group.id],
)
pulumi.export("public_ip", server.public_ip)
pulumi.export("public_dns", server.public_dns)
```

Code 4.3: Create an AWS ec2 instance using terraform code

How to use this code:

1. **Save the code**: Save this code as a **.py** file (e.g., **main.py**).

2. **Initialize Pulumi**: Run `pulumi init` in the directory where you saved the file.

3. **Plan the changes**: Execute `pulumi up` to see what Pulumi will create.

4. **Apply the changes**: Run `pulumi up` to create the EC2 instance and security group.

This Python script using Pulumi will create an AWS EC2 instance and a security group. However, the team has better control on resource creation programmatically.

- **Crossplane (2018)**: Crossplane is an open-source Kubernetes extension that enables your cluster to serve as a universal control plane. This innovative technology empowers platform teams to create custom APIs and abstractions, leveraging the full potential of Kubernetes features like namespaces, role-based access controls, and policies. With Crossplane, you can seamlessly manage diverse resources from various sources through standard Kubernetes APIs. Platform teams can design custom APIs that ensure security and compliance enforcement across resources or clouds without burdening developers with unnecessary complexity.

Crossplane's power lies in its ability to create multiple resources with a single API call, streamlining your workflow and simplifying management. Create a `.yaml` file and use **kubectl** to create an **ec2** instance. However, you need to setup Crossplane and create provider (AWS) configuration:

```
apiVersion: ec2.aws.crossplane.io/v1alpha1
kind: Instance
metadata:
  name: sample-instance
spec:
  forProvider:
    region: ap-south-1
    imageId: ami-0ecc74eca1d66d8a6
    instanceType: t2.micro
    keyName: my-crossplane-key-pair
  providerConfigRef:
    name: awsconfig
```

Code 4.4: Create an AWS ec2 instance using Crossplane in declarative manner

How to use this code:

1. **Save the code**: Save this code as a `.yaml` file (e.g., **instance.yaml**).

2. **AWS provider configuration**: Create a separate YAML file (e.g., **awsconfig. yaml**) containing the AWS provider configuration, including access key, secret key, and region.

3. **Apply the configuration**: Use the Crossplane CLI to apply the configuration files: `crossplane apply -f awsconfig.yaml -f instance.yaml`

This will create an EC2 instance in the **ap-south-1** region using the specified AMI, instance type, and key pair.

- **OpenTofu (2023)**: OpenTofu is an open-source Terraform fork and replacement. OpenTofu is a community-driven project in response to HashiCorp's license changes announcement and is an official Linux Foundation project. OpenTofu is making progress to join **Cloud Native Computing Foundation** (**CNCF**). OpenTofu is a fork of Terraform and is an IaC framework that enables DevOps, SREs, and platform teams to provision and manage cloud resources using declarative language and automating infrastructure creation.

Create a declarative script to create an S3 bucket:

```
resource "aws_s3_bucket" "data-bucket" {
  bucket = "data-tofu-bucket"
  tags = {
  Name  = "Data bucket"
  }
}
```

Code 4.5: AWS S3 bucket creation using OpenTofu code

How to use this code:

1. **Save the code**: Save this code in a file named **main.tf** (or any **.tf** file).

2. **Initialize Terraform**: In your terminal, navigate to the directory where you saved the file and run **terraform init**. This will initialize Terraform and download the necessary provider plugins.

3. **Plan and apply**: Run **terraform plan** to see what Terraform will do. If everything looks good, run terraform apply to create the S3 bucket.

Following is a quick comparison of some of the key features of IaC tools used by most of the companies:

Feature	Terraform	OpenTofu	Pulumi	Crossplane	Ansible
Cloud compatibility	Wide range (AWS, Azure, GCP, etc.)	Kubernetes-native, works across clouds	Wide range (AWS, Azure, GCP, etc.)	Kubernetes-native, works across clouds	Wide range (AWS, Azure, GCP, on-prem)
Programming model	Declarative (HCL)	Declarative (HCL, planned support for other languages)	Imperative (Go, Python, TypeScript, etc.)	Declarative (YAML, with Go controllers)	Imperative (YAML playbooks)

Feature	Terraform	OpenTofu	Pulumi	Crossplane	Ansible
Community support	Large and active community, extensive documentation	Growing community, HashiCorp's support	Growing community, strong company backing	CNCF project, growing community	Large and active community, Red Hat support
Primary focus	Infrastructure provisioning and management	Managing Kubernetes deployments and infrastructure	General-purpose IaC with focus on developer experience	Building and managing cloud-native platforms	Configuration management, application deployment
Strengths	Mature, widely adopted, extensive provider ecosystem	Kubernetes-native, strong focus on platform engineering	Flexibility of general-purpose languages, strong for complex logic	Extensibility, enables platform as a product	Agentless, simple to learn, good for existing infrastructure
Weaknesses	Can be verbose for complex deployments, HCL can be limiting	Relatively new, ecosystem still developing	Steeper learning curve for some languages	Can be complex for simple use cases	Less suited for complex infrastructure provisioning

Table 4.1: Key IaC tool features comparison

IaC a code paradigm for infrastructure

IaC is a reliable method to automate the provisioning and management of infrastructure using declarative code.

IaC uses the software engineering methodologies, principles, and tools in the cloud infrastructure. IaC's major benefit is that developers could now create a consistent, repeatable workflow, and help in wider-scale deployments across a range of resources, environments, and locations.

If we look into details, IaC provisions infrastructure and application resources creation achieved using machine-readable definition files instead of through configuration tools:

- **As Code paradigm for platform engineering**: As Code paradigm is aligned with the everything as code and core of platform engineering. Different parts of the infrastructure and things can be codified using different toolsets. A partial list of things to consider be codified includes:

- o Virtual servers

- o Hardware devices

- o Application deployments

- o Delivery pipelines

- o Platform services

- o Tests

We will go into the detail of IaC in modern cloud-based application development. IaC involves managing and provisioning infrastructure through code, enabling greater speed, agility, and consistency. Key benefits include repeatability, accountability, improved productivity, and collaboration. The following sections cover key elements of IaC, such as tools, versioning, testing, and CI/CD pipelines. It emphasizes the shift towards cloud-based infrastructure and the need for automation to manage frequent changes. We will begin with guidance on starting with IaC, including defining a target state and codifying existing infrastructure. Overall, it highlights IaC as a crucial practice for organizations seeking to optimize their cloud infrastructure and streamline their development processes.

Versioning of infrastructure code

Code and configuration for infrastructure and other system elements should be versioned. This code shall be stored in a **version control system** (**VCS**) or **source code management** (**SCM**) system. These VCS keep track of code changes, compare versions, and allow recovery of infrastructure using old code in case of any issue with the new infrastructure setup. VCS can also trigger actions automatically when changes are committed for CI/CD pipelines. Versioning helps in some of the core aspects of infrastructure management:

- **Increased efficiency and automation**: Versioning infrastructure code allows for automation and increased efficiency in managing your infrastructure. By automating infrastructure provisioning and updates through CI/CD pipelines, deployments become faster and require less manual effort. Managing infrastructure changes programmatically reduces the need for error-prone manual intervention. Additionally, the ability to define reusable infrastructure components and modules promotes consistency and reduces code duplication, further streamlining the management process. This approach treats infrastructure as code, enabling faster, more reliable, and efficient deployments.

- **Disaster recovery**: Versioned infrastructure code is crucial for robust disaster recovery It enables rapid rebuilding of infrastructure in a new environment, minimizing downtime and business impact. Version control ensures consistent configurations during recovery, reducing errors and inconsistencies. The following are the key benefits of version controlled infrastructure code:

o **Faster recovery**: In a disaster scenario, having versioned infrastructure code allows you to quickly rebuild your infrastructure in a new environment. This minimizes downtime and reduces the impact on your business operations.

o **Consistency**: Version control ensures that you rebuild your infrastructure with the same configurations and settings as the original environment. This reduces the risk of errors and inconsistencies during recovery.

o **Reproducible disaster recovery drills**: You can use versioned code to create reproducible disaster recovery drills. This allows you to test your recovery procedures and ensure they are effective.

o **Reduced risk of configuration drift**: Configuration drift occurs when the actual state of your infrastructure deviates from the desired state defined in your code. Version control helps minimize this risk by providing a single source of truth for your infrastructure configuration.

- **Compliance audit**: Versioning infrastructure code provides a clear and auditable history of all changes, fostering accountability and understanding of infrastructure evolution. Following are the key benefits of version controlled infrastructure code:

o **Traceability and auditability**: Version control systems like Git provide a detailed history of changes to your infrastructure code. This allows auditors to track who made what changes, when, and why. This granular audit trail is crucial for demonstrating compliance with regulations and internal policies.

o **Reproducibility**: With versioned code, you can recreate the exact state of your infrastructure at any point in time. This is invaluable for audits, as you can demonstrate the state of your infrastructure at a specific date or during a particular incident.

o **Evidence of compliance**: Version history serves as documented evidence of your adherence to compliance requirements. You can show how your infrastructure has evolved to meet specific standards and regulations over time.

o **Rollback to compliant state**: If an audit reveals a non-compliant configuration, you can easily revert to a previous, compliant version of your infrastructure code.

Branching strategy for infrastructure code

Branching strategies for infrastructure code are crucial for managing and deploying infrastructure changes in a controlled and organized manner, similar to how they are used for application code. They help teams collaborate effectively, ensure quality, and minimize risks when updating infrastructure:

- **Main or master branch**: Represents the production environment. Only stable and thoroughly tested code should be merged here.

- **Development branch**: Used for ongoing development and integration of new features and changes.

- **Feature branches**: Created for specific features or bug fixes. Developers work on these branches in isolation before merging them back into the development branch.

- **Release branches**: Created from the development branch when preparing for a release. Used for final testing and bug fixes before merging into main.

- **Hotfix branches**: Created from the main branch to address urgent issues in production. After fixing the issue, the hotfix branch is merged back into both the main and develop branches.

Example workflow using the Git branching strategy:

1. **Feature development**: A developer creates a new feature branch from the develop branch to work on a new feature (e.g., adding a new database server).

2. **Testing**: Once the feature is complete, it is tested in a development environment.

3. **Merge to develop**: If the tests pass, the feature branch is merged into the development branch.

4. **Release preparation**: When a release is planned, a release branch is created from development.

5. **Testing and deployment**: The release branch is deployed to a staging environment for final testing.

6. **Merge to main**: After successful testing, the release branch is merged into the main branch and deployed to production.

7. **Hotfix**: If a critical bug is found in production, a hotfix branch is created from main, the bug is fixed, and the hotfix branch is merged back into both main and develop.

Popular version control systems

GitHub and GitLab are two of the most popular VCS in the world, and they play a crucial role in enabling IaC. Here is a brief summary of the features of these two popular choices:

- **GitHub**: With its vast community and tight CI/CD integration through GitHub Action, it allows for version-controlled infrastructure, automated deployments, and collaborative infrastructure development.

- **GitLab**: A comprehensive DevOps platform, it offers built-in CI/CD pipelines, a strong security focus, and an integrated approach to managing the entire IaC lifecycle, from code to deployment and security. Both platforms empower teams to implement IaC effectively, ensuring reliable, scalable, and secure infrastructure management.

Importance of infrastructure as code

There is a big change in Infrastructure provisioning and management after the migration of applications to the cloud and the cloudification of all applications. There is a big shift in the SDLC process, and organizations can deliver changes very quickly. Some large organizations can do thousands of new feature releases in a single day, which is not possible without IaC. The following are some significant trends:

- **The transition to the cloud**: The first trend is the migration of all digital native business applications to the cloud, as more organizations move workloads from on-premises or data center environments to cloud-based infrastructure. Cloud service providers like AWS, Microsoft Azure, and Google Cloud are driving this shift. With cloud environments, teams can seamlessly manage resources without manual provisioning or configuration. Instead, these cloud providers offer APIs for provisioning and management, making it possible to manage infrastructure as code.

- **Cloud modernization**: After organizations transition to the cloud, organizations tend to look for opportunities to maximize the value they get from their cloud environment.

  o Companies are embracing innovative technologies such as serverless computing, containers, and Kubernetes to modernize their infrastructure.

  o Cloud service providers offer managed services for cloud migration, allowing organizations to benefit from expert guidance without maintaining specialized teams.

  o This shift enables businesses to reap the advantages of ephemeral, stateless workloads that exist only temporarily, making it easier to decommission them after meeting specific needs or scaling requirements.

  o All the preceding methods enable teams to deliver value quickly and without any failure.

- **Frequent infrastructure changes**: Organizations are recognizing the need for speed and agility in releasing new features or changes. They are finding that embracing the cloud's inherent elasticity allows them to move faster. While managing a few dozen cloud resources with scripts or interactive tools might be manageable, teams often find themselves dealing with tens of thousands of resources that change daily or hourly. In such cases, manual management becomes impractical, and automation is essential.

  This can only be achieved by IaC. IaC can help manage dynamic infrastructure, which requires to be upscaled or downscaled and needs frequent changes.

Key elements of IaC

The key elements of IaC are similar to software engineering practice:

- **Tools**: To start with IaC, you need a tool or engine that translates the IaC understandable by the cloud provider as instructions. Some of the key considerations for the selection of IaC tools are:

  o Cloud providers may support their IaC tools, such as AWS CloudFormation, Terraform, or Pulumi, which are vendor agnostic.

  o Tools understand machine declarative language such as YAML or JSON.

  o DSL or general-purpose programming languages such as Go, Python, and Java may be used by the tools.

- **Versioning**: When infrastructure is defined using code, it becomes possible to track changes, collaborate with teams, and ensure security through traditional software development practices. With version control systems, such as GitLab, GitHub, and Bitbucket, and infrastructure as code, you can:

  o Check-in your configurations into source control systems like GitHub, Bitbucket, or Azure DevOps.

  o Version control your configurations to maintain a record of changes:

    ▪ *What* changes were made.

    ▪ *When* the changes were made.

    ▪ *Who* made the changes.

  o Perform code reviews by team members or security scanners to ensure compliance and integrity.

- **Test**: As complex systems grow, it is natural to feel nervous about making changes without thoroughly verifying their impact. IaC empowers teams to write tests for their infrastructure, ensuring correctness and confidence in the face of change. By implementing policies, teams can guarantee that all provisioned infrastructure and configurations adhere to required security frameworks, eliminating uncertainty and promoting compliance.

- **CI/CD pipelines**: To maintain the consistency and immutability for infrastructure, IaC and application code are deployed through CI/CD pipelines, enabling the deployment of infrastructure configurations through existing CI/CD tools. This approach automates the process of building and deploying infrastructure, mirroring the same workflow used for application code, ensuring consistency and efficiency in managing both applications and infrastructure.

Benefits of infrastructure as code

IaC uses similar SDLC principles and adds an abstraction for infrastructure creation and management. This is easy to provision, de-provision, and scale the required infrastructure for applications.

Here are some of the key benefits IaC provides:

- **Repeatability and consistency**: Infrastructure created and managed via IaC can be deployed consistently without failure. The team requires a development environment that dynamically mirrors the production environment and must ensure infrastructure is deployed consistently across single or multiple regions. This is easily achieved with IaC.

- **Accountability**: Changes to the infrastructure without change management can be prevented and easily tracked using version control for your IaC files, allowing teams to identify modifications accurately.

- **Improved productivity**: Developers typically use an **integrated development environment** (**IDE**) regularly. When infrastructure is coded, it leverages IDE features such as autocompletion and method parameter lookups. Additionally, with the assistance of Gen AI, infrastructure teams can generate and use IaC more efficiently.

- **Better collaboration**: IaC facilitates closer collaboration between infrastructure and software development teams by adopting DevOps principles. When infrastructure is coded as part of the SDLC process, it creates a common language and set of practices that all stakeholders understand. This common understanding creates cross-team collaboration, which is a core principle of DevOps.

Start with infrastructure as code

Starting IaC in a startup with new projects is not very difficult and can be straightforward. However, for other companies, it is not so easy. Most of the companies, whether large or small, have a lot of infrastructure that was created by the console of a cloud provider or through batch scripts. This might be maintained by a team with documentation created, which may or may not be maintained. These recommendations provide a starting point for IaC adoption in your company. The following section discusses a few recommendations.

Define a target state

Before starting your IaC journey, look at your current journey of automation. It depends on your company's requirements and the set of tools used by your company currently. You shall look at the **current** state of your automation, and the target state is viewed with milestones:

- The scale of your infrastructure.
- Interconnectivity between environments.
- The deployment frequency of your application and the rate of changes in your infrastructure.
- Your team and their capabilities to support the infrastructure.
- Infrastructure code should be integrated into your CD pipeline, where you are ready to deploy after infrastructure creation.

You and your team need to look at the target state to achieve with its cloud infrastructure, with required security, compliance, quality, and cost factors.

Codifying existing infrastructure

As stated previously, it is easy to start the IaC journey with greenfield projects, but for many companies, infrastructure is created and managed without code. So, you cannot directly start using IaC tools for existing infrastructure; you can start importing existing infrastructure into new IaC tools. For example, you might have an application server that you want to manage as IaC; you can start codifying the infrastructure required, stored in VCS, create a pipeline with required security and compliance guardrails, and test integration as part of your codification.

Security policies

One of the worst nightmares is not having common templates with policies enforced for the entire organization. The team shall have standard guardrails and policies that apply consistently for infrastructure build. It is very important to plan security and respective policies as part of IaC design. This empowers the development teams with the required flexibility to incorporate required security controls and policies.

In a nutshell, you might start with a new project so you do not disrupt existing projects. Once the initial implementation is successful, apply the same process and change the existing infrastructure. Pick a project where you can see value early and then start implementing it.

Challenges and limitations with IaC

Platform engineering is a nascent field, and finding skilled professionals can be tough. Reskilling your existing teams is a smart strategy. The following are the challenges and possible solutions to address the following challenges:

- **Challenge 1: Skillset of team members**

    In many places, infrastructure or operations teams are not well-versed in version control systems (Git) or programming in the organization. This is a major hurdle to reskilling the existing teams in VCS and coding.

Solution: It is not possible to replace existing DevOps engineers working on Infrastructure provisioning and automation with new resources skilled in platform engineering. Organizations need to look at the following options to reskill existing team members:

o   **Targeted training**: Invest in training programs specifically focused on Git, scripting languages (Python, Bash), and IaC tools (OpenTofu, Pulumi, etc.).

o   **Pair programming**: Encourage collaboration between experienced developers and infrastructure team members to facilitate knowledge transfer. Another option is to bring one expert team member on platform engineering to train existing team members.

o   **Gradual transition**: Start with simple IaC tasks and gradually increase complexity as the team's skills develop.

o   **Internal workshops**: Organize internal workshops and knowledge-sharing sessions to foster learning and collaboration.

- **Challenge 2: Learning new tools**

Solution: IaC tools can have a steep learning curve, requiring time and effort to master. It is not straightforward to run the tools and start creating and managing infrastructure. The team needs some learning before the adoption of new technology within an organization.

o   **Structured learning paths**: Create clear learning paths with well-defined milestones and practical exercises.

o   **Hands-on labs**: Provide access to sandbox environments where team members can experiment with IaC tools without fear of impacting production systems.

o   **Dedicated learning time**: Encourage dedicated time for learning and experimentation.

- **Challenge 3: Hiring**

Solution: There is a high demand for skilled people with DevOps and automation. So, there is always a challenge to hire good people in IaC. This is making hiring competitive. Organizations have having following options to build a platform engineering team:

o   **Reskilling existing teams**: Prioritize reskilling existing employees to fill IaC roles.

o   **Competitive compensation and benefits**: Offer attractive salaries and benefits packages to attract top talent.

o   **Internship programs**: Develop internship programs to train and recruit promising candidates.

o **Partnerships with educational institutions**: Collaborate with universities and training providers to source skilled individuals.

The journey to managing your environments using IaC will typically start with a small deployment or new small projects where the risks of failure are lower. Once you are successful in the initial journey, you can increase the footprint by growing the adoption. Once you have the required team and process, the organization is ready to move on the right path for the adoption of IaC.

Declarative versus imperative

There is a very important aspect of DevOps and platform engineering that is automation. These automations are handled by the tool, and users do not need to go into lower-level execution.

Declarative tools have gained widespread popularity across the industry, particularly in the IaC space for automation. When using declarative code, changes and updates typically fall to the infrastructure team.

Declarative tools are idempotent, meaning you define the target state of the solution. This ensures that the process can be executed multiple times with the same result. On the other hand, imperative approaches involve defining a set of steps to achieve a desired goal, like procedural programming. Imperative tools offer more control and flexibility when writing instructions. These tools are most useful in situations where you need to deploy once without maintaining any state, such as scripting or automating manual steps.

An imperative approach allows you to define a set of steps, like procedural programming, to reach the desired goal. Imperative tools give you more control over writing your instructions. These tools are most useful when you need to deploy once without maintaining any state, such as writing a script or automating manual steps.

Internal developer platform and IaC

IDPs streamline the software development lifecycle by providing a centralized platform for developers to access tools, services, and infrastructure. When combined with IaC, IDPs can further enhance developer productivity and operational efficiency. IaC tools like Terraform, Pulumi, or AWS CloudFormation enable developers to define and manage infrastructure as code, which can then be integrated into the IDP. This integration allows developers to easily provision and manage the infrastructure they need to build and deploy their applications, while also ensuring consistency and repeatability. There is a reference architecture and platform tooling available for IDP.

You can refer to the latest toolset using: **https://platformengineering.org/platform-tooling**

Refer to the following figure:

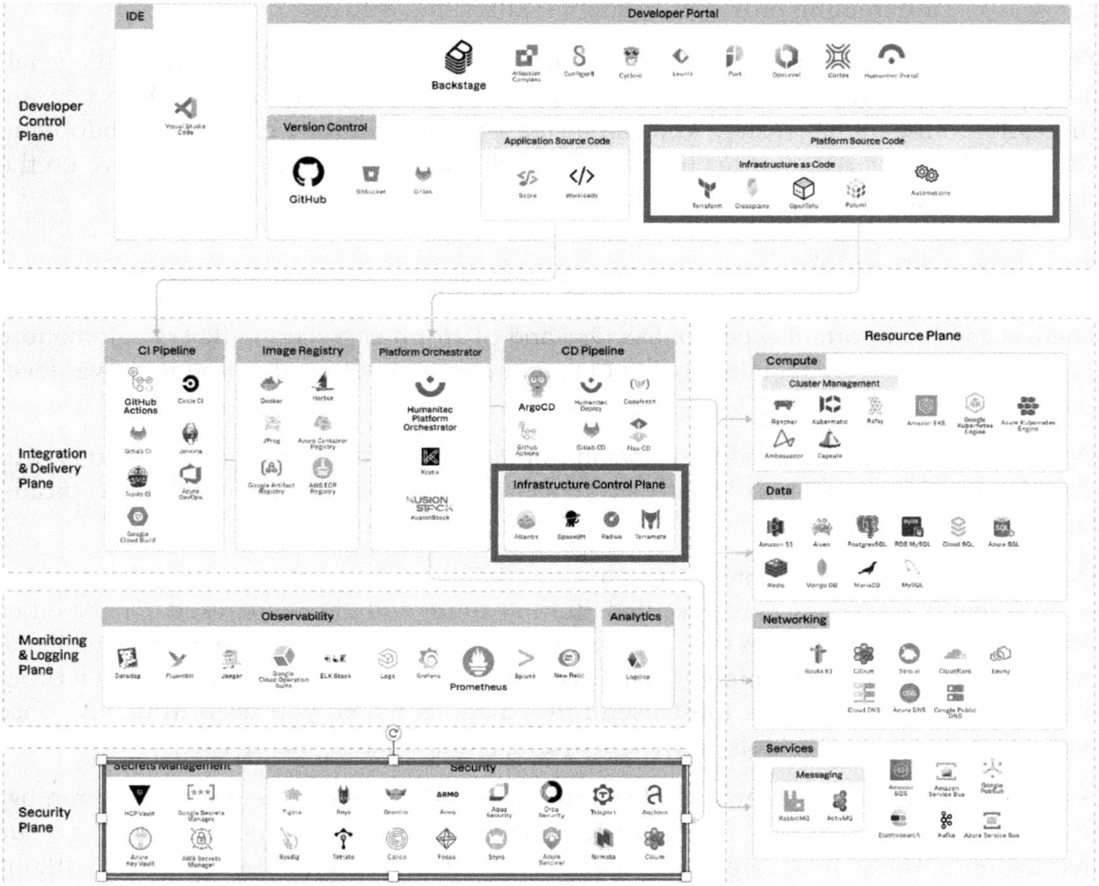

Figure 4.2: Platform engineering toolset with IaC and security toolsets

Source: https://platformengineering.org/

To integrate IaC in an internal developer platform, you can leverage various tools and services that provide a seamless experience for developers. We have already discussed some of the well-known IaC tools such as Terraform, OpenTofu, Pulumi, and **Azure Resource Manager** (ARM). Here are some ways to integrate IaC in an IDP:

- **IaC as a service**: Use any of the IaC tools as a service within the IDP, allowing developers to use existing code templates or write new templates using the in-built process in the IDP.

- **Cloud-agnostic infrastructur**e: Provide a cloud-agnostic infrastructure management system that can be integrated with various IaC tools like Terraform, CloudFormation, or ARM.

- **IaC-driven (CI/CD)**: Integrate IaC with CI/CD pipelines to automate the deployment of infrastructure and applications.

- **Integrated code editor**: Offer an integrated code editor within the IDP that allows developers to write IaC code using tools like Terraform, OpenTofu, or CloudFormation JSON.

- **IaC-based deployment**: Provide a feature for deploying infrastructure and applications using IaC, allowing developers to manage their entire stack from within the IDP.

- **Integration with other tools**: Integrate IaC with other tools and services used in the IDP, such as version control systems like Git or SVN.

OpenTofu is a new era of IaC for platform engineering

Emergence of OpenTofu, a significant development in the IaC landscape, and its impact on platform engineering. It started with Terraform as IaC and its role in fostering innovation and collaboration within the platform engineering ecosystem.

The licensing shift and OpenTofu's emergence

HashiCorp's decision to transition Terraform's licensing from the permissive **Mozilla Public License** (**MPL**) to the more restrictive **Business Source License** (**BSL**) sparked widespread concern among users. The BSL limits commercial use of Terraform by competitors and restrains innovations.

OpenTofu emerged as a direct response to this licensing change. As a community-driven fork of Terraform, it aims to preserve the open-source ethos and collaborative development.

How OpenTofu addresses licensing challenges:

- **Open-source license**: OpenTofu remains under the MPL v2.0, ensuring its free use, modification, and distribution, even for commercial purposes. This removes the restrictions imposed by Terraform.

- **Community governance**: OpenTofu is stewarded by the Linux Foundation, guaranteeing a transparent and collaborative development process. This fosters community involvement and prevents any single entity from controlling the project's direction.

Key benefits of OpenTofu for platform engineering:

- **Freedom and flexibility**: OpenTofu empowers platform engineers with the freedom to use, modify, and distribute the tool without licensing constraints. This is crucial for building and managing IDPs without vendor lock-in, allowing for customization and integration tailored to specific organizational needs.

- **Cost-effectiveness**: OpenTofu eliminates the potential costs associated with Terraform's BSL, making it a more budget-friendly option for organizations of all sizes, particularly startups and smaller companies with limited resources.

- **Community support**: The vibrant community behind OpenTofu ensures active development, timely bug fixes, and a collaborative environment for knowledge sharing. This provides platform engineers with access to a wealth of expertise and support, accelerating their IaC initiatives.

- **Compatibility**: OpenTofu strives for full compatibility with Terraform, enabling teams to migrate existing Terraform codebases with minimal effort. This ensures a smooth transition and minimizes disruption to existing workflows.

OpenTofu's role in the platform engineering ecosystem

OpenTofu is rapidly gaining traction as a key player in the platform engineering ecosystem. It empowers platform engineers to:

- **Build and manage infrastructure**: Provision and manage a wide range of infrastructure resources, including cloud services, on-premises infrastructure, and other components of their IDPs, using a consistent and declarative approach.

- **Automate infrastructure deployments**: Create reproducible and reliable infrastructure deployments through code, ensuring consistency and reducing the risk of human error.

- **Integrate with other tools**: Seamlessly integrate with existing CI/CD pipelines, version control systems, and other DevOps tools, streamlining workflows and enhancing automation.

OpenTofu, while a relatively new project, has quickly established itself as a strong contender in the IaC space. Its commitment to open-source and community-driven development positions it as a key driver of innovation in infrastructure management. As platform engineering continues to evolve, OpenTofu is poised to play a significant role in shaping the future of how organizations build, manage, and scale their infrastructure.

Security policies and benchmarking

It is expensive to detect security vulnerabilities at a later stage of the SDLC process. There is a huge cost for data breaches, which leads to a drop in company valuation, brand value, and customer trust. A gain in popularity of the IDP to build the security guardrails to detect and resolve security vulnerabilities at each stage of the SDLC processes.

An IDP can help baseline the security policies and implement the required security controls as part of infrastructure creation and software build processes. In *Chapter 5, Platform and DevSecOps*, we will be discussing the security framework and security benchmark in detail. Some of the required security practices are part of the release process using the IDP.

Baseline security posture

A cybersecurity baseline serves as a foundational set of information security standards for your organization. It provides valuable insights into your security posture, pinpoints potential security gaps, and helps meet regulatory requirements.

The most widely accepted and adopted cybersecurity baselines are those recommended by the **National Institute of Standards and Technology (NIST)** Cybersecurity Framework, the *SANS Top 20 Critical Security Controls*, and the **Center for Internet Society (CIS)** benchmark. These frameworks offer a structured approach to assess, monitor, and improve your organization's overall security posture.

Shift left in platform engineering

Shift left is an agile methodology that involves performing tasks, processes, and activities earlier on in the development cycle rather than waiting until later stages of development or deployment. By shifting left, teams can proactively identify and address issues, conduct thorough testing, and ensure high-quality deliverables, ultimately reducing errors, rework, and costs.

Shift left is an approach that relocates security, quality, and testing initiatives to earlier stages of the development cycle. This proactive strategy enables teams to identify issues sooner, minimize costs, and ultimately enhance overall product quality. In platform engineering, shift left involves seamlessly integrating security, compliance, and monitoring capabilities into the platform's design and development process from the outset. By doing so, organizations can create a robust, secure, and compliant foundation for their platforms, reducing the risk of costly rework or post-deployment issues.

The following are the key principles for implementing shift left in platform engineering:

- **Continuous integration (CI)**: Integrate platform components early in development using CI pipelines. The platform should trigger automated builds and tests for any infrastructure creation or changes.

- **Automated testing**: Integrate automated testing tools to ensure platform functionality and security. This includes a range of tests: integration, functional, performance, and security, integrated into CI/CD pipelines triggered by the platform.

- **Compliance monitoring**: Implement monitoring and reporting mechanisms to track compliance with regulatory requirements. The platform shall have an integrated compliance list, such as ISO 27001, PCI DSS, HIPAA, for quick adoption, along with the flexibility to define new compliance rules using the **Unified Compliance Framework (UCF)** that helps organizations address the often overlapping and complex requirements of multiple regulatory frameworks and standards.

- **Security scanning**: Integrate regular security scanning and vulnerability assessments to identify security vulnerabilities. The platform team shall integrate.

- **Observability**: Build observability into the platform from the start. This means incorporating logging, monitoring, and tracing to gain insights into platform behavior and identify potential issues proactively.

By embracing shift left principles, organizations can create platforms that are not only efficient and scalable but also secure and compliant by design.

Supply chain management

The goal is to achieve **secure by design** and **secure at runtime**, ensuring that security is embedded throughout every stage of the software development process. To accomplish this, it is crucial to understand the concept of a software supply chain, which refers to all the artifacts, third-party libraries, and software components that come together to create a software application. With the proliferation of open-source frameworks, libraries, and operating systems, many modern software applications rely on these freely available components. In fact, most modern software is built utilizing open-source software suppliers. This shift away from proprietary, in-house code has been driven by the adoption of cloud-native and DevSecOps methodologies, which prioritize speed and agility in software delivery. As a result, the inclusion of open-source software suppliers has increased significantly, bringing both benefits and challenges for securing the software supply chain. One of the ways this new supply chain complexity is being regularized is with the help of a **software bill of materials** (**SBOM**). An SBOM is a critical component of developed software that provides a comprehensive inventory of the various software artifacts, modules, and libraries that are included within the software. This inventory includes information about each software component, such as its name, version, and dependencies.

The foundation of your app might look solid, but there is always the potential risk of finding a vulnerability in software that could compromise the entire software delivery.

Security and quality gates

The initial step in establishing security and quality gates involves formalizing the policies. Creating machine-friendly policies makes it easier to integrate them as validation in the SDLC pipeline. Policy formalization can be accomplished with tools like Inspec, OPA, Kyverno, etc.

Vulnerability management

Vulnerability management is an essential process that ensures the continuous identification, classification, prioritization, remediation, and reduction of software vulnerabilities in your organization. This ongoing process helps protect against potential security threats and minimizes the impact of successful attacks. It is a crucial aspect of computer and network security and should not be mistaken for vulnerability assessment. Vulnerabilities can be found using a vulnerability scanner, which examines a computer system to identify known vulnerabilities. All identified vulnerabilities at each stage of the SDLC are centrally managed and monitored.

Security controls

Besides the preceding processes, there is the following list of security controls that are part of the IDP:

- **Access control**: Define role-based access controls to restrict access to sensitive data, applications, and infrastructure.

- **Authentication and authorization**: Implement strong authentication mechanisms, including MFA, and authorize users based on their roles and permissions.

- **Data encryption**: Ensure that all data stored or transmitted within the IDP is encrypted using industry-standard encryption algorithms.

- **Secure communication**: Use secure communication protocols (e.g., HTTPS, SSH) for all interactions between developers, applications, and infrastructure components.

- **Vulnerability management**: Establish a process for identifying, reporting, and remediating vulnerabilities in the IDP's software, infrastructure, and configurations.

- **Compliance and governance**: Ensure that the IDP complies with relevant organizational, industry, and regulatory requirements (e.g., HIPAA, PCI-DSS).

- **Backup and recovery**: Implement a backup and recovery process to ensure business continuity in case of data loss or system failure.

Security benchmarking in IDP

There are industry-recognized benchmarks for IDP and used by many organizations for security and compliance:

- **NIST Cybersecurity Framework**: The NIST Cybersecurity Framework provides a comprehensive framework for managing cyber risks. The NIST CSF provides a structure for managing cybersecurity risks across the entire lifecycle of your IDP. It consists of five core functions: identify, protect, detect, respond, and recover. The following are the details for all five functions and applicable controls in details:

  1. **Identify**:
     - **Asset management**: Identify all critical assets within your IDP, including infrastructure components (servers, databases, network devices), platform services, code repositories, and sensitive data.
     - **Risk assessment**: Conduct a thorough risk assessment to identify potential threats and vulnerabilities to your IDP. Consider threats like unauthorized access, data breaches, denial-of-service attacks, and insider threats.
     - **Governance**: Establish clear security policies, standards, and procedures for the development, deployment, and operation of your IDP.

2. **Protect**:

   o **Access control**: Implement strong authentication and authorization mechanisms to control access to your IDP. This includes:

   - **Multi-factor authentication (MFA)** for all users.

   - **Role-based access control (RBAC)** to restrict access based on user roles and responsibilities.

   o **Data security**: Protect sensitive data within your IDP through encryption, data masking, and secure storage practices.

   o **Protective technology**: Deploy security tools like firewalls, **intrusion detection/prevention systems (IDS/IPS)**, and anti-malware software to safeguard your IDP infrastructure.

   o **Configuration management**: Establish secure configuration baselines for all IDP components and enforce them through automated tools.

3. **Detect**:

   o **Security monitoring**: Implement continuous security monitoring to detect suspicious activity and potential security incidents. This includes:

   - Log management and analysis.

   - **Security Information and Event Management (SIEM)** systems.

   - Intrusion detection systems.

   o **Vulnerability scanning**: Conduct regular vulnerability scans to identify and remediate security weaknesses in your IDP infrastructure and applications.

   o **Anomaly detection**: Utilize tools and techniques to detect unusual behavior that may indicate a security breach.

4. **Respond**:

   o **Incident response plan**: Develop and regularly test an incident response plan to effectively handle security incidents.

   o **Communication**: Establish clear communication channels for reporting and escalating security incidents.

   o **Mitigation**: Implement measures to contain and mitigate the impact of security incidents.

5. **Recover**:

o **Recovery planning**: Develop a recovery plan to restore your IDP to normal operations following a security incident.

o **Data backup and recovery**: Implement regular data backups and ensure you can restore data in case of data loss or corruption.

o **Disaster recovery**: Establish a disaster recovery plan to ensure business continuity in case of a major outage.

By aligning your IDP security practices with the NIST CSF, you can establish a robust security posture, protect your critical assets, and ensure the continued availability and integrity of your platform.

- **CIS benchmarking**: The **Center for Internet Security (CIS)** provides a set of best practices and benchmarks for securing IT systems, networks, and applications. The CIS benchmarks are based on a set of 18 controls that cover critical security areas as:

  o **Hardening your operating system**: The following are the measures to harden the operating system to be used for infrastructure creation:

    ▪ **Minimizing attack surface**: Disabling unnecessary services, closing unused ports, and configuring firewalls.

    ▪ **Secure user account management**: Implementing strong password policies, enforcing least privilege, and regularly reviewing user accounts.

    ▪ **System hardening**: Configuring security settings for file systems, logging, and auditing.

  o **Security controls**: The following are CIS-recommended security controls to protect the database to be provisioned:

    ▪ **Access control**: Restricting database access to authorized users and applications.

    ▪ **Encryption**: Protecting sensitive data at rest and in transit.

    ▪ **Auditing**: Logging database activity to detect unauthorized access or modifications.

  o **Secure network devices**: Use devices like routers, switches, and firewalls using CIS benchmarks for networking equipment using following security controls:

    ▪ **Access control lists (ACLs)**: Controlling network traffic flow and restricting access to sensitive network segments.

    ▪ **Secure protocols**: Using secure protocols like SSH and HTTPS for remote management.

    ▪ **Regular firmware updates**: Keeping network devices up-to-date with the latest security patches.

- o **Containerization**: Platform leverages containerization technologies like Kubernetes, and the following are the security controls to be implemented:

  - **Control plane security**: Securing the Kubernetes API server, etcd, and other control plane components.

  - **Worker node security**: Hardening the operating system and container runtime on worker nodes.

  - **Network policies**: Controlling network traffic between pods and namespaces.

The other two key security benchmarks used across the industry are the following. We will not cover in detail the applicable controls for these security benchmarks or compliance. Please explore the applicable controls for the following security benchmarks:

- **OWASP ASVS**: The **Open Web Application Security Project's Application Security Verification Standard** (**OWASP ASVS**) provides guidelines for assessing the security of web applications.

- **HIPAA Security Rule**: The **Health Insurance Portability and Accountability Act** (**HIPAA**) Security Rule provides guidelines for securing **electronic protected health information** (**ePHI**).

By establishing clear security policies and benchmarking the performance of your **internal developer platform** (**IDP**), you can ensure that it meets industry standards, reduces risk, and supports business continuity.

Following is a quick table comparison for reference:

Feature	CIS benchmarks	NIST Cybersecurity Framework	HIPAA Security Rule	OWASP ASVS
Focus	Secure configuration of IT systems, networks, and applications	Comprehensive cybersecurity risk management	Protecting ePHI	Secure development and assessment of web applications
Scope	Provides specific, prescriptive guidance for securing various technologies (OS, databases, network devices, etc.)	Offers a flexible, risk-based approach to managing cybersecurity across five core functions (Identify, protect, detect, respond, recover)	Focuses on administrative, physical, and technical safeguards for ePHI	Provides security requirements and testing guidance for web applications, categorized by sensitivity levels

Feature	CIS benchmarks	NIST Cybersecurity Framework	HIPAA Security Rule	OWASP ASVS
Relevance to IDP	Helps secure the underlying infrastructure and components of the IDP, ensuring a strong foundation	Guides the overall security strategy for the IDP, addressing risk management, security controls, incident response, and recovery	Mandates specific security measures if the IDP handles ePHI	Secures the web-based components of the IDP (e.g., dashboards, APIs) against common web application vulnerabilities
Key benefits	<ul><li>Reduces risk by adhering to established security best practices</li><li>Improves compliance with various security standards</li><li>Increases efficiency through standardization</li></ul>	<ul><li>Provides a holistic approach to IDP security</li><li>Prioritizes security efforts based on risk</li><li>Offers flexibility and adaptability</li></ul>	<ul><li>Ensures compliance with HIPAA regulations for protecting ePHI</li><li>Safeguards patient data and privacy</li></ul>	<ul><li>Reduces the risk of web application vulnerabilities in the IDP</li><li>Improves the security posture of IDP web components</li><li>Promotes secure coding practices</li></ul>
Examples	<ul><li>Secure configuration of operating systems, databases, and network devices</li><li>Implementing strong authentication and access control mechanisms</li><li>Regular vulnerability scanning and patching</li></ul>	<ul><li>Identifying and assessing risks to the IDP</li><li>Implementing security controls (access control, data security, protective technology)</li><li>Developing incident response and recovery plans</li></ul>	<ul><li>Access control to ePHI</li><li>Audit trails</li><li>Data encryption</li></ul>	<ul><li>Secure authentication and authorization</li><li>Input validation to prevent injection attacks</li><li>Secure session management</li><li>Data protection (encryption, secure storage)</li><li>Security testing (penetration testing, code review)</li></ul>

Table 4.2: Security benchmarks comparison

Case study in security guardrails for IDP

There are many case studies of the successful adoption and implementation of security guardrails within their IDP by companies. However, *Airbnb* is a very good example of the successful implementation of security guardrails for IDP.

Their initial challenge was to enable hundreds of engineers to rapidly deploy and iterate on their applications while maintaining a high level of security and compliance. They achieved this by building an IDP with the following robust security guardrails integrated:

- **Automated security checks**: Integrated security scanning tools (e.g., SAST, DAST) directly into their CI/CD pipeline. This ensured that the code was automatically checked for vulnerabilities before deployment.

- **IaC**: Used IaC to define and manage their infrastructure as templates and declaratively, ensuring consistent security configurations across all environments.

- **Least privilege access control**: Implemented role-based access and strict access controls, granting developers only the necessary permissions to perform their tasks.

- **Continuous monitoring and auditing**: Implemented continuous monitoring and auditing of their platform and applications to detect and respond to security threats in real-time.

This approach leads to the following benefits for the Airbnb security team:

- **Reduced security incidents**: By embedding security checks early in the SDLC, Airbnb significantly reduced the number of security incidents.

- **Increased developer productivity**: The IDP automated many security-related tasks, freeing up developers to focus on building and shipping features.

- **Improved compliance**: The platform ensured that all applications and infrastructure met regulatory and compliance requirements.

Some of the key takeaways from this case study:

- **Shift left security**: Integrating security checks early in the SDLC is crucial for identifying and mitigating vulnerabilities before they reach production.

- **Automation**: Automating security tasks reduces the burden on developers and ensures consistent enforcement of security policies.

- **Least privilege**: Implementing RBAC and strict access controls minimizes the risk of unauthorized access and data breaches.

By incorporating these principles into their IDP, Airbnb successfully created a secure and efficient development environment that empowers engineers to innovate while maintaining a high level of security.

Policy as code

In today's fast-paced digital landscape, where microservices-based applications have become the norm, traditional process-based security and compliance approaches are no longer sufficient. With organizations able to scale their applications multiple times in a single day, manual methods like written documents and spreadsheets simply cannot keep pace with the rapid changes. PaC is a modern approach that enables organizations to manage and enforce security policies more efficiently. By using code to define and implement rules and procedures, PaC provides a scalable and automated solution for managing security policies, ensuring they remain relevant and effective in today's rapidly evolving IT environments.

Policy as code components

PaC is the use of codified artifacts. PaC aims to enhance security, compliance, and governance within the IaC framework in IDP. PaC consists of:

- **Policies**: To manage and apply rules and conditions. The following is the basic composition of any policy:
    - o **Policy identifier**: A unique name assigned to the policy, serving as a label.
    - o **Policy purpose**: The objective and reason for implementing this policy, including any required enforcement measures.
    - o **Policy context**: The system, environment, or scenario in which the policy will be applied.
    - o **Policy rules**: Controls or prescriptive behaviors defined by checking specific conditions. Policies can have multiple rules.
    - o **Policy actions**: The actions taken by the system if a policy rule is violated or not met.

    Policies definition provides a clear and comprehensive outline for defining policies by code, ensuring that all necessary information is included to effectively manage and enforce security controls.
- **Policy engine**: A program that interprets policy artifacts to apply policy decisions using the required rules and conditions.

Organizational standards and policies that are created or adopted contain rules and conditions defined in the policy definition.

Policy as code features and benefits

Here are some key benefits of PaC used to apply security, compliance, governance, and best practices decisions to prevent and react to unwanted changes within the systems:

- **Automation**: Teams can leverage rule-based, predefined, curated, or custom policies that are triggered and automatically enforced, minimizing the risk of human error and inconsistency. The following are a few examples:

    o **Standardizing naming conventions to maintain consistency**: An organization wants to enforce consistent naming conventions for its cloud resources. They can define a policy that requires all resources to be tagged with a specific prefix:

```
package naming
deny[msg] {
    input.request.kind.kind == "aws#CreateResource"
    not startswith(input.request.resource.tags.Name, "dev-")
    msg := "Resource names must start with 'dev-'"
}
```

Code 4.6: Rego policy code for all resources to be tagged

    o **Enforcing resource limits**: To prevent developers from provisioning overly expensive cloud resources. We can define a policy in Rego that limits the instance size that can be created:

```
package cloud.cost
deny[msg] {
input.request.kind.kind == "aws#RunInstances" input.request.
instanceType == "m5.24xlarge"
msg := "Instances larger than m5.16xlarge are not allowed"
}
```

Code 4.7: Rego policy code for not allowing big instances

    o **Default S3 bucket encryption**: To prevent developers from accessing S3 buckets without server-side encryption. We can define a policy in Rego that denies any request to create an S3 bucket without server-side encryption:

```
package aws.s3
deny[msg] {
    input.request.kind.kind == "s3#PutBucketEncryption"
    not input.request.resource.serverSideEncryptionConfiguration
    msg := "All S3 buckets must be encrypted"
}
```

Code 4.8: Rego policy code for default encryption of S3 buckets

- **Tracking**: Changes to policies can be tracked and controlled, ensuring that teams work with the latest version added to the version control system.

- **Machine-readable**: Policies are created in machine-readable formats (JSON, YAML) and can be integrated with other systems and tools, such as automation frameworks and security platforms.

- **Collaboration**: Policies are easy to share and collaborate on within or across organizations, fostering a culture of transparency and consistency.

- **Compliance**: Automation using PaC enables organizations to quickly comply with industry regulations and standards, reducing the risk of non-compliance.

By leveraging these benefits, PaC helps organizations streamline their security management processes, improve compliance, and reduce the risk of human error.

Policies are written in programming languages such as JSON, YAML, or Python, creating machine-readable code that can be easily understood by both humans and machines. These policy files are then stored in a version control system, allowing for version tracking and collaboration among teams. When deployed to relevant systems, the policies are executed and monitored, and the system automatically generates an alert for teams or takes corrective action. This automation ensures consistent adherence to standards and minimizes the risk of human error, promoting efficiency in managing complex systems. Some of the key features of PaC:

- PaC seamlessly integrates with IaC and **security as code (SaC)** practices as well, implementing policy enforcement to code-defined infrastructures and enforcing required security policies:

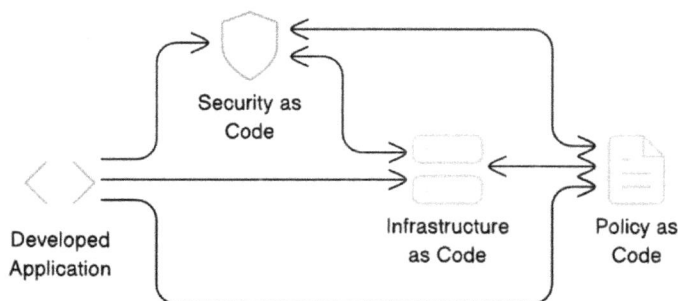

Figure 4.3: SaC, IaC, and PaC as everything is code

- o **Continuous compliance**: PaC facilitates compliance by conducting automated policy checks at various stages of the development lifecycle.

- o **Continuous validation**: It ensures that systems consistently meet specified rules and compliance and reduces the likelihood of post-deployment issues.

- o **Automation**: It maintains consistency in policy enforcement with accuracy.

- o **Consistency**: PaC benefits from version control, enabling organizations to manage changes systematically and roll back to previous versions, enhancing governance and auditability.

o **Continuous integration**: Integrates flawlessly into CI/CD pipelines, embedding policy checks within automated testing and deployment processes.

o **Audit**: Reduce efforts in audit and reporting capabilities and provide clear insights into compliance status.

o **Unified policies**: Provides a unified solution for enforcing policies across multi-cloud environments.

o **Standardized framework**: A standardized framework for defining, interpreting, and enforcing policies.

Working of policy as code

PaC has a very simple architecture:

- PaC can be created and maintained as a readable, scripted file with all the required rules and validations.

- Policies are created using declarative language (JSON or YAML).

- Policies are written as code and are input to the policy engine in the form of queries. The policy engine processes the policy code and outputs the result.

- The result creates a decision after processing the current policies. It helps in automated decisions for security scanning, quality testing, or infrastructure creation.

- Policies can also be implemented through API calls integrated in the CI pipeline, which helps in running security checks without breaking any code.

The following figure shows the workflow for PaC:

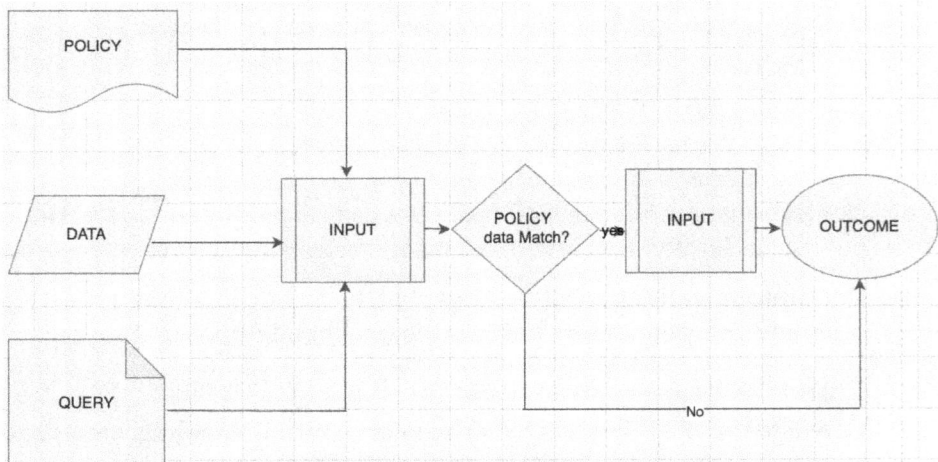

Figure 4.4: *Policy as code flow diagram*

To function, the PaC utilizes three elements:

- **Codified policy**: PaC uses a written policy with code inside to facilitate comparison and decision-making.

- **Collected data**: PaC uses data and context provided by software application, environment, or service for comparison and validation.

- **Decision making**: A query triggers the process of decision-making based on provided data and configured policy to the policy engine for decision-making by the system.

Policy language

We have seen the difference between declarative and imperative programming languages and the use of these in the digital native world. The kind of automation and integration is in progress, and it was not possible with the XML or properties files. DevOps and platform engineering use JSON and YAML formats to support automation. The main basis of modern infrastructure is containerization, and container technologies use JSON and YAML formats in all activities (setup, configuration, deployment, etc).

Getting started with policy language

If you are interested in getting started with PaC, here are a few steps you can take:

1. **Create goals**: Determine which policies you want to automate and what benefits you hope to achieve.

2. **Suitable tool**: Evaluate different options and choose one that best suits your requirements.

3. **Policy development**: Start by writing simple policies for a few cases, and then gradually expand.

4. **System integration**: Configure your chosen PaC tool to work with your existing systems and tools.

5. **Monitoring**: Regularly test your policies and monitor for any issues.

PaC stores policy definitions as single or multiple files in JSON or YAML as a machine-readable format. This can be processed later by the policy engine.

Problem it addresses

It needs lots of manual work and leads to human errors by developers and reviewers to check applications and infrastructure against documented policies. Manual processes also do not meet the processing speed and scale requirements of cloud-native applications. This can help in enforcing the following codified policies in the applications and infrastructure building:

- Do not allow storing secrets in source code

- Running a container with superuser permissions

- Storing some data outside a specific geo region due to compliance requirements

Creating the guardrails

Before PaC days, it was very difficult for the compliance team to engage the software engineering team and make them understand the policies. In the examples given previously, PaC has helped software engineering teams to understand and prevent unnecessary changes or system behaviors by users or automation. These codified policies are guardrails, and these operations are not restricted. Any drift from the prescribed path and violation of the rules and conditions set by policies are restricted by enforced policies. Teams that are not able to manage security, compliance, and governance could put the business at risk and need automated controls.

Popular PaC tools

The following are the popular PaC tools:

- **Open Policy Agent (OPA)**: OPA is a policy engine that can be seamlessly integrated into your system in various ways.

  o **Sidecar**: Run OPA alongside your container service as a separate process

  o **Host-level daemon**: Install OPA as a system-level daemon to monitor and enforce policies

  o **Library**: Incorporate OPA into your application or library as a policy enforcement module

  This is one widely used general-purpose engine and can be used for the policy validation required for containers, systems, data filtering, and CI/CD pipeline too.

  OPA allows you to keep and manage policies separated from infrastructure, service, or application. The team responsible for policy management can maintain control over the policy independently of the underlying service or system, ensuring a clear separation of concerns and allowing for more effective governance.

  OPA uses Rego, a query language that leverages structured data models such as JSON, to create policies. This language enables teams to write code for policies using the OPA framework, providing a powerful toolset for policy management. In this way, OPA allows teams to define and enforce policies in a clear and concise manner, decoupling policy management from the underlying system or service.

An example of policy validation using **The Rego Playground**:

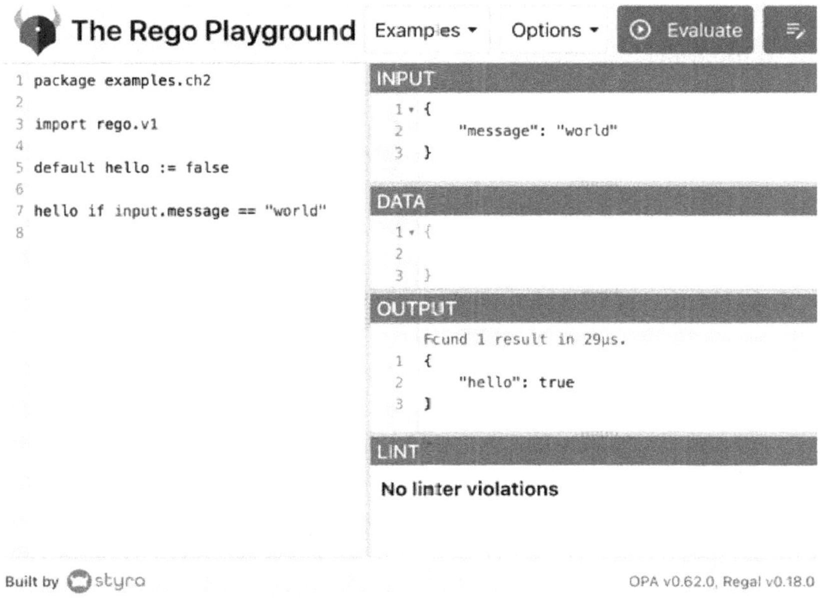

Figure 4.5: Rego Playground

- **Kyverno**: Kyverno is a Kubernetes policy engine utilizing a declarative language to formulate policies for modifying, validating, or generating resources and configurations. Unlike OPA, Kyverno operates on declarative code, leveraging YAML to define policies, which are then recognized as Kubernetes resources. Kyverno seamlessly integrates with developer tools such as Git and Kubectl.

In Kyverno's policy validation process, there are two stages. Firstly, the **pre-admission controller** (**PAC**) can influence inbound requests. The mutating admission webhook interacts with a configured policy engine, allowing for resource mutation.

The following object schema validation is a second stage, where a data plane service can impact inbound requests. The validating admission webhook connects to a configured service to validate the current payload. In cases where the data plane service is integrated with a policy engine:

- o It is done by policies that match the criteria. If the validation returns true, then it goes ahead with the change after object schema validation.

- o The validating admission webhook calls out to a configured service to have the current payload validated.

- o In the case where the data plane service is connected to a policy engine, the validation is done by any policies that match. Changes persisted to etc., if validation returns true, and led to a change in the cluster status.

o   However, if the validation results in a false or exception return, then the request stops and the status is immediately returned.

Refer to the following figure:

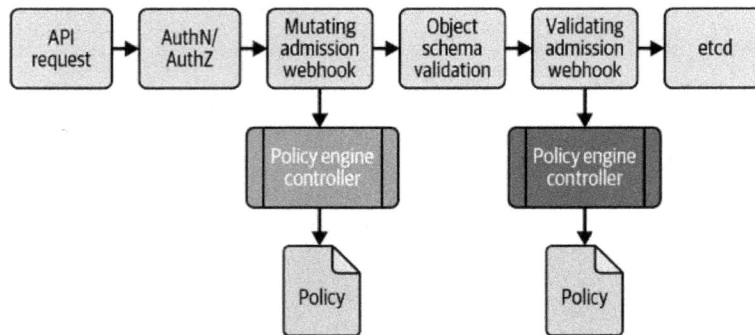

Figure 4.6: Policy validation using Kyverno

- **ConfTest**: ConfTest is a popular open-source tool for testing configuration files, including Kubernetes configurations and Terraform scripts. It helps detect potential security vulnerabilities. This tool was created by the Google Cloud Security team to help organizations ensure the security and integrity of their infrastructure by testing IaC. Infra developers can add policies in the policy folder in the desired location of the tool.

- **Chef Inspec**: It is an open-source framework that enables teams to test and audit their applications and infrastructure with ease. By comparing the actual state of your system against the desired state defined in Chef InSpec code, it detects any violations and presents findings in a clear report. Chef InSpec empowers you to take control of remediation by providing actionable insights without imposing prescriptive fixes. This allows you to address issues at your own pace, leveraging your organization's specific expertise and processes.

It is a runtime framework that uses the rule language to specify compliance, security, and policy requirements. The InSpec tool uses the available open-source profiles or written profiles to inspect the infrastructure code. This is one of the prominent tools to help compliance as code achieve with the help of a set of controls documented by the compliance team as a profile, and can be used to inspect and audit the applications or infrastructure. There are different open-source compliance or baseline profiles available to use with InSpec.

A sample control file to check the correct version of software used (ssh-v2):

```
control "sshd-11" do
  impact 1.0
  title "Server: Set protocol version to SSHv2"
  desc "Set the SSH protocol version to 2. Don't use legacy
```

```
     insecure SSHv1 connections anymore."
  tag security: "level-1"
  tag "openssh-server"
  ref "Server Security Guide v.1.0", url: "http://..."

  describe sshd_config do
    its('Protocol') { should eq('2') }
  end
end
```

Code 4.9: SSH version control inspection

- **jsPolicy**: It is an open-source policy engine specifically designed for Kubernetes that allows users to create policies using JavaScript or TypeScript. By leveraging the popularity of JavaScript, jsPolicy provides a more straightforward and less complex policy management experience compared to other engines like OPA or Kyverno. The use of JavaScript as a programming language makes jsPolicy a natural choice for many developers, thanks to the widespread adoption of JavaScript frameworks, libraries, and modules. jsPolicy's integration with **Node Package Manager** (**npm**) packages simplifies policy creation and packaging. It can use the JavaScript SDK for creating and packaging policies.

The following is a feature comparison for the three most popular PaC tools:

Feature	OPA	Kyverno	ConfTest
Language	Rego	YAML, **Common Expression Language** (**CEL**)	YAML, JSON, HCL
Policy enforcement	Admission controllers (Kubernetes), Gatekeeper, Envoy, Terraform, etc.	Admission controllers (Kubernetes)	Standalone CLI, CI/CD pipelines
Focus	General-purpose policy engine	Kubernetes-native policy management	Testing and validation of configuration files
Strengths	Expressive Rego language for complex policies Strong community and wide adoption Extensive integrations with various tools and platforms	Simple YAML-based policies for easier adoption Kubernetes-native with seamless integration Built-in support for mutations and validations	Lightweight and easy to use Supports various configuration formats Good for testing IaC before deployment

Feature	OPA	Kyverno	ConfTest
Ideal use cases	Complex authorization policies API security Data filtering Microservices governance General-purpose policy enforcement across different platforms	Enforcing security policies in Kubernetes Managing resource configurations Validating and mutating Kubernetes resources	Testing Kubernetes manifests Validating Terraform configurations Ensuring IaC best practices

Table 4.3: Key PaC tool features comparison

Applying PaC to IaC

We use PaC to apply controls: security, compliance, governance, FinOps, and best practices, to IaC resources and processes. These controls are usually arranged into three categories:

- **Detective**: Detective controls records and catalogs noncompliant issues. These controls are usually consolidated and send the notifications for awareness and further disposition or action by the team. Generally, when the PaC tool runs in Audit mode, it discovers policy violations as detective controls.

- **Preventive**: Preventive controls are used as **guardrails** and are most effective at stopping non-compliant behavior and enforcing best practices, and are executed before resource creation or modification. Preventive controls are also directly triggered by system events and prevent changes from happening before they change the state of the system.

- **Corrective**: Corrective controls are like both preventive and detective controls. They are used to avoid or record noncompliant changes or behavior, and their application is triggered by internal system events. However, the reactive-control event triggers occur after the system changes have been made and the system state has been modified. Corrective controls become more effective as their time to react to system events decreases. Corrective controls that react within single-digit seconds, or sub-seconds. These are useful where you do not have preventive control, and you have a way to detect and react to correct the policy violation. Some of the above controls can be used for:

  o **Access security**: It helps in defining and enforcing access control rules for IT systems.

  o **Regulatory compliance**: Automating compliance checks for regulations like ISO 27001, HIPAA, or PCI DSS.

o **Infrastructure management**: Scan the infrastructure using setup policies and highlight the issues.

The following are the key activities where PaC can be utilized to help implement organizational policies or regulatory compliance.

Policy as code integration into pipeline

PaC can be integrated into a pipeline to automate policy enforcement and ensure continuous compliance. By integrating PaC into the development pipeline, organizations can detect policy violations early in the development process, preventing issues from reaching production. Automated enforcement ensures consistent compliance and reduces human error, while continuous integration with CI/CD pipelines enables ongoing compliance throughout the software development lifecycle. Furthermore, a shared policy repository fosters collaboration between development, security, and operations teams, promoting a unified approach to security and compliance. The following figure explains the PaC integration in pipeline tools (Jenkins, GitHub, etc.):

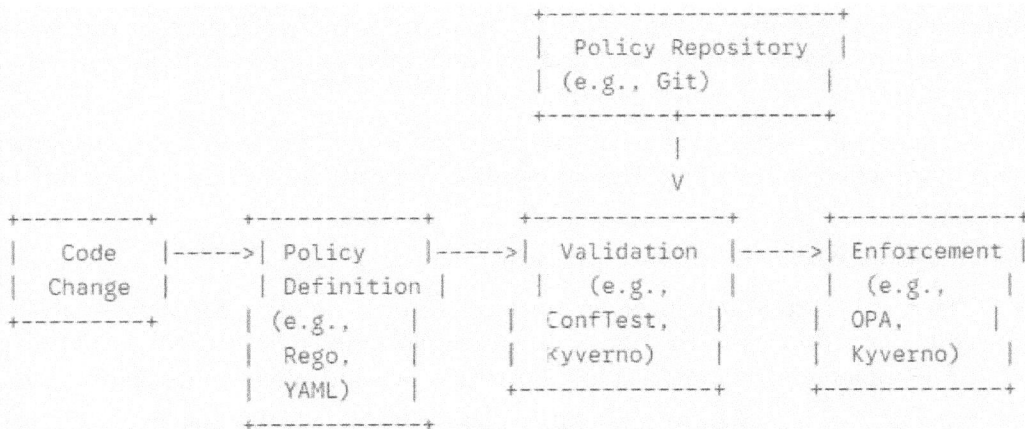

```
                              +----------------------+
                              |  Policy Repository   |
                              |  (e.g., Git)         |
                              +---------+------------+
                                        |
                                        V
 +----------+      +--------------+      +----------------+      +---------------+
 |  Code    |----->|  Policy      |----->|  Validation    |----->| Enforcement   |
 |  Change  |      |  Definition  |      |  (e.g.,        |      |  (e.g.,       |
 +----------+      |  (e.g.,      |      |  ConfTest,     |      |  OPA,         |
                   |  Rego,       |      |  Kyverno)      |      |  Kyverno)     |
                   |  YAML)       |      +----------------+      +---------------+
                   +--------------+
```

Figure 4.7: *PaC integration to pipeline tool*

The following is the explanation of PaC integration with pipeline tools:

- **Code change**: The process starts with a code change, which could be a modification to infrastructure code (e.g., Terraform, Kubernetes manifests) or application code.

- **Policy definition**: Policies are defined using a policy language (e.g., Rego for OPA, YAML for Kyverno) and stored in a central repository (e.g., Git). These policies define the rules and constraints that must be enforced.

- **Validation**: Before the code change is deployed, the policies are validated to ensure their correctness and prevent any unintended consequences. This validation can be done using tools like ConfTest or Kyverno, which can check the policies against specific criteria or test cases.

- **Enforcement**: Once the policies are validated, they are enforced through various mechanisms, such as:

    o **Admission controllers**: In Kubernetes, admission controllers intercept requests to the API server and enforce policies before resources are created or modified.

    o **Gatekeeper**: A Kubernetes-native project that extends the functionality of admission controllers with OPA integration.

    o **Envoy proxy**: Enforce policies at the network level, controlling access to microservices or APIs.

    o **Terraform providers**: Integrate policy checks into Terraform deployments to validate infrastructure configurations before they are applied.

Infrastructure provisioning

PaC can automate the compliance, security, and operations as part of provisioning resources (such as services, databases, etc.). Apart from these activities, it can include tagging instances, networking configuration, and other resources. It also scans the container images as part of policy governance.

PaC is useful for provisioning infrastructure resources in environments like development, sandbox, production, and staging. This allows us to write different policy sets for different environments.

Some of the tools to scan the provisioned infrastructure:

- **Tfsec**: It is a comprehensive open-source security solution for static analysis of your Terraform code for potential misconfigurations. This tool has led to the development of Trivy, another Infrastructure code and image vulnerability scanner.

- **Terrascan**: It is a powerful static code analyzer that helps organizations ensure the security and compliance of their IaC. It is widely used in automated development and deployment pipelines, where it plays a critical role in policy enforcement and infrastructure security. It can be installed and run in multiple ways.

- **AWS Inspector**: Amazon Inspector is a cloud-based vulnerability management service that continuously scans your AWS workloads for software vulnerabilities and unintended network exposure, helping you to identify and remediate potential security threats. With Amazon Inspector, you do not need to manually scan your environments. The service automatically discovers and scans running Amazon EC2 instances, container images in **Amazon Elastic Container Registry (Amazon ECR)**, and AWS Lambda functions for known software vulnerabilities and unintended network exposure.

- **Prowler**: Prowler is an open-source security tool that enables organizations to perform comprehensive security assessments, audits, and compliance checks across multiple cloud platforms, including AWS, Azure, Google Cloud, and Kubernetes. This powerful tool helps ensure the security and integrity of your cloud environments. It helps in audits, incident response, continuous monitoring, hardening, forensics readiness, and remediation.

Kubernetes controls

PaC is most suitable for Kubernetes infrastructure. You can create policies in a declarative way in YAML or JSON format for Kubernetes resources like nodes, namespaces, Pods, etc. You can also setup and configure resource limits (CPU, memory) for your containers. In a virtualized environment, this helps prevent resource hogging and run applications optimally. Teams can also setup policies for a maximum and minimum number of replicas to meet the resource demands.

Some of the following tools help to discover any issues with the Kubernetes YAML files:

- **Kubebench**: Kubebench is an open-source tool for auditing and hardening Kubernetes clusters. It provides a comprehensive assessment of the security, compliance, and performance of Kubernetes deployments.

- **Kubesec**: Kubesec is another open-source tool for auditing Kubernetes clusters. It provides a comprehensive security assessment and remediation guidance to help organizations ensure the integrity, confidentiality, and availability of their Kubernetes environments.

- **Falco**: It is an open-source tool managed by Sysdig. Falco is a powerful runtime threat detection tool that helps organizations improve their threat detection and incident response capabilities and reduce the risk of data breaches and system compromise.

- **Checkov**: Checkov is an open-source tool that helps organizations ensure the security and integrity of their cloud infrastructure by scanning and discovering misconfigurations in cloud configurations. This powerful tool analyses IaC scan results across various platforms, including Terraform, CloudFormation, Kubernetes, Helm, ARM Templates, and Serverless framework.

- **Sonobuoy**: It is used for conformance testing. It is a diagnostic tool that makes it easier to understand the state of a Kubernetes cluster by running a choice of configuration tests in an accessible and non-destructive manner.

Access and authorization controls

The biggest advantage of PaC for access control is to use RBAC for Kubernetes. It helps the creation of policy where authorization rules are outlined to get the required access, you are following the authorization rules, and increasing the security of the application. You can create policies such that:

- Only HTTPS connections are allowed

- Setting a policy to deny a specific type of service that is not in the scope of the application

This will help improve the security posture.

Auditing and compliance

Modern organizations face the mandate of adhering to governmental and industry-specific regulations, encompassing standards such as HIPAA, GDPR, and PCI DSS, among others. These mandates dictate protocols for data storage, computation, and networking. However, the challenge lies in the dynamic nature of these regulations, subject to frequent updates based on evolving conditions, making an organization's diligent tracking difficult and time-consuming.

Using PaC, offering a solution by encoding these regulations into machine-readable formats like YAML or JSON, and seamlessly integrating them into the SDLC. By codifying policies, inputs, and modifications, organizations can streamline compliance efforts, ensuring comprehensive documentation and logging of query results.

FinOps

Effectively controlling and managing operational costs stands as a crucial aspect of infrastructure management. To achieve this, implementing PaC to mandate resource labeling, annotations, and distributing machine types can prove invaluable:

- By tagging resources according to product, service, or department, organizations can generate detailed reports showcasing expenditure breakdowns, aiding in cost analysis.

- Implementing restrictions on allowable instance types and resources, coupled with code optimization, enables the creation of comprehensive reports. Empowering stakeholders with these insights allows for informed decision-making regarding infrastructure resource optimization.

- Establishing policies to cap project costs across various infrastructure environments, such as production, development, sandbox, and staging, helps maintain financial discipline and ensures budget adherence.

Conclusion

This chapter centered on applying everything as code to infrastructure. It explored IaC, SaC, and PaC, all of which were integrated through platform engineering. It highlighted how this approach automates resource provisioning with built-in security and compliance, fostering faster development cycles. It explored the evolution of IaC tools and modern solutions like Terraform, Pulumi, and Crossplane, emphasizing their declarative nature and benefits such as automation, disaster recovery, and compliance auditing through version control. The importance of branching strategies for infrastructure code, using systems like Git, GitHub, and GitLab, was also covered, along with their role in efficient, secure, and collaborative infrastructure management.

The next chapter will focus on following DevSecOps principles and how they can help you to make a more robust, secure, and automated SDLC.

Multiple choice questions

1. **Which is a configuration management tool?**
   a. Terraform
   b. Chef
   c. Python
   d. None of the above

2. **IaC has key properties:**
   a. Tools
   b. Versioning
   c. CI/CD pipelines
   d. All of the above

3. **GitOps processes use the:**
   a. Application code
   b. Scripts
   c. IaC
   d. None of the above

4. **Microsoft Azure uses the tools or services for IaC:**
   a. Terraform
   b. CloudFormation templates
   c. Azure Resource Manager
   d. None of the above

5. **Which is the framework used for the security baseline?**
   a. ISO 9001
   b. NIST CF

    c.   RISK-MF

    d.   All of the above

6. **Policy as code:**

    a.   Developers can use any programming language to enforce policies

    b.   The developer needs a specific policy engine and programming language

    c.   None of the above

    d.   Both

7. **Policy as code can enforce regulatory compliance and is managed by the compliance team:**

    a.   True

    b.   False

8. **Which is the most widely used PaC tool?**

    a.   Sonar

    b.   Snyk

    c.   OPA

    d.   All of the above

9. **Policy as code has the following elements:**

    a.   Policy

    b.   Data

    c.   Query

    d.   All of the above

10. **PaC can help to enforce the following compliance:**

    a.   HIPPA

    b.   PCIDSS

    c.   ISO 27001

    d.   All of the above

Answers

1. a

2. d

3. c

4. c

5. b

6. b

7. a

8. c

9. d

10. d

References

1. **https://geekflare.com/policy as code/**

2. **https://platformengineering.org/**

3. **https://www.pulumi.com/docs/clouds/aws/guides/**

4. **https://developer.hashicorp.com/terraform/tutorials/aws-get-started/aws-build**

5. **https://www.openpolicyagent.org/docs/latest/**

6. **https://kyverno.io/docs/**

Join our Discord space

Join our Discord workspace for latest updates, offers, tech happenings around the world, new releases, and sessions with the authors:

https://discord.bpbonline.com

## CHAPTER 5

Platform and DevSecOps

Introduction

In today's software development landscape, combining development, security, and operations is crucial for ensuring the reliability and security of digital systems. Platform engineering is at the core of this integration within the DevOps paradigm. It provides the infrastructure, tools, and frameworks needed to streamline the development lifecycle while incorporating security and operational efficiency at every stage. Platform Engineers coordinate the interaction between development teams, security protocols, and operational frameworks, serving as a linchpin for innovation, resilience, and security in software engineering. This chapter of the book will cover the platform engineering and DevSecOps, which, when combined, will accelerate the DevSecOps maturity and improvement in **DevOps Research and Assessment (DORA)** metrics and compliance level across the organization.

Structure

The chapter covers the following topics:

- DevSecOps
- Baselining the security posture
- Security frameworks

- Shift left in platform engineering

- Platform engineering in a nutshell

- AI, ML, and DevSecOps platforms engineering

Objectives

By the end of this chapter, you will understand how platform engineering following DevSecOps principles can help you to make a more robust, secure, and automated **software development life cycle (SDLC)**.

DevSecOps

DevSecOps is a methodology that emphasizes the integration of security practices throughout the entire software development lifecycle. It focuses on incorporating security as a shared responsibility across development, security, and operations teams. This approach involves creating a culture that prioritizes security, implementing automation to streamline security processes, and designing platforms with built-in security measures. Integrating development, security, and operations, a DevSecOps approach ensures seamless collaboration, embedding security throughout the software lifecycle for robust and efficient delivery. Refer to the following figure:

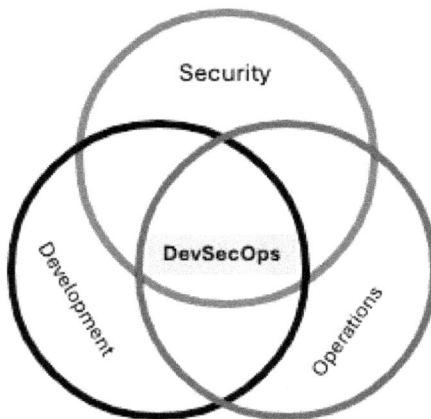

Figure 5.1: Dev, Sec, and Ops integrated as DevSecOps

By implementing DevSecOps, teams can strengthen their applications and infrastructure's security. It allows for early detection and resolution of security issues in the SDLC, making it easier and more cost-effective to safeguard your projects. Thereby, the teams can avoid future compliance issues and ensure uninterrupted development without costly reworks.

Checkpoint's research report on DevSecOps throws the following insights about ROI on DevSecOps:

- The organizations that do DevSecOps right deploy code 46 times more frequently and are two times more likely to exceed in profitability and market share.

- Businesses can save as much as 50% in time costs by automating security and compliance processes in the cloud.

- The organizations with high DevSecOps maturity are 144 percent more likely to resolve flaws quickly, closing the window faster on vulnerabilities that trigger costly incidents.

DevSecOps, when adopted, will help organizations achieve better DORA metrics.

Having learned the importance of DevSecOps, let us move to understand more about the DevSecOps framework.

The following are some crucial topics within the DevSecOps framework that help to achieve DevSecOps maturity:

- **Secure development practices**: Foster a culture of secure coding with training, tools, and policies for developers. Minimize risks by addressing vulnerabilities during development. The following are some of the steps related to securing the development lifecycle. It can go as exhaustively as possible:

  o   Secure coding standards:

      ▪   **Secrets scanning**: GitLeaks, GitGuardian, Trufflehog etc.

      ▪   **IDE plugins**: SonarLint, etc.

  o   Automated code checks and reviews

  o   Security design review

  o   Pre-commit and pre-receive hooks

      A sample **.pre-commit-config.yaml** is given for your reference as follows:

```
---
default_language_version:
    ruby: 2.7.0
repos:
  # Linting
    - repo: https://github.com/pre-commit/pre-commit-hooks
      rev: v4.4.0
      hooks:
          - id: trailing-whitespace
          - id: end-of-file-fixer
          - id: check-yaml
          - id: check-added-large-files
```

```
                    - id: check-json
                    - id: check-executables-have-shebangs
                    - id: check-shebang-scripts-are-executable
                  - id: no-commit-to-branch # both main and master protected
      by default
                    - id: detect-private-key
                    - id: detect-aws-credentials
                      args:
                          - --allow-missing-credentials
```

Code 5.1: Pre-commit hook

- **Security in the CI or CD pipeline**: Integrate security at every stage of your CI/CD process to identify vulnerabilities early. Enhance software delivery speed while ensuring robust protection:

  o **Automated security testing:** Incorporating security checks in **continuous integration or continuous deployment (CI or CD)** pipelines.

  o **Static Application Security Testing (SAST):** Analyzing source code for vulnerabilities.

  o **Software Composition Analysis (SCA):** SCA is a process that analyzes the dependencies and relationships between software components, such as libraries, frameworks, and services. The goal of SCA is to provide insights into how these components interact with each other, identify potential vulnerabilities or issues, and suggest improvements for better maintainability, scalability, and security.

  o **Dynamic Application Security Testing (DAST):** Testing running applications for vulnerabilities.

  o **Interactive Application Security Testing (IAST):** IAST is a type of application security testing that involves interacting with the application in real-time to identify vulnerabilities. IAST tools analyze the application's behavior and interactions at runtime, providing more accurate results.

  o **Secrets scan**: These tools scan the code repositories and detect and notify any secrets (passwords, access keys, **application programming interface (API)** keys, etc.).

  Refer to the following code:

```
pipelineJob('Security-Scanning-Pipeline') {
    definition {
        cps {
            script('''
```

```
pipeline {
    agent any
    environment {
        SONAR_TOKEN = credentials('sonar-token')
        JFROG_USER = credentials('jfrog-user')
        JFROG_PASS = credentials('jfrog-pass')
        JFROG_URL = 'https://your.jfrog.io/
artifactory'
        ZAP_DOCKER_IMAGE = 'owasp/zap2docker-
stable'
    }
    stages {
        stage('Checkout Code') {
            steps {
                checkout scm
            }
        }

        stage('Gitleaks - Secrets Detection') {
            steps {
                sh 'gitleaks detect --source .
--verbose --redact'
            }
        }

        stage('SonarQube Analysis') {
            steps {
                withSonarQubeEnv('SonarQube') {
                    sh 'sonar-scanner -Dsonar.
projectKey=my-project -Dsonar.sources=.'
                }
            }
        }

        stage('JFrog Xray Scan') {
            steps {
                sh "jfrog rt scan my-repo/
--user=${JFROG_USER} --password=${JFROG_PASS}"
            }
        }
```

```
                            stage('Anchore Image Scan') {
                                steps {
                                    sh 'anchore-cli image add
myimage:latest'
                                    sh 'anchore-cli image wait
myimage:latest'
                                    sh 'anchore-cli image vuln
myimage:latest all'
                                }
                            }

                            stage('Checkov - Terraform & Kubernetes
IaC Scanning') {
                                steps {
                                    sh 'checkov -d .'
                                }
                            }

                            stage('ZAP DAST Scan') {
                                steps {
                                    sh 'docker run -v $(pwd):/zap/wrk
-t ${ZAP_DOCKER_IMAGE} zap-baseline.py -t http://yourapp.com -g
gen.conf -r zap_report.html'
                                }
                            }
                        }
                    }
                ''')
            }
        }
}
```

Code 5.2: Security in the CI/CD pipeline

- **IaC security:** Embed security in your infrastructure code to prevent misconfigurations and enforce compliance. Automate security checks to enable secure, rapid deployments:

  o **IaC tools security:** Securing tools like Terraform, Ansible, and Chef.

  o **Kubernetes:** Workload and helm manifests.

- **Container security:** Safeguard containerized environments with comprehensive security measures from build time to runtime. Ensure compliance, vulnerability management, and workload integrity:

- o **Container scanning**: Scanning container images for vulnerabilities.
- o **Runtime security**: Monitoring containers during execution for security issues.
- o **Orchestration security**: Securing Kubernetes and other container orchestration platforms:
  - Container security (Docker, Kubernetes)
- **Cloud security:** Secure your cloud environment with continuous monitoring, policy enforcement, and advanced threat protection. Mitigate risks while enabling seamless cloud operations:
  - o **Cloud provider security**: Leveraging and securing services from AWS, Azure, GCP, etc.
  - o **Cloud configuration security**: Ensuring secure configurations in cloud services.
  - o **Cloud Security Posture Management (CSPM):**
    - Serverless security
    - **Cloud Workload Protection Platforms (CWPP)**
- **Application security:** Build resilient applications by embedding security into every stage of the development lifecycle. Protect against vulnerabilities with proactive assessments and robust defenses:
  - o **Secure coding practices:** Adopting coding practices that reduce vulnerabilities, as discussed in the section with the same name.
  - o **Third-party libraries:** Managing and securing open-source and third-party components.
- **Identity and access management (IAM):** Protect resources by enforcing secure, role-based access and managing identities at scale. Empower seamless user authentication and authorization across your ecosystem:
  - o **Authentication and authorization**: Implementing robust IAM practices.
  - o **Secrets management**: Securely managing secrets, keys, and certificates:
    - **Role-based access control (RBAC)**
    - **Multi-factor authentication (MFA)**
    - **Identity federation and single sign-on (SSO)**
    - **Privileged access management (PAM)**
- **Monitoring and logging:** Enable proactive system health management with real-time monitoring and centralized logging. Ensure timely issue detection and resolution while maintaining a comprehensive activity record for analysis and compliance:

- o **Security monitoring**: Continuous monitoring of applications and infrastructure for security incidents.
- o **Log management**: Collecting and analyzing logs for security events.
- **Compliance and governance**: Simplify governance and ensure alignment with regulatory standards through automated, policy-driven frameworks. Foster trust and accountability with continuous monitoring and enforcement of compliance controls:
  - o **Compliance automation**: Automating compliance checks and reporting.
  - o **Policy as code**: Implementing policies in code to enforce compliance.
  - o **Compliance as code:**
    - Regulatory compliance (for example, GDPR, HIPAA, PCI-DSS)
    - Audit and reporting
- **Threat modeling and risk management:** Anticipate and mitigate risks by identifying vulnerabilities and evaluating potential threats. Build resilient systems by aligning risk management strategies with evolving threat landscapes:
  - o **Threat modeling:** Identifying and mitigating potential security threats.
  - o **Risk assessment**: Continuously assessing risks in the development lifecycle:
    - Threat modeling
    - Attack surface management
    - Security posture management
- **Security automation and orchestration:** Elevate your cybersecurity posture by automating repetitive tasks and integrating tools for seamless workflows. Empower your team to focus on high-priority threats while minimizing response times and improving efficiency:
  - o Automated vulnerability management
  - o Automated compliance checking
  - o **Security Orchestration, Automation, and Response (SOAR)**
    - **Security tools integration**: Integrating security tools into the DevOps toolchain.
    - **Automation**: Automating repetitive security tasks to improve efficiency.
- **Security monitoring and incident response**: Proactively safeguard your organization with comprehensive security monitoring and incident response, ensuring rapid detection, analysis, and mitigation of threats to protect your critical assets and maintain business continuity.

o **Incident response planning**: Preparing for and responding to security incidents.

o **Post-mortem analysis**: Conducting post-incident analysis to improve security:

- Continuous security monitoring
- **Intrusion detection systems (IDS)**
- **Security Information and Event Management (SIEM)**
- Incident response automation

- **Collaboration and culture:** Collaboration and culture in a DevSecOps environment emphasize shared responsibility across development, security, and operations teams, fostering a mindset, where security is a collective priority and integrated throughout the entire SDLC:

  o **Security champions**: Identifying and training security advocates within teams.

  o **Cross-functional teams**: Encouraging collaboration between development, operations, and security teams:

  - DevSecOps culture and mindset
  - Cross-functional collaboration
  - Security training and awareness
  - DevSecOps metrics and **key performance indicators (KPIs)**

- **Vulnerability management**: Vulnerability management is a critical process in identifying, assessing, and mitigating security weaknesses within systems and applications. By proactively addressing vulnerabilities, organizations can reduce their exposure to cyber threats and strengthen their overall security resilience:

  o **Vulnerability scanning**: Regularly scanning for vulnerabilities.

  o **Patch management**: Efficiently managing and applying patches.

- **Security training and awareness**: Security training and awareness are crucial components in building a strong cybersecurity culture, empowering individuals to recognize, prevent, and respond to potential threats. By fostering a proactive security mindset, organizations can significantly reduce risks and enhance their overall defense posture.

  o **Training programs**: Conducting regular security training for developers and operations teams.

  o **Awareness campaigns:** Promoting security awareness across the organization.

- **Emerging technologies and practices**: Emerging technologies and practices are transforming the DevSecOps landscape, driving innovation in how security is integrated throughout the development lifecycle. As organizations embrace these advancements, they must balance agility with robust security measures to ensure secure, efficient, and scalable software delivery:

o   **DORA Report 2023:** The 2023 DORA Report highlights key factors contributing to improved software delivery and organizational performance.

The following are the key insights:

- **User-centered approach**: Teams that prioritize user feedback and needs see a 40% boost in organizational success.

- **Technical excellence**: High-performing teams leverage trunk-based development, modular architecture, continuous integration, and fast code reviews to enhance efficiency.

- **Documentation matters**: Well-maintained documentation strengthens the impact of technical practices.

- **Cultural influence**: A positive work culture significantly enhances key performance outcomes.

- **AI in development**: While AI is gaining traction, the report finds no conclusive evidence linking AI adoption to better performance, yet.

Success in software engineering depends on continuous improvement, a user-first mindset, and fostering a strong team culture.

o   **Artificial intelligence and machine learning in security**: AI-driven security tools have significantly evolved, with advancements in LLM-powered security assistants, automated threat modeling, and AI-driven vulnerability management. Here are some key trends and tools in this space:

- **LLM-powered security assistants:**

  - ❖ **Microsoft Security Copilot**: Uses GPT-powered AI to analyze security incidents, automate threat response, and enhance security operations.

  - ❖ **IBM Watson for Cybersecurity**: AI-powered assistant that provides threat intelligence and context for security incidents.

  - ❖ **Google Chronicle AI**: AI-driven security operations platform for faster incident response.

  - ❖ **OpenAI-powered SOC bots**: Custom GPT models trained for **Security Operations Center** (**SOC**) tasks like log analysis, SIEM queries, and threat hunting.

- **AI-driven security scanners:**

  - ❖ **DeepCode by Snyk**: AI-powered code security analysis that identifies vulnerabilities and suggests fixes.

- ❖ **GitHub Copilot Security Features**: AI-assisted code security recommendations and vulnerability prevention.

- ❖ **Rezilion**: AI-driven vulnerability management platform that prioritizes threats based on real exploitability.

  - ▪ **Automated threat modeling solutions:**
    - ❖ **IriusRisk**: Automates threat modeling with AI-generated attack trees and security countermeasures.

    - ❖ **ThreatModeler**: AI-assisted automated threat modeling for DevSecOps workflows.

    - ❖ **Microsoft Threat Modeling Tool (TMT)**: AI-enhanced tool for identifying and mitigating security threats early.

  - ▪ **AI-powered attack surface management**
    - ❖ **Censys** AI: Uses AI to continuously monitor and identify exposed assets.

    - ❖ **Darktrace**: AI-powered anomaly detection for proactive cyber defense.

    - ❖ **Horizon3.ai**: AI-driven autonomous penetration testing.

o **Blockchain for security:** Blockchain technology has emerged as a powerful tool in cybersecurity, offering decentralization, immutability, and transparency to enhance security frameworks across various industries. Here is how blockchain is transforming security:

  - ▪ **Decentralized identity management (Self-Sovereign Identity (SSI)):** Users control their identity without relying on a central authority.

  - ▪ **Secure data integrity and protection:** Once recorded, data cannot be altered or tampered with. This ensures transparency and accountability in data transactions. Some of the use cases are secure medical records, legal documents, and audit logs.

  - ▪ **Blockchain for secure transactions (cyber fraud prevention)**: Cryptographic signatures ensure authenticity. Transactions are validated by consensus mechanisms. Some of the use cases are secure payments, **anti-money laundering (AML),** and fraud detection.

o **Quantum computing security implications:** Quantum computing threatens traditional encryption methods by enabling rapid decryption of RSA and ECC-based cryptographic keys. Organizations must adopt **post-quantum cryptography (PQC)** and quantum-resistant algorithms to safeguard sensitive data. Additionally, **quantum key distribution (QKD)** provides a secure communication method leveraging quantum mechanics to prevent eavesdropping.

o **Zero Trust Architecture (ZTA):** ZTA is a security framework that **eliminates implicit trust** and enforces **continuous verification** of every user, device, and application before granting access.

Key principles of Zero Trust:

- **Verify every request**: Always authenticate and authorize users and devices, regardless of their location.

- **Least privilege access:** Grant only the minimum permissions necessary to reduce attack surfaces.

- **Assume breach mentality:** Continuously monitor for threats, detect anomalies, and enforce segmentation to limit lateral movement.

Implementing Zero Trust strengthens defenses against modern cyber threats, securing both cloud and on-prem environments.

These important topics collectively ensure that security is deeply integrated into every phase of the software development lifecycle. This includes the initial design phase, deployment, and beyond. This approach fosters a culture where every individual takes responsibility for security. Each of these topics includes a wide range of best practices, advanced tools, and innovative methodologies that focus on seamlessly integrating and automating security throughout the software development lifecycle. This proactive approach ensures that security is not an afterthought but rather a fundamental and proactive component of the entire process.

Platform engineering simplifies DevOps by providing an internal development platform that serves as a **golden path** for developers. This platform streamlines the practice of DevSecOps, which involves a cultural shift, known as **shift left**, in processes and tools across development, security, and operations teams. This shift makes security a shared responsibility, requiring everyone to integrate security into the DevOps **continuous integration and continuous delivery (CI/CD)** workflow. This includes testing for security vulnerabilities and building business-driven security services. By ensuring that security is an integral part of the entire development lifecycle, DevOps teams can deliver secure applications with speed, quality, and agility, thus preventing future vulnerabilities.

Development teams have a centralized view of vulnerabilities, enabling them to incorporate vulnerability resolution into their release plan. Let us explore various aspects to be considered as part of the DevSecOps journey:

- Baseline security posture
- Shift left in platform engineering
- Supply chain management
- Security and quality gates
- Vulnerability management

Baseline the security posture

The term **security posture** refers to an enterprise's overall cybersecurity readiness. According to the **National Institute of Standards and Technology** (**NIST**), it is defined as the security status of an enterprise's networks, information, and systems based on the information security resources (for example, people, hardware, software, policies) and capabilities in place to manage the defense of the enterprise and to react as the situation changes. There are various frameworks and tools available to assess your security posture and identify ways to mitigate threats.

CIS benchmarks

The CIS benchmarks are prescriptive configuration recommendations for more than 25 vendor product families. They represent the consensus-based effort of cybersecurity experts globally to help you protect your systems against threats more confidently. Refer to the following link:

https://www.cisecurity.org/cis-benchmarks

The teams can use the above benchmarks to baseline their security posture across various tools like AWS, Azure, Linux, Webserver, Kubernetes, etc.

Well-Architected Frameworks

A Well-Architected Framework provides recommendations and best practices to design and operate cloud solutions that are secure, robust, resilient, performant, and cost-optimized. Several cloud providers offer their own version of Well-Architected Frameworks specific to their cloud.

Most of the Well-Architected Frameworks cover the following pillars:

- Operational excellence
- Security
- Cost optimization
- Performance
- Reliability

One can use the security pillar section of one's cloud provider to baseline the security posture. Once baselined, the framework can be used to do periodic assessments to continuously improve the security posture.

Security frameworks

The NIST **Secure Software Development Framework** (**SSDF**) and **Cybersecurity Assessment Framework** (**CAF**) are frameworks that organizations can use to evaluate their security position and address supply chain threats. These frameworks cover the software development lifecycle and other aspects of software security, including incident response plans.

Supply-chain Levels for Software Artifacts (SLSA) is designed to simplify assessment and mitigation implementation. It outlines supply chain threats and their mitigations, provides examples of tools for implementing mitigations, and organizes security posture strengthening requirements into levels for prioritized and incremental changes. SLSA primarily focuses on the software delivery pipeline, so it should be used in conjunction with other assessment tools such as SSDF and CAF.

NIST CSF

NIST is a body that handles the technology, metrics, and standards used within the technology and science industries. The NIST CSF is supported by governments and industries worldwide as a recommended baseline for use by any organization, regardless of its sector or size. Refer to the following list:

- **NIST SP 500-291 (2011**) identifies the existing standards landscape for security, portability, interoperability standards or models, studies, or use cases, etc., relevant to cloud computing.

- **NIST SP 500-293 (2014)** contains ten high-level priority requirements in security, interoperability, and portability for the government's adoption of cloud computing.

- **NIST SP 800-53 Rev. 5 (2020**) provides a catalog of security and privacy controls for information systems, also relevant to cloud environments.

- **NIST SP-800-210 (2020)** presents cloud access control characteristics and a set of general access control guidance for cloud service models: IaaS, **platform as a service (PaaS)**, and **software as a service (SaaS)**.

ISO 27001 and ISO 27002

The **International Organization for Standardization (ISO)** created ISO 27001 certifications, which are recognized as the global cybersecurity standard for validating cybersecurity programs within an organization and across third parties. With an ISO certification, companies can demonstrate to stakeholders that they are effectively managing cyber risk. *ISO or IEC Technical Report 22678:2019* is a great reference for cloud policy guidelines.

Service organization controls

Service organization control (SOC) type 2 is a trust-based cybersecurity framework and auditing standard developed by the **American Institute of Certified Public Accountants (AICPA)** to verify that vendors and partners securely manage client data. SOC type 2 involves over 60 compliance requirements and rigorous auditing processes for third-party systems and controls, which can take up to a year to complete. It has a set of trust service principles for organizations to comply with. It is particularly challenging for organizations in the finance or banking sector due to their higher compliance standards.

NERC-CIP

The **North American Electric Reliability Corporation-Critical Infrastructure Protection** (**NERC-CIP**) was introduced to address the increase in attacks on U.S. critical infrastructure and third-party risks. It is a set of cybersecurity standards designed to help organizations in the utility and power sectors reduce cyber risk and ensure the reliability of bulk electric systems. NERC-CIP requires organizations to identify and manage third-party cyber risks in their supply chain and includes controls for systems and critical assets, personnel training, incident response and planning, recovery plans for critical cyber assets, and vulnerability assessments.

Health Insurance Portability and Accountability Act

The **Health Insurance Portability and Accountability Act** (**HIPAA**) is a cybersecurity framework that requires healthcare organizations to implement controls for securing and protecting the privacy of electronic health information. Compliance includes training employees and conducting risk assessments to manage and identify emerging risks.

GDPR or CCPA

The **General Data Protection Regulation** (**GDPR**) was adopted to strengthen data protection procedures and practices for citizens of the **European Union** (**EU**). It impacts all organizations established in the EU or any business that collects and stores the private data of EU citizens, including U.S. businesses. The framework includes 99 articles related to data access rights, data protection policies and procedures, data breach notification requirements, and more. Similarly, the **California Consumer Protection Act** (**CCPA**) is enacted in the USA to provide privacy protection to consumers. Other countries are also working on or enacting privacy acts to protect consumers' data.

Federal Information Security Management Act

The **Federal Information Security Management Act** (**FISMA**) is a comprehensive cybersecurity framework that protects federal government information and systems against cyber threats. It also extends to third parties and vendors working on behalf of federal agencies and is aligned closely with NIST cybersecurity standards.

Payment Card Industry Data Security Standard

The **Payment Card Industry Data Security Standard** (**PCI DSS**) is an information security standard used to handle credit cards from major card brands. Administered by the PCI DSS, it aims to control cardholder data and reduce credit card fraud.

Utilizing these frameworks or others as recommended by your **Chief Information Security Officer (CISO)** or cybersecurity team, the security posture should be baselined:

- Security baseline assessment.

- Provides a snapshot of your company's cybersecurity posture in comparison with industry best practices.

- Identifies maturity level.

- Compares against industry standards and peers.

- Any security baseline starts with the risk assessment and risk tolerance level of the organization.

- Connects security performance with financial performance and overall business risk.

- Ensures adherence to internal governance and compliance.

- Assesses the level of security awareness and training requirements.

- Identifies current gaps.

- Prescribes controls that can be codified to make them automation-friendly.

Shift left in platform engineering

Shift left refers to the practice of moving tasks, processes, and activities earlier in the development lifecycle rather than addressing issues and conducting tests in the later stages of development or during deployment. Any issues resolved at a later stage will cost more than if they were fixed earlier in the SDLC. Shifting left speeds up development efficiency and reduces costs. This approach also aims to reduce the feedback loop, thereby improving developer experience and productivity. By implementing prescriptive quality gates and guardrails, developers will have a clear path to perform their development activities, leading to improved productivity.

Platform engineering implements the shift left approach by automating and orchestrating all the related tools with codified policies as gates and guardrails. These are shifted as far left as possible so that the feedback loop is shorter, allowing developers to fail fast.

Figure 5.2 is an example implementation of how a VCS secrets audit can be achieved using a pre-commit framework and an asynchronous workflow that is event-driven based on each commit by the developer into the version control. Many organizations use a cloud-hosted version control (SaaS version) that does not provide pre-receive hooks functionality. This opens a risk, as pre-commit hooks can be overridden by developers.

The approach, shown in the following figure, provides a method to enhance a pre-commit with an event-driven scan that publishes the scan result to a central vulnerability dashboard and assigns tickets on the project tracker:

Cloudnative Event Driven VCS Audit

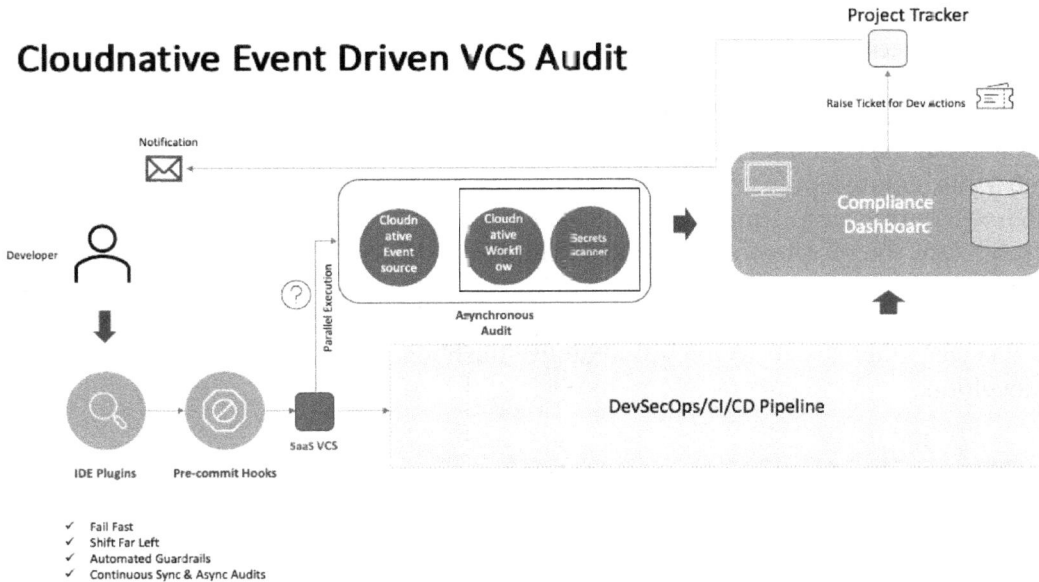

Figure 5.2: *Version control system audit process*

IDE plugins should be consistent with downstream guardrails. If a code quality analysis tool like SonarCloud or SonarQube is integrated as part of the pipeline, related IDE plugins like SonarCloud should be recommended for the developers to adopt. This way, the platform engineering team can help developers shift left their code quality analysis. The same would be applicable to other guardrails.

Note: **All guardrails may not have IDE plugins.**

This is where the platform engineering teams will be playing a greater role. They should carefully assess buy versus build and standardize IDE plugins for different technologies and IDEs based on their guardrails landscape.

Git based version control systems support two types of hooks. Client-side hooks are triggered by operations such as committing and merging, while server-side hooks run on network operations such as receiving pushed commits.

Pre-commit hooks will play a greater role where the SDLC setup uses a SaaS version of VCS. Pre-receive hooks are not supported by those offerings. If the teams want a proven way to validate commits, they should go for a self-hosted version control system, as pre-receive hooks can play a greater role in those setups. Pre-commit hooks can also be overridden by intelligent developers. Therefore, this should be viewed more as an additional guardrail, and the platform engineering team cannot solely rely on pre-commit hooks.

Pre-commit can be setup using several frameworks like pre-commit, Talisman, etc., or the platform engineering team may go with a simple approach of making use of scripts under. Git or hooks (by removing the scripts with the suffix `.sample`).

Imagine a developer, John, is working on an important update for a product hosted on AWS. If John accidentally hard-codes the AWS access key or secret access key, the secrets scanner IDE plugin will alert him when he pastes the access key. Let us say he chooses to ignore the alert and commits the code. The pre-commit, which is set to enable a secret scan hook, will fail the commit. Despite this, John decides to commit his changes, including the secret, to his remote repository. He then uses the **no-verify** switch to push the changes to the remote repository. Unfortunately, the remote repository is a SaaS version of, for example, GitHub. Now, the secret has been leaked. The event-driven VCS audit established by the information security team will trigger an Argo Workflow. This workflow, which works asynchronously with respect to the CI or CD pipeline, conducts audits, identifies the leaked secret, publishes it to the vulnerability dashboard, and raises a Jira ticket against the developer.

Supply chain management

In the earlier part of this chapter, we discussed various SDLC controls. Now, let us take a broad look at the entire SDLC with some indicative controls in mind. These controls are also called **Guardrails**, which will help the developers to fail fast in the SDLC and provide a feedback loop. The following figure details the integration of various tools throughout the SDLC:

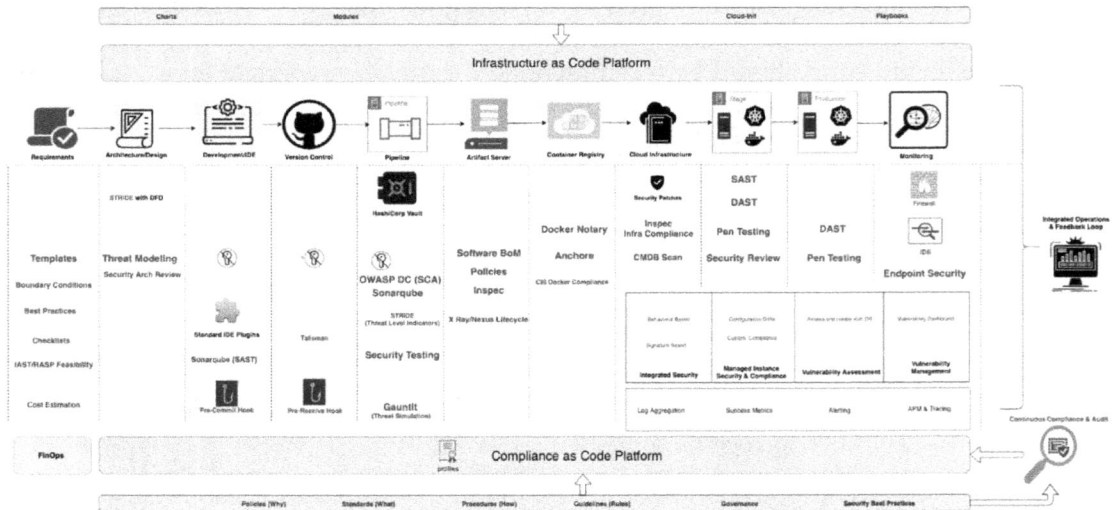

Figure 5.3: Toolset for supply chain management

The main goal is to achieve **secure by design** and **secured at runtime**, ensuring security at every stage. One potential issue to watch out for is tool sprawl and overlaps among the tools. It is important to carefully assess and minimize redundancies. Implementing tools to achieve a secure SDLC is just one part of the puzzle. The other crucial aspect is orchestrating these tools, which is where platform engineering plays a significant role.

Security and quality gates

The initial step in establishing security and quality gates involves formalizing the policies. Creating machine-friendly policies makes it easier to integrate them as validation in the SDLC pipeline. Policy formalization can be accomplished with tools like Inspec, **Open Policy Agent** (**OPA**), Kyverno, etc.

Not all policies can be codified, but it is worth trying to achieve the highest possible coverage. You cannot codify policies using a single tool. It could be one or more tools.

The second step is to classify the controls as follows:

- Detective
- Preventive
- Corrective

A general guideline is to begin with only **detective** controls when implementing for the first time. This phase is more about discovery. Preventive controls come into play while tightening the security measures. Corrective controls can be planned once maturity has improved and strong collaboration and alignment are observed among the stakeholders.

A sample continuous compliance architecture is illustrated in the following. Every validation is captured and published on a central vulnerability dashboard:

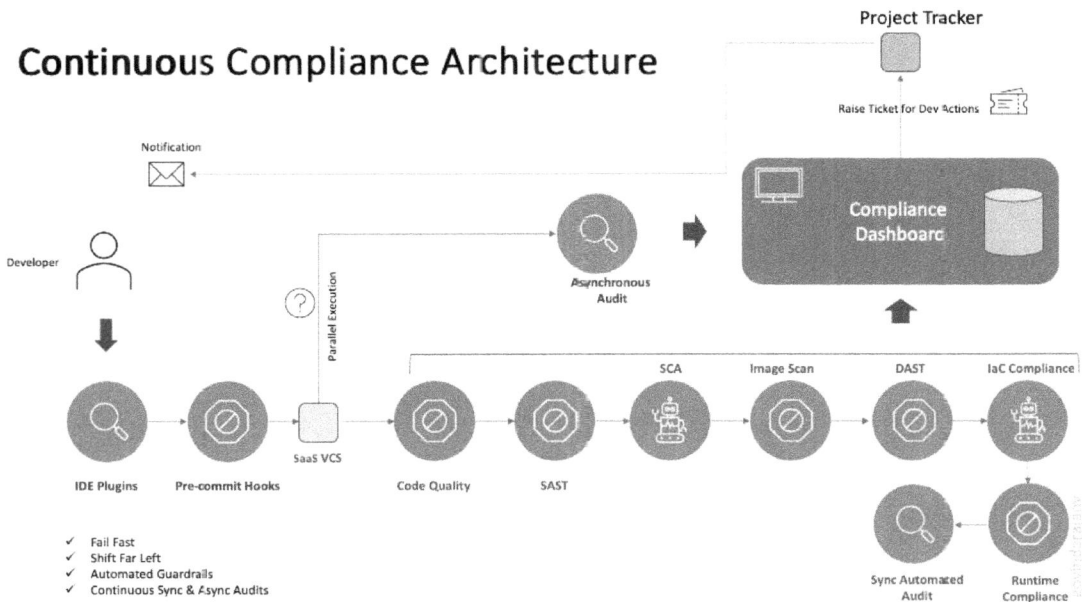

Figure 5.4: Continuous compliance architecture

Here is a sample OPA policy for validating container images, ensuring they come from trusted registries and do not contain vulnerabilities:

```
package kubernetes.admission

# Define allowed image registries
allowed_registries := {
    "docker.io",
    "gcr.io",
    "quay.io",
    "your-private-registry.com"
}

# Define maximum allowed vulnerability severity
allowed_severity := ["LOW", "MEDIUM"]

# Check if the image registry is trusted
deny[msg] {
    image := input.review.object.spec.containers[_].image
    not is_trusted_registry(image)
    msg := sprintf("Image %s is not from an allowed registry", [image])
}

is_trusted_registry(image) {
    some registry
    registry := split(image, "/")[0]
    registry == allowed_registries[_]
}

# Enforce vulnerability scanning results
deny[msg] {
    vuln := input.review.object.metadata.annotations["vulnerability.
severity"]
    not is_allowed_severity(vuln)
    msg := sprintf("Image contains vulnerabilities with severity: %s",
[vuln])
}

is_allowed_severity(severity) {
    severity == allowed_severity[_]
}
```

Code 5.3: OPA policy for validating container images

The following is the equivalent Kyverno policy to enforce image validation, ensuring that images are pulled only from trusted registries and do not contain high-severity vulnerabilities:

```
apiVersion: kyverno.io/v1
kind: ClusterPolicy
metadata:
  name: validate-trusted-image-registry
spec:
  validationFailureAction: Enforce
  rules:
    - name: enforce-trusted-image-registry
      match:
        resources:
          kinds:
            - Pod
      validate:
        message: "Container images must be pulled from a trusted registry."
        pattern:
          spec:
            containers:
              - image: "^(docker.io|gcr.io|quay.io|your-private-registry.
com)/.*$"

    - name: block-high-severity-vulnerabilities
      match:
        resources:
          kinds:
            - Pod
      validate:
        message: "Images with HIGH or CRITICAL vulnerabilities cannot be
deployed."
        deny:
          conditions:
            all:
              - key: "{{ request.object.metadata.annotations.vulnerability.
severity }}"
                operator: AnyIn
                value:
                  - HIGH
                  - CRITICAL
```

Code 5.4: Kyverno policy for validating container images

InSpec can also be used to codify policies and continuously audit for conformance. Here is an InSpec profile that replicates the Kyverno policy we described, ensuring that container images are pulled only from trusted registries and do not contain high-severity vulnerabilities:

```
# InSpec Profile: Image Validation for Kubernetes
title 'Kubernetes Image Security Compliance'

control 'trusted-image-registry' do
  impact 1.0
  title 'Ensure container images come from trusted registries'
  desc 'Only allow images from approved registries like docker.io, gcr.io,
quay.io, and private registries.'

  allowed_registries = ['docker.io', 'gcr.io', 'quay.io', 'your-private-
registry.com']

  kubernetes_pods.namespace('default').items.each do |pod|
    pod.containers.each do |container|
      registry = container.image.split('/')[0]
      describe registry do
        it { should be_in allowed_registries }
      end
    end
  end
end

control 'block-high-severity-vulnerabilities' do
  impact 1.0
  title 'Deny images with HIGH or CRITICAL vulnerabilities'
  desc 'Ensure that deployed container images do not have vulnerabilities
with HIGH or CRITICAL severity.'

  disallowed_severities = ['HIGH', 'CRITICAL']

  kubernetes_pods.namespace('default').items.each do |pod|
    vuln_annotation = pod.metadata.annotations['vulnerability.severity']
    next unless vuln_annotation # Skip if annotation is missing

    describe vuln_annotation do
```

```
        it { should_not be_in disallowed_severities }
      end
   end
end
```

Code 5.5: *Inspec profile for validating container images*

Vulnerability management

Vulnerability management involves the ongoing process of identifying, classifying, prioritizing, addressing, and reducing software vulnerabilities. It is a crucial aspect of computer and network security and should not be mistaken for vulnerability assessment. Vulnerabilities can be found using a vulnerability scanner, which examines a computer system to identify known vulnerabilities. All identified vulnerabilities at each stage of the SDLC are centrally managed and monitored.

This vulnerability dashboard should help with the following needs:

- Support for integration with all the tools

- Monitor vulnerabilities in a central place

- Reduce duplications

- Categorize findings

- Trend analysis

- Identify and manage false positives and false negatives

- Actionize findings

Our recommendation is **DefectDojo**, which meets most of the requirements mentioned previously. The platform engineering team may need to write some custom code and build specific integrations to address any gaps in DefectDojo. You can also explore commercial tools that offer ready-made features. Tenable and CrowdStrike provide vulnerability management dashboards, but commercial tools may have their own limitations, so it is important to conduct a thorough assessment before choosing the right tool.

The following figure is an example of implementing centralized vulnerability management using DefectDojo, AWS Security Hub, and Argo Workflows:

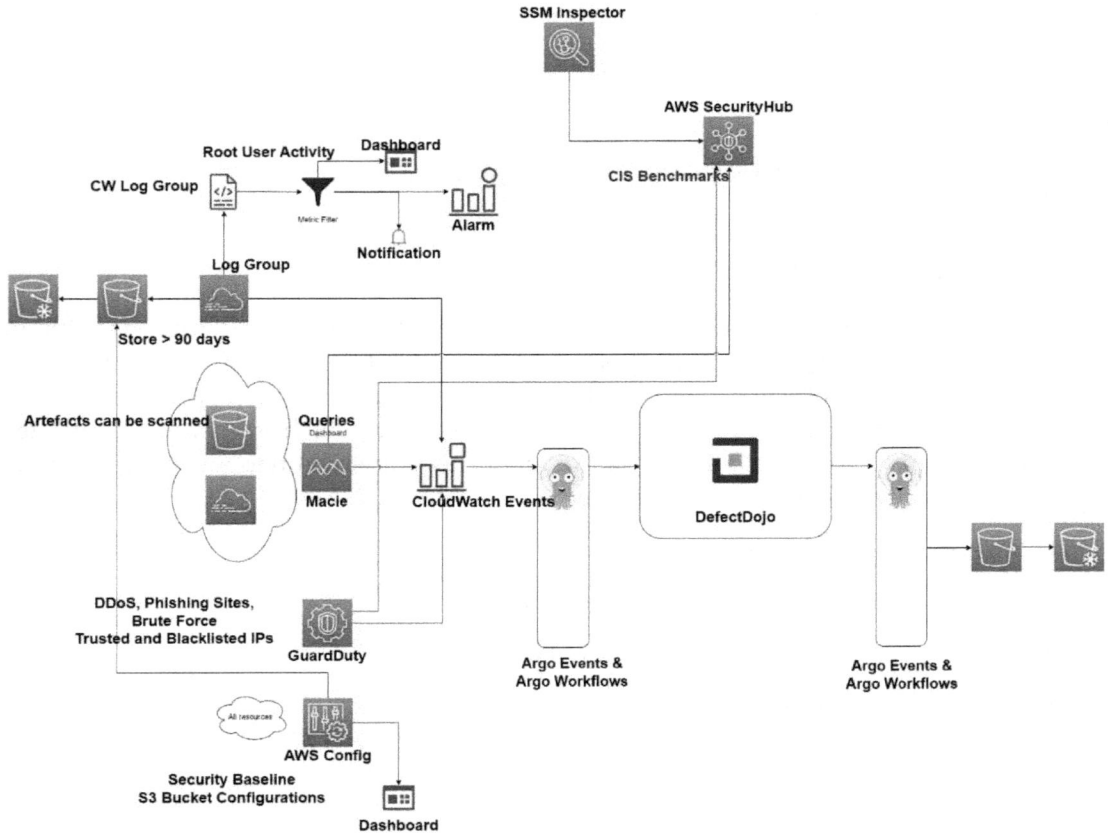

Figure 5.5: *Centralized vulnerability management workflow*

Another implementation of capturing vulnerabilities across the SDLC is given in *Figure 5.6*. The following figure shows how DefectDojo can play the role of a compliance dashboard and raise tickets on Jira. At each stage of scanning, generated reports can be pushed to DefectDojo for centralized tracking and resolution:

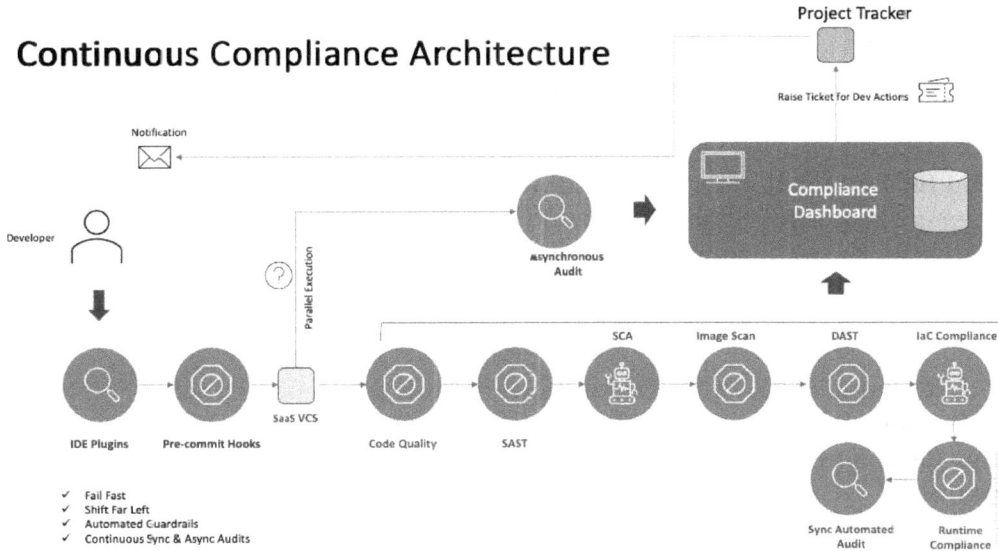

Figure 5.6: *Continuous compliance using DefectDojo as compliance dashboard*

Platform engineering in a nutshell

Having considered various aspects, it is now time for us to consolidate our understanding and explore how we can use platform engineering to manage them effectively and effortlessly.

The following figure is the logical diagram of a platform engineering solution:

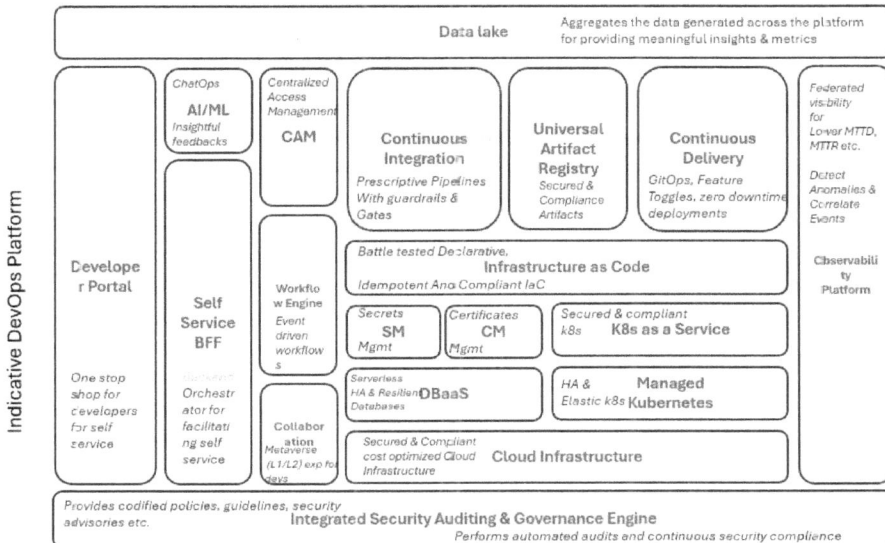

Figure 5.7: *Platform engineering logical diagram*

Let us discuss only security-related components from the above proposal.

Centralized access management

This is a **centralized access management (CAM)** layer. The developer portal, self-service **Backend for Frontend (BFF)**, and workflow engines act on this layer and perform access management requests initiated by developers. This also takes care of approval flows, validates privilege escalations, policy adherence, etc.

CI or UAR or CD

Security related to SDLC (CI, CD, and universal artifact registry). Integration of CI/CD and **universal artifact registry (UAR)** with required guardrails helps teams achieve secure software development. We have discussed enough on these topics. So, we can move on to the next one.

Observability

This helps not only to observe infrastructure and application observability, but also security and thread-level indicators should be made observable. Integrating security observability with application observability is the right step to have a holistic view of application health, which should cover performance, reliability, **Total Cost of Ownership (TCO)**, availability, and security.

Integrated security auditing and governance engine

This will be the heart of security orchestration and intelligence. This uses codified policies, governance controls, gates, etc., and enforces the policies across the SDLC. This layer also helps to continuously monitor the security posture and perform the required actions to mitigate and remediate the vulnerabilities.

The following is a sample implementation of DevSecOps with integrated security auditing and governance engine. The tools are indicative as per the knowledge based on implementing similar solutions.

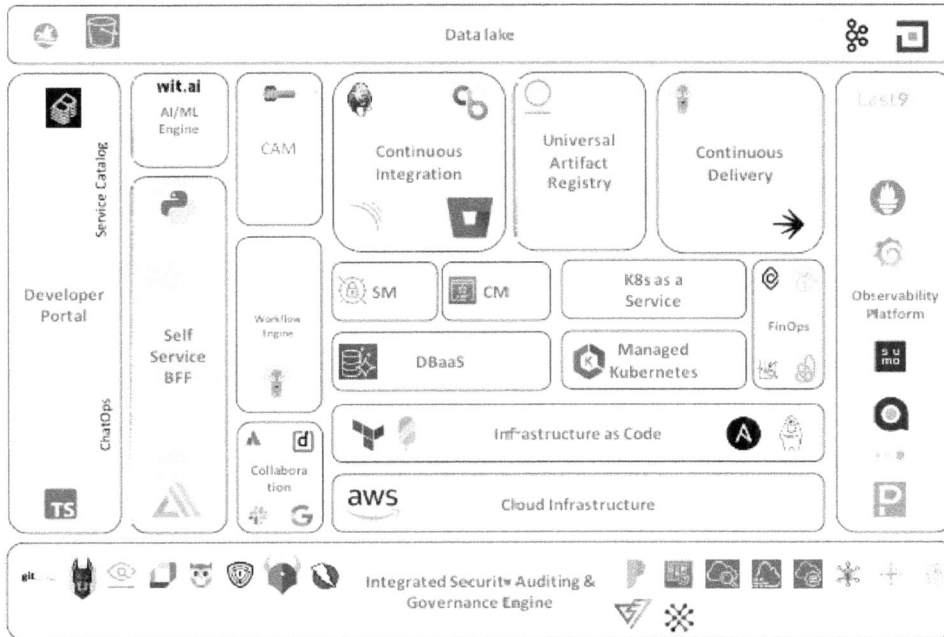

Figure 5.8: *Integrated security auditing and governance engine*

AI, ML, and DevSecOps platforms engineering

In this section, we will learn about AI, ML, and DevSecOps with platform engineering. A significant challenge in promoting organization-wide security is the cognitive load faced by developers. Understanding and effectively incorporating security practices into the SDLC can be overwhelming due to the inherent complexity of information security. This cognitive overload is a serious cyber threat, as it can lead to critical security oversights. To mitigate this, we propose an AI-driven model designed to reduce cognitive load and enhance security awareness and adoption among developers.

Artificial intelligence

One of the challenges in promoting security across the organization is the cognitive load that ordinary developers face when trying to understand and incorporate security into the SDLC.

Cognitive overload poses a serious cyber threat, as overwhelmed brains do not make good soldiers. Information security is inherently complex, and teaching it can lead to cognitive overload among developers. To address this, we propose a model that leverages AI to reduce cognitive load and improve security awareness and adoption.

Prompt engineering involves designing inputs for AI tools to produce optimal outputs. We can utilize prompt engineering tools like OpenAI to act as a 24/7 cybersecurity evangelist for InfoSec teams. This chat client can receive questions from developers and respond in a more developer-friendly language. These chatbots can access InfoSec policies, best practices, and knowledge bases about internal implementations of similar problems and requirements. They can also provide invulnerable code snippets for a given vulnerable code snippet, and more.

Refer to the following figure:

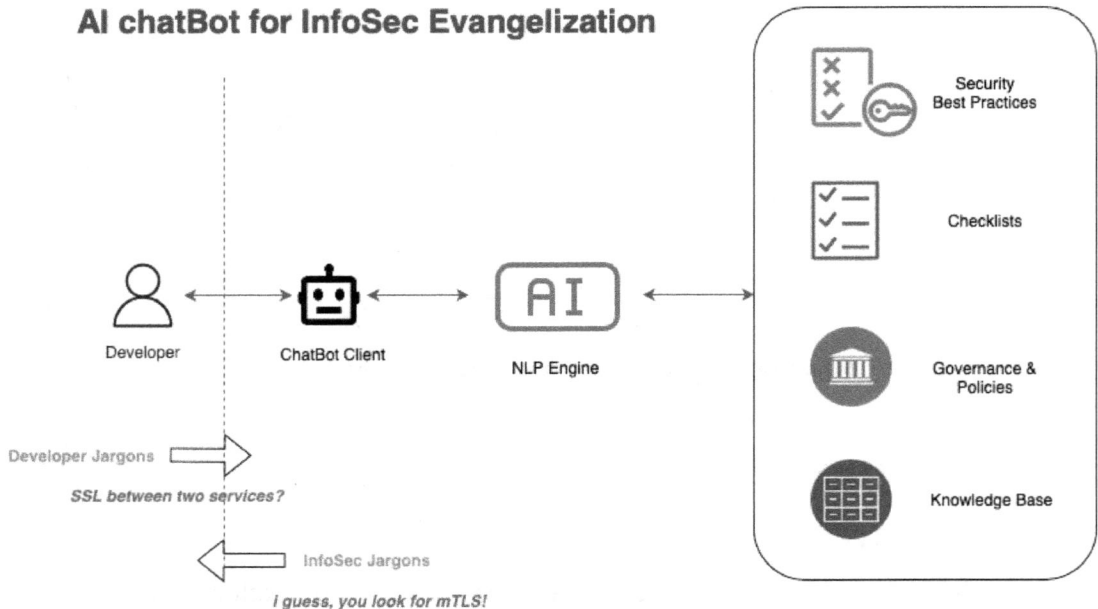

Figure 5.9: AI chatbot

Machine learning

An organization's tech team with a long history of operations will have left lots of data and trails. A machine learning algorithm can use that data to learn and predict outcomes.

In a typical SDLC, pipeline failures can be learned from historical data. An **integrated development environment (IDE)** plugin can be developed to act as a client, scanning the code in real-time and alerting the developer about possible failures in later stages of the SDLC. This decision will be based on a machine learning model using historical data. This should help reduce the cognitive load not only on the development teams but also on the information security team. It will also help us achieve the shift left principle, which helps the organization achieve all validations far left of the software development lifecycle. Refer to the following figure:

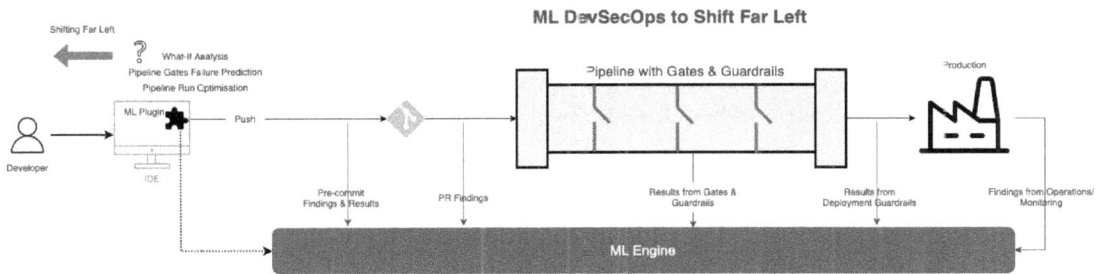

Figure 5.10: *ML DevSecOps*

Conclusion

In this chapter, we covered the platform engineering and DevSecOps, when combined, will accelerate the DevSecOps Maturity and improvement in DORA metrics and compliance level across the organization.

In the next chapter, readers will explore platform engineering and containerization, exploring how leveraging Kubernetes as a platform for engineering operations can streamline development workflows, boost operational efficiency, and drive innovation in today's software development landscape.

Exercises

1. What is the purpose of threat modeling in DevSecOps?

2. Why are pre-commit hooks not a foolproof solution?

3. Why is UAR considered the core of DevSecOps?

4. What is the shift left in DevSecOps?

5. Please list the types of controls discussed in this chapter.

6. Under ISO, which policy provides a great reference for cloud policy guidelines?

Answers

1. Threat modeling is a process by which potential threats, such as structural vulnerabilities or the absence of appropriate safeguards, can be identified and enumerated, and countermeasures prioritized.

2. Developers can override pre-commit validations using no-verify switch, which is the reason why pre-commit is not a fool-proof solution. However, it can be a good additional layer of guardrail.

3. Unified artifact registry is a secured, compliant, and invulnerable storage of all artifacts like application packages, third-party libraries, helm charts, Ansible playbooks, Terraform modules, etc. This is considered a first step for organizations starting with their DevSecOps journey.

4. The core principles and practices of DevSecOps revolve around the idea of shifting security left, meaning that security considerations are introduced as early as possible in the SDLC. The idea is to fail fast and have a shorter feedback loop so that developers are able to turn around faster.

5. There are three types of controls discussed in this chapter. They are as follows:

   - Detective

   - Corrective

   - Preventive

6. ISO/IEC Technical Report 22678:2019

Join our Discord space

Join our Discord workspace for latest updates, offers, tech happenings around the world, new releases, and sessions with the authors:

https://discord.bpbonline.com

CHAPTER 6
Platform Engineering and Containerization

Introduction

Kubernetes, a container orchestration platform, is open-source and offers a flexible, reliable, and scalable environment for running containerized applications. Engineers can easily package and manage applications using containers, automate deployment, scale systems dynamically, and ensure high availability with Kubernetes. It simplifies the complexities of deploying, scaling, and managing containerized applications by providing an abstract layer. Utilizing Kubernetes as a platform for engineering operations allows organizations to streamline development workflows, increase operational efficiency, and foster innovation in the modern software development landscape. Among the available platforms, Kubernetes is a standout, serving as an ideal platform for running complex distributed applications.

Structure

The chapter covers the following topics:

- Features of Kubernetes
- Platform engineering with Kubernetes
- Key concepts and tools
- Platform engineering on K8s architecture

- DOITBACK
- Platform engineering maturity model

Objectives

By the end of this chapter, you will understand how platform engineering following DevSecOps principles can help you to make a more robust, secure, and automated **software development lifecycle** (**SDLC**). This chapter provides a comprehensive guide to platform engineering on Kubernetes. You will learn the core concepts, the role of Kubernetes, and key tools and technologies. You will also learn how to design a platform architecture and apply these principles to real-world scenarios. Finally, you will be able to assess your organization's platform engineering maturity.

Features of Kubernetes

Kubernetes has become the standard platform for managing containerized workloads in modern software development, offering several benefits for platform engineering and gaining popularity in recent times:

- **Elasticity**: By adding or removing instances of containers based on demand, Kubernetes enables horizontal scaling, ensuring optimal resource utilization and effortless handling of high traffic loads for applications.

- **Self-healing and fault tolerance**: Kubernetes possesses self-healing capabilities, automatically restarting or rescheduling affected containers if a container or node fails. This maintains the system's desired state, ensuring high availability and minimizing disruptions to applications.

- **Service discovery**: Kubernetes includes built-in service discovery mechanisms, allowing applications to be exposed as services and discovered using **Domain Name Service** (**DNS**) or environment variables. Its seamless load-balancing features ensure even distribution of traffic among application instances.

- **Cloud native observability**: Kubernetes offers integrations with monitoring and observability tools to provide insights into resource utilization, application metrics, and logs, facilitating efficient troubleshooting, performance optimization, and capacity planning.

- **Cloud Native Computing Foundation (CNCF) community support**: With a vibrant ecosystem and strong community backing, Kubernetes boasts numerous plugins, tools, and extensions that complement and expand its capabilities.

Platform engineering with Kubernetes

Kubernetes is a powerful platform for building self-service tools that make life easier for developers. This is because it is so good at managing containers (lightweight packages of software), Kubernetes makes it simple to deploy and scale applications. It also provides a layer of abstraction that hides the complexity of the underlying infrastructure, and it can be customized with add-ons to meet specific needs. Plus, with its huge community and wide range of supporting tools, Kubernetes offers a solid foundation for building robust and efficient developer platforms.

In short, by using Kubernetes and applying platform engineering best practices, organizations can create an environment where developers can focus on what they do best: building and deploying great software.

Let us look at some of the details of why Kubernetes has become the leading platform for building modern, efficient platforms for developers.

Optimized resource utilization

Kubernetes allows applications to efficiently handle varying workloads by enabling automatic scaling and resource allocation. This is achieved through several mechanisms:

- **Resource requests and limits**: Developers can define the minimum (requests) and maximum (limits) CPU and memory resources for their containers. This enables Kubernetes to intelligently schedule pods onto nodes with sufficient capacity and prevents individual applications from monopolizing resources, ensuring fair distribution and preventing noisy neighbour issues.

- **Horizontal Pod Autoscaler (HPA)**: HPA automatically scales the number of pod replicas up or down based on observed CPU utilization or other custom metrics. This ensures that applications can handle fluctuating loads without manual intervention, optimizing resource consumption during peak times and reducing waste during idle periods.

- **Vertical Pod Autoscaler (VPA)**: VPA automatically adjusts the CPU and memory requests and limits for individual containers based on their historical and real-time usage. This helps to right-size pods, ensuring they have just enough resources to perform optimally, minimizing over-provisioning and under-provisioning.

- **Cluster Autoscaler**: This component dynamically adjusts the number of nodes in the Kubernetes cluster itself based on pending pods and resource requirements. If there are unscheduled pods due to insufficient resources, the Cluster Autoscaler can provision new nodes. Conversely, it can remove underutilized nodes, leading to significant cost savings in cloud environments.

- **Quality of Service (QoS) classes**: Kubernetes assigns QoS classes (Guaranteed, Burstable, Best-Effort) to pods based on their resource requests and limits. This helps the scheduler prioritize critical workloads during resource contention, ensuring that essential applications maintain performance even under stress.

- **Monitoring and observability**: Tools like Prometheus and Grafana integrate seamlessly with Kubernetes to provide deep insights into resource usage across the cluster. This data is invaluable for identifying bottlenecks, optimizing resource configurations, and making informed decisions about capacity planning and cost optimization.

Resource isolation

Teams can work independently and manage their resources by using namespaces, which provide logical separation within a Kubernetes cluster. Individual teams or projects can utilize separate namespaces, providing a dedicated space for each entity. This isolated environment ensures that distinct workflows and configurations remain self-contained, reducing the likelihood of development project conflicts. If cost and operational overheads are not constraints, cluster-level isolation could be a preferable option.

Enhanced collaboration

Enhance communication and coordination by using collaboration tools like chat platforms and project management systems. Integration with Kubernetes' APIs and popular tools like Kubernetes Dashboard and kubectl, teams can effortlessly collaborate and streamline their workflow, leveraging the power of these powerful automation and orchestration tools.

GitOps-friendly architecture

GitOps framework uses Git as a single source of truth for managing Kubernetes configurations and ensures version control of configurations. This allows teams to track changes, roll back to previous versions, and collaborate effectively. It promotes the IaC approach and enables teams to apply software engineering practices, resulting in more reliable and reproducible deployments. With GitOps, deployments can be triggered automatically whenever changes are successfully committed to the Git repository. Rollback capabilities enable swift recovery from errors or unexpected changes, allowing teams to quickly revert to a prior version of their application. This feature ensures minimal disruption and maintains the integrity of the application, preserving stability and uptime.

Reconciliation loop

Kubernetes streamlines processes, reduces errors, and accelerates application delivery by offering robust features for automating deployment and scaling operations. Kubernetes's reconciliation loop automates application management. Example of Kubernetes reconciliation loop for automating application lifecycle management:

- **Desired state**: User defines the intended application configuration (replicas, images, etc.).
- **Controllers**: Kubernetes components responsible for specific resource types (e.g., Deployments).
- **Actual state**: The current state of running resources.

- **Reconciliation loop**: Continuous comparison of desired vs. actual state by controllers.
- **Reconciliation**: Actions taken by controllers to match actual to desired state (scaling, updates, restarts).
- **Benefits**: Self-healing, automation, declarative management, reduced errors, faster delivery.

The reconciliation loop is a fundamental pattern in Kubernetes that enables its powerful automation and self-healing capabilities. It is what allows you to manage complex applications with confidence and efficiency.

Deployment strategy for every need

Kubernetes deployments enable declarative management of application deployments. The desired state of the application can be defined, allowing Kubernetes to handle the orchestration. Deployments ensure that the required number of replicas are running, automatically scaling up or down as necessary. Rolling updates and deployment features facilitate seamless application upgrades while minimizing downtime. Kubernetes services offer a dependable endpoint for accessing a group of pods. By defining a service, the application is separated from the underlying network, enhancing resilience to changes in pod IP addresses. Services facilitate load balancing across multiple replicas of an application, guaranteeing exceptional availability and optimized traffic distribution. By intelligently routing traffic to the most suitable instance, services ensure that your application remains responsive and performant even in high-traffic scenarios.

Automating scaling with Kubernetes autoscaling features

Kubernetes provides robust autoscaling features that automatically adjust the number of running replicas based on application demand. HPA scales the number of pods in a deployment automatically based on CPU utilization or custom metrics. It guarantees that the application has adequate resources to handle increased traffic and optimizes resource utilization during periods of lower demand. Cluster Autoscaler automates the scaling of the underlying Kubernetes cluster by dynamically adding or removing nodes based on workload demands. It ensures optimal resource allocation and cost efficiency, scaling nodes up or down in response to the overall workload.

Customizing Kubernetes with operators

Kubernetes operators and **custom resource definitions** (**CRDs**) operators are Kubernetes controllers that expand the platform's capabilities for managing applications or services. Custom operators can be created to automate the setup and teardown of development and testing environments.

These operators serve as comprehensive managers for resource lifecycles, provisioning the necessary infrastructure and enforcing consistent configurations across diverse environments. By automating these tasks, they simplify the process of deploying and maintaining complex applications. CRDs allow teams to define custom resources that expand Kubernetes' native capabilities. CRDs enable the specification of environment configurations as custom resources, making it easier to create, manage, and tear down environments as needed. CRDs enable consistent and predictable environment configurations, significantly reducing manual intervention and ensuring the reproducibility of complex deployments. By standardizing setup procedures, CRDs streamline the process of creating and managing heterogeneous environments.

Advanced traffic control and routing using service meshes

Service meshes, such as Istio and Linkerd, offer advanced traffic management and control, enabling teams to define routing rules, implement traffic splitting, and conduct canary deployments. They also allow development teams to perform A/B testing, gradually roll out new features, and handle blue-green deployments seamlessly. Additionally, they provide powerful observability features, including distributed tracing, metrics collection, and logging. These features empower developers to quickly identify and troubleshoot problems early in the development cycle, facilitating swift resolution and minimizing downtime. By providing real-time insight into application performance and behavior, they enable more effective debugging and issue resolution.

Service meshes also facilitate fault injection, enabling teams to simulate failures and test the resiliency of their applications. Service meshes also provide circuit-breaking and rate-limiting mechanisms that help maintain application stability and prevent cascading failures. These features allow development teams to control traffic flow, enforce resource limits, and ensure the reliability of their applications under various load conditions.

Key concepts and tools

Modern software development demands speed and efficiency. Platform engineering has become essential to meet these demands by creating robust, self-service platforms. These platforms empower developers to build and deliver high-quality applications rapidly. To achieve this, platform engineering leverages a core set of concepts and powerful tools that streamline development processes, automate infrastructure management, and foster collaboration between teams.

Chaos engineering

Chaos engineering helps to fulfill resilience requirements by proactively creating controlled failures to ensure that applications, infrastructure, and platforms can recover without impacting users. The purpose of chaos experiments is to identify weaknesses and improve communication during critical incidents, ultimately increasing confidence in complex systems.

OpenTelemetry

OpenTelemetry is a set of APIs, **software development kits** (**SDKs**), and tools designed for instrumenting, collecting, and exporting telemetry data such as metrics, logs, and traces. This open-source observability framework, developed by the CNCF, aims to standardize protocols and tools for routing telemetry data to monitoring platforms. Furthermore, OpenTelemetry offers vendor-neutral SDKs, APIs, and tools, enabling the transmission of data to any observability backend for analysis.

Feature flags

Feature flags, also called feature toggles, are a method in software development that enables teams to activate or deactivate features in a system without the need to deploy new code. This method facilitates the management of new feature releases, the execution of A/B testing, the implementation of continuous delivery, and the handling of rollbacks more effectively.

Feature flags allow for the gradual introduction of features to a subset of users, providing the ability to monitor and adjust before a full release. With feature flags, features can be deployed to production in an inactive state and activated when ready. This decouples deployment from release, enabling more frequent and safer releases. In the event that a new feature results in issues, it can be promptly disabled through the feature flag, avoiding the need for a complete rollback of the deployment. Several tools and libraries are accessible to assist with feature flag implementation, such as LaunchDarkly, Unleash, and Split.io.

CloudEvents

Events are omnipresent, but event publishers often use different descriptions. This makes the platform engineering teams write glue code and duct piping to handle and process each of those events separately.

CloudEvents is a standard used to describe event data consistently. The goal is to simplify event declaration and delivery across various services and platforms. The CloudEvents working group has garnered substantial interest from industry players, including major cloud providers and popular **software as a service** (**SaaS**) companies. The specification is currently managed under the CNCF. In the absence of a standard way to describe events, developers are required to create new event-handling logic for each event source. The absence of a common event format results in a lack of consistent libraries, tooling, and infrastructure for transmitting event data across different environments.

CloudEvents offers SDKs for languages such as Go, JavaScript, Java, C#, Ruby, PHP, PowerShell, Rust, and Python, which can be utilized for constructing event routers, tracing systems, and other utilities. The overall hindrance to event data's portability and productivity is attributable to the lack of consistency in this area.

With the advent of CloudEvents, the event lifecycle will have consistency, portability, and accessibility.

Continuous Delivery Events

A common specification for Continuous Delivery Events. Redefine your builds with the freedom to select and customize as you wish, liberate your continuous delivery approach from being tied to a specific vendor, and embrace broad reusability. With **Continuous Delivery Events (CDEvents)**, you can choose the continuous delivery approach that best fits your product's requirements and integrate the tools that align with your specific needs. CDEvents provides a unified framework for the continuous delivery of events, fostering seamless collaboration and integration across the entire software development lifecycle.

It expands on the **Continuous Delivery Foundation's (CDF)** efforts to establish best practices in continuous delivery and create a common language for CI/CD ecosystem events. This allows for the separation of pipeline descriptions from physical implementations, making it easier to scale a decoupled CI/CD architecture and enhance the resilience of CI/CD pipelines, especially in increasingly intricate end-to-end software production and delivery pipelines, such as those found in microservices architecture with numerous independent pipelines. By utilizing CDEvents, you can easily link workflows from different systems, accelerating the transition to a fully automated continuous delivery process for your organization. The use of standardized events simplifies the enhancement of observability and auditability in workflows across diverse technology platforms. Employing a common descriptive language makes it easier for your staff to comprehend all your workflows, regardless of the team or platform they support. Additionally, it facilitates the seamless transition between tools or infrastructure vendors if necessary.

The specification for CDEvents is an extension of the CloudEvents specification and is designed to offer vocabulary suitable for CI/CD events. The aim of the CDEvents specification is to establish compatibility between systems, enabling services to generate or consume events independently, without being reliant on each other. Producers can create events even when no consumer is listening, and consumers can express interest in events that are not currently being produced. CDEvents are characterized as declarative events, meaning the producer conveys information about an occurrence without needing to know how the event will be used on the receiving end, or who the recipient will be. The primary application is to enable interoperability, allowing one CI/CD tool to consume events generated by another tool without requiring fixed, specific definitions. This application focuses on facilitating the collaboration of CI/CD tools in an automated, more efficient manner. The secondary application of CDEvents is in observability and metrics. A crucial aspect of enhancing the CD workflow involves the pipeline's ability to gather events from various CI/CD tools. Standardized events from all participating tools enable a unified, end-to-end process that spans multiple tools.

Here are some of the CDEvents:

- **Source code control events**: Represent events standardized event types for representing important events related to the management of source code assets, such as commits, builds, and deployments. This enables consistent tracking, analysis, and reporting of critical software development activities.

- **Continuous integration events**: Represent events related to the software development lifecycle, including builds, tests, packages, and releases of software artifacts. This enables efficient tracking, analysis, and reporting of critical software development activities.

- **Testing events**: Represent events related to testing activities, such as test runs, failures, and passes. This enables consistent tracking, analysis, and reporting of critical testing results.

- **Continuous deployment events**: Represent events representing important occurrences related to environments where software artifacts are deployed or intended to run, such as production, staging, or development environments. This enables efficient tracking, analysis, and reporting of critical deployment activities.

- **Continuous operations events**: This standardizes the representation of key events related to continuous operations, including incident occurrences and subsequent resolutions. This enables consistent tracking, analysis, and reporting of critical events across your organization.

- **Core events**: Core event types provide a standardized way to represent significant occurrences in the context of continuous operations, including incidents and their subsequent resolutions. This enables streamlined tracking, analysis, and reporting of critical events.

Open application model

Open application model (OAM) provides a standardized framework for modeling cloud-native applications on top of diverse hybrid and multi-cloud environments.

By focusing on the application rather than the container or orchestrator, OAM enables modular, extensible, and portable design for defining deployment configurations using a higher-level API. By adopting OAM, organizations can streamline application deployment and management across a broad range of hybrid environments, encompassing Kubernetes, cloud platforms, and even **Internet of Things (IoT)** devices. This unified approach simplifies the process of delivering applications, reduces complexity, and improves overall operational efficiency.

The following figure provides a high-level architecture for the open application model:

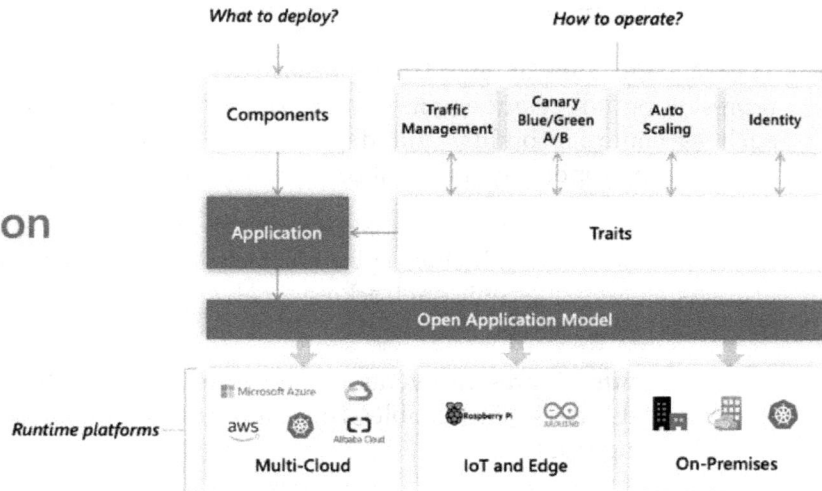

Figure 6.1: *Open application model for modelling cloud application*

In contemporary hybrid deployment settings, delivering applications without their specific context poses a significant challenge. This is apparent as developers often find themselves focusing on intricate infrastructure elements such as clusters, ingress, labels, DNS, and the complexities of adapting infrastructure across diverse environments, rather than the application itself. This approach proves to be limited in its adaptability, as the introduction of a higher-level platform typically fails to meet the evolving requirements of an application. Additionally, the close coupling of app deployment with service providers and infrastructure leads to vendor lock-in, impacting the configuration, development, and operation of apps across hybrid environments. To address these issues, the OAM promotes an app-centric approach. Emphasizing the application as the central focus, this model suggests defining app deployment using a self-contained model, incorporating operational behaviors as an integral part of the app definition and independent of the underlying infrastructure, enabling straightforward deployment. It also offers a clear and scalable solution by standardizing app delivery into reusable components, allowing for customized deployment plans and promoting self-service functionality. Furthermore, the model advocates for a vendor-neutral approach, providing a consistent high-level abstraction for app delivery across various environments, thus reducing the risk of vendor lock-in.

Let us break down the key points about OAM and its relationship to platform engineering:

- **Declarative approach**: Imagine you are ordering a pizza. A declarative approach is like telling the pizza place exactly what you want: *I want a large pizza with pepperoni, mushrooms, and extra cheese.* You do not tell them how to make it (knead the dough, cook it, etc.), just the *result* you desire.

  OAM works similarly. Instead of telling the platform how to deploy your application (step-by-step instructions), you declare the desired state in a simple configuration file. For example, *I need a web service with two replicas, connected to a database, and exposed on port 80*. The platform then figures out how to provision servers, configure networks, etc. This simplifies deployment and makes it more consistent.

- **Composable components**: Think of *LEGOs*. You have different bricks (components) like wheels, windows, and blocks. You can combine these in various ways to build different things.

  OAM treats application components like LEGOs. A database, a service, a load balancer, these are all individual components. You can define them separately and then combine them to build your application. This makes applications more modular, reusable, and easier to manage. For example, you might have a database component that can be reused across multiple applications.

- **Flexibility and abstraction (OAM)**: Imagine you are driving a car. You do not need to know how the engine works or how the transmission shifts gears. You just steer, accelerate, and brake. The car's mechanics are abstracted away.

  OAM does the same for infrastructure. It hides the complex details of the underlying cloud or Kubernetes from developers. They do not need to worry about which specific servers or network configurations are used. This abstraction makes applications more portable (you can move them between different environments easily) and simplifies the deployment process. It allows developers to focus on the application itself, not the infrastructure.

OAM helps platform engineering by providing a standardized, declarative way to define and deploy applications. This makes applications more manageable, portable, and reusable, ultimately simplifying the job of the platform engineering team and allowing developers to focus on building features.

The following are the real-world examples of OAM:

- **Backstage:** Think of *Backstage* as a one-stop shop for developers. It is a portal where they can find everything they need to build and manage their applications: documentation, APIs, services, infrastructure components, and even monitoring dashboards.

  Backstage uses OAM-like concepts to organize and present this information. It treats each application, service, or infrastructure component as a distinct entity with its own metadata and configuration. This allows Backstage to create a unified view of the entire software ecosystem, making it easier for developers to discover and interact with different parts of the system.

- **KubeVela:** Without OAM, you might have to write a bunch of YAML files to define deployments, services, ingress, and other Kubernetes resources. KubeVela, using OAM principles, simplifies this. You define your application in a higher-level, more declarative way. You specify the components (e.g., *I need a web service with this image, this many replicas, and connected to this database*), and KubeVela translates that into the necessary Kubernetes YAML. The following section covers more details.

These applications are growing examples of OAM and show the great adoption of it.

KubeVela

KubeVela is a modern application delivery platform that makes deploying and operating applications across today's hybrid, multi-cloud environments easier, faster, and more reliably. The following figure depicts the KubeVela integration with IDP:

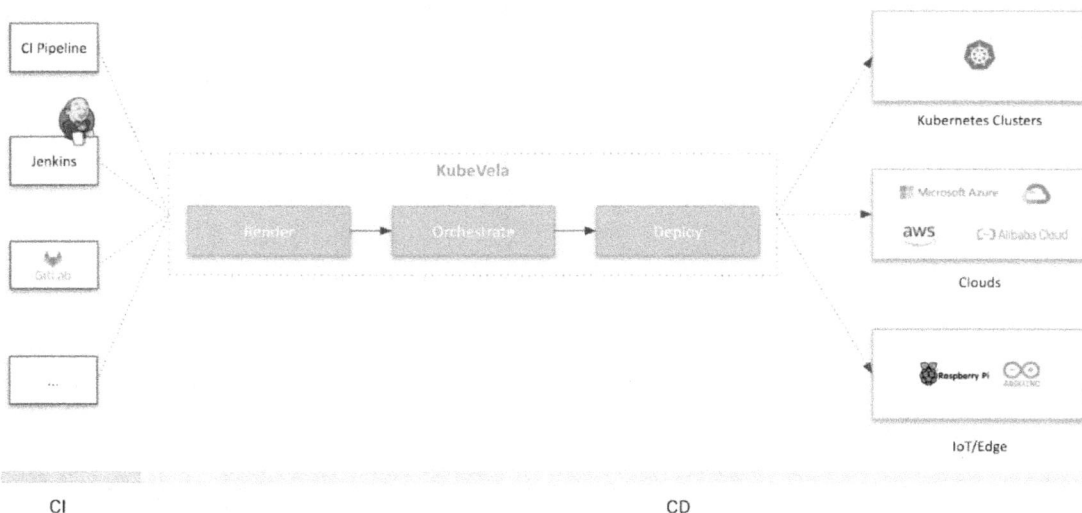

Figure 6.2: *KubeVela integration in internal developer platform*

Declare your deployment plan as a workflow and run it automatically with CI, CD, or GitOps systems. Benefit from built-in observability, multi-tenancy, and security support with **Lightweight Directory Access Protocol (LDAP)** integrations and RBAC modules. Multi-cloud or hybrid-environment app delivery is supported as a first-class citizen. The lightweight but highly extensible architecture minimizes control plane deployment and allows easy orchestration of infrastructure capabilities with reusable modules. KubeVela is a project that is worth exploring. The following are some examples of KubeVela:

- **Scenario:** A company needs to deploy its application to multiple Kubernetes clusters, perhaps for high availability or to support different environments (dev, test, prod).

  How KubeVela helps: KubeVela provides built-in support for multi-cluster deployments. You can define your application once and then deploy it to multiple clusters with different configurations. KubeVela handles the orchestration and ensures that the application is deployed consistently across all clusters.

Benefits: Simplified management of multi-cluster applications, improved disaster recovery.

- **Building internal platforms**

  Scenario: A company wants to build an internal platform for its developers, providing them with a self-service way to deploy and manage their applications.

  KubeVela can be used as the foundation for building such a platform. It provides a declarative and extensible framework for defining and deploying applications. Platform engineers can use KubeVela to create customized workflows and abstractions that meet the specific needs of their company.

Platform engineering on K8s architecture

We need to look into various components that can be integrated as building blocks to build a platform on top of Kubernetes. These building blocks are only indicative, and the actual building blocks will depend on your requirements, the existing toolsets, available bandwidth to administer these tools, etc. Please refer CNCF landscape: **https://landscape.cncf.io**.

Identity and access management

A fundamental building block for any platform is a robust **identity and access management (IAM)** solution that provides single sign-on, social login, and federated identity brokering. This component is crucial for securely authenticating and authorizing users and services interacting with your Kubernetes-based platform. An effective IAM solution should offer:

- **Single sign-on (SSO)**: Enabling users to access multiple platform services with a single set of credentials, improving user experience and reducing credential fatigue.

- **Federated identity brokering**: Allowing users to authenticate with their existing enterprise identities (e.g., Active Directory, LDAP) and seamlessly access the Kubernetes platform, which is critical for large organizations.

- **Centralized user management**: Providing a single pane of glass for managing user accounts, roles, and permissions across the entire platform. This includes creating, updating, and deleting user profiles, and assigning them to groups and roles.

- **Role-based access control (RBAC) integration**: Tightly integrating with Kubernetes' native RBAC system to define granular permissions. It ensures users and applications only have the minimum necessary access to resources (least privilege principle), enhancing security. For example, a developer might only have access to deploy applications within a specific namespace, while an administrator has broader control.

- **Multi-factor authentication (MFA) support**: Enhancing security by requiring multiple forms of verification for user authentication, reducing the risk of unauthorized access even if passwords are compromised.

- **Audit logging and reporting:** Maintaining comprehensive logs of all authentication and authorization events is crucial for security auditing, compliance, and incident response. It allows administrators to track who accessed what, when, and from where.

- **API for programmatic access:** Offering a well-documented API for managing identities and access programmatically, facilitating automation and integration with other systems.

Tools like **Keycloak** are excellent candidates for this role, providing a comprehensive open-source solution that can be self-hosted or managed. Other considerations might include commercial solutions like Okta or Auth0, or cloud-native IAM services such as AWS IAM, Azure Active Directory, or Google Cloud Identity, depending on your cloud provider strategy. The choice should prioritize strong security features, ease of integration with Kubernetes, and alignment with organizational security policies.

Logging

Logging records detailed information about application behavior and system events, which is crucial for identifying issues and gaining insights into system performance. It works alongside metrics and tracing to offer a complete perspective on an application's health and functionality. The possible choices are FluentD, Loki, etc.

Chaos testing

We previously covered Chaos testing in *Key concepts and tools*. We recommend looking at tools like Litmus Chaos or ChaosToolKit.

Middleware

Middleware serves as a middle layer that eases communication and data handling between different software applications, ensuring smooth integration. It delivers important services like authentication, logging, and message queuing, thereby improving the overall operation and effectiveness of complex systems. A tool like the NATS messaging system would be a good choice.

Artifact registry

An artifact registry acts as a repository for storing and managing build artifacts, such as binaries, container images, and packages, ensuring effective version control and distribution. It simplifies the CI or CD process by offering a centralized platform for developers to securely and reliably publish and retrieve artifacts.

Cluster virtualization

Kubernetes cluster virtualization involves abstracting underlying hardware resources to establish a scalable, multi-tenant environment for containerized applications. This virtualization enables efficient resource management, isolation, and deployment of applications across diverse infrastructures seamlessly. VCluster will fit this requirement well.

Virtual clusters, comprising full-fledged Kubernetes environments, are seamlessly embedded within a physical host cluster. This architecture enables robust isolation and adaptability, empowering the coexistence of multiple tenants or applications while maintaining efficient resource utilization. This setup allows multiple teams to function independently within the same physical infrastructure, minimizing conflicts, maximizing autonomy, and reducing costs. Virtual clusters operate within host cluster namespaces but act as distinct Kubernetes clusters, featuring their own API server, control plane, syncer, and set of resources. Virtual clusters leverage the underlying infrastructure of the host environment to access shared resources like CPU, memory, and storage. By self-managing these resources, they optimize usage and scalability, ensuring flexible and efficient operations.

Developer portal

A developer portal serves as a centralized hub where developers can access documentation, APIs, tools, and resources necessary for efficient software development. It enhances productivity by providing a streamlined, user-friendly interface for discovering and integrating various development services and platforms. Backstage, Port, and Cortex are some of the tools that you can look at.

Timeseries database

A timeseries database stores data points along with timestamps efficiently, making it perfect for analyzing trends and patterns over time in monitoring and IoT applications. Prometheus, an effective monitoring and alerting toolkit originally created at SourdCloud, is known for its reliability and scalability and is widely used for monitoring cloud-native applications. It gathers metrics from specified targets at regular intervals, stores them locally, and enables users to query and visualize these metrics using a versatile query language called **PromQL**.

VictoriaMetrics is a time series database and monitoring solution engineered for optimal performance and efficiency. It is specifically designed to handle large-scale time series data, with a focus on rapid ingestion, querying, and storage. VictoriaMetrics supports Prometheus-compatible APIs and is commonly utilized as a backend for Prometheus. It provides additional capabilities such as long-term storage and enhanced querying performance. Either tool can be picked based on your needs.

Service mesh

Service mesh handles communication between microservices and offers features such as load balancing, encryption, and observability, ensuring secure and reliable interactions. A service mesh is an indispensable layer in a microservices architecture, addressing many of the inherent challenges that arise when dealing with numerous interconnected services. It acts as a dedicated infrastructure layer for inter-service communication, abstracting away the complexities of network management and providing a consistent set of features across your microservices. Here is how a service mesh helps:

- **Traffic management**: Service meshes offer fine-grained control over traffic flow. This includes features like load balancing (distributing traffic across service instances), routing (directing traffic based on various criteria like headers or versions), canary deployments (gradually rolling out new versions), and fault injection (testing resilience by simulating failures).

- **Security**: Security is paramount in microservices. A service mesh simplifies the implementation of **mutual TLS** (**mTLS**) to encrypt communication between services, ensuring that only authorized services can communicate with each other. It also provides features like authorization and access control to enforce security policies.

- **Observability**: Service meshes provide rich observability features, including metrics, tracing, and logging. This gives developers deep insights into service performance, latency, and dependencies, enabling them to identify and resolve issues quickly.

- **Resilience**: Microservices are prone to failures. A service mesh helps build resilient applications by implementing features like retries (automatically retrying failed requests), circuit breaking (preventing cascading failures), and timeouts (preventing services from hanging indefinitely).

- **Simplified development**: By abstracting away network complexities, a service mesh allows developers to focus on business logic rather than the intricacies of inter-service communication.

- **Consistent policy enforcement:** A service mesh enables consistent application of policies across all services, including security policies, traffic management rules, and observability configurations. This ensures uniformity and reduces the risk of misconfigurations.

You may want to compare Istio and Linkerd to determine which one better suits your requirements. Choosing the right service mesh is crucial for managing microservices effectively. Istio, with its comprehensive feature set, offers advanced traffic management, robust security, and detailed observability, making it ideal for complex applications and organizations with dedicated expertise. However, its complexity and resource demands can be a significant consideration.

Linkerd, on the other hand, prioritizes simplicity and performance. Its lightweight design and ease of use make it an excellent choice for teams seeking a less complex solution with minimal performance overhead, although it offers a smaller set of features. The decision ultimately hinges on a careful evaluation of your team's skills, your application's specific requirements, and your infrastructure constraints. Testing both options in your own environment is often the most effective way to determine the best fit.

The following table shows a quick comparison between Istio and Linkerd:

Feature	Istio	Linkerd
Complexity	High	Low
Resource consumption	Higher	Lower
Feature set	Comprehensive	Smaller
Flexibility	High	Lower
Security	Advanced	Default mTLS
Community	Large and active	Growing

Table 6.1: A comparison between Istio and Linkerd

Distributed tracing

Tracing software development monitors and displays the movement of requests across distributed systems, aiding in identifying performance bottlenecks and optimizing application performance:

- **Canary releases:** Deploying to a small user group for initial real-world testing.
- **A/B testing:** Comparing different versions to inform decisions.
- **Feature flags:** Enabling or disabling features without redeploying.
- **Blue/green deployments:** Switching between two environments for near-zero downtime.
- **Rolling updates:** Updating instances gradually to minimize disruption.
- **Traffic splitting:** Directing traffic percentages to different versions.
- **Phased or ramped rollouts:** Gradually increasing user access.
- **Observability and monitoring:** Tracking key metrics for early issue detection.
- **Automated rollbacks:** Automatically revert on errors. These processes combined improve reliability and user satisfaction.

These processes are often used in combination. For example, you might use feature flags to control access to a new feature, canary releases to test it with a small group of users, and rolling updates to gradually roll it out to the rest of your user base. The specific techniques you choose will depend on your application, your team's practices, and your risk tolerance.

DOITBACK

We coined the abbreviation when we wanted to build a cloud-native platform on Kubernetes. We used **DOITBACK**, which is the first letter of the following key tools that we have chosen:

- **D**: Dapr
- **O**: OpenFeature
- **I**: Istio
- **T**: Terraform or OpenTofu
- **B**: Backstage
- **A**: Argo family of tools
- **C**: Crossplane
- **K**: Kyverno

We have prefixed **DOIT** to the **BACK** stack used by many of the platform engineering communities these days.

A real-world example:

A financial services company is deploying a new microservice for processing transactions. They have strict security and compliance requirements. They want to automate the process as much as possible while ensuring all deployments adhere to their standards. They have a tech stack as DOITBACK:

- **Development:** Developers build the transaction processing microservice using Dapr for inter-service communication (e.g., to a fraud detection service) and OpenFeature for feature flags (e.g., to enable or disable certain transaction types).

- **Infrastructure provisioning (Crossplane):** The application requires a secure, managed MySQL database. Developers define a Crossplane ManagedResource for a MySQL instance on their cloud provider (e.g., AWS RDS, Azure Database for MySQL, Google Cloud SQL). They have created an infrastructure as code using OpenTofu.

- **Kyverno policies:** The company has defined several Kyverno policies:
  - **Required labels:** All deployments must have labels like team, environment, application, and cost-center.
  - **Resource limits:** Pods must define resource requests and limits to prevent resource starvation.
  - **Security context:** Containers must run with a non-root user and have appropriate security context constraints.
  - **Network policies:** All services exposed externally must have NetworkPolicies defined to restrict access.

    o **Dapr sidecar injection:** Deployments that use Dapr must have the Dapr sidecar automatically injected.

- **CI/CD (Argo CD):**

They have created an Argo Workflow as follows:

    o Developers commit their code and the Crossplane ManagedResource definition to a Git repository.

    o Argo CD detects the changes and initiates the deployment process.

- **Kyverno validation and mutation:**

    o Before the deployment is applied to Kubernetes, Kyverno intercepts the request.

    o Kyverno validates the deployment manifest against all defined policies.

        ■ If any policy is violated (e.g., a required label is missing), the deployment is rejected, and the developer receives feedback.

        ■ If all policies are met, Kyverno mutates the deployment. For example: It automatically adds any missing required labels or injects the Dapr sidecar container.

- **Crossplane resource provisioning:** Argo CD, recognizing the Crossplane ManagedResource definition, triggers Crossplane to provision the MySQL database. Crossplane interacts with the cloud provider's API to create the database instance. It then creates a Kubernetes Secret containing the connection details.

- **Deployment (Kubernetes):** Once Kyverno has validated and mutated the deployment, and Crossplane has provisioned the database, Argo CD applies the manifest to Kubernetes. Kubernetes schedules the pods.

- **Service mesh (Istio):** Istio manages traffic to the new microservice, including routing, security (mTLS), and observability.

- **Runtime (Dapr):** The microservice uses Dapr for communication with other services, including the fraud detection service.

- **Feature flags (OpenFeature):** The operations team uses Backstage to control the rollout of new features by managing the feature flags via OpenFeature.

- **Monitoring and cost optimization (Istio, DoiT/Google Cloud):**

    o Istio provides metrics for monitoring the microservice's performance.

    o DoiT (Google Cloud) monitors the costs associated with the microservice and the provisioned database.

- **Backstage (developer portal):** Developers can use Backstage to view the status of their deployments, manage feature flags, monitor performance, and access documentation.

This workflow demonstrates a more mature and secure approach to deploying microservices in a regulated environment. It emphasizes automation, policy enforcement, and infrastructure as code. It significantly reduces the risk of human error and ensures consistency across deployments.

Distributed application runtime

Distributed application runtime (**Dapr**) is a Microsoft-developed open-source project aimed at simplifying the creation of microservices-based applications. Dapr simplifies the process of building microservices by offering a collection of standardized, language-agnostic building blocks. This enables developers to concentrate on business logic rather than the complexities of distributed systems.

Dapr is compatible with multiple programming languages and frameworks. Its modular architecture allows developers to integrate different components as needed, whether it is state management, pub/sub messaging, service invocation, or resource bindings. Each capability can be independently configured and extended. Dapr's decentralized approach involves each application instance having its own Dapr sidecar, ensuring scalability and fault tolerance. This architecture allows applications to scale independently and recover from failures without impacting the overall system. Dapr comes with built-in observability features, including distributed tracing, metrics, and logging. By offering pre-built solutions for common microservice challenges, Dapr significantly decreases the time and effort needed to develop and maintain distributed applications. This increase in productivity allows developers to deliver features more quickly and focus on innovation.

We can leverage Dapr into an existing architecture incrementally. Dapr applications can call non-Dapr endpoints. Dapr's component model decouples the integrated API from the underlying resources. For example, if you are utilizing the Dapr publish-subscribe API, you have the flexibility to switch the message broker from RabbitMQ to Kafka (or any other supported broker) by substituting a YAML component file, all without needing to modify your application code.

Using Dapr as shown in the following figure, you can switch the message broker:

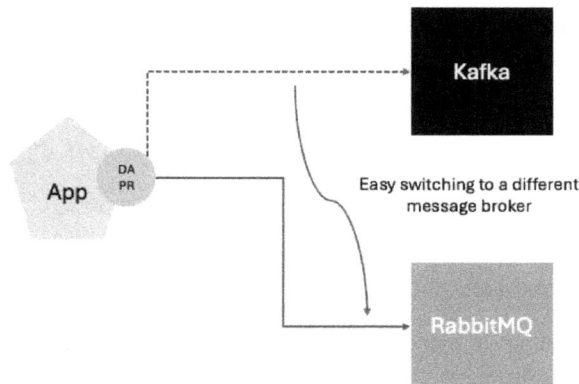

Figure 6.3: Switching of message broker (Dapr project)

OpenFeature

OpenFeature provides a flexible platform for organizing feature management and experimentation for software development teams. It enables developers to easily switch features on and off in real-time, aiding controlled rollouts and A/B testing. This helps teams make data-driven decisions on feature releases, ensuring improved user experiences and quicker iteration cycles. With its user-friendly interface and strong API, OpenFeature encourages collaboration and agility, assisting teams in delivering impactful features confidently while maintaining operational stability.

Refer to the link **https://openfeature.dev/**.

Istio

Istio is an open-source service mesh platform that provides a consistent method for connecting, managing, and securing microservices. It improves the visibility and control of service communication within a Kubernetes cluster or other environments by adding features such as traffic management, security, and observability. Istio simplifies the intricacies of microservices architecture by providing capabilities like load balancing, fine-grained access control, and metrics collection without necessitating changes to the application code. Its robust feature set makes Istio a powerful tool for enhancing reliability, resilience, and security in modern distributed systems.

Terraform or OpenTofu

Terraform is a tool for IaC that is open-source and allows users to define and manage infrastructure resources in a declarative manner. It works with multiple cloud providers and other service providers, enabling consistent provisioning, management, and deployment of infrastructure across different environments. Terraform's configuration files outline the components required for applications and their dependencies, aiding in automation and reducing operational complexity. OpenTofu, formerly OpenTF, is an open-source, community-led initiative, now governed by the Linux Foundation. This Terraform fork fosters collaboration and innovation in IaC management. You can choose between Terraform or OpenTofu based on your organization's licensing policies.

Backstage

Spotify developed the open-source platform Backstage to function as a centralized developer portal for managing and visualizing the entire software development lifecycle. It offers a unified interface for engineering teams to discover, use, and collaborate on various tools, services, and documentation needed for building and operating software applications. Backstage's key features include a customizable plugin architecture that integrates with existing CI or CD pipelines, monitoring tools, and other services to enhance visibility and control over the development process. It supports teams in maintaining consistency across projects, improving productivity through streamlined workflows, and fostering collaboration by promoting transparency and knowledge sharing. Backstage is designed to scale with organizations of all sizes, making it a valuable asset for modern software development teams striving for efficiency and innovation.

Argo

The Argo project is a collection of open-source tools aimed at enhancing Kubernetes workflows for continuous delivery, event-driven automation, and workflow orchestration. Here are some of the benefits of Argo:

- Argo CD simplifies continuous delivery in Kubernetes environments by automating deployment processes and ensuring application consistency across clusters with GitOps principles.

- Argo Events enables event-driven architecture in Kubernetes, allowing applications to respond to events from various sources and facilitating automation through event-driven workflows.

- Argo Rollouts enrich Kubernetes deployment strategies by introducing advanced deployment techniques such as blue-green and canary deployments, automating rollback upon failures, and providing metrics-driven analysis for safe and controlled updates.

- Argo Workflows orchestrate complex workflows and pipelines in Kubernetes, allowing teams to define, manage, and execute multi-step processes as code while supporting tasks like parallel execution, conditional logic, and retry mechanisms.

Together, these tools form a powerful toolkit for Kubernetes-native automation, offering scalable solutions for CI or CD, event-driven architectures, progressive deployments, and workflow orchestration in modern cloud-native environments.

Crossplane

Crossplane, created by upbound, is a Kubernetes extension that is open-source and expands the platform's capabilities for managing and coordinating cloud infrastructure and services across different providers. It introduces the idea of IaC to Kubernetes, allowing teams to define and provision cloud resources through Kubernetes-style APIs. Crossplane enables organizations to embrace a unified approach to managing infrastructure and applications, capitalizing on Kubernetes' strengths in automation, scalability, and adaptability across various cloud environments.

Kyverno

Kyverno serves as an open-source Kubernetes policy engine and management tool that offers native Kubernetes policy enforcement. It enables cluster administrators and developers to establish and enforce policies that automatically validate, mutate, and generate configurations for Kubernetes resources. The key functionalities of Kyverno include the following:

- **Policy enforcement**: Users can define policies with Kubernetes CRDs to enforce security, compliance, and operational best practices across clusters, ensuring consistency and adherence to organizational standards.

- **Mutating webhooks**: Kyverno supports dynamic policy enforcement through mutating webhooks, automatically altering Kubernetes resource configurations based on defined policies, simplifying the implementation of default configurations or application of transformations.

- **Policy validation**: It provides real-time validation of Kubernetes resources against defined policies, preventing non-compliant configurations from being deployed or modifying existing resources.

- **Integration with CI or CD pipelines**: Kyverno integrates with CI or CD pipelines to enforce policies early in the development lifecycle, aiding in the detection of policy violations before deployments, reducing risks, and ensuring smoother deployments.

Overall, Kyverno streamlines Kubernetes policy management by leveraging Kubernetes-native mechanisms, enhancing security, compliance, and operational efficiency in cloud-native environments.

Now, that we have discussed some key tools, let us take a final look at what our build blocks view of the platform looks like. Some of the tools for platform engineering are as follows:

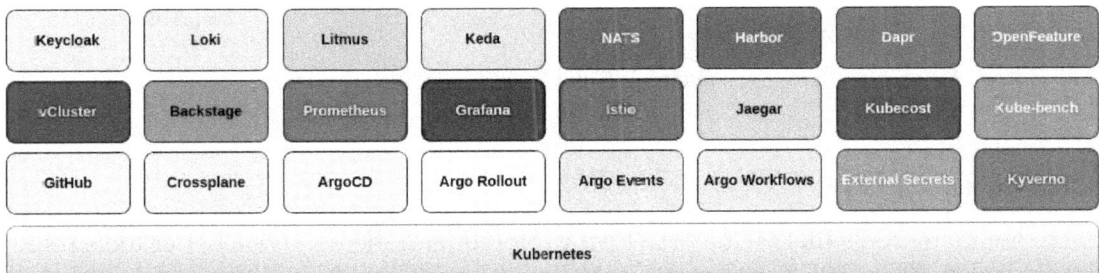

Figure 6.4: All the key components of platform engineering

Platform engineering maturity model

The **platform engineering maturity model (PEMM)** evaluates an organization's capacity to construct and oversee platform services in cloud-native setups. It examines elements such as automation of infrastructure, CI/CD methodologies, scalability, robustness, and developer satisfaction to measure maturity levels from early adoption to sophisticated orchestration and enhancement phases.

If you are just starting your platform engineering journey, a platform maturity assessment will help you understand the gaps and determine where your organization stands in terms of maturity. Even after the platform is built, the platform engineering maturity model offers an excellent way to continually improve the platform's maturity level.

It is crucial to understand that the ways in which platforms are implemented differ from one organization to another. Ensure that you assess your organization's current status of transitioning to cloud-native solutions. The cloud-native maturity model is an excellent tool to utilize for this assessment.

The following is the maturity model defined by cloud-native app delivery, and the same can be referred to using **https://tag-app-delivery.cncf.io/whitepapers/platform-eng-maturity-model/**:

	Aspect	Provisional	Operational	Scalable	Optimizing
Investment	How are staff and funds allocated to platform capabilities?	Voluntary or temporary	Dedicated team	As product	Enabled ecosystem
Adoption	Why and how do users discover and use internal platforms and platform capabilities?	Erratic	Extrinsic push	Intrinsic pull	Participatory
Interfaces	How do users interact with and consume platform capabilities?	Custom processes	Standard tooling	Self-service solutions	Integrated services
Operations	How are platforms and their capabilities planned, prioritized, developed and maintained?	By request	Centrally tracked	Centrally enabled	Managed services
Measurement	What is the process for gathering and incorporating feedback and learning?	Ad hoc	Consistent collection	Insights	Quantitative and qualitative

Figure 6.5: Platform maturity model

Conclusion

There are many tools that we have not yet explored, and there may be better tools under development. The CNCF landscape is evolving rapidly, and we cannot claim to have covered everything in this book. The cloud-native world is constantly evolving, with new tools and technologies emerging all the time. It is crucial for platform engineers to stay informed and be ready to adapt, continuously reviewing and updating their platform's building blocks to take advantage of the latest and greatest solutions. Kubernetes offers a solid foundation for building robust and flexible platforms, allowing for the creation of loosely coupled components that can be managed consistently. This chapter provided a comprehensive overview of platform engineering with Kubernetes, covering its key features, essential concepts, tools, and the benefits it offers. Now, let us move on to explore the critical area of security and compliance integration in the next chapter.

In the next chapter, readers will go through embedding security and compliance in the development using the **internal developer platform (IDP)**. Next chapter will go in-depth about the integration of security and compliance tools and processes in IDP as security gates.

Exercises

1. What is the reconciliation loop in Kubernetes?

2. How do feature flags differ from the properties file?

3. What is a progressive delivery?

4. How can one extend Kubernetes to implement custom functionalities?

5. Which is the tool under IaC category that leverages Kubernetes reconciliation loop?

6. How can the platform team stay updated with the latest tools and projects in the CNCF ecosystem?

Answers

1. The Kubernetes reconciliation loop is a continuous control loop managed by the kube-controller-manager that ensures the current state of cluster objects matches the desired state declared in Kubernetes manifests. It monitors changes, reconciles discrepancies, and maintains system reliability by automating the deployment, scaling, and management of containerized applications.

2. The feature flags offer more dynamic and runtime-controlled capabilities for managing feature releases and experimentation, whereas properties files are static configuration files used primarily for setting up application environments and behaviors at deployment time.

3. Unified artifact registry is a secure, compliant, and invulnerable storage of all artifacts like application packages, third-party libraries, helm charts, Ansible playbooks, Terraform modules, etc. This is considered a first step for organizations starting with their DevSecOps journey.

4. The core principles and practices of DevSecOps revolve around the idea of shifting security left, meaning that security considerations are introduced as early as possible in the SDLC. The idea is to fail fast and have a shorter feedback loop so that developers are able to turn around faster.

5. Crossplane uses a controller-based continuous reconciliation model.

6. You can stay updated about the latest tools and projects using **https://landscape.cncf.io**.

References

1. https://loft.sh/blog/platform-engineering-on-kubernetes-for-accelerating-development-workflows/

2. https://github.com/kubevela/kubevela

3. https://github.com/oam-dev/spec

4. https://cdevents.dev/#td-block-1

5. https://tag-app-delivery.cncf.io/wgs/platforms/

Join our Discord space

Join our Discord workspace for latest updates, offers, tech happenings around the world, new releases, and sessions with the authors:

https://discord.bpbonline.com

CHAPTER 7

Embed Security and Compliance in Platform

Introduction

Platform engineering goes beyond application-level security to focus on securing the entire platform, including the underlying infrastructure and tools that host and manage applications. Here, embedding security and compliance baked into the platform helps in the **software development life cycle (SDLC)**:

- **Embedding security and compliance early**: Security and compliance are integrated into the SDLC from the start, ensuring that it is a top priority throughout the development process.

- **Focusing on applications**: The platform focuses on securing software applications.

- **Utilizing specialized tools**: Platform teams use specialized tools, such as **Static Application Security Testing (SAST)** and **Dynamic Application Security Testing (DAST)**, to scan for and fix security vulnerabilities in applications.

- **Incorporating security or policy as code**: Security policies are incorporated into the application code, making them an integral part of the deployment process.

This chapter of the book will cover embedding security and compliance in the development using the **internal developer platform (IDP)**. This chapter will go in-depth about the integration of security and compliance tools and processes in IDP as security gates. This integration and update can be maintained with the help of security tools and the as code approach. This will help organizations enforce application security and required compliance policies across all phases of the SSDLC, achieved with the help of platform engineering. This helps the developer teams to develop faster without any dependencies. All security attributes and checks are built in as part of platform engineering.

Structure

The chapter covers the following topics:

- DevSecOps versus platform engineering
- Security and compliance by design
- Workflow and tools for security and compliance
- IDP security and compliance integration

Objectives

By the end of this chapter, you will learn the required security and compliance processes, tooling, and guardrails embedded into the IDP. This chapter will cover the different workflows to be embedded as part of the platform, and shifting security left and making it a core part of the development process from day one. It differentiates platform engineering from DevSecOps, highlighting how platform engineering offers a more comprehensive and self-service approach that empowers developers to build secure applications without getting bogged down in infrastructure complexities. The chapter emphasizes that security and compliance should be foundational elements, baked into the IDP's design to ensure applications and infrastructure meet required standards. It also provides a detailed look at the different control planes within an IDP, including the developer control plane, integration and delivery plane, monitoring and logging plane, and security plane, along with the associated tools and workflows. Finally, the chapter presents use cases for integrating security tools into the IDP to address common challenges such as access control, secret management, vulnerability tracking, and compliance monitoring.

DevSecOps versus platform engineering

This is a common myth that DevSecOps is the same as platform engineering. DevSecOps is a cultural change in the way of working of the developers, security, and operations teams and requires collaboration for faster releases of software. This also needs integration of security and operations into the software development process.

Platform engineering is the practice of designing, building, and maintaining the foundational infrastructure that helps in software development. This also needs a cultural change in the way of working of an organization, where dev teams can focus on their core function, which develops the applications. They do not need to learn the infrastructure, and rather, they can use the abstraction available in the in-service catalog with the help of self-service. The DevOps team also does not need to rely on automation scripts but rather develop the IDP as a product with a roadmap defined for them. While both DevSecOps and platform engineering aim to enhance software delivery, they have distinct focuses and methodologies. The following table outlines a comparison of their core attributes:

Attribute	DevSecOps	Platform engineering
Focus	Cultural shift to integrate security, operations, and development processes	Building and maintaining infrastructure to empower developers
Primary goal	Secure and automate the software development lifecycle with a focus on faster releases	Provide developers with reliable, abstracted infrastructure and self-service tools
Main responsibilities	Integrating security practices into the CI/CD pipeline, fostering collaboration between security, dev, and Ops teams	Designing, building, and maintaining the infrastructure platform, providing an abstraction layer for developers
Tools used	Security tools (SAST, DAST, IAST), CI/CD tools, security scanners, threat detection tools	Kubernetes, Docker, Terraform, cloud platforms (AWS, GCP, Azure), service catalog tools
Collaboration	Cross-team collaboration between development, security, and operations for seamless, secure releases	Works with development and DevOps teams to ensure platform reliability, focusing on abstraction for self-service
Key skills	Security integration, automation, vulnerability management, collaboration facilitation	Cloud architecture, infrastructure automation, self-service enablement, platform product development
Key focus areas	Continuous security, compliance, and incident response within development pipelines	Scaling and optimizing platform services, reducing friction for developers by abstracting infrastructure complexity
Workflows involved	Embedding security into the entire software lifecycle, automating security tests, ensuring compliance	Building infrastructure tools that abstract complexities for dev teams and supporting self-service catalog development
Impact on development cycle	Speeds up secure software development with integrated security and operational controls	Enables developers to focus on code and application development without worrying about infrastructure
Cultural change	Requires collaboration between dev, sec, and Ops for faster, secure releases	Requires a shift toward infrastructure as a service, allowing dev teams to focus on coding without infrastructure concerns and have product mindset for addressing problems around development lifecycle

Table 7.1: Comparison of DevSecOps and platform engineering's core attributes

DevSecOps approach

DevSecOps approach for integration of security practices. Some of the benefits of DevSecOps approach:

- It integrates security practices into the DevOps workflow. The main aim of the DevSecOps approach is to integrate security into each stage of development. The following are the examples:

    o The team is working on the design phase, starting to do the threat modeling to understand the security risks and make the design decisions.

    o A team member is using the design document and starts doing the development. Here, an integrated SAST scanner in the **integrated development environment (IDE)** or a **command-line interface (CLI)** looks for security vulnerabilities and advises the user to correct them.

    o They can complete the development and ignore the suggestion from the IDE, a prehook commit check fails her commit.

    o They can disable the prehook commit and commit the code in the repository. Another integration in the pipeline code fails the build.

    o They can use the **Software Composition Analysis (SCA)** tool to identify vulnerabilities in third-party libraries and dependencies.

    o They can scan the IaC templates (Terraform or CloudFormation) using the IaC scanning tools such as Checkov, TFLint, Terrascan, etc.

    o They can scan the container images for vulnerabilities using tools such as Trivy, Clair.

    o They can use the secret management tools to securely manage and rotate secrets, keys, and credentials, such as Azure key vault, AWS secret manager, and HashiCorp vault.

    o They can build and deploy the code, but it leads to a runtime security vulnerability. A DAST scanner will run after the deployment to identify vulnerabilities, such as OWASP ZAP and Burp Suite.

    o They need continuous monitoring tools to monitor applications and infrastructure for security threats and anomalies, such as Splunk, ELK Stack, and Prometheus.

- Security policies and controls are implemented as security as code into the development and deployment processes.

- Automated security and compliance checks are integrated into the CI/CD pipeline.

- It encourages collaboration between development, operation, and Infosec teams.

- The system needs continuous monitoring using monitoring and observability tools.

DevSecOps approach allows security and compliance teams to enforce security and compliance gates for new development or changes deployed in the production applications.

An example of building a Jenkins pipeline with security checks is as follows:

```
pipeline {
    agent any
    stages {
        stage('Build') {
            steps {
                script {
                    // Build the application
                    sh 'mvn clean install'
                }
            }
        }
stage('Static Code Analysis') {
        steps {
            script {
                // Run static code analysis
                sh 'sast-cli scanner'
            }
        }
    }
        stage('Dependency Check') {
            steps {
                script {
```

Code 7.1: Security stages in pipeline

Platform engineering approach

There has been a significant shift in the working methods of development teams. They have transitioned from the waterfall SDLC methodology to an agile way of working. When organizations started moving to the public cloud for digital transformation, and development architecture started moving to microservices-based architecture, the focus of the development team remained on the faster release of features. The developers should not have to worry about cognitive load.

The following are the benefits of the platform engineering approach:

- Platform engineering is the practice of creating and managing a shared platform that is used by developers to build, deploy, and run their applications. This abstracts the underlying infrastructure complexities and provides a set of tools and services that help teams accelerate development.

- Platform engineering helps developers with self-service capabilities to provision resources without having much experience with infrastructure.

- This establishes the standards and best practices for application development and releases.

- This automated infrastructure provisioning, configuration, and management reduces manual efforts and increases efficiency.

- It has integrated tools for logging, monitoring, and tracing to ensure the performance and health of the infrastructure.

You need to build security features as part of IDP development as a minimal viable security plan. Here, security is integrated as a layered approach with platform engineering:

- **Code security**: Integrate required toolsets for code vulnerability, store secrets, and identify vulnerable libraries. This toolset shall be available to the developers at different stages of their code development, pushing their code to the **version control system** (**VCS**) or the build or deployment process.

- **Infrastructure security**: Provide standard templates for infrastructure provisioning, an integrated toolset to identify and detect infrastructure cloud misconfiguration, and hardening of cloud accounts.

- **Runtime security**: Integrated tools for continuous scanning of app runtime vulnerabilities and API security.

- **CI/CD security**: Securing VCS, detecting container vulnerabilities, and securing pipelines. Security toolset to be integrated as part of the continuous integration and continuous delivery blocks. Any security vulnerabilities or findings are to be pushed to the data lake for centralized view and tracking.

- **Data security**: It supports role-based access controls, service-to-service authentication, and data encryption for data security.

- **Vulnerability management**: All the vulnerabilities are to be pushed to a data lake and available as a centralized dashboard for the action of different teams. The engineering team can view dashboards and pull reports to review vulnerabilities in their product, application, or services.

- **Third-party tools or APIs integration**: Support extensibility and interfaces for easy integration of tools or APIs.

- **Operational security**: Easy onboarding and offboarding of the people, tools, or services using the self-service platform. This helps new team members become productive from the beginning.

- **Incident management**: Integration of observability and monitoring as part of the platform. Provide interfaces for quick search of activities and investigation capabilities.

By integrating platform engineering, security, and compliance at the forefront of your technology strategy, the business is well-equipped to minimize business risk and ensure business sustainability.

Security and compliance by design

It means that security and compliance should be the basic pillars of every IT project or initiative. They cannot be the afterthoughts but a foundational element and must be built into every aspect of an organization's technology, infrastructure, and operations. The core elements of it are the following. The following is the list of security and compliance requirements for IDP:

- **Security requirements**:
    o Protecting sensitive data and assets.
    o Meeting regulatory requirements and industry standards.
    o Reducing risks and minimizing potential threats.

- **Compliance requirements**:
    o Understanding of applicable laws and regulations.
    o Identifying and addressing compliance risks.
    o Creating and enforcing policies to ensure compliance.
    o Continuous compliance through regulatory auditing and reporting on compliance status.

For development organizations, security and compliance are important and cannot be overlooked because the organization needs faster delivery of software. This has become much more important after organizations have started moving to the public cloud, where security and compliance are shared responsibilities. Cloud service provider (AWS, GCP, Azure) provides the default security for any of the services used in the public cloud. Application and security teams need to make sure that the correct configurations are used to meet their security needs.

A similar approach is also used while building IDP for organizations. Developers using the IDP for building software need not worry about security and compliance. The platform engineering team will ensure that default security and compliance are embedded into the IDP, and different configurations and templates shall be available to the development teams to meet their security goals.

It is very important that organizations consider security and compliance requirements at different stages of development. Application teams shall consider the following requirements during different stages of development:

- Ensure that applications created are tested and do not have any security vulnerabilities.

- Different components used, such as **cloud, container, cluster, and code (4Cs)**, are secure and meet compliance requirements.

- Security and compliance cannot be achieved in a traditional manner where security and compliance teams are custodians and provide sign-off.

- Security and compliance are built at each stage of software development, including build, deploy, and runtime.

Security and compliance are not optional features; they are non-negotiable requirements that must be built into every stage of the software development lifecycle. Refer to the following figure:

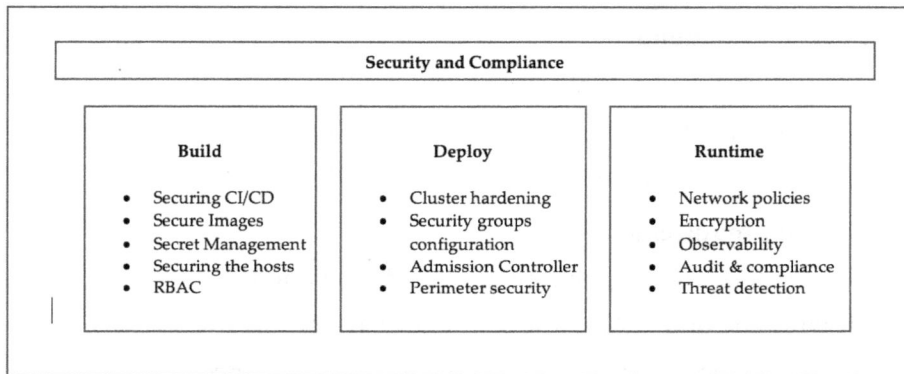

Figure 7.1: *Security and compliance to be embedded at each stage of software development*

Modern software development lifecycle: For business organizations, it is critical to ideate and release services faster into the market. They have to create a standard framework for development. Some organizations do thousands of builds in a single day. Meeting security requirements for all builds with a traditional approach will be a hindrance.

Platform engineering streamlines the software development lifecycle by providing developers with self-service tools and automated workflows. The following figure illustrates how a platform-driven approach facilitates rapid iteration and continuous delivery while incorporating essential feedback mechanisms:

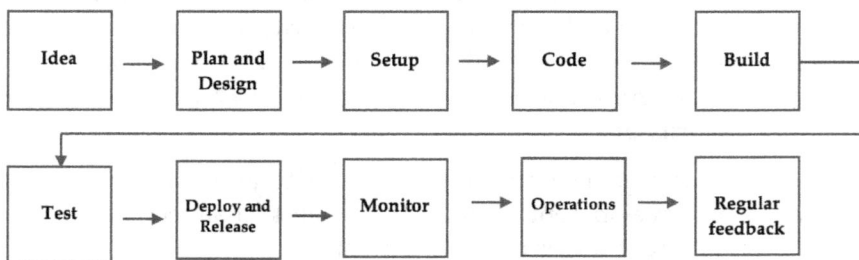

Figure 7.2: *Software development lifecycle*

The security hurdles faced by developers: For most developers, security is a black hole, and it is the job of the information security team to take care of security and compliance requirements. For example:

- Not knowing where and why to start
- Need to be taken care at the end of development
- Not my team, must be security / compliance team
- Tools enforced are too complex
- Too many vulnerabilities to take care

Figure 7.3: Security is complex for developers

The following are the principles and challenges for the development teams:

- **Platform key principles**: To achieve faster release with security and compliance embedded as part of IDP, there are some core principles followed for IDP development. They are as follows:

  o **Customer-first**: The main goal is to remove customer hindrances in the software development lifecycle. IDP will encourage self-service with required security and quality checks built in as part of the platform.

  o **Enabler over gatekeeper**: The platform engineering team enables the development team for faster release. Their focus shall be on development rather than security or quality parameters. These are built-in and are available by default.

  o **Products over projects**: Use a product approach to keep a roadmap and deliver new features to solve development challenges.

  o **Provide paved road**: An approach to streamline and standardize development, deployment, and operation processes for developers. The platform handles the complexities of infrastructure, security, and compliance.

- **Platform engineering to solve security and compliance challenges**: The platform engineering team takes a productization approach to build the IDP and embeds security and compliance requirements to solve the above challenges. The platform engineering team consists of developers, DevOps, security, and quality SMEs to build the platform capabilities. The security team will focus on the integration of security capabilities in IDP. The following is the range of security measures integrated into the platform, emphasizing a comprehensive and layered approach to security:

  o **Static analysis**: Scan the source code for vulnerabilities without executing the code. Some of the popular tools are SonarQube, Checkmarx, and Fortify.

  o **Dependency vulnerability scanning**: Scan all the third-party libraries or open-source components used.

o **Versioning**: The code is versioned and merged after review or approval.

o **Infrastructure scanning**: Infrastructure is created through code, and code is scanned for security issues.

o **Image scanning**: Scan all the images created and stored as part of the repository. These container images are scanned for vulnerabilities, and security policies are enforced on these images.

o **Container or cluster scanning**: Scan the configuration for containers or clusters.

o **CI or CD pipelines**: The required security gates are available in CI or CD.

o **Dynamic analysis**: Test the running applications for security vulnerabilities before going live in production.

o **Logging, monitoring, and alerting**: The required logging, alerting, and monitoring have been setup.

o **Incident management**: All security events are tracked as incidents.

o **Service-to-service authentication**: Authentication and authorization services are available.

o **Secret management and scanning**: The secrets are stored safely, and the code is scanned for any hard-coding.

o **Audit for compliance**: The regular auditing of the system for required compliance and regulatory requirements.

The platform engineering team does not have to build all capabilities together, and they can take an incremental approach to build a **minimum viable platform (MVP)** first and keep on developing other capabilities.

Platform engineering helps in the consolidation of diverse tools and teams into a single unified platform. This leads to effective collaboration, data-driven automation, and facilitates faster software delivery and infrastructure management. Platform engineering offers a compelling solution to many of the security and compliance challenges faced by organizations today. By adopting a platform approach, teams can realize several key benefits:

o **Security as a foundation**: Security is integrated into every part of the software development process. The internal developer platform provides a standard framework that integrates security tools and practices as security by default. This is a more proactive approach.

o **Encourage more collaboration**: One of the core issues in many organizations, is development, security and operations teams work in silos, and many of the tools are independently driven by each of the groups. This problem is addressed by IDP, where standard tools are integrated and increase collaboration between different teams who speak a similar language.

o **Provide a unified platform**: Many organizations start with the DevSecOps approach, but have different ways of adoption by different teams and groups. A unified platform solves this issue for organizations where security, compliance, and quality are integrated as core requirements of each software development process.

o **Codify security and compliance**: This is very difficult to manage automation and configurations unless you codify the security governance and embed policies and regulations directly into development and deployment processes. This helps in minimizing human error, versioning your security requirements or policies, and streamlining them.

o **Create consistency and auditability**: The platform engineering ensures that processes are consistent and auditable.

With the advent and increased footprint of AI or ML, a unified platform is going to help organizations where your data and events are captured and can be used for more automation and data-driven decisions using AI or ML.

Workflow and tools for security and compliance

The reason for the popularity of the IDP is a centralized environment where developers can build, deploy, and manage applications efficiently. This also helps the integration of common tools and workflows to provide similar experiences across the organization. This makes it easier for organizations and developers to work across different cloud service providers and platforms. Some benefits include enhancing workflow efficiency, reducing errors, and cost reduction with enhanced operational efficiency.

There are different control planes in IDP, as shown in *Figure 7.4*. These are different layers of tools that are integrated with different control planes. The platform engineering reference architecture provides the following control planes:

- Developer control plane

- Integration and delivery plane

- Monitoring and logging the plane

- Security plane

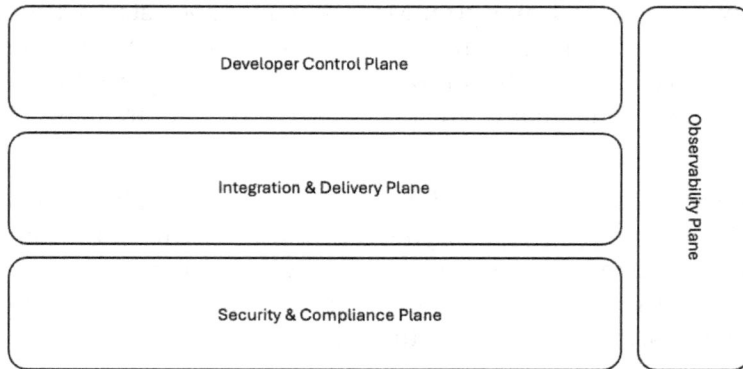

Figure 7.4: Control planes in internal developer platform

We will be looking into the details of these control planes and the tools and workflows associated with them.

Developer control plane

This plane in the IDP is a primary configuration layer and direct interaction point for the developers. A **developer control plane (DCP)** is a centralized interface that provides developers with the required tools, resources, and controls to manage the software development life cycle, as shown in the following figure:

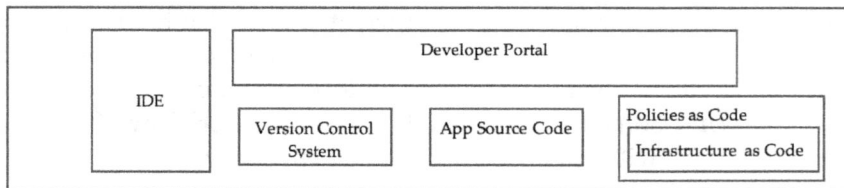

Figure 7.5: Developer control plane in platform engineering reference architecture

The DCP allows developers to control and customize the whole development process and ship their code faster. Developers can use DCP for faster coding, integrating, and deploying their services. Typically, this control plane has the following three components:

- Code
- Configurations
- Self-service portal

In today's world, developers' onboarding in organizations is very quick. They do not need to wait for a long process to complete their onboarding. They are just a few clicks away from being onboarded and ready to contribute. They have the required tools available to start development for their services. The developer control plane enables them to build a quick, local development workflow.

They can start coding in their local environment in their preferred IDE, quickly test it, and integrate it with other services or a continuous integration workflow. This helps them to be productive on day one. The team does the code management using the following:

- **Version control system**: This code is stored in popular version control systems, for example, GitHub, GitLab, or Bitbucket. This contains the following two main types of repositories:
  - o Application source code
  - o Platform source code or automation code
- **Configurations**: The developer control plane also offers standardized templates and configuration management tools to simplify and automate configuration tasks, along with a self-service portal for easy access to tools, documentation, and resources. This comprehensive approach ensures that developers can be productive from the moment they join the team, while maintaining consistency, security, and compliance across the platform.
- **Self-service portal**: A portal (for example, Backstage, Port) is a self-service portal.

The platform engineering team follows the design principle of everything as code. Both the application source code and platform source code are stored in VCS, which includes configurations and infrastructure code as well.

Toolset in this DCP is the following:

- **IDE**: Developers use an IDE for their development and integrate plugins to automate other tasks such as unit tests, code review, and security review. One of the most popular IDEs used by developers is **Visual Studio Code** (**VCS**). Developers are free to use the IDE of their choice, such as IntelliJ, Eclipse, or JDeveloper.
- **Developer portal**: The developer portal is a self-service portal for developers that can integrate with APIs exposed by all tools and workflows. This provides abstraction and helps developers to focus on development. They do not need to learn the internal details of working on tools and automation workflows. Some of the popular developer portals are the following:
  - o Backstage
  - o Atlassian Compass
  - o Configure8
  - o Port
  - o OpsLevel
  - o Cortex
- **Version control**: This helps you to keep versioning and management of your code using VCS. Some of the popular VCS are the following:

- o GitHub
- o Bitbucket
- o Gitlab

- **Platform source code**: This contains your IaC and automation to build your platform. You need to make sure that you are building the required guardrails for your IaC. IaC offers significant benefits, but it also introduces potential risks if not managed carefully. To ensure security and reliability, it is crucial to establish robust guardrails for your IaC using any of the IaC tools:

  - o Terraform
  - o Crossplane
  - o OpenTofu
  - o Pulumi
  - o Custom automations

- **Integration and delivery plane**: Modern software development platforms often incorporate a range of tools and services to streamline the development process. *Figure 7.6* provides a high-level overview of the architecture of such a platform, showing how different components interact to facilitate efficient software delivery:

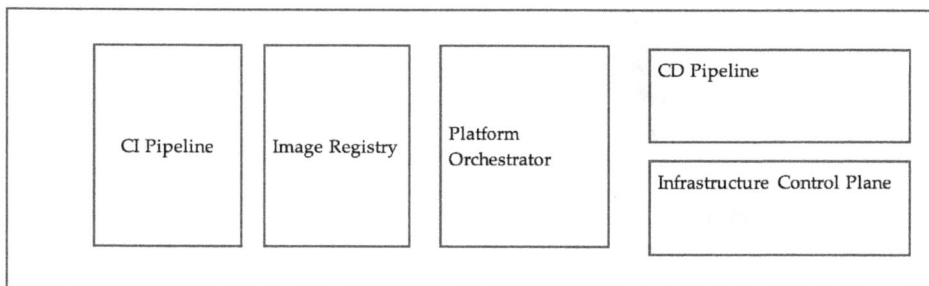

Figure 7.6: Integration and delivery plane in platform engineering reference architecture

This plane requires tools and workflow to build and store code as an image, creating deployable apps and infrastructure configurations to deploy it as a final stage. This plane contains the following four different tools:

- o **CI pipeline**: It can be any continuous integration tool. Popular CI tools are the following:

  - ▪ Jenkins
  - ▪ GitHub Action
  - ▪ CircleCI
  - ▪ Azure DevOps

o **Image registry**: This holds your container images. Popular choices of image registry are the following:

- AWS ECR registry
- Docker
- Harbor
- Jfrog
- Azure container registry

o **Orchestrator**: This can be your custom build, or you can use popular tools such as the Humanitec platform orchestrator.

o **CD system**: This helps platform orchestrators have deployment capabilities. Usually, deployment events are triggered by webhooks for external systems or workflow systems like Argo CD. Some of the popular CD systems:

- Argo CD
- GitHub Action
- Gitlab CD
- Flux CD

This streamlines the process of building and deploying code by providing a seamless and automated workflow. Let us look at how it works.

Developers can start developing code quickly, merge with the existing code base, and have automated reviews and tests conducted. There are different guardrails built into the delivery platform. Developers can integrate and deploy their code into the production system quickly. The following are examples of shipping a new application code:

o The developer does a **Pull Request (PR)**.

o After a PR merge, a continuous integration process starts.

o The task builds a new image and uploads it to a container registry.

o A second pull request is generated to update the Kubernetes specs with the new configuration.

o The pipeline also notifies the platform orchestrator about the new image and, with the help of specifications, triggers a deployment with the newly generated image.

- **Monitoring and logging plane**: *Figure 7.7* illustrates the tools and technologies that enable comprehensive observability and analytics within a modern software development platform. It highlights the key components for:

o **Observability**: Gaining insights into the health and performance of applications and infrastructure through real-time monitoring and data collection.

o **Analytics**: Analyzing collected data to identify trends, troubleshoot issues, and improve overall system efficiency, shown as follows:

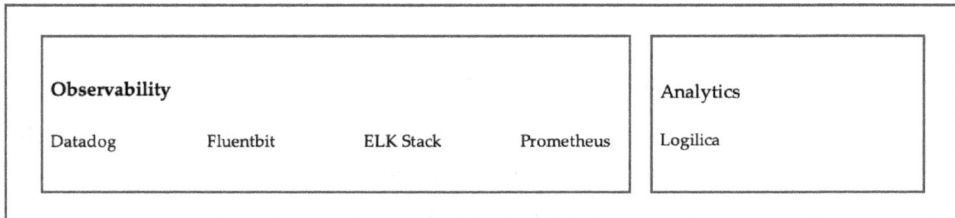

Observability				Analytics
Datadog	Fluentbit	ELK Stack	Prometheus	Logilica

Figure 7.7: *Monitoring and logging plane in the platform engineering reference architecture*

This layer ensures the platform's performance, reliability, and security. The following layer is essential for customer experience:

o **Performance**: This helps in monitoring the platform's performance to identify any bottlenecks, optimize resource utilization, and build a seamless experience for the users. This layer can identify any performance impact on the system and provide alerts to the users.

o **Reliability**: This logs errors and continuously monitors the system and business metrics. This helps in detecting errors before they affect users, enabling teams to prompt remediation and minimizing downtime.

o **Security**: This helps in monitoring and logging security-related events to detect potential threats and track suspicious activities. This also helps organizations maintain compliance and regulatory requirements.

Some of the well-known tools in this layer are the following:

o Datadog

o Fluentbit

o Jaeger

o ELK stack

o Grafana

o Prometheus

o Splunk

o New Relic

• **Security plane**: The following figure showcases the essential security tooling integrated into a robust software development platform. It highlights two key areas:

o **Secrets management**: Securely storing and managing sensitive information like API keys, passwords, and certificates.

o **Security tooling**: A collection of tools used to identify and mitigate vulnerabilities throughout the software development lifecycle. This includes static and dynamic analysis, software composition analysis, container security, and runtime application self-protection, as shown in the following figure:

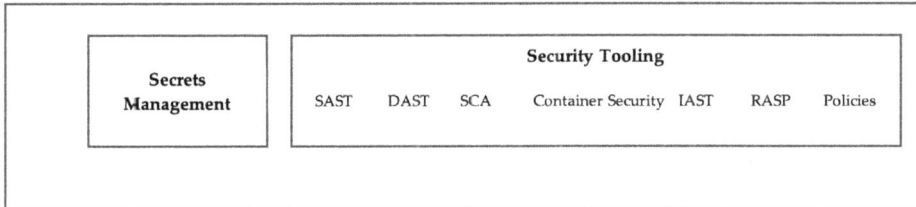

Figure 7.8: Security plane in the platform engineering reference architecture

The security plane is focused on the following two key security enforcement:

o **Secrets management**: This helps in storing secret configurations such as database passwords, API keys, and TLS certificates required by the application. It allows access to these secrets by platform and injects them into the running workloads (apps) dynamically. Several robust secret management solutions are available to securely store and manage your sensitive information. Popular choices include:

   ▪ HCP vault

   ▪ AWS secrets manager

   ▪ Google secrets manager

   ▪ Azure key vault

o **Security and policy controls**: This helps in enforcing security and compliance policies during application development, infrastructure creation, and runtime. Technologies and tools that are integrated into the following layer:

   ▪ **SAST tools**: Snyk

   ▪ **Container security**: Aqua security

   ▪ **Cloud Security Posture Management/Cloud-native application protection platform**: Sentinel One, Orca security, Sysdig

   ▪ **K8 policies**: Nirmata, Styra, Cilium

• **Resource plane**: This plane is where actual application infrastructure is created, such as clusters, databases, storage, or DNS services. Resource configuration is taken care of by platform orchestrators, which dynamically create app and infrastructure configurations with every deployment and create, delete, or modify resources accordingly. The following figure breaks down the resource plane of a platform, showing the key components and services that make up the foundation of your applications:

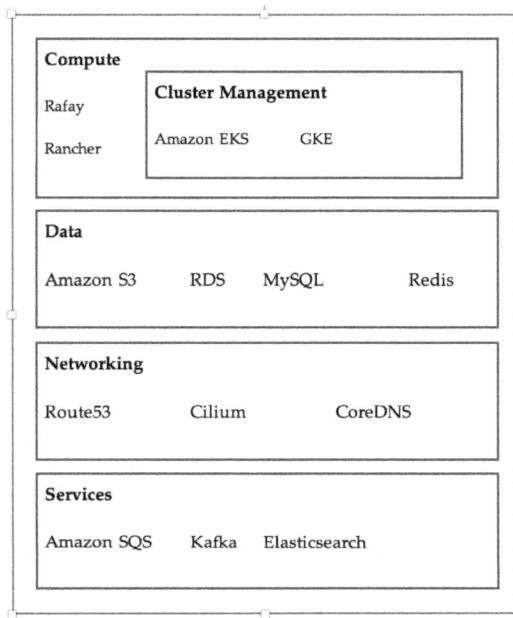

Figure 7.9: Resource plane in platform engineering reference architecture

We can further divide this layer into the following sub-layers:

o **Compute**: It refers to the hardware and software components that provide the processing power, storage, and memory for running applications and services. This includes CPUs, GPUs, memory, storage, VMs, containers, etc. For example, Amazon EKS, GKE, Rancher, Rafay, etc.

o **Data**: This layer refers to the components and processes responsible for storing, processing, and transmitting data. This layer is responsible for managing the flow of data between different parts of a system, application, or network. For example, Amazon S3, RDS, Redis, MongoDB, MariaDB, etc.

o **Networking**: It refers to the components and processes responsible for connecting and transmitting data between devices, applications, and services. This layer enables the communication, data exchange, and connectivity between different components of the system. For example, Route 53, Cilium, Cloudflare, Cloud DNS, etc.

o **Services**: It refers to the software components and applications that provide specific functionalities and capabilities as application features. Services are built using compute, data, storage, networking, and security resources, Elasticsearch, Kafka, Google PubSub, etc.

IDP security and compliance integration

IDP is a set of tools, services, and standards with built-in guardrails that help developers build, deploy, and manage applications in a self-service way and more efficiently. Bootstrapping an IDP requires setting up the initial infrastructure, tools, and processes to support internal development by different teams. Security and compliance are paramount for any organization, and the IDP enables the different teams to meet the requirements.

We will cover some use cases where the integration of different security tools can help different teams engaged in the software development lifecycle, consider the following questions:

- How do I create an account?

- How will my credentials be setup?

- How will I get the API key to start development or testing?

IDP shall have an in-built **centralized access management** to allow them to be productive from the beginning. IDP has integration of identity-based security, identity brokering solutions, and centralized management of credentials. This allows teams to move away from the ticket-driven process to **just in time (JIT)** access and Zero Trust security.

Success criteria for effective IDP implementation include measurable improvements in DORA metrics.

Identity brokering

This workflow might work as follows:

- A human, application, or service initiates a request.

- Identity providers validate the provided identity against the **single source of truth (SSOT)**.

- After authentication and authorization, a response is sent to the requestor.

- The identity system should be centralized.

- **Identity and access management (IAM)** controls are implemented for identity providers.

- This is integrated and configured in the IDP using IaC.

Managing user access across multiple services and applications can be complex. The following figure illustrates how a centralized identity broker simplifies authentication and authorization, streamlining access control within a platform:

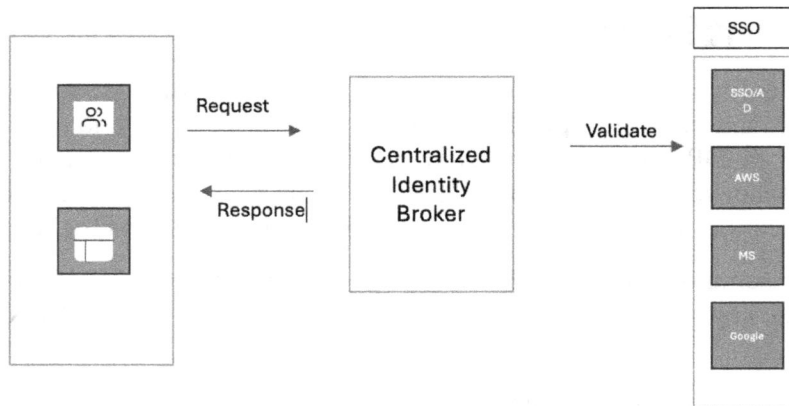

Figure 7.10: Access management using a centralized identity broker

- **Securely handling secrets and encryption within the platform**: The platform shall have an automated mechanism to support secret management (secret vault), encryption, and hashing functions available for the development teams. The platform has an integration of required tools and can support the following:

    o   Retrieving a secret (credential, password key, etc.).

    o   Brokering access.

    o   Managing secure data (encryption, hashing, and masking).

    Refer to the following figure:

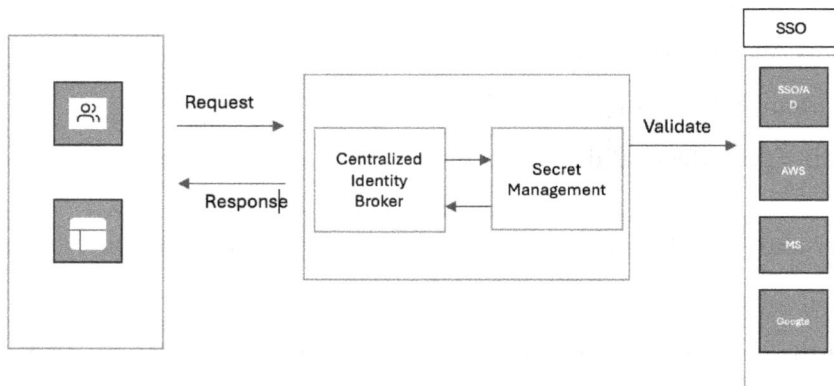

Figure 7.11: Secret management integration in the platform

- **Managing the system (privileged access management)**: The introduction of ephemeral resources in the Cloud needs a different approach to connect with the system. Traditional approaches of persistent **Secure Shell** (**SSH**), **Virtual Network Computing** (**VNC**), or a bastion host with resources are not fully secure. You need to build secure remote access tools with auditability and a Zero Trust model. Users with a scoped role and JIT access can get time-based access to resources. The platform shall have the capabilities for the following:

o Services can register with the service catalog dynamically.

o Identity-based model shall be implemented.

o Authentication with multiple sources shall be available.

o Implemented as code and API-enabled.

o Support role-based access control.

o Having capabilities to record actions, commands, and sessions to provide full audit trails.

o Highly available and supports multiplatform and multi-cloud capabilities.

The following figure illustrates how a centralized identity broker integrates with secret management to provide secure access to platform resources:

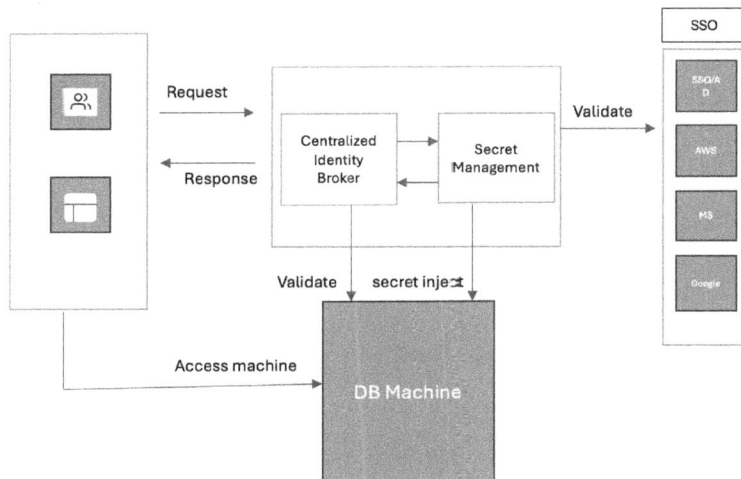

Figure 7.12: Privileged access management

Here is a breakdown of the process:

• **Constantly monitoring the vulnerabilities and tracking them**: Vulnerability management is an ongoing and regular process of identifying, assessing, reporting, managing, and remediating security vulnerabilities. These vulnerabilities can be identified in multiple ways, including manual security assessment, pen-testing, bug bounty, or integration of automated SAST, SCA, and DAST solutions. To track and timely resolve these vulnerabilities, you need a centralized tool. There are multiple tools available, but DefectDojo, as an open-source and web-based system, can help with the following:

o Tracking vulnerabilities of all security engagements.

o   Tracking products or components.

o   Custom field support.

o   Auto-closure of vulnerabilities if not detected in the scan.

o   Dashboard and benchmarks for tracked products.

o   API based.

You can create and map multiple products with DefectDojo.

The following figure provides the detailed metrics available to the development teams:

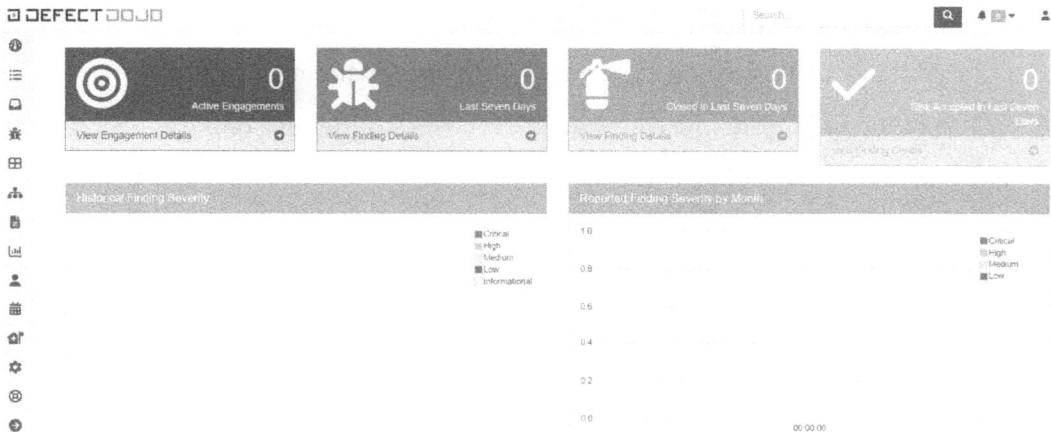

Figure 7.13: DefectDojo dashboard screen

The detailed dashboards are shown as follows:

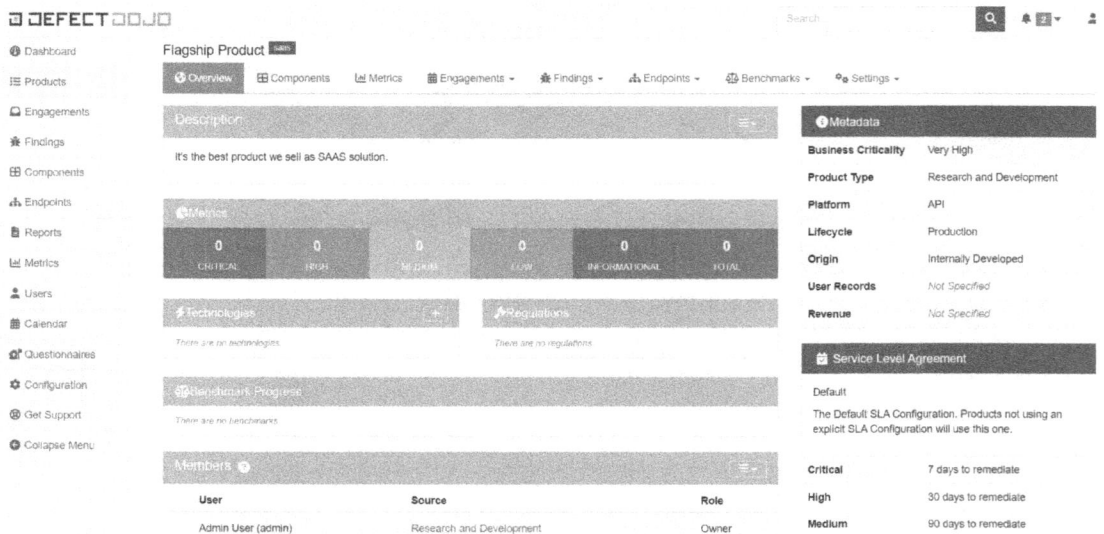

Figure 7.14: DefectDojo detailed dashboards

- **Managing compliance with all software**: One of the key aspects of software development is to manage required security and regulatory compliance. This cannot be an afterthought and shall be built with your development practices, that is, your developer platform. You need to have the following:

  o **Built-in controls**: The compliance is built-in, integrated workflow and processes. For example, access control and encryption are built into all the workflows integrated into the developer platform.

  o **Policy automation**: The codified policies as part of your solution. Some of the integrated policy tools, such as OPA or Kyverno, are integrated with the developer platform and help you to monitor the compliance of all developed software using the platform.

  o **Shift compliance**: The codified policies are part of your pipeline and allow you to fail to build or deploy in case of failure of key policies.

  o **Compliance framework**: The support of different compliance frameworks such as ISO 27001, NIST-CF, PCI DSS, etc.

- **Platform to manage incidents**: The developer platform shall support different personas (Developer, DevOps, SRE, Infosec, etc.) to use and support different activities. This shall have the integration of an incident management tool with capabilities to trigger, escalate, and manage incidents. This allows organizations to configure the on-call rotation, trigger alerts based on events, and notify the on-call team. This allows you to respond to an incident and close the incident when it is resolved.

The platform team keeps developing runbooks to automate an incident. For analysis of an incident, a person on-call needs to have all the details available to them. Integration of logging and monitoring systems to track all the events, a service catalog to identify services and ownership, and automation for incident response allows a person to close the incident quickly. They can perform the following tasks if the automated response does not work:

  o Correct the permissions.

  o Rollback a service.

  o Scale up resources.

  o Toggle off a feature.

The team can use all the tracking available in the system for learning and implementing preventive measures.

Conclusion

This chapter explored the crucial role of platform engineering in embedding security and compliance into the software development lifecycle. By integrating security and compliance tools and processes into the IDP, organizations can shift left and ensure that security is a top priority from the start. This approach not only strengthens the security posture of applications and infrastructure but also fosters collaboration among development, security, and operations teams.

We delved into the different control planes within an IDP, examining the tools and workflows associated with each. We also discussed various use cases for integrating security tools into the IDP to address challenges such as access control, secret management, vulnerability tracking, and compliance monitoring.

By adopting the principles and practices outlined in this chapter, organizations can create a robust and secure development environment that enables them to deliver high-quality software while effectively managing risks.

In the next chapter, we will explore self-service for developers, further expanding our understanding of how platform engineering can transform the software development landscape and provide a self-service platform to developers.

Exercises

1. **An internal developer platform helps organizations achieve**:
   a. Good developer experience
   b. Better customer experience
   c. Both
   d. None

2. **What is a policy automation tool?**
   a. Snyk
   b. Burp
   c. OPA
   d. NA

3. Why security is hard for developers?

4. What are the 4Cs of cloud native security?

5. What does the developer control plane consist of?

6. Which tool is used for centralized vulnerability management?

7. What is a secret management tool provided by HashiCorp?

Answers

1. c

2. c

3. Developers feel that security is blocking for them and is the job of the security and compliance team

4. Cloud, cluster, container, and code

5. Code, configuration, self-service portal

6. DefectDojo

7. HashiCorp vault

References

1. **https://platformengineering.org/platform-tooling**

Join our Discord space

Join our Discord workspace for latest updates, offers, tech happenings around the world, new releases, and sessions with the authors:

https://discord.bpbonline.com

CHAPTER 8
Self-service for Developers

Introduction

Self-service DevOps marks a significant shift in how companies handle and optimize their software development and IT operations. In the past, DevOps concentrated on dismantling barriers between development and operations teams to expedite software delivery while upholding reliability and stability. With a growing number of deliveries by companies, developers are also responsible for managing the infrastructure that runs their applications, but it is impractical to expect all developers to acquire a deep understanding of all insights into infrastructure. Self-service elevates this cooperation and effectiveness to the next level by granting development teams the necessary tools and independence to oversee their infrastructure, deployments, and operations, and DevOps to build the necessary tool chains and automation as a platform. This chapter will cover platform engineering and self-serve DevOps, covering various challenges and approaches to be adopted for achieving developer delight and DevOps excellence.

Structure

The chapter covers the following topics:

- Self-service DevOps
- Benefits of self-serve DevOps
- Self-serve DevOps building blocks

- Challenges
- Approaches

Objectives

By the end of this chapter, you will understand the significance and evolution from agile methodology to DevOps to a self-serve **internal developer platform** (**IDP**). This chapter will also explain its benefits, like enhanced agility and efficiency, and the practical strategies for implementation using key tools and approaches. You will explore self-service for developers, a critical component of modern software development. You will explore its evolution from traditional DevOps practices, driven by technologies like infrastructure as code, cloud computing, and IDP. You will also learn the practical implementation strategies and methods to address challenges such as security and tool sprawl using different approaches, including service catalogs, facade layers, and iterative adoption, which are analyzed to guide you in selecting the optimal strategy for your organization. By embracing self-service, you can unlock greater efficiency and innovation in the software delivery lifecycle. This chapter will also explain metrics-based outcomes such as a reduction in onboarding time, deployment time, or reduced **mean time to response** (**MTTR**).

Self-service DevOps

Self-service DevOps is a methodology used in software development and operations where teams independently handle and automate the processes of infrastructure creation, deployment, monitoring, and scaling applications and infrastructure. It gives teams the power to use tools, platforms, and workflows that enable self-service capabilities, reducing reliance on centralized IT and promoting agility, efficiency, and innovation throughout the software development lifecycle.

Self-service DevOps incorporates core DevOps principles, such as automation, collaboration, and continuous delivery. It extends autonomy and responsibility to development and operations teams, driving overall organizational efficiency and effectiveness. Overall, the industry is moving towards self-service DevOps, which is platform engineering, to leverage its benefits in terms of speed, efficiency, agility, empowerment, and scalability. Teams are productizing the self-service capabilities as an IDP and focusing on releasing features as a roadmap item. Organizations adopting platform engineering are better equipped to innovate quickly, effectively respond to market demands, and achieve sustainable growth in today's competitive landscape.

You do not need to write front-end or integration capabilities from scratch. You can use the existing platforms called **service catalog** to implement the self-service pipelines, empowering developers to manage their deployments with minimal operational overhead. Some examples of these service catalogs are:

- AWS Service Catalog

- Backstage
- Harness
- Azure DevOps
- GitLab CI/CD

The following are some of the benefits of using these platforms:

- **Centralized catalog**: These tools allow you to create and manage a catalog of approved IT services, including pre-configured pipelines. This ensures consistency and compliance.

- **Self-service portal**: These tools provide an intuitive interface with a defined catalog and request pipelines without needing an IT or operations team.

- **Automation**: This service catalog provides plugins or easy integration of the API to automate workflows.

- **Governance**: These tools allow policy integration to maintain control of security and usage of services.

The following is an example of Backstage implementation where developers see the services available through a **service catalog**:

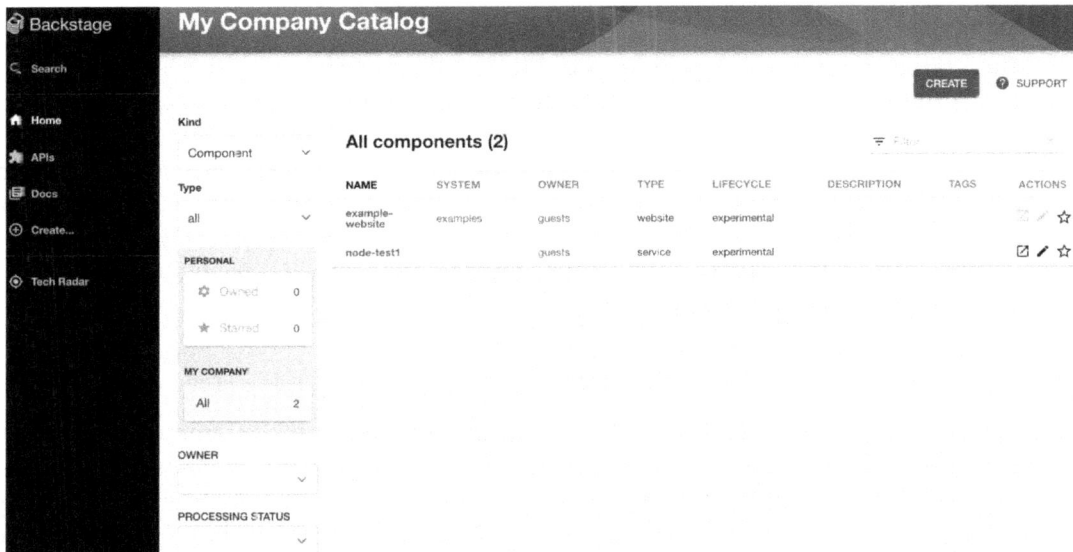

Figure 8.1: Backstage self-service portal

Evolution

The shift from traditional software development to a cloud-based approach has revolutionized development and operations. This transformation has propelled the industry from a few monthly releases to a dynamic environment where numerous deployments occur daily. Let us look at the evolution in the software development lifecycle and the role of DevOps and platform engineering in this evolution.

DevOps culture and principles

At first, DevOps arose to address the necessity for closer teamwork between development and operations teams, emphasizing automation, CI/CD, and a shared responsibility culture for software delivery and infrastructure management. Developers need to focus more on writing code and software development, while the Platform Team needs to focus on building self-service capabilities for developers. Developers do not need to understand the infrastructure complexities and security or compliance required for it. These are available as default with the required guardrails.

Shift to infrastructure as code

The move to **infrastructure as code (IaC)** was crucial in the progression towards self-serve DevOps, enabling automated provisioning and management of infrastructure through code, and allowing teams to programmatically define and deploy infrastructure resources. This also includes different infrastructure templates available to the developers to create the desired infrastructure with ease.

Cloud computing and platforms

The emergence of cloud computing provided scalable infrastructure and platforms managed through APIs and automated tools, abstracting away the complexity of infrastructure management and supporting self-service capabilities for development teams. Cloud computing is still very complex for traditional developers. Modern cloud architectures, such as microservices and serverless, have increased the complexity of managing infrastructure, too, so developers and **site reliability engineering (SRE)** teams need a platform to abstract these complexities from them. IDP provides these abstractions to the development and SRE teams.

Containerization and orchestration

The popularity of containerization technologies like Docker and container orchestration platforms such as Kubernetes further accelerated the evolution of self-serve DevOps, providing consistent deployment environments and automating deployment, scaling, and management of containerized applications. Containerization has helped in the cloudification of applications and achieving a large-scale.

Microservices architecture

The adoption of microservices architecture, breaking down applications into smaller, loosely coupled services, aligns well with self-serve DevOps principles, enabling teams to independently develop, deploy, and scale their services, fostering autonomy and agility. This has led to service-wise and faster deliveries.

Focus on automation and efficiency

There has been a continuous emphasis on automation to enhance efficiency and reduce manual intervention in software delivery processes, including automation of testing, deployment pipelines, monitoring, and incident response as integral components of self-serve DevOps practices.

Expansion of DevOps tooling

The proliferation of specialized DevOps tools and platforms tailored for self-service capabilities further broadened opportunities for teams to automate and manage their workflows, supporting diverse organizational needs and workflows in areas such as CI or CD, security and compliance validations, configuration management, monitoring, and collaboration.

A cultural shift towards empowerment

Beyond technical advancements, the evolution of self-serve DevOps signifies a cultural shift towards empowering development and operations teams, promoting a culture of ownership, autonomy, and continuous improvement, and encouraging teams to innovate and take responsibility for their work. In summary, the development of self-serve DevOps has been steered by technological advancements, cultural changes, and a growing emphasis on speed, efficiency, and collaboration in software development and operations. It continues to progress as organizations strive to utilize automation, cloud-native technologies, and agile methodologies to achieve faster time-to-market and maintain a competitive edge in the digital era.

Benefits of self-serve DevOps

Self-service DevOps empowers developers to accelerate software delivery by independently managing environments and deployments. They can spin up new environments, provision cloud resources, and deploy code with ease. Operations teams provide pre-approved infrastructure templates, ensuring consistency and efficiency. Security is baked in with automated compliance checks integrated into the self-service pipeline. This collaborative approach streamlines the entire process, from development to production. The following are the benefits of using self-service DevOps:

- **Agility**: Self-service DevOps empowers teams to deploy and iterate applications more rapidly and independently. This agility is crucial in fast-paced industries where rapid innovation and time-to-market provide competitive advantages.

- **Empowerment of developers**: Empowering teams to manage their infrastructure and deployments fosters a culture of ownership, collaboration, and innovation. It allows teams to experiment, iterate, and innovate more freely, fostering a dynamic and responsive organizational culture. They do not have to worry about the costs and security that are inherent to the self-service platform.

- **Scalability:** As organizations expand and scale, self-service DevOps offers scalable solutions that can adapt to changing business needs and technological advancements. It allows seamless integration of new tools and technologies, supporting continuous improvement and adaptation.

- **Efficiency**: Streamlining workflows, reducing manual intervention, and optimizing resource usage through automation and self-service capabilities lead to cost savings and improved operational efficiency, enabling organizations to achieve more with existing resources. Self-service DevOps breaks down traditional DevOps models' dependencies on centralized IT or operations teams for infrastructure provisioning and deployment. It enables cross-functional teams to work more autonomously and collaboratively.

There are some credible market survey reports available that explain the clear benefit of using a self-service portal and enhanced time to market for their features.

- **Accelerate State of DevOps Report (DORA, 2023):** Organizations with self-service DevOps toolchains (e.g., automated CI/CD, IaC, containerization) achieve 50% to 70% faster time-to-market compared to teams relying on manual processes.

  Key drivers: Self-service reduces bottlenecks by empowering developers to provision infrastructure, deploy code, and test without waiting for approvals.

- **Gartner's Market Guide for DevOps Value Stream Management (2023)**: Organizations adopting self-service DevOps tools see 30% to 50% faster release cycles, driven by streamlined workflows and reduced dependency on siloed teams.

- **Forrester's Total Economic Impact of DevOps (2022)**: A global enterprise reduced time-to-market by 65% after implementing self-service IaC (Terraform) and Kubernetes orchestration.

  Key drivers: Elimination of manual infrastructure provisioning (saving 15 to 20 hours per week). Automated rollbacks and testing in CI/CD pipelines.

By embracing self-service DevOps, organizations can create a more agile, efficient, and innovative software development environment that benefits everyone involved.

Self-serve DevOps building blocks

Several building blocks need to be in place to have a robust self-serve DevOps platform. Self-service DevOps empowers developers with access to a catalog of pre-approved infrastructure components and services to deploy applications and manage resources independently. IaC ensures consistency and reproducibility. Security is baked in with automated compliance checks. These building blocks accelerate delivery, foster developer autonomy, and free operations teams to focus on strategic initiatives. Let us discuss them in detail in the following sub-sections.

Infrastructure as code

Teams can use tools such as Terraform and CloudFormation to define and manage infrastructure using code, which automates the provisioning and configuration of resources, ensuring consistency and scalability. This method enables rapid infrastructure deployment, reduces configuration drift, and supports version control and auditability of infrastructure changes. Standardized IaC embedded with guardrails and gates is crucial as a first step to achieving self-service DevOps. It should align with the cloud governance framework followed by the respective organizations.

These IaC modules ensure compliance and cost guardrails, easing the cognitive load on developers while managing the infrastructure lifecycle. Service catalog and approval flows can help managers monitor non-standard requests effectively. The following are a few examples of IaC modules that can be considered:

- Terraform modules
- AWS CloudFormation templates
- **Azure Resource Manager (ARM)** templates
- Pulumi component resources
- Ansible playbooks
- Helm charts

The following figure explains the indicative self-service DevOps platform, highlighting the core components: IaC for provisioning of infrastructure and Kubernetes for containerization and orchestration:

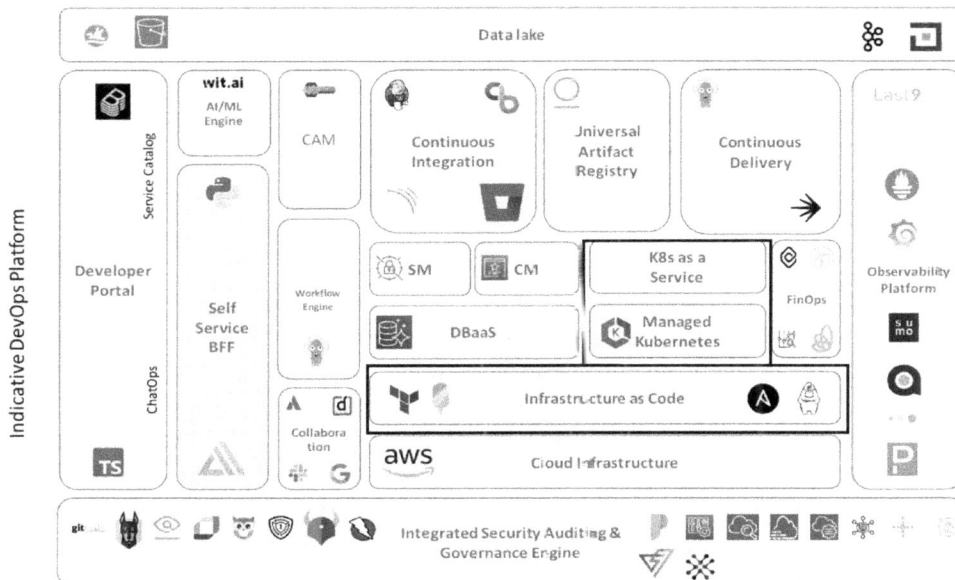

Figure 8.2: Indicative self-service DevOps platform

Prescriptive CI/CD

Prescriptive CI/CD offers a systematic method for implementing automated software delivery pipelines, enabling organizations to achieve faster, more reliable, and higher-quality releases while promoting collaboration and innovation across teams. From code development to application deployment and continuous operation, there will be a defined set of steps that developers must follow without deviation.

Here is a CI/CD pipeline view that explains the different stages of the pipeline and integration of IaC and Kubernetes tools:

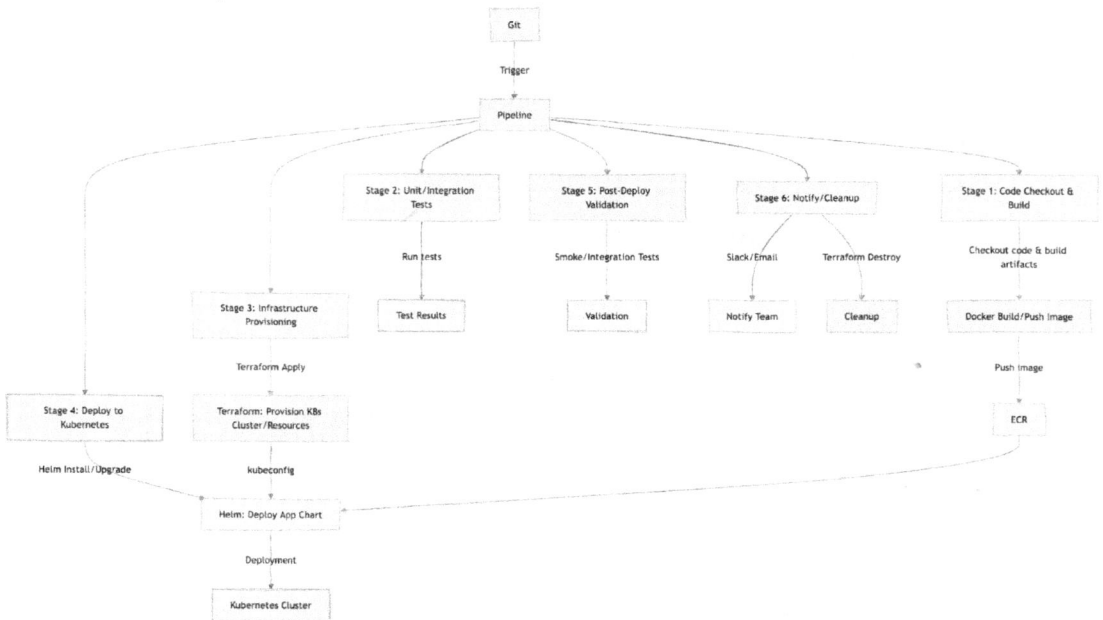

Figure 8.3: Sample Jenkins pipeline with stages of infrastructure provisioning and deployment

Observability stack

An observability stack is essential for modern IT operations as it provides comprehensive insights into the performance and behavior of complex distributed systems. It enables organizations to proactively monitor, troubleshoot, and optimize their applications and infrastructure, ensuring reliability, scalability, and agility in today's dynamic digital landscape. It should support metrics, logs, traces, and events. Additionally, it should cover cost and DevOps metrics such as **DevOps Research and Assessment (DORA)**, which will be displayed on developer portals for the respective development teams and summarized for organizational leadership. Refer to *Chapter 10, Data Lake and Observability,* to review how observability tools such as Grafana or Prometheus are used for metric visualization as part of the overall self-service portal.

Managed Kubernetes services

Managed Kubernetes services within self-serve DevOps significantly reduce cognitive load on developers by abstracting the complexities of cluster management. These services automate tasks such as provisioning, scaling, and monitoring Kubernetes clusters, allowing developers to focus on application development and deployment rather than infrastructure maintenance. This streamlined approach improves efficiency, speeds up deployment cycles, and enhances overall agility within DevOps workflows, enabling teams to innovate more rapidly and effectively.

The following are key considerations when choosing **managed Kubernetes services**:

- **Existing cloud infrastructure**: If you are already heavily invested in a particular cloud provider, their Kubernetes service is usually the best choice for integration.

- **Ease of use**: GKE is often praised for its ease of use, especially with Autopilot.

- **Cost**: Carefully compare pricing models, including control plane costs, worker node costs, and any additional charges.

- **Features**: Evaluate the specific features you need, such as serverless options, advanced networking capabilities, and integration with other services.

- **Support**: Consider the level of support offered by each provider.

Here are some key differences between different providers (AWS, GCP, and Azure):

Feature	AWS EKS	GCP GKE	Azure AKS
Control plane management	Fully managed (you manage worker nodes, but managed node groups and Fargate simplify this)	Fully managed (includes worker nodes with Autopilot)	Fully managed (you manage worker nodes, but managed node pools and Virtual Nodes simplify this)
Worker Node management	You manage (EC2 instances or managed node groups, Fargate)	Mostly managed (auto-provisioning, auto-upgrades, Autopilot)	You manage (Virtual machines or managed node pools/virtual nodes)
Networking	Integrates with AWS VPC, security groups	Integrates with GCP VPC, firewall rules	Integrates with Azure Virtual Network, Network Security Groups
IAM	Integrates with AWS IAM	Integrates with Google Cloud IAM	Integrates with **Azure Active Directory** (**AAD**)

Feature	AWS EKS	GCP GKE	Azure AKS
Serverless option	Fargate	Autopilot	Virtual Nodes
Ease of use	Can be more complex (but improving with managed node groups)	Generally considered easiest (especially with Autopilot)	Can be more complex (but improving with managed node pools)

Table 8.1: Key differences between managed Kubernetes services

Developer control plane

In self-serve DevOps, a developer control plane refers to a dedicated environment or platform that empowers developers to independently manage and orchestrate their applications and infrastructure. This control plane typically includes tools and interfaces tailored for developers to deploy, scale, monitor, and troubleshoot their applications with minimal reliance on centralized operations teams. By granting developers control over their environments, organizations foster agility and innovation while reducing bottlenecks in the software delivery lifecycle. This approach not only enhances developer productivity but also aligns with DevOps principles by promoting collaboration, continuous integration, and rapid deployment of code changes.

A good example of a developer control plane is **Backstage**, an open-source developer portal originating from Spotify, which helped the developer workflow by consolidating essential tools, services, and documentation into a single, unified platform. This significantly reduces friction and boosts productivity. The following are some of the core capabilities of Backstage:

- **Centralized service catalog**: Provides a comprehensive inventory of all services, APIs, and infrastructure components. Instead of reinventing the wheel, developers can easily discover and reuse existing resources. For example, a developer can search for an authentication service rather than build one from scratch.

- **Documentation-as-code (TechDocs)**: Integrates documentation directly with the codebase using Markdown. Teams document their APIs within their repositories, and Backstage automatically renders them into a searchable, accessible site. This ensures documentation stays up-to-date and easily discoverable.

- **Automated project scaffolding (software templates)**: Offers pre-configured templates for new projects, enabling rapid setup and consistent configurations. A **React Microservice** template, for instance, could include pre-configured CI/CD pipelines, linting, and monitoring.

- **Seamless CI/CD integration**: Integrates with popular CI/CD platforms like Jenkins and GitHub Action, allowing developers to monitor pipelines and trigger deployments directly within Backstage. This eliminates the need for constant context switching.

- **Kubernetes integration**: Provides visibility into Kubernetes deployments, pods, and logs directly within the portal. Developers can debug production issues by examining pod logs without leaving Backstage, simplifying troubleshooting.

- **Extensible plugin ecosystem**: Backstage's open architecture allows for extension through plugins. This enables integration with a wide range of tools, including monitoring solutions like Grafana and Prometheus.

- **Role-based access control (RBAC)**: Ensures secure access to sensitive resources by implementing granular permissions. This allows, for example, restricting database credentials to only authorized backend team members.

- **Dependency visualization**: Provides a visual representation of the relationships between different services, allowing developers to understand the impact of changes before they are made. This helps prevent outages by identifying downstream dependencies.

- **Customizable extensibility**: Beyond plugins, Backstage supports custom API integrations, enabling deeper integration with existing systems.

- **Industry-wide adoption**: Leading companies like Splunk, HP, and DoorDash have adopted Backstage to unify their fragmented development tools, significantly improving developer productivity and efficiency.

Backstage significantly enhances developer productivity by addressing the following key workflow challenges:

- The unified portal reduces cognitive load by consolidating all essential development tasks, minimizing context switching, and ensuring readily accessible information.

- This streamlined approach also facilitates faster developer onboarding, allowing new hires to quickly become productive by leveraging the service catalog and pre-configured project templates.

- Backstage fosters improved consistency across projects. Standardized workflows and project setups, enforced through templates, minimize errors, promote best practices, and contribute to a more predictable and efficient development process.

By centralizing critical tools and automating key workflows, Backstage empowers developers to focus on what matters most: writing code and building great products. It streamlines the entire software development lifecycle, leading to increased efficiency, improved collaboration, and faster time to market.

Automated administration of tools

Automated management of tools in self-service DevOps involves automating tasks related to managing and maintaining the various tools and platforms used in the software development process. This automation is essential for enabling teams to work efficiently and independently within a self-service system. The following are the main aspects of automated management in self-service DevOps:

- **Provisioning and configuration**: Automated scripts and templates are utilized to setup and configure development tools, CI/CD pipelines, infrastructure, and other essential resources. This ensures uniformity and reduces the time taken for manual setup.

- **Monitoring**: Automated monitoring tools constantly monitor the health and performance of development environments, applications, and infrastructure. Automated alerts notify teams of potential issues or performance degradation, allowing for proactive maintenance and troubleshooting. This helps in maintaining **service level objectives** (**SLO**) and uptime for their applications.

- **Backup and disaster recovery** (**DR**): Automated backup processes make certain that data and configurations are regularly backed up, scanned for conformity, and can be quickly restored in case of failures or disasters. This minimizes downtime and reduces the risk of data loss.

- **Security and compliance**: Automated security scans and compliance checks are built into the pipeline to enforce security policies and regulatory requirements. This ensures that tools and environments are secure and compliant throughout the development lifecycle.

- **Scaling and efficiency**: Automated scaling capabilities adjust resources dynamically based on demand, optimizing usage and performance without manual intervention. This elasticity supports efficient resource management and cost savings.

- **E2E lifecycle management**: Automated tools oversee the lifecycle of software and infrastructure components, managing tasks such as version upgrades, patch management, and retirement of outdated resources. This ensures that environments remain current and secure. By automating these administrative tasks, self-service DevOps empowers teams to concentrate more on development, innovation, and delivering business value rather than on routine maintenance and management activities. This approach not only enhances operational efficiency but also improves collaboration and agility within the organization, fostering a culture of continuous improvement and rapid iteration.

The teams can use template repositories to have boilerplate codes, use developer portals like Backstage to host these golden standards and paths, standardized Terraform modules, templatized pipelines as golden paths, etc. To foster consistency and efficiency across development teams, organizations can implement standardized tools and resources:

Template	Indicative tool	Benefits
Template repo	GitHub template repository	QuickStart boilerplates with all guardrails and best practices
Template pipelines	Azure DevOps Template pipeline, Jenkins Groovy Libraries, GitHub Action, etc.	Prescriptive paved ways or Golden Paths
Battle-tested IaC modules	Terraform modules, Ansible Roles, helm charts	Invulnerable, standardized, compliant, and reusable IaC
Golden AMI, packages, libraries	Packer, JFrog, Nexus Artifact servers, Docker	Secured and compliant packages and artifacts

Table 8.2: Standardized tools and resources

IaC tools vs. containerization

IaC and containerization are foundational pillars of modern cloud-native development and DevOps practices. These are building blocks of platform engineering and self-service IDP as well.

IaC automates the provisioning and management of infrastructure using code (e.g., Terraform, AWS CloudFormation), enabling teams to define servers, networks, and services in reusable, version-controlled templates. This approach eliminates manual setup errors, ensures consistency across environments (dev, staging, prod), and accelerates deployments. However, challenges like state management (e.g., Terraform's state files) and vendor lock-in (e.g., AWS CloudFormation) require careful planning.

Containerization (e.g., Docker, Kubernetes) complements IaC by packaging applications and dependencies into lightweight, portable containers. Containers ensure that software runs uniformly across environments, solving the *works on my machine* problem. Docker simplifies building and sharing containerized apps, while Kubernetes orchestrates complex deployments with auto-scaling, self-healing, and load balancing. Together, IaC and containerization streamline end-to-end automation. This synergy enhances agility, scalability, and reproducibility, critical for microservices architectures and CI/CD pipelines.

However, there are certain key differences between the two, and the use of the right IaC tool or container technologies needs to be planned carefully to avoid complexities like orchestration overhead or security concerns, e.g., image vulnerabilities.

The following table is a summary of the pros and cons of some of the IaC and containerization tools:

	Infrastructure as code (IaC)			Containerization		
Pros	**Terraform**	**AWS Cloud-Formation**	**Pulumi**	**Docker**	**Kubernetes**	**OpenShift**
	Cloud-agnostic	Native AWS integration	Uses general-purpose languages (Python, Go)	Lightweight, portable containers	Robust orchestration	Enterprise-grade Kubernetes
	Declarative syntax (HCL)	Supports JSON/YAML	Multi-cloud support	Easy to use	Auto-scaling/self-healing	Built-in CI/CD and security
	Large ecosystem	Managed state		Strong isolation	Ecosystem	GUI
Cons	State management complexity	AWS-locked	Smaller community	No built-in orchestration	Steep learning curve	Proprietary (Red Hat)
	The steep learning curve for HCL	Verbose templates	Complex setup for large teams	Limited scalability out of the box	Complex setup/maintenance	Resource-heavy
	Limited configuration management	Slower deployments	Limited scalability out-of-the-box		Overkill for small apps	Costly for small teams

Table 8.3: Key differences between IaC tools and containerization

IaC and containerization empower teams to manage **infrastructure** and **applications** as code, fostering collaboration, reducing downtime, and enabling rapid iteration: key drivers for modern, cloud-first organizations, and paved the way for self-service portals.

Challenges

While se3lf-service DevOps offers greater agility and reduces reliance on centralized IT, it also introduces challenges. These include the increased complexity of managing a self-service platform, heightened security risks, potential cost overruns, and the need for standardized practices and upskilling. Here is the list of challenges and difficulties to be faced in self-service DevOps:

- **Cultural shift:**

o New team members might encounter a challenging learning curve when acclimating to self-service systems, which could potentially hamper productivity.

o The adoption of a self-service DevOps model often involves a shift in the organizational culture. Teams need to embrace ownership and accountability, which may be challenging if they are accustomed to relying on centralized DevOps and support.

- **Tool sprawl and glue code:**

o In the absence of central oversight, different teams might utilize different tools for the same tasks, leading to a fragmented and inconsistent environment.

o Integrating different tools and platforms to establish a seamless workflow can be intricate. Challenges may arise concerning compatibility, data synchronization, and maintaining the integration over time.

- **Security and compliance:**

o Providing developers with extensive access to tools and infrastructure can create security vulnerabilities if not managed properly. This necessitates strict controls and monitoring to prevent unauthorized access or changes. The tools access shall be job role basis.

o Ensuring that all developers adhere to security policies and compliance requirements can be demanding, especially in a decentralized and independent environment.

- **Process efficiency tradeoffs:**

o Self-service models can result in inefficient resource usage, as developers might overprovision infrastructure or neglect to decommission unused resources. This can lead to efficiency in operational costs.

o Guaranteeing efficient resource usage and optimized performance across various services can be complex in a self-service environment.

o Effectively monitoring all changes, deployments, and resource usage across teams necessitates robust monitoring and reporting systems. A lack of visibility can result in unnoticed issues until they become critical.

o As the organization expands, scaling the self-service infrastructure to accommodate a growing number of users and services can be demanding. This involves scaling both the technical infrastructure and the support systems surrounding it.

Policy as code to solve these challenges

Kyverno and Open Policy Agent are two well-known solutions to enforce policies as code. This ensures that all resources deployed to the cluster adhere to the organization's security and compliance standards. It solves challenges in the following manner:

- These solutions can validate resources against predefined rules, preventing the creation of non-compliant resources. For example, we can enforce requirements for mandatory labels, annotations, or security contexts.

- These solutions can automatically modify resources to ensure compliance. For example, you can automatically add missing labels or enforce specific resource limits.

- These systems can generate new resources based on existing ones.

Benefits and examples of the policy as code

Here are the following benefits of the policy as code:

- **Improved security**: Enforce security best practices and prevent the deployment of vulnerable resources.

- **Reduced risk**: Minimize the risk of compliance violations and potential security breaches.

- **Increased efficiency**: Automate compliance checks and reduce manual efforts.

- **Centralized policy management**: Manage all your compliance policies in one place.

- **Audit trails**: Track policy violations and generate audit reports.

Example 1: Automating project tagging

The following policy automatically adds a **project** label to namespaces. It uses the namespace name as the value, which can be useful for organizing resources by project.

```
apiVersion: kyverno.io/v1
kind: ClusterPolicy
metadata:
  name: auto-project-tag
spec:
  rules:
  - name: add-project-tag
    match:
      any:
      - resources:
          kinds:
          - Namespace # Or other resource types like Pod, Deployment, etc.
    mutate:
      patchStrategicMerge:
        metadata:
          labels:
```

```
                    project: "{{request.object.metadata.name}}" # Use the namespace
name as project tag
```

Code 8.1: Policy example for automated project tagging

Example 2: Adding cost center tag based on namespace

The following example adds a cost-center tag to pods, using the pod's namespace as the value. You could enhance this by having a mapping of namespaces to cost centers stored in a ConfigMap or custom resource and using Kyverno's lookup functionality to apply the correct tag.

```
apiVersion: kyverno.io/v1
kind: ClusterPolicy
metadata:
  name: add-cost-center-tag
spec:
  rules:
    - name: add-cost-center
      match:
        any:
          - resources:
              kinds:
                - Pod
      mutate:
        patchStrategicMerge:
          metadata:
            labels:
              cost-center: "{{request.object.metadata.namespace}}" # Or a
lookup based on namespace
```

Code 8.2: Policy example for cost center tagged for namespace

These policy code examples can be used with your Kubernetes infrastructure and the Kyverno tool implemented. Setting up these tools is out of the scope of this book, and you can refer to books on these specific topics.

By combining these tools, teams can enforce guardrails **proactively** (during development) and **reactively** (runtime scans), reducing risks and optimizing costs.

Addressing these difficulties requires thorough planning, suitable tooling, and a strong focus on governance, training, and cultural alignment. By acknowledging these potential pitfalls, organizations can better prepare for and mitigate the risks associated with a self-service DevOps model.

Approaches

Organizations seeking to embrace self-service DevOps can choose from a variety of implementation approaches, each with its advantages and considerations. These approaches dictate how developers gain access to resources and tools, and how much control and standardization the organization maintains. Let us explore some of the most common approaches, including top-down, bottom-up, facade layer, and green field setups, to understand their unique characteristics and identify the best fit for different organizational needs.

Top-down approach

In a top-down approach to self-service DevOps, the initiative is spearheaded by organizational leadership or central IT teams. This approach prioritizes standardization and control, aiming to establish a unified platform with pre-approved tools, technologies, and workflows for developers to utilize. Let us look into the details:

- **Service catalog-based approach**: In a self-service DevOps environment, a service catalog is a centralized assortment of standardized, pre-defined services, applications, and infrastructure resources that are provided to development and operations teams for easy consumption and provisioning. This catalog acts as a menu of IT services that teams can request and deploy on demand without undergoing traditional procurement or manual setup processes.

  The catalog outlines standardized offerings of services and resources that are pre-approved and compliant with organizational policies and best practices. This guarantees uniformity and dependability across deployments. It enables developers and operations teams to peruse the catalog, choose the services or resources they require, and start the provisioning process independently.

  This self-service approach empowers teams to be more agile and decreases reliance on centralized IT operations. Teams can observe the available resources, feasible configurations, and cost implications before selecting. It ensures that deployments via the service catalog adhere to organizational policies, security requirements, and compliance standards. It establishes controls over who can access specific services and the permissible configurations. It aids in managing and optimizing infrastructure and service costs by offering insights into usage patterns, cost allocations, and resource budgeting.

  The service catalog in a self-service DevOps context plays a crucial role in facilitating the rapid and consistent deployment of applications and infrastructure resources while advancing automation, collaboration, and efficiency across development and operations teams. It aligns with DevOps principles by promoting agility, continuous delivery, and innovation within the organization.

These may include quick-start boilerplate code templates with self-contained code bases with codified pipelines. The developers can pick based on their requirements. The entire deployment occurs with a single click. The templates will include golden versions that are invulnerable and compliant. This approach helps the development community with the reduced cognitive load and simplified options to pick, as there will be a finite set of choices to make.

The service catalog can focus on providing abstraction, composability, or both. In the case of **abstraction**, the developers are provided with a standard and finite set of options to choose from, and they may not be able to provide granular options. This approach has the benefits of having limited variations to manage, while the **composability** approach gives greater autonomy to the developers, and they get the freedom to explore within the paved way. Developers get golden standards at a granular level, and these granular items can be used to compose the desired service. The platform engineering team may have to support many permutations and combinations, as this approach may lead to wider varieties in the hands of the developers.

When designing a service catalog for self-service DevOps, organizations must determine the level of composability they want to offer developers. An example is the following figure:

Figure 8.4: Sample service catalog following the composition principle

Service catalogs can offer varying levels of abstraction to cater to different developer needs and organizational preferences. The following figure illustrates how a service catalog can present different abstraction levels, ranging from specific cloud providers and deployment models to more generalized infrastructure options:

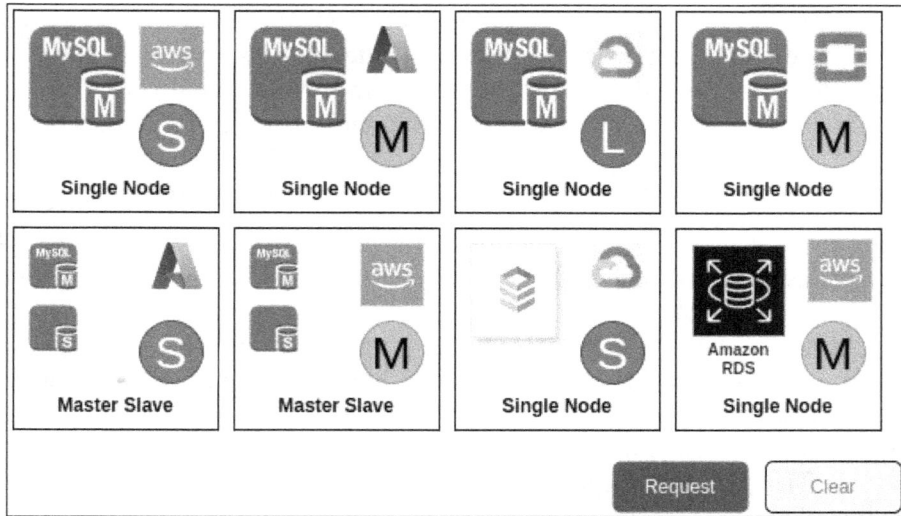

Figure 8.5: A sample service catalog following the abstraction principle

- **Facade layer approach:** The illustration seems to show a self-serve platform engineering model that includes a **Facade** layer connecting a developer with different existing tools.

  The following is an explanation of the elements:

  o **Developer**: Represents the user or developer interacting with the system.

  o **Facade layer**: This acts as a new interface mediating between the developer and the existing tools, streamlining and consolidating interactions into a single entry point.

  o **Existing tools**: The tools integrated with the facade layer include:

    ▪ **Continuous integration (CI)**: Tools for frequently integrating code changes into a shared repository.

    ▪ **Continuous deployment (CD)**: Tools automating the deployment of new software releases.

    ▪ **Monitoring**: Tools for tracking performance, availability, and application health.

    ▪ **Operations**: Tools for managing and maintaining software infrastructure.

    ▪ **Infrastructure provisioning**: Tools for setting up and managing the infrastructure required for running applications.

    ▪ **Other tools**: Every organization is unique. There will be a plethora of tools a developer needs to interact with or consume as part of the **software development life cycle (SDLC)**.

A facade layer can simplify interactions with complex backend systems in self-service DevOps. An example is shown in the following figure:

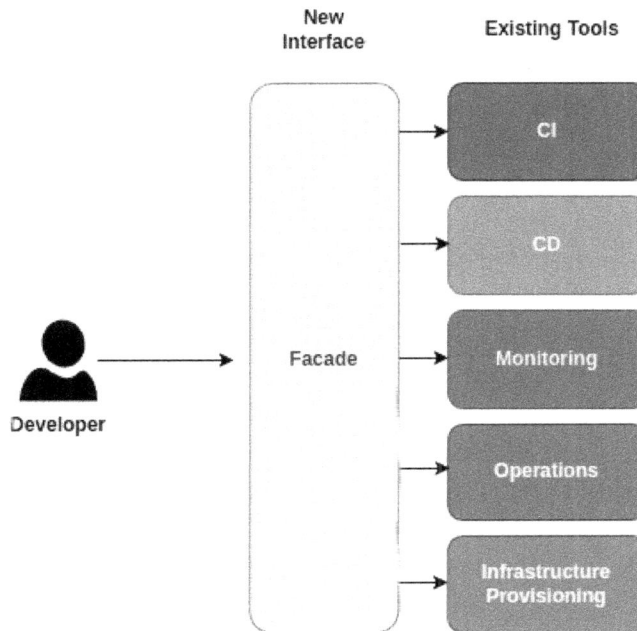

Figure 8.6: A façade layer approach

The facade layer provides developers with a simplified and unified interface for interacting with various tools. It abstracts complexities and streamlines workflows, potentially boosting productivity and simplifying the management of development and deployment processes. The platform engineering team has the flexibility to easily integrate or remove tools without affecting the developer experience. Another advantage is the loose coupling with underlying tools and workflows, as the facade layer allows the platform engineering team to handle complex tasks in the background, reducing the cognitive load on developers when interacting with different tools directly.

IDPs play a crucial role in enabling self-service DevOps by providing a centralized hub for golden paths, tools, and resources. The following figure shows an example:

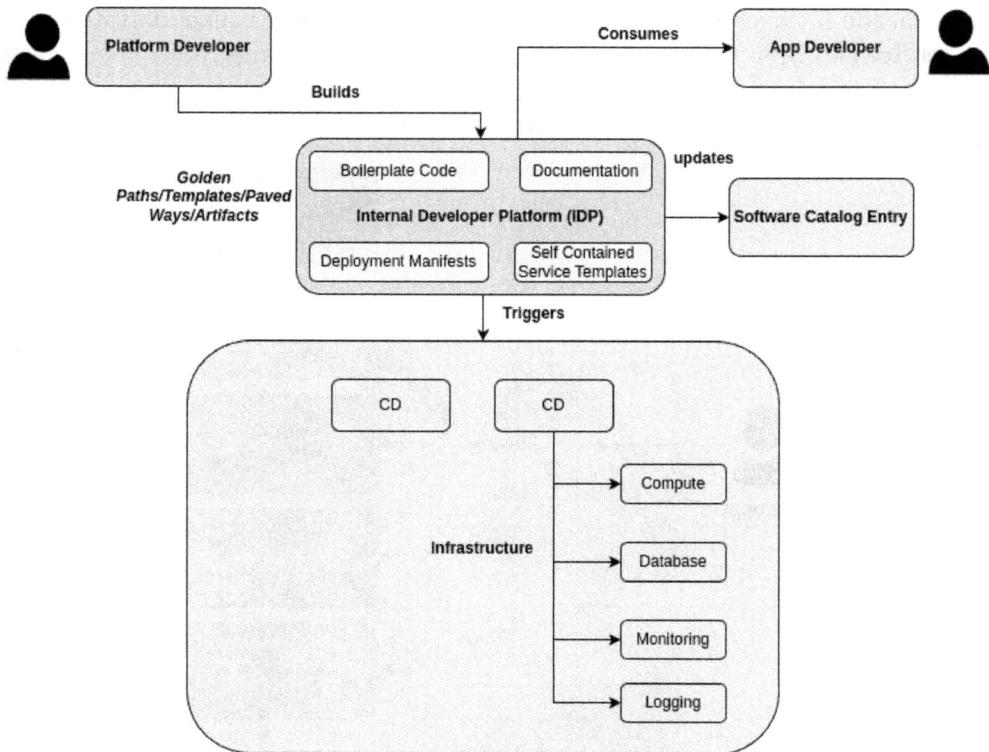

Figure 8.7: Workflow for a developer platform

The figure depicts a workflow for a developer platform involving platform developers, app developers, an IDP, and infrastructure components. Platform developers are responsible for building and maintaining the IDP, which includes boilerplate code, documentation, deployment manifests, and self-contained service templates. These resources are used by app developers to streamline application development and deployment. The IDP updates the software catalog entry with new resources, making them accessible to app developers. The infrastructure includes components such as CD, compute, database, monitoring, and logging systems. The IDP triggers deployments to the infrastructure, ensuring efficient application management. Platform developers create and update the IDP, providing necessary tools and templates. App developers utilize these resources to speed up the building and deployment of applications. The software catalog entry serves as a searchable repository for platform resources. This workflow ensures a smooth and efficient development cycle, from resource creation to application deployment and monitoring.

Greenfield setup

The greenfield setup is likely focused on updating the development and deployment processes by potentially incorporating newer technologies or methodologies to enhance efficiency, security, and scalability. This gradual transition approach is designed to reduce the risks associated with significant changes in infrastructure and tools.

The following is a breakdown of the components and flow:

- **Developer:** The user or developer interacts with the system.
- **Existing tools:** These tools consist of the following:
  - **Continuous integration:** Tools that facilitate the integration of code changes into a shared repository.
  - **Continuous deployment:** Tools that automate the deployment process.
  - **Monitoring:** Tools for monitoring the performance, health, and availability of applications.
  - **Operations:** Tools that handle operational aspects of the infrastructure.
  - **Provisioning:** Tools for establishing and managing the required infrastructure.
  - **Greenfield setup (new platform):** This denotes a new or updated setup, possibly integrating new tools, technologies, and methodologies. It may involve elements for improved development environments, faster SDLC, simplified workflow, optimized **Total Cost of Ownership (TCO)**, and enhanced security.

A greenfield setup allows organizations to build a self-service DevOps platform from the ground up, often alongside existing systems and gradual transition, as shown in the following figure:

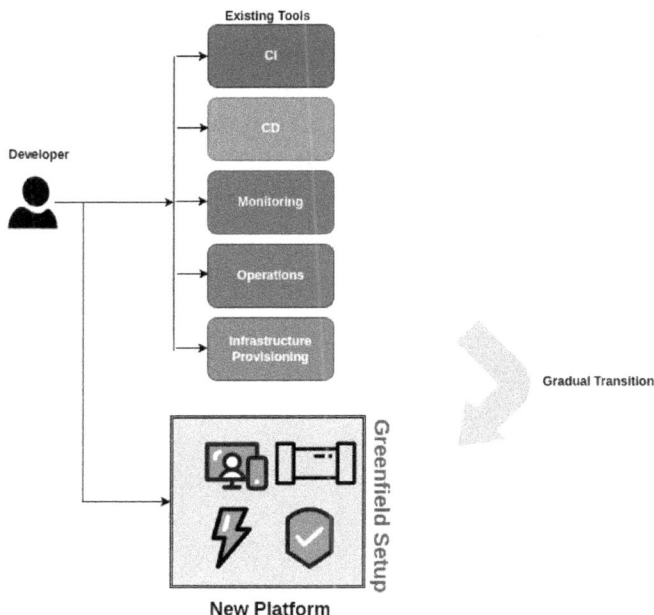

Figure 8.8: Greenfield setup

The preceding figure indicates a phased approach to migrating from the existing tools to the new platform. This allows for a seamless transition without disrupting existing workflows, ensuring that both systems can run concurrently until the migration is finished.

Here are some phased migrations to a greenfield self-service DevOps platform. The five suggested phases to guide the transition are as follows:

1. **Assessment and planning**: Define goals, stakeholders, current and target states, and roadmap.

2. **Proof of concept**: Pilot a small project with an MVP, iterating based on feedback.

3. **Pilot expansion**: Onboard more teams, expand features, and refine processes.

4. **Production rollout**: Migrate applications, automate processes, and monitor performance.

5. **Continuous improvement**: Gather feedback, track metrics, and enhance the platform. Key considerations include parallel operations, communication, training, support, and a rollback plan.

With this phased approach and addressing these key considerations, organizations can effectively transition to a greenfield self-service DevOps platform, realizing the benefits of increased agility, efficiency, and developer empowerment.

After discussing the greenfield setup, let us consider our **Please Help Yourself** (**PHY**). All these building blocks can be created as a completely new green field setup alongside the existing toolchain. Alternatively, each block can be viewed as an independent entity. We can then decide whether to opt for a greenfield setup of that building block, optimize the existing toolchain to integrate it into the target platform, or purchase an off-the-shelf component that perfectly suits our needs. Implementing self-serve DevOps is a journey that should be planned and executed based on organizational culture, available budget, the learning curve required for successful adoption, and, most importantly, alignment from the developer community.

A comprehensive self-service DevOps (PHY) platform can empower developers with a wide range of tools and services while ensuring compliance and observability. Refer to the following figure:

PHY (Self-Serviced DevOps Platform)

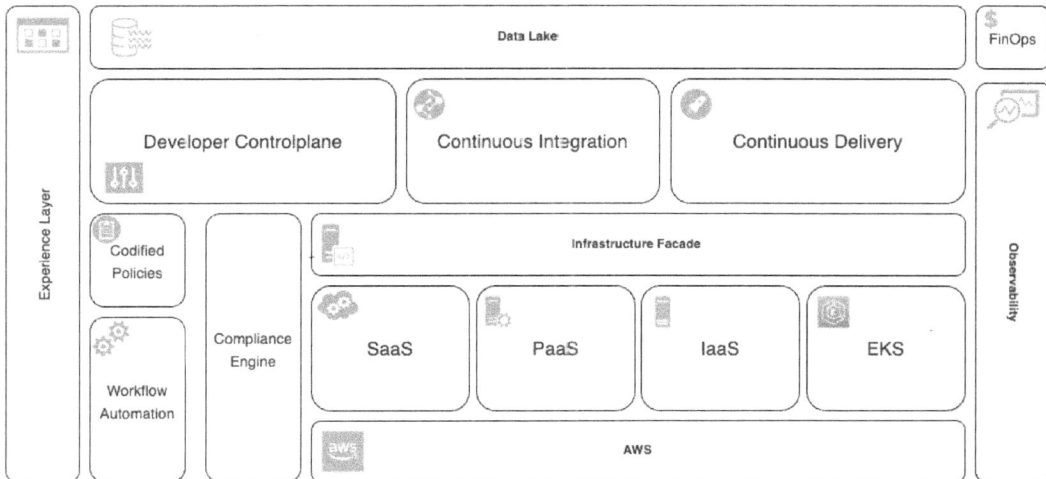

Figure 8.9: A self-service developer platform

Bottom-up approach

The bottom-up approach to self-service DevOps empowers individual development teams to a culture of experimentation and innovation, allowing developers to choose the tools and workflows that best suit them. While this approach can boost developer satisfaction and agility, it is important to be mindful of potential challenges like fragmentation and inconsistencies across teams. Let us discuss the following benefits, drawbacks, and key considerations of this grassroots approach to self-service DevOps:

- **Incremental adoption approach:** Encourages a strategic and methodical approach for upgrading or changing an organization's tools and practices. By utilizing iterations, the organization can effectively manage change, ensuring stability and enabling adjustments based on feedback and evolving needs. This method reduces disruptions and risks linked with large-scale transformations. The transition comprises multiple iterations, with each iteration progressively transforming into different components.

  The process is segmented into several iterations (Iteration 1, Iteration 2, Iteration 3, ..., Iteration N), illustrating a step-by-step approach to transformation. The blue wrench and screwdriver icon symbolize the current state, indicating existing tools or methods. The green version of the same icon represents the goal state, indicating the desired future setup or tools. In each iteration, specific components are shifted from the current state to the target state. For example, in Iteration 2, CI and CD are portrayed in green, indicating that these components have been shifted to the new setup.

The following figure progresses with subsequent iterations, gradually converting all components to the target state:

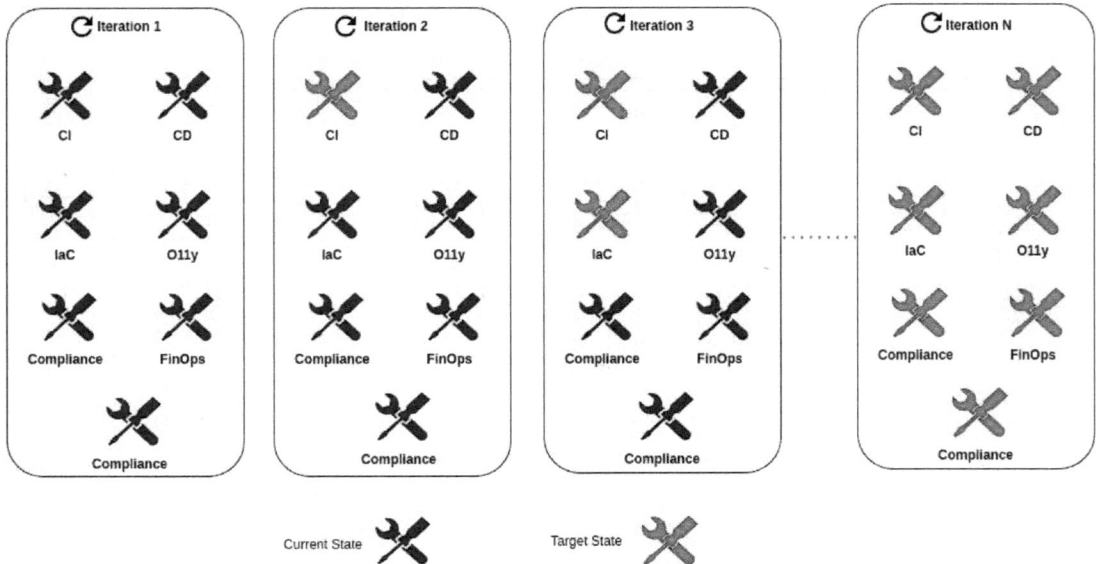

Figure 8.10: An iterative development for IDP

- **Toolchain orchestration:** Orchestration of the toolchain involves bringing together and managing different development tools and workflows to establish a smooth and effective software development lifecycle. It requires synchronizing the various phases of software development, from creating code to deployment and monitoring, using a unified set of tools and methodologies. This improves productivity, ensures uniformity, and speeds up the delivery of high-quality software. Orchestration combines different tools into a coherent workflow. For example, a commit to a version control system such as Git can initiate a CI pipeline that encompasses building the application, running tests, and deploying to a staging environment. Automation is crucial for toolchain orchestration. Automated pipelines reduce the necessity for manual involvement, expediting the development process and minimizing errors. By automating repetitive tasks and guaranteeing seamless integration, orchestration heightens the efficiency of the development process.

The following figure shows a toolchain orchestration depicting the interconnections between various tools and components in a software development and IT operations environment, specifically highlighting a scenario **without an orchestrator**. Each tool or component is independently linked to the CI Tool, forming a web of interconnected systems that work together without an orchestrator to manage or streamline the interactions. This setup results in the complexity and potential challenges of managing these connections manually or without a central orchestration mechanism:

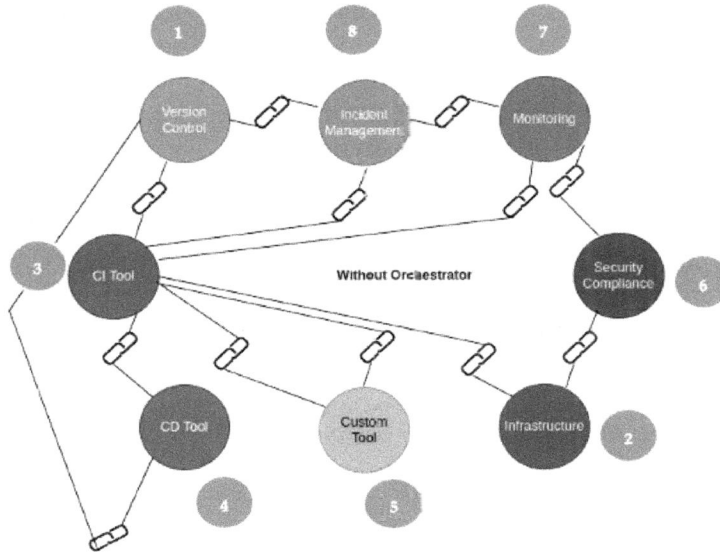

Figure 8.11: *Toolchain orchestration for IDP*

Figure 8.12 shows a toolchain orchestration like the previous one, but introduces an **orchestrator** into the setup. The orchestrator acts as an intermediary, centralizing and managing the interactions between various tools and components. This central orchestration mechanism simplifies and streamlines the communication and coordination between the different tools and components, reducing complexity and improving efficiency. The orchestrator ensures that each tool can integrate seamlessly, facilitating a more cohesive and manageable system architecture:

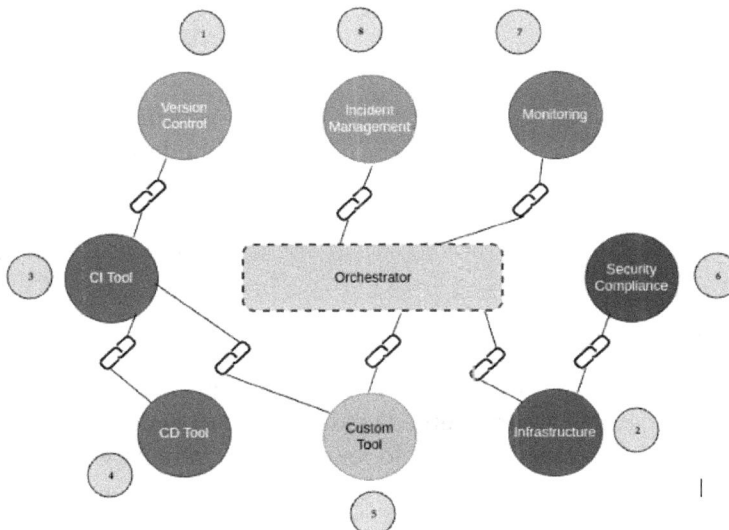

Figure 8.12: *A toolchain orchestration for IDP*

Here, self-service DevOps implementations can be categorized into four main approaches: top-down (centralized control, standardized tools), bottom-up (decentralized, developer-driven), facade layer (simplified interface to existing tools), and greenfield setup (building a new platform). Each approach has trade-offs in complexity, speed, cost, control, and flexibility. The following table shows the comparison of a few approaches discussed in the chapter:

Feature	Top-down	Bottom-up	Facade layer	Greenfield setup
Complexity	High (initial setup), Low (ongoing)	Low (initial setup), High (ongoing)	Medium	High
Speed	Slow (initial setup), Fast (ongoing)	Fast (initial setup), Slow (ongoing)	Medium	Slow (initial setup), Fast (ongoing)
Cost	High (initial investment), Low (ongoing)	Low (initial investment), High (ongoing)	Medium	High (initial investment), Low (ongoing)
Control	High	Low	Medium	High
Consistency	High	Low	Medium	High
Flexibility	Low	High	Medium	High
Maintainability	High	Low	Medium	High
Scalability	High	Low	Medium	High
Developer satisfaction	Medium	High	Medium	High
Best for	Large organizations, strict governance	Small, agile teams, rapid innovation	Gradual modernization, existing tools	New platforms, significant change

Table 8.4: Key differences between self-service DevOps approaches

Most used workflows

Figure 8.10 shows a detailed flowchart of the different phases involved in software development and IT operations as perceived by developers. Let us consider a representative list of the journeys undertaken by developers. A comprehensive self-service DevOps platform should streamline the entire software development lifecycle, from onboarding new developers to managing infrastructure:

- **Onboarding**: The journey commences with **onboarding**, encompassing tasks like new developer orientation, setting up workstations, managing access and privileges, documentation, and training.

  Although there can be several factors such as complexity of setup, maturity of DevOps practices, size of the organization, and tooling platform, the organization still reduces setup time for user onboarding between 20% and 80%.

- **Creating artifacts**: After onboarding, the **artifact creation** phase covers repository establishment, template creation for pipelines, implementation of guardrails, ensuring artifact security, and setting up artifact servers. These automated workflows can help in the reduction of 70% to 80% of time for the organizations, depending on the factors cited previously. For example:

Task	Manual time (hours)	Automated time (hours)	Time saved (hours)
Repository establishment	4	0.5	3.5
Pipeline template creation	8	2	6
Guardrail implementation	12	4	8
Artifact security setup	6	1	5
Artifact server setup	10	1.5	8.5
Total	40	9	31

Table 8.5: Time-saving in artifact creation by automation workflows

- **Deploying releases**: The subsequent phase, **releasing deployments**, includes deployment processes, feature toggle management, database operations, rollbacks, and workload management. These automated workflows can help reduce 70% to 80% time for the organizations. For example:

Task	Manual time (hours)	Automated time (hours)	Time saved (hours)
Deployment execution	4	0.5	3.5
Feature toggle mgmt	6	1	5
Database operations	8	2	6
Rollback execution	12	0.5	11.5
Workload management	4	1	3
Total	34	5	29

Table 8.6: Time-saving in deployment releases by automation workflows

- **Managing infrastructure**: **Infrastructure management** is the next stage, concentrating on infrastructure provisioning, configuration management, managing certificates, and handling secrets management. Optimizing **infrastructure management** is crucial for efficiency. The following table highlights the significant time savings achieved by automating various infrastructure tasks, from provisioning to secrets management, demonstrating a clear advantage over manual processes:

Task	Manual time (hours)	Automated time (hours)	Time saved (hours)
Infrastructure prov	24	2	22
Configuration mgmt	16	4	12
Certificate mgmt.	8	1	7
Secrets management	4	0.5	3.5
Total	52	7.5	44.5

Table 8.7: Time-saving in managing infrastructure by automation workflows

- **Monitoring and operations**: The final phase, **monitoring and operations**, encompasses log management, capturing metrics, analyzing TCO, ensuring service security, and publishing. Automated workflow can help the organization reduce the MTTR by approximately 80%.

The following figure highlights the platform engineering from onboarding new developers to managing infrastructure and ongoing operations:

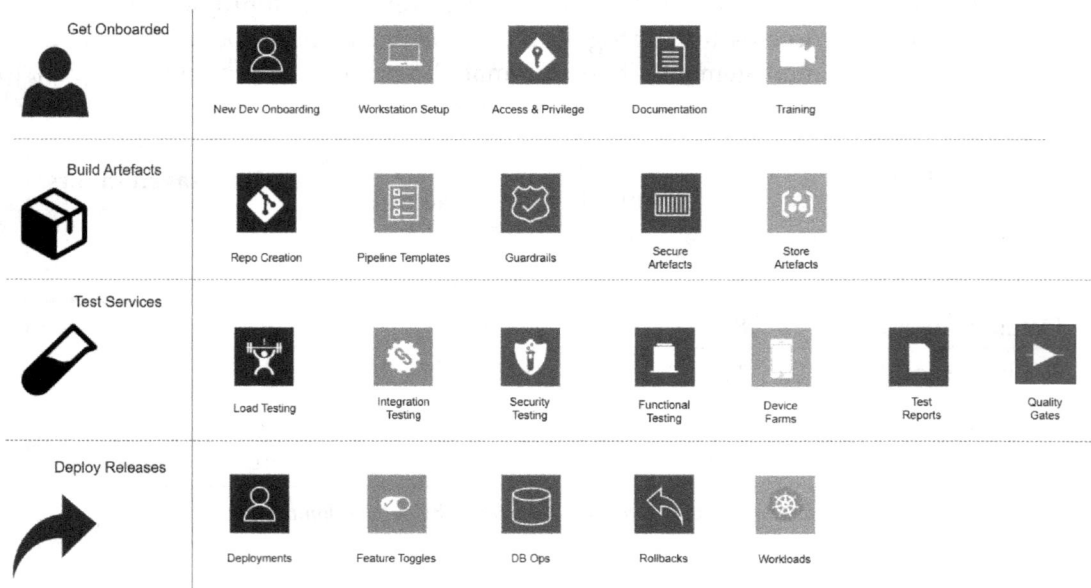

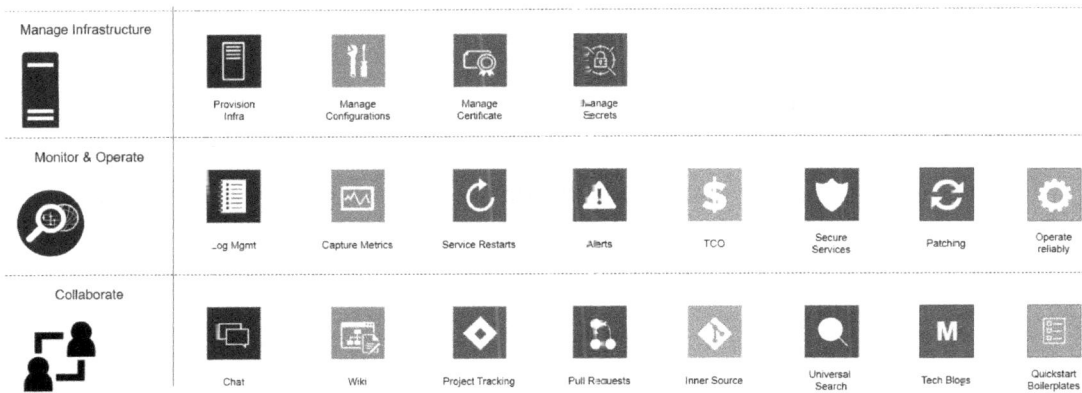

Figure 8.13: Platform engineering toolset for different SDLC stages

When an organization is moving towards a platform engineering culture with self-service DevOps, one approach is to identify key journeys that can significantly enhance the developer experience and productivity across the development community. According to the *Pareto principle*, only 20% of such journeys will be utilized 80% of the time. Enabling self-service for these 20% of journeys will yield a better return on investment compared to attempting to solve all the problems at once.

Conclusion

The chapter explores how self-service DevOps can transform modern software development. It emphasizes the significance of a well-organized implementation strategy, appropriate governance, and a supportive culture. By providing development teams with the necessary tools and independence, organizations can attain increased agility, effectiveness, and innovation in their software delivery procedures. Besides this, this chapter explored various implementation approaches, including top-down, bottom-up, facade layers, and greenfield setups, each with its trade-offs and considerations. By carefully evaluating these approaches and addressing potential challenges like security risks and tool sprawl, organizations can effectively implement self-service DevOps to optimize their software delivery lifecycle.

Modernizing legacy applications is a complex task, and choosing the right approach is crucial for success. A greenfield setup combined with a facade layer offers a compelling strategy, balancing risk and reward. This approach allows development teams to build new functionalities using modern technologies in a separate codebase (the **greenfield**) while the facade layer acts as a bridge, seamlessly integrating these new features with the existing legacy system. This enables a gradual, iterative migration, minimizing disruption to ongoing operations and allowing for continuous delivery of value. Starting with a well-defined pilot project focused on a specific set of functionalities is highly recommended. This pilot serves as a proof-of-concept, validating the chosen approach and allowing teams to refine their processes before tackling a full-scale migration.

In the next chapter, we will shift our focus to productization and collaboration using platform engineering.

Exercises

1. What is the approach you would choose if you were to provide a single interface that can offer a seamless experience across a diverse set of tools and processes?

2. What are the challenges if you plan to perform toolchain orchestration without a central orchestrator?

3. What does the PHY model stand for?

4. Which control plane is built for developer experience?

5. Which control plan helps in customer experience?

Answers

1. Facade layer.

2. Without a central orchestrator, the setup will be very complex, posing challenges in managing these connections manually or without a central orchestration mechanism.

3. **Please Help Yourself** (**PHY**), where all features are available to the developer in self-service mode.

4. Developer control plane.

5. Monitoring and observability.

References

1. *DORA Report: Google Cloud DevOps Research:* **https://cloud.google.com/devOps**

2. *Self Service Portal:* **https://Backstage.io/**

3. *IaC Tool:* **https://www.pulumi.com/**

    https://aws.amazon.com/cloudformation/

4. **https://mermaid.live/** *for generating code as a diagram*

CHAPTER 9
Productization and Collaboration

Introduction

The field of software development has experienced rapid change, resulting in frequent releases and multiple daily deployments now being considered standard practice across organizations. Platform engineering represents a significant advancement; it is a discipline that bridges development, operations, and infrastructure. Platforms have transitioned from simple tool collections to foundational components of modern software delivery, empowering organizations to build, deploy, and scale applications with speed and reliability. However, the success of these platforms relies on their technical capabilities, and their perception and management within the organization: **productization** and **collaboration** are critical.

Productization involves treating platforms as products by having dedicated roadmaps, user-centric design, and continuous improvement cycles. This ensures that the platform evolves according to the needs of its users, typically developers and operations teams rely on it to deliver high-quality software.

By adopting a product mindset, platform teams can create functional, intuitive, reliable, and scalable systems, driving greater adoption and user satisfaction. Collaboration connects platform teams to the rest of the organization. In the age of DevOps and agile methodologies, collaboration between development, operations, security, and platform teams is crucial for developing platforms that meet the organization's needs. This chapter explores the dynamics of productization and collaboration within platform engineering and how platforms can be turned into products that deliver tangible value to users. It looks at how collaboration across teams unlocks this potential. From the technical aspects of designing scalable platforms to the cultural shifts needed to break down silos, this chapter helps organizations enhance their platform engineering practices.

Structure

The chapter covers the following topics:

- Productization in platform engineering
- Technical aspects of productization
- Collaborations in platform engineering
- Cultural and organizational differences
- Challenges and solutions
- Measuring KPIs
- Cultural and organizational differences

Objectives

By the end, readers will have a deeper understanding of how to create, manage, and scale platforms as products that not only meet but exceed the expectations of their users. This chapter will provide an interlink between and details of productization and collaboration in achieving secure platform engineering. It highlights the importance of treating platform components as products, complete with defined APIs, documentation, and SLAs, to enhance efficiency and reusability. It also addresses the cultural and organizational factors that influence collaboration, offering strategies to foster a shared responsibility for security across different teams. By combining practical solutions with real-world examples and measurable KPIs, this chapter provides a roadmap for organizations to build and scale secure platforms through effective productization and collaborative efforts.

Productization in platform engineering

In the context of traditional software development, platforms have frequently been viewed as a set of tools and services designed to address specific, immediate requirements. These tools are usually created independently and with a narrow focus, often solving a particular issue or facilitating a specific procedure. Following deployment, these tools or services typically receive minimal maintenance, with attention given only when there are issues or when a critical update is necessary. While this method is functional, it often leads to inconsistent, fragmented user experiences and platforms that do not adapt to their users' evolving needs.

Need for platform as a product mindset

The concept of **platform as a product** represents a significant shift in thinking, transforming internal platforms from static tools into evolving products that consistently cater to the needs of their users, primarily developers, operations, and other technical teams.

Like any consumer-oriented product, a platform viewed through the product lens undergoes continuous development, iteration, and enhancement:

- It is driven by a clear vision, managed through a roadmap, and evaluated based on its capacity to meet user needs and generate business value.

- Transitioning from treating platforms as one-time tools to continuously maintained products necessitates a fundamental shift in the approach of platform teams. Rather than exclusively focusing on addressing immediate technical challenges, teams must embrace a **long-term outlook**, perceiving the **platform as a dynamic entity** that evolves.

One of the very good examples is Spotify's Backstage for treating a **DevOps platform as a product** that transformed developer productivity and organizational efficiency. The key to the development of Backstage was adopting a product mindset and fostering a community-driven ecosystem. This led to the creation of a platform by Spotify that not only solved its internal challenges but also became a valuable product across the globe. Here are some of the insights into how Spotify treated **Backstage as a Product**:

- **Product mindset**: Backstage was developed with a clear focus on the end users (developers). The product team gathered feedback from engineering teams to prioritize features and improvements.

- **Dedicated team**: A dedicated platform engineering team was responsible for building, maintaining, and evolving Backstage. This team was responsible for defining the roadmap, sprints, and user research.

- **Iterative development**: Backstage was rolled out incrementally, starting with a few teams and gradually expanding across Spotify. The feedback loop was followed, and continuous improvements were made.

- **Metrics and KPIs**: The product team tracked metrics such as developer productivity, time-to-market, and platform adoption to measure the success of Backstage. These metrics helped in the future investment of the product.

This platform as a product approach built a Backstage portal and benefited a large number of organizations across the globe by adopting Backstage as a self-service portal.

Long-term vision

A productized platform is constructed with a long-term vision in focus:

- This vision is typically aligned with the broader objectives of the organization, guaranteeing that the platform not only caters to current needs but is also scalable and adaptable to future requirements.

- Roadmaps play a critical role in managing platform development. These roadmaps describe the planned evolution of the platform, encompassing new features, enhancements, and integrations, and are regularly updated based on user feedback and shifting priorities.

User-centric design and approach

Treating a platform as a product involves placing its users at the forefront, and keeping their needs and user-centric design is the key approach for **platform as a product**. Some of the considerations are:

- This signifies that the experiences of developers, operations, and other stakeholders are central to the decision-making processes. Continuous feedback loops are established to ensure that the platform effectively meets user needs.

- Regularly collecting and analyzing feedback enables the platform team to prioritize improvements and promptly address any emerging issues or new requirements.

- To ensure the success of a platform as a product, it should closely meet the requirements of its users. In platform engineering, the primary users are usually internal teams like developers, operations, security, and at times, external partners or customers.

- The first step in aligning platform objectives with user needs is to fully comprehend the different user personas that engage with the platform. This not only involves understanding their technical needs but also their workflows, pain points, and objectives. For instance, developers may require a platform that facilitates quick and reliable deployments, while operations teams might prioritize monitoring, security, and scalability. Grasping these varied needs assists in developing a platform that is adaptable and user-friendly.

Regular interaction with users is crucial to ensure the platform progresses in a manner that continues to fulfill their needs. This can be achieved through:

- Direct communication channels
- User feedback surveys
- Beta testing of new features
- Regular review meetings

By involving users in the development process, platform teams can anticipate needs, pinpoint potential issues before they arise, and ensure that the platform remains in line with its users' changing requirements.

Continuous maintenance

Unlike one-time tools, which are often neglected after initial use, a productized platform benefits from continuous investment. This dedication manifests in several key areas:

- **Ongoing investment**: Resources are consistently allocated for maintenance, security patches, and performance enhancements, guaranteeing the platform's long-term viability.

- **Proactive maintenance**: Updates are not merely reactive fixes; they encompass regular improvements to usability, scalability, and integration, ensuring the platform evolves with changing needs.

- **Security improvements**: Regular security updates address vulnerabilities, safeguarding the platform and its users from potential threats.

- **Performance optimization**: Continuous fine-tuning ensures the platform operates efficiently and effectively, delivering a consistent and reliable user experience.

- **Resilience and relevance**: Through these sustained efforts, the platform maintains its resilience and relevance, avoiding outdated and providing lasting value.

This ensures that the platform remains resilient and pertinent over time.

Loosely coupled architecture

The adoption of microservices and toolchain architecture, breaking down applications, tools, and services into smaller, loosely coupled services, aligned well with self-serve DevOps principles, enabling teams:

- Independently develop, deploy, and scale their services, fostering autonomy and agility.

- This will help with the easier adoption of the platform and make the end users see the entire orchestration as a single product

- This also helps in achieving faster evolution with the change in needs and technology.

User needs vs. organization goals trade-off

Balancing user needs with the organization's broader goals is essential:

- Strategic decisions may need to be made about which features to prioritize based on their potential impact on the business.

- A key aspect of effective product management is making trade-offs between different user needs and aligning these decisions with the organization's long-term strategy. For example, enhancing security might be given priority over improving usability if security is a crucial organizational objective.

Data-driven decisions

Aligning platform goals with user needs often necessitates a data-driven approach:

- By monitoring how users engage with the platform, analyzing performance metrics, and tracking adoption rates, platform teams can make informed decisions about where to direct their efforts.

- Data-driven insights help identify the most valuable features to users, any functionality gaps, and how the platform can be enhanced to better serve its users.

Cultural shift toward empowerment

The **platform as a product** approach signifies a cultural shift that empowers development and operations teams by fostering a collaborative and innovative environment. Key aspects of this approach include:

- **Empowerment**: Providing teams with the tools, autonomy, and resources they need to take ownership of their work.

- **Culture of ownership**: Encouraging teams to take responsibility for the entire lifecycle of their services, from development to deployment and maintenance.

- **Autonomy**: Enabling teams to make decisions and innovate without excessive dependencies on centralized teams.

- **Continuous improvement**: Promoting iterative development, feedback loops, and a mindset of constant learning and optimization.

- **Innovation**: Creating an environment where teams are encouraged to experiment, take risks, and drive creative solutions.

This approach not only enhances productivity but also builds a sense of accountability and collaboration across the organization.

Embedded security and compliance

From the perspective of the **platform as a product**, the platform's lifecycle incorporates security and compliance, aiming at proactive risk management and continuous adherence to regulations. Important elements involve:

- Integrating security into the architecture from the outset and automating compliance checks during development. This strategy utilizes automation in CI or CD pipelines to continually scan for security issues and verify compliance, ensuring the early identification of vulnerabilities.

- Components of the platform, such as microservices and **application programming interfaces (APIs)**, are protected through authentication and encryption. **Role-based access control (RBAC)** is used to enforce least privilege access. Monitoring tools are integrated to detect and respond to security and compliance issues in real-time.

- A DevSecOps culture fosters collaboration between development, operations, and security teams, ensuring that security is a shared responsibility. By offering self-service security and compliance tools, platform users can easily configure settings and manage risks. Built-in auditability guarantees platform transparency and automatic generation of compliance reports.

Overall, this approach promotes faster, more secure delivery, cost reduction, and increased user trust.

Technical aspects of productization

We have already touched upon the benefits of productization at the start of this chapter. We will explore the concept of **everything as code or service**:

- This emphasizes managing and provisioning all platform components through code or APIs, enabling automation, consistency, and scalability.

- Furthermore, we will examine how integrating workflows into the platform can streamline processes and enhance collaboration across teams. By automating key features and functionalities, we can create a self-service platform that empowers diverse users, such as developers, to easily access and utilize resources with minimal friction, ultimately improving their experience.

Approaches

When it comes to platform engineering, it is essential to create systems that are strong, scalable, and simple to maintain. Achieving these objectives often involves embracing architectural principles like modularity and microservices, which naturally support adaptability and scalability:

- **Scalability and adaptability**: These principles allow platform teams to create platforms that can grow with the organization, adapt to changing requirements, and remain resilient amidst complexity.

- **Modular design**: Platforms are built as a collection of distinct, self-contained modules, each handling specific functions or groups of functions. Unlike monolithic systems, where all functions are tightly integrated into a single, often cumbersome system, modular platforms are more flexible and manageable.

- **Independent development and maintenance**: By dividing the platform into smaller, independent modules, teams can develop, test, and maintain each component separately, reducing the risk of system-wide issues.

- **Focused effort**: Teams can concentrate on individual modules without worrying about the broader impact on the entire platform, improving efficiency and innovation.

One of the most significant decisions in platform engineering, and indeed in any area of software development, is whether to purchase a solution off the shelf or develop it in-house. This **buy vs. build** dilemma has significant implications for time, cost, flexibility, and long-term maintenance. Making the correct choice requires careful consideration of the organization's objectives, technical capabilities, resources, and the specific requirements of the platform.

Buying a solution entails acquiring or subscribing to an existing product or service that meets the organization's needs. Some of the benefits include speed to market, cost efficiency, reduced risk, and focusing on core competencies rather than reinventing the wheel.

Developing a solution in-house involves creating a custom product tailored to the organization's specific needs. Although this approach can be resource-intensive, it offers substantial advantages, including long-term cost savings, flexibility, customizability, and better control.

A hybrid approach of **buying a solution** and **customization** or **developing** some part of it helps the organizations most. For instance, they might purchase a core platform and build custom modules or extensions to meet specific needs. This approach combines the strengths of both strategies, enabling organizations to benefit from the speed and reliability of purchased solutions while still achieving the customization and control that come with building.

Everything as code or everything as a service

In the world of platform engineering and modern IT infrastructure, two significant paradigms are changing how organizations create, manage, and deliver technology:

Everything as code (**XaC**) and **everything as a service** (**XaaS**) are both concepts that are crucial for improving automation, flexibility, and scalability in IT environments. They are often interconnected, enabling organizations to achieve greater agility and efficiency.

- **Everything as code (XaC)**

  Extends **infrastructure as code** (**IaC**) principles to manage the **entire IT stack** (infrastructure, security, configurations, deployments) through code. This philosophy involves managing the entire technology stack, including infrastructure, security policies, configuration management, and application deployment through code.

- o **Key features**:

    - **Automation**: Scripted management reduces manual intervention.

    - **Version Control**: Track changes and enable rollbacks via tools like Git.

    - **Consistency**: Uniform environments (dev, staging, production) minimize errors.

Some examples of XaC are tools (Terraform, Ansible) for infrastructure, code-driven security policies (e.g., AWS IAM roles defined in YAML), and CI/CD pipelines (GitHub Action).

- **Everything as a service (XaaS)**

Delivers IT resources (infrastructure, platforms, software) **over the internet** via subscription models rather than through traditional on-premises hardware and software installations. XaaS includes various **service** models, such as **infrastructure as a service (IaaS)**, **platform as a service (PaaS)**, **software as a service (SaaS)**, and more. The platform engineering team can provide overlay services on top of traditional workflows involving multiple tools and make them available as services for consumption by users or downstream systems.

All companies get key advantages such as reduced overhead, scalability, and accessibility (e.g., **overlay services** abstracting complex workflows into consumable services).

XaC and XaaS often work together in modern IT environments:

- o **Automated provisioning**: XaC practices can be used to automate the provisioning, configuration, and management of cloud resources within XaaS environments. For example, IaC can ensure consistent and reproducible infrastructure deployments for IaaS resources.

- o **Consistent scalability**: By combining XaC and XaaS, organizations can achieve scalable and consistent environments that are easy to manage and adapt to changing business needs. For instance, a platform built using PaaS can be configured and managed entirely through code, ensuring consistent deployments across development, staging, and production environments.

- o **Agility and innovation**: The combination of XaC and XaaS enables organizations to innovate faster, respond quickly to market changes, and deploy new features and services with minimal friction. This is particularly important in highly competitive industries where time-to-market is critical.

- **Use cases of XaC and XaaS in practice**

The following are code examples to illustrate how XaC (e.g., IaC, CI/CD pipelines) and XaaS (e.g., Kubernetes, cloud services) work in practice:

o **IaC with Terraform**: Here, one of the team members is working on a new service and provisioning an AWS EC2 instance (IaaS resource) using Terraform (XaC):

```
# main.tf
terraform {
  required_providers {
    aws = {
      source  = "hashicorp/aws"
      version = "~> 4.0"
    }
  }
}

provider "aws" {
  region = "us-west-2"
}

resource "aws_instance" "web_server" {
  ami             = "ami-0c55b159cbfafe1f0" # Ubuntu 22.04 LTS
  instance_type = "t3.micro"
  tags = {
    Name = "XaC-UMS-Server"
  }
}
```

Code 9.1: IaC code to provision a server required in a developed service

The preceding code automates cloud infrastructure provisioning (XaaS) using Terraform code (XaC).

o The development team has created a small service to allow all users to log in to the portal, and now they need to deploy their microservice as a containerized app to Kubernetes (XaaS) via declarative YAML file (XaC):

```
# deployment.yaml

apiVersion: apps/v1
kind: Deployment
metadata:
  name: xac-user-management-app
spec:
  replicas: 3
```

```
  selector:
    matchLabels:
      app: xac-ums
  template:
    metadata:
      labels:
        app: xac-ums
    spec:
      containers:
      - name: nginx
        image: nginx:1.25
        ports:
        - containerPort: 80
---
# service.yaml
apiVersion: v1
kind: Service
metadata:
  name: xac-ums-service
spec:
  selector:
    app: xac-ums
  ports:
    - protocol: TCP
      port: 80
      targetPort: 80
  type: LoadBalancer
```

Code 9.2: YAML code to deploy the user management service to K8s

o   Now, the development team is automating the build, test, and deployment for a SaaS app using GitHub Action:

```
# .github/workflows/deploy.yml
name: Deploy to AWS

on:
  push:
    branches: [ "main" ]

jobs:
```

```
build-and-deploy:
  runs-on: ubuntu-latest
  steps:
    - name: Checkout code
      uses: actions/checkout@v4

    - name: Install dependencies
      run: npm install

    - name: Run tests
      run: npm test

    - name: Deploy to AWS S3 (Static Site)
      uses: aws-actions/configure-aws-credentials@v4
      with:
        aws-access-key-id: ${{ secrets.AWS_ACCESS_KEY_ID }}
        aws-secret-access-key: ${{ secrets.AWS_SECRET_ACCESS_
KEY }}
        aws-region: us-east-1
    - run: aws s3 sync ./dist s3://xac-demo-bucket –delete
```

Code 9.3: *GitHub Action code for build, test, and deploy*

o   Policy as code allows the development team to enforce policies declaratively:

```
# iam-policy.yaml
Version: "2012-10-17"
Statement:
  - Effect: Allow
    Action:
      - s3:GetObject
      - s3:PutObject
    Resource: "arn:aws:s3:::xac-ums-bucket/*"
```

Code 9.4: *Codification of IAM security policy*

The following summarizes the XaC and XaaS relationship:

Scenario	XaC tool	XaaS resource	Outcome
Spin up cloud servers	Terraform	AWS EC2 (IaaS)	Automated, repeatable infrastructure.

Deploy a microservice	Kubernetes YAML	Managed Kubernetes (PaaS)	Scalable, code-managed app environments.
Roll out a SaaS feature	GitHub Action	AWS S3 / SaaS endpoints	Zero-downtime deployments via pipelines.
Enforce security policies	IAM policy as code	Cloud IAM (XaaS)	Consistent governance across environments.

Table 9.1: Everything as a Code and service

Toolchain orchestration as workflows

As organizations expand and scale, self-service DevOps offers scalable solutions that can adapt to changing business needs and technological advancements. It allows seamless integration of new tools and technologies, supporting continuous improvement and adaptation.

In the world of platform engineering, efficiency is paramount. Developers need to move quickly, and anything that slows them down hinders innovation. That is where toolchain orchestration helps in the scalability of operations. By streamlining and automating the tools developers use daily, we can create a smoother, more productive experience.

The benefits of toolchain orchestration:

- **Increased speed:** Automated workflows eliminate manual handoffs and bottlenecks, accelerating everything from infrastructure provisioning to application deployments.

- **Empowered developers:** By providing self-service access to tools and resources, we reduce the cognitive load on developers, allowing them to focus on what they do best: writing code.

- **Operational stability:** Standardized, automated processes minimize errors and ensure consistency, leading to more reliable systems.

Examples of toolchain orchestration in platform engineering:

- **Infrastructure as code (IaC):** Workflows can automate the provisioning and management of infrastructure resources using tools like Terraform, Ansible, or Pulumi.

- **CI/CD pipelines:** Workflows can orchestrate the build, test, and deployment processes using tools like Jenkins, GitLab CI/CD, or GitHub Action.

- **Security and compliance:** Workflows can automate security scanning, vulnerability analysis, and compliance checks using tools like SonarQube, Snyk, or Burp for SAST or DAST scanning.

Code-driven toolchain orchestration examples

Code-driven toolchain empowers developers to provision resources, deploy applications, and manage workflows independently through automated, code-driven pipelines. Toolchain orchestration ties together tools (IaC, CI/CD, security scanners) into cohesive workflows, reducing manual toil and accelerating delivery.

IaC with Terraform

Automate cloud infrastructure provisioning (AWS S3 bucket) with Terraform:

```
# main.tf
terraform {
  required_providers {
    aws = { source = "hashicorp/aws", version = "~> 5.0" }
  }
}
provider "aws" {
  region = "us-east-1"
}
resource "aws_s3_bucket" "data_bucket" {
  bucket = "my-org-data-${var.environment}"
  tags   = { Environment = var.environment }
}
# Define variables for the environment (dev/prod)
variable "environment" {
  description = "Deployment environment (dev/staging/prod)"
  type        = string
}
```

Code 9.5: S3 bucket creation for dev, stage & prod environment

CI/CD pipeline with GitHub Action

The following are code examples to create build and deploy pipelines for a Python app:

```
# .github/workflows/pipeline.yml
name: Python App CI/CD
on:
  push:
    branches: [ "main" ]
jobs:
  build-and-test:
```

```
    runs-on: ubuntu-latest
    steps:
      - name: Checkout code
        uses: actions/checkout@v4
      - name: Setup Python
        uses: actions/setup-python@v4
        with:
          python-version: "3.11"
      - name: Install dependencies
        run: pip install -r requirements.txt
      - name: Run tests
        run: pytest
  deploy-to-ecs:
    needs: build-and-test
    runs-on: ubuntu-latest
    steps:
      - name: Deploy to AWS ECS
        uses: aws-actions/amazon-ecs-deploy-task-definition@v1
        with:
          task-definition: task-definition.json
          cluster: my-cluster
          service: my-service
```

Code 9.6: Build and deploy pipeline

Security automation with Snyk and GitHub Action

We can integrate Snyk into the CI/CD pipeline:

```
# Add this step to the CI/CD pipeline above
- name: Snyk Security Scan
  uses: snyk/actions/python@v3
  with:
    command: test
    args: --severity-threshold=high
  env:
    SNYK_TOKEN: ${{ secrets.SNYK_TOKEN }}
```

Code 9.7: Snyk integration

End-to-end workflow orchestration

Combine all tools into a unified pipeline:

- **Developers commit code**: Triggers GitHub Action.

- **Terraform provisions infrastructure**: For example, AWS ECS cluster.

- **Snyk scans for vulnerabilities**: Blocks the build if risks are found.

- **App deploys to ECS**: Post-deployment, run smoke tests.

This example covers the workflow: *Code | Build | Test | Secure | Deploy.*

End-to-end automation

Streamlining workflows, reducing manual intervention, and optimizing resource usage through automation and self-service capabilities lead to cost savings and improved operational efficiency, enabling organizations to achieve more with existing resources. Self-service DevOps breaks down traditional DevOps models' dependencies on centralized IT or operations teams for infrastructure provisioning and deployment. It enables cross-functional teams to work more autonomously and collaboratively.

The following are the benefits to the organizations:

- **Reduced operational costs:** By automating repetitive tasks and minimizing manual intervention, organizations can reduce the need for additional staff, minimize errors that lead to costly rework, and optimize resource allocation. This translates directly into lower operational costs and higher profit margins.

- **Improved resource utilization:** Automation ensures that resources are provisioned and utilized based on actual demand, preventing over-provisioning and waste. This efficient use of resources further contributes to cost savings and allows organizations to scale their operations without significant increases in expenditure.

- **Increased productivity and throughput:** Streamlined workflows and reduced manual handoffs accelerate various processes, enabling teams to complete tasks faster and serve more customers or clients efficiently. This increased throughput leads to higher productivity and potentially increased revenue generation.

Self-service DevOps further amplifies these benefits by breaking down the traditional dependencies on centralized IT or operations teams for infrastructure provisioning and deployment. This empowers cross-functional teams to:

- **Work autonomously:** Teams gain the freedom to manage their infrastructure and deployments without relying on a separate operations team, reducing bottlenecks and wait times. This autonomy fosters a sense of ownership and accountability within teams.

- **Increase collaboration:** Self-service capabilities promote collaboration by providing shared access to tools and resources. Teams can work together more effectively, share knowledge, and contribute to a more cohesive development process.

- **Accelerate innovation:** By removing operational barriers and empowering teams to work independently, self-service DevOps fosters a culture of experimentation and innovation. Teams can quickly test new ideas, iterate on solutions, and bring products to market faster.

In essence, streamlining workflows through automation and self-service capabilities not only leads to cost savings and improved operational efficiency but also creates a more agile and innovative organizational culture. This empowers organizations to thrive in today's dynamic and competitive landscape.

Security, compliance, and observability

The platform is equipped with embedded compliance mechanisms to ensure that it remains auditable at all times:

- Automatic generation of audit trails captures changes, access events, and compliance violations. These trails allow organizations to track and review platform activities in real-time, helping them adhere to internal policies and external regulations.

- Platforms with built-in reporting capabilities streamline compliance audits by automatically generating compliance reports, thereby saving time and reducing manual effort.

- Platforms designed with a focus on products often offer self-service capabilities for users, allowing them to configure security settings, manage compliance requirements, and monitor security risks. This ensures that platform users, such as developers, DevOps teams, and business units, can conveniently access and configure security and compliance features.

- Embedded observability tools continuously monitor the platform for security events, vulnerabilities, and compliance violations.

- These tools provide real-time visibility into platform operations, facilitating proactive detection and response to threats. By integrating security and compliance monitoring into the platform's observability stack, organizations can detect anomalies, flag compliance drift, and ensure that security policies are being actively enforced.

Let us break down security, compliance, and observability in platform engineering with practical examples and code snippets to illustrate how these principles are embedded into modern platforms. We will focus on actionable implementations like policy as code, audit logging, compliance automation, and observability integrations:

- **Security as code**: It enforces security policies using **Open Policy Agent** (**OPA**) for admission control in Kubernetes. The following example automatically blocks privileged containers or root-user pods in Kubernetes:

```
# security/policy.rego
package kubernetes.admission

deny[msg] {
  input.request.kind.kind == "Pod"
  not input.request.object.spec.securityContext.runAsNonRoot
  msg := "Pods must run as non-root users"
}

deny[msg] {
  input.request.kind.kind == "Pod"
  input.request.object.spec.containers[_].securityContext.privileged
  msg := "Privileged containers are not allowed"
}
```

Code 9.8: Security as code example

- **Compliance as code:** The following example makes sure that S3 buckets have encryption enabled as per PCI DSS and GDPR compliance requirements:

```
# checkov --framework terraform_plan -f terraform.plan
# Sample Checkov policy (YAML)
# compliance/checkov-policy.yaml
metadata:
name: "S3 Bucket Encryption Enforcement"
 id: "CKV_AWS_19"
category: "ENCRYPTION"
scope:
provider: "aws"
  resource_type: "aws_s3_bucket"
definition:
  cond_type: "attribute"
  resource_types: ["aws_s3_bucket"]
  attribute: "server_side_encryption_configuration"
  operator: "not_empty"
```

Code 9.9: Compliance as a code example

- **Audit trails and logging**: The following code example captures all AWS API activity (who, when, and what):

```
# audit/cloudtrail.tf
resource "aws_cloudtrail" "platform_audit" {
  name                         = "platform-audit-trail"
  s3_bucket_name               = aws_s3_bucket.audit_logs.id
  include_global_service_events = true
  is_multi_region_trail        = true
  enable_log_file_validation   = true
}

resource "aws_s3_bucket" "audit_logs" {
  bucket        = "platform-audit-logs-${var.env}"
  force_destroy = false
}
```

Code 9.10: Audit trail and logging example

- **Observability with security integration**: The following example detects suspicious login attempts using Prometheus alerts:

```
# observability/Prometheus-alerts.yaml
groups:
- name: security-alerts
rules:
- alert: ExcessiveFailedLogins
expr: rate(aws_cloudtrail_failed_login_events_total[5m]) > 5
    for: 10m
    labels:
      severity: critical
    annotations:
      summary: "Potential brute-force attack detected"
      description: "More than 5 failed logins per minute over 10
minutes."
```

Code 9.11: Security alerts as code integration in observability

By embedding security, compliance, and observability into the platform (via code and automation), organizations reduce risk, accelerate audits, and empower teams to innovate safely.

Collaborations in platform engineering

Effective collaboration is vital for successful platform engineering, enabling teams to streamline infrastructure management and foster innovation. By leveraging IaC tools, organizations can automate resource provisioning, ensuring consistency and scalability. In platform engineering, the choice of collaboration model significantly impacts team effectiveness. Various models, such as cross-functional teams, pod-based structures, matrix organizations, and platform product teams, are designed to optimize development and break down traditional silos. These models promote diverse perspectives, encourage ownership, and streamline communication, ultimately enhancing platform development and management. Several building blocks need to be in place to have a robust self-serve DevOps platform. Let us discuss them in detail.

Need for collaboration

Teams can use tools such as Terraform and CloudFormation to define and manage infrastructure using code, which automates the provisioning and configuration of resources, ensuring consistency and scalability. This method enables rapid infrastructure deployment, reduces configuration drift, and supports version control and auditability of infrastructure changes. Standardized IaC embedded with guardrails and gates is crucial as a first step to achieving self-service DevOps. It should align with the cloud governance framework followed by the respective organizations. These IaC modules ensure compliance and cost guardrails, easing the cognitive load on developers while managing the infrastructure lifecycle. Service catalog and approval flows can help managers monitor non-standard requests effectively. The following are a few examples of IaC modules that can be considered:

- Terraform modules
- AWS CloudFormation templates
- **Azure Resource Manager** (**ARM**) templates
- Pulumi component resources
- Ansible playbooks
- Helm charts

Collaboration models and techniques

In platform engineering, the collaboration model can significantly impact how effectively teams develop and manage the platform. The following are some common collaboration models for a product mindset in platform engineering:

- **Cross-functional teams**: Teams consist of members from different disciplines (for example, engineers, designers, and product managers) working together on the platform. To truly optimize platform development and break down traditional silos, we need to foster collaboration across different disciplines. This is where the power of cross-functional teams comes into play. Here are some benefits, tools, and techniques for cross-functional teams:

o **Benefits**: Promotes diverse perspectives, speeds up problem-solving, and enhances communication between different functions.

o **Tools:** Some of the best collaboration tools available for platform integration:

- Slack or Microsoft Teams for communication.

- Jira or Trello for task and project management.

- Confluence or notion for documentation.

o **Techniques:** Techniques to be used for productization and collaboration:

- Regular stand-ups and sprint planning meetings.

- Establish shared objectives to ensure all team members understand the product vision and their role in achieving it.

- Encourage team members to share their unique insights and expertise to enhance problem-solving and innovation.

- Cross-functional workshops and brainstorming sessions.

- Retrospectives to assess team performance and processes.

- **Pod-based model:** Teams are organized into pods, each responsible for a specific feature or service of the platform. Pods are typically small, autonomous, and cross-functional. Here are some benefits, different tools to be used, and techniques for the pod-based model:

  o **Benefits**: Encourages ownership, enables rapid iteration, and allows for more focused expertise.

  o **Tools:** Some of the best tools available for pods:

  - Asana or *Monday.com* for tracking pod-specific tasks and projects.

  - GitHub or GitLab for version control and collaboration on code.

  - Jenkins or Azure DevOps for continuous integration and deployment.

  o **Techniques**: Some of the guidelines and techniques for the pod-based model:

  - Clear pod objectives and ownership.

  - Give pods the freedom to make decisions while holding them accountable for their results.

  - Regular pod meetings to sync on the progress and challenges and avoid duplication of effort.

  - Cross-pod knowledge sharing sessions.

- **Matrix structure:** Team members report to both a functional manager and a project manager. Functional managers handle skill development, while project managers oversee the delivery of specific platform initiatives. Here are the benefits, tools, and techniques for matrix structure:

- o **Benefits**: Balances the need for specialized skills and project-focused execution.

- o **Tools:** Some of the tools to be used in matrix structure:
  - Smartsheet or Wrike for managing multiple reporting lines and project tasks.
  - Workday or SAP SuccessFactors for managing functional and project-based roles.

- o **Techniques:** Some of the techniques for matrix structure:
  - Defined roles and responsibilities for both functional and project managers.
  - Regular alignment meetings between functional and project managers.
  - Performance reviews that consider both functional expertise and project contributions.

- **Platform product teams:** Teams are organized around specific platform products or components. Each team is responsible for the lifecycle of their product, including development, maintenance, and support. Here are some benefits, tools and techniques for platform product teams:

  - o **Benefits**: Clear accountability for product success, streamlined communication, and easier alignment with business goals.

  - o **Tools**: Some of the tools to be used for platform product teams:
    - Productboard or Aha! for product management and roadmap planning.
    - JIRA or Azure DevOps for issue tracking and agile project management.

  - o **Techniques:** Some of the techniques to be used for platform product teams:
    - Product-specific roadmaps and **Objectives and Key Results (OKRs)**.
    - Regular product review meetings and customer feedback sessions.
    - End-to-end ownership of product lifecycle by the team.

- **Community of practice:** Groups of individuals with similar interests or expertise come together to share knowledge, and best practices, and collaborate on common challenges. Here are some benefits, tools, and techniques for community of practice:

  - o **Benefits**: Fosters knowledge sharing, innovation, and continuous improvement across teams.

  - o **Tools:** Some of the tools to be used for the community of practice:

- Discourse, MS Teams, or Slack communities for discussions and knowledge sharing.

- SharePoint, confluence, or GitHub Wiki for collaborative documentation.

o **Techniques**: Some of the techniques to be used for community of practice:

- Regular community meetups and knowledge-sharing sessions.

- Shared best practices and resource libraries.

- Encourage experienced members to mentor others, fostering growth and knowledge transfer.

- **Centralized vs. decentralized model**: Here is a comparison between the centralized and decentralized models:

o **Centralized**: A single team or group is responsible for the entire platform, making decisions and driving changes.

o **Decentralized**: Multiple teams or groups manage different aspects of the platform, with each having a degree of autonomy.

o **Benefits**: Centralized models can ensure consistency and coherence, while decentralized models can offer more flexibility and responsiveness.

o **Tools:** Here are some tools to be used for the centralized vs decentralized model:

- **Centralized**: ServiceNow or Atlassian suite for unified management and control.

- **Decentralized**: Kubernetes or Docker Swarm for managing multiple services across teams.

o **Techniques:** Here is a comparison of techniques for centralized vs. decentralized models:

- **For centralized**: Centralized planning and decision-making processes. Implement unified processes and decision-making frameworks to maintain consistency across the platform.

- **For decentralized**: Clear service boundaries and inter-team communication protocols. Define clear boundaries and communication protocols to ensure that teams can operate independently while still coordinating effectively.

- **DevOps and agile integration:** Teams adopt DevOps practices and agile methodologies to enhance collaboration, speed up delivery, and improve platform reliability. Here are the benefits, tools, and techniques for DevOps and agile integration:

- o **Benefits**: Streamlined workflows, faster feedback loops, and enhanced collaboration between development and operations.

- o **Tools:** Here are some of the recommended tools:

  - GitLab or Bitbucket for version control and CI or CD pipelines.

  - Jira or Azure DevOps for agile project management and tracking.

  - Docker and Kubernetes for containerization and orchestration.

- o **Techniques:** Here are some recommended techniques:

  - CI and CD practices.

  - Agile sprints and iterative development.

  - DevOps metrics and monitoring for continuous improvement.

- **External partnerships:** Collaboration with external vendors, partners, or open-source communities to extend platform capabilities or integrate third-party services. Here are some of the benefits, tools, and techniques:

  - o **Benefits**: Access to additional resources, expertise, and innovation.

  - o **Tools**: Here are some of the recommended tools:

    - Zapier or Integromat for integrating third-party services.

    - Postman for API testing and integration.

  - o **Techniques**: Here are some of the recommended techniques:

    - Hold joint workshops and planning sessions to align on goals and address any challenges.

    - Define clear contracts and SLAs to set expectations and manage relationships effectively.

    - Regularly test integrations with external services to ensure compatibility and performance.

Choosing the right model often depends on the organization's size, goals, and existing culture. A combination of these models may also be used to address different aspects of platform engineering.

Challenges and solutions

Collaboration in platform engineering can face several challenges, but understanding these issues and implementing effective solutions can significantly enhance team effectiveness and project success. The following are some common collaboration challenges and their solutions:

- **Misalignment:** Team members with varying objectives or priorities can cause conflicts and inefficiencies. It is important to set and communicate clear, shared goals and objectives for the entire team using OKRs or KPIs. Holding workshops to align team members on goals, priorities, and expectations is essential. Regular review meetings should be conducted to evaluate progress toward goals and make necessary adjustments to priorities.

- **Resistance to change:** Resistance from team members towards changes in processes, tools, or structures can hinder collaboration and adoption. Establish a structured change management process encompassing communication, training, and support. Involve team members in the change process to gather feedback and address concerns. Clearly articulate the advantages of changes and how they align with team and organizational objectives.

Measuring KPIs

Measuring the impact of productization and collaboration requires tangible metrics. Here are some examples of KPIs that provide valuable insights.

- **Developer satisfaction:** At the heart of a successful platform is a positive developer experience. We prioritize understanding how developers perceive our platform, ensuring it empowers them to work efficiently and effectively. To achieve this, we actively collect feedback through surveys and direct interactions, focusing on key aspects that impact their satisfaction.

  o **Measurement methods:**

    ▪ **Surveys:**

      ❖ **Net Promoter Score (NPS):** Ask developers how likely they are to recommend the platform to a colleague.

      ❖ **Customized surveys:** Include questions about ease of use, documentation quality, support responsiveness, and overall experience. Use Likert scales (e.g., 1-5, strongly disagree to strongly agree).

      ❖ **Example questions:**

        1. How satisfied are you with the platform's reliability?
        2. How easy is it to find the documentation you need?
        3. How responsive is the platform support team?

    ▪ **Feedback sessions:**

      ❖ Regularly scheduled feedback sessions with development teams.

> ❖ Office hours where developers can directly interact with the platform team.

- **Usage data analysis:**
  - ❖ Analyze patterns in platform usage. For example, are developers consistently using specific features or avoiding others?
  - ❖ Analyze support ticket volume and resolution times.

Some specific examples are as follows:

o **NPS score:** Track changes in NPS over time to gauge overall satisfaction.

o **Average satisfaction score:** Calculate the average score for each survey question to identify areas for improvement.

o **Support ticket resolution time:** Measure the average time it takes to resolve support tickets.

- **Platform adoption:** To assess the platform's reach and effectiveness, we track a range of usage and adoption metrics. These measurements provide concrete data on how widely the platform is utilized and how efficiently new services are integrated.

  o **Measurement methods:**

    - **Usage metrics:**
      - ❖ Number of active users.
      - ❖ Number of deployments through the platform.
      - ❖ Number of services onboarded to the platform.
      - ❖ Frequency of feature usage.

    - **Onboarding rate:**
      - ❖ Track the time it takes for new teams or services to onboard to the platform.
      - ❖ Measure the completion rate of onboarding processes.

    - **Feature adoption rate:** Track the percentage of users who adopt new platform features.

    - **API usage:** Track the number of calls to the platform APIs.

Some specific examples are as follows:

o **Percentage of teams using the platform:** Track the percentage of development teams that have adopted the platform.

o **Number of deployments per month:** Monitor the number of deployments made through the platform to assess adoption and usage.

    o **Time to onboard a new service:** Measure the time it takes for a new service to be successfully onboarded to the platform.

- **Deployment frequency:** A key indicator of our platform's effectiveness is the speed and reliability with which we can deploy changes. We measure this through CI/CD pipeline metrics, release cadence, and automation levels, providing insights into our deployment frequency.

    o **Measurement methods:**

        ▪ **CI/CD pipeline metrics:**

            ❖ Track the number of deployments per day, week, or month.

            ❖ Measure the time between deployments.

        ▪ **Release cadence:** Monitor the frequency of software releases.

        ▪ **Automation metrics:** Track the percentage of deployments that are fully automated.

Specific examples are as follows:

    o **Deployments per day or week:** Track the average number of deployments per day or week to assess the frequency of releases.

    o **Lead time for changes:** Measure the time it takes for a code change to go from commit to production.

    o **Deployment success rate:** Track the percentage of deployments that are successful without requiring rollbacks.

- **Using metrics to drive continuous improvement**: To effectively utilize the data gathered from our KPI measurements, we implement a comprehensive continuous improvement framework. This framework encompasses the following key steps:

    o **Establish baseline metrics:**

        ▪ Start by establishing baseline metrics to understand the current state of the platform.

        ▪ Regularly track these metrics to identify trends and changes over time.

    o **Identify areas for improvement:**

        ▪ Analyze the metrics to identify areas where the platform is performing below expectations.

        ▪ For example, low developer satisfaction scores or low feature adoption rates may indicate areas that need attention.

    o **Prioritize improvements:**

        ▪ Prioritize improvements based on their potential impact on developer satisfaction, platform adoption, and deployment frequency.

- Focus on improvements that will have the greatest positive impact.

o **Implement changes and monitor results:**

  - Implement changes to the platform based on the identified areas for improvement.

  - Continuously monitor the metrics to assess the impact of the changes.

o **Iterate and refine:**

  - Use the data to iterate and refine the platform over time.

  - Continuously seek feedback from developers and other stakeholders.

o **Set goals and targets:**

  - Set realistic goals and targets for each KPI.

  - For example, increase developer satisfaction by 10% or reduce deployment lead time by 20%.

  - Celebrate when goals are achieved.

o **Create feedback loops:** Ensure that there are good feedback loops in place. Use the metrics to drive conversations with the development teams and to inform future platform development.

By using these metrics and following these steps, platform engineering teams can create a culture of continuous improvement and deliver a platform that meets the needs of its users.

Cultural and organizational differences

Teams from different departments or locations may possess distinct cultures, practices, and expectations. Provide training to enhance understanding of diverse team cultures and practices. Cultivate an inclusive environment where diverse perspectives are esteemed and taken into consideration. Implement standardized processes and practices to promote consistency across teams.

Conflicting priorities

Coordinating tasks and projects across multiple teams or pods can be intricate and susceptible to duplication or gaps. Maintain a centralized roadmap outlining key milestones and dependencies to effectively coordinate efforts. Conduct regular meetings between teams to synchronize activities and address any coordination issues or conflicting priorities.

Technical integration issues

Integration of different systems, tools, or technologies might be challenging and could affect collaboration. Utilize standardized APIs and integration platforms to simplify connections between systems. Implement thorough testing and validation processes to ensure integrations function as intended. Maintain detailed documentation of integration processes and interfaces to facilitate troubleshooting and future updates. Maintaining flexibility in approach can help correct any initial assumptions going wrong and converge on the path to the desired state.

Cognitive load

Teams might feel overwhelmed by excessive information, leading to confusion and decreased productivity. Use prioritization techniques to concentrate on critical information and tasks. Implement tools and procedures to filter and organize information to reduce clutter. Conduct regular reviews to ensure that information and tasks are relevant and up-to-date.

By addressing these challenges with targeted solutions, teams can improve collaboration, enhance productivity, and achieve better outcomes in platform engineering projects.

Platform as a service in large-scale enterprises

PaaS has become a cornerstone of digital transformation in large-scale enterprises, evolving beyond basic application hosting to a robust ecosystem enabling rapid innovation, scalability, and cross-functional collaboration.

- Modern PaaS offerings integrate cutting-edge technologies like Kubernetes-driven container orchestration, serverless computing (e.g., AWS Lambda, Azure Functions), and AI/MLOps pipelines (e.g., Kubeflow, SageMaker) to streamline development and deployment workflows.

- Enterprises are increasingly adopting multi-cloud PaaS architectures (e.g., Red Hat OpenShift, Google Anthos) to avoid vendor lock-in and optimize workloads across hybrid environments.

- These platforms now embed **security as code** tools (e.g., OPA, HashiCorp Vault) and observability stacks (e.g., Prometheus-Grafana, OpenTelemetry) to enforce compliance and provide real-time insights into performance and threats.

- Meanwhile, **low-code or no-code PaaS solutions** (e.g., Salesforce Platform, OutSystems) empower business units to build applications autonomously, accelerating time-to-market.

- Leading organizations also leverage **service meshes** (e.g., Istio, Linkerd) to manage microservices communication at scale.

- Edge-native PaaS frameworks to support IoT and latency-sensitive workloads.

- By combining developer self-service portals (e.g., Backstage), GitOps-driven CI/CD pipelines, and automated compliance guardrails, enterprises are transforming PaaS into a unified **innovation engine** that balances agility with governance.

GitOps and Argo CD for platform governance

GitOps, when used together, creates a robust and efficient platform engineering ecosystem. The platform provides the foundational infrastructure and services, while GitOps adds the governance and automation layer, ensuring consistency, security, and scalability. GitOps is a concept where Git repositories serve as the single source of truth. GitOps has emerged as a gold standard for platform governance in enterprises. Argo CD, a declarative GitOps tool for Kubernetes, automates deployments by continuously syncing the live state of clusters with the desired state defined in Git. This approach allows platform teams to enforce policies like **no direct cluster modifications** by routing all changes through Git pull requests, which are reviewed, versioned, and automatically applied by Argo CD.

Key governance features

Modern platform governance hinges on four pillars of GitOps-driven automation:

- **Declarative configuration**: Define infrastructure or apps as code (YAML, Helm, Kustomize) in Git.

- **Policy enforcement**: Integrate OPA or Kyverno to validate manifests in CI/CD or during Argo CD syncs.

- **RBAC and audit trails**: Argo CD's built-in RBAC restricts who can deploy what, while Git commit history provides immutable audit logs.

- **Drift detection**: Argo CD flags deviations from Git-defined states and auto-reconciles them (if configured).

Enterprise use cases

To govern distributed, enterprise-scale platforms with precision, Argo CD and GitOps converge on the following practices:

- **Multi-cluster governance**: Sync identical configurations (e.g., network policies, quotas) across hundreds of clusters.

- **Compliance as code**: Store compliance rules (e.g., **encrypt all S3 buckets**) in Git, enforced via Argo CD hooks or admission controllers.

- **Self-service with guardrails**: Let developers deploy via git PRs while platform teams review and approve changes via merge requests.

There are the following real-life examples of Argo CD for platform governance:

- When a developer merges a pull request to the main branch of a git repository, Argo CD will detect the change and automatically deploy the new version of the application to the Kubernetes cluster. This removes the need for manual deployments.

- If a developer attempts to deploy a container that does not meet security policies, OPA will block the deployment and provide feedback to the developer.

Large-scale platforms

In cloud-native ecosystems where stability and scale are non-negotiable, Argo CD and GitOps unlock enterprise resilience in the following ways:

- **Risk reduction**: All changes are traceable (Git history) and reversible (rollback via Git revert).

- **Scalability**: Manage thousands of services with GitOps patterns like **app-of-apps** for hierarchical deployments.

- **Unified observability**: Argo CD's UI or API provides real-time visibility into deployment status, health, and sync history.

By combining GitOps' transparency with Argo CD's automation, enterprises achieve platform governance that balances developer agility with operational rigor, ensuring compliance without stifling innovation.

Conclusion

This chapter has explored the critical role of productization and collaboration in platform engineering. Treating platforms as products, with a focus on continuous improvement, user-centric design, and alignment with organizational goals, transforms them into dynamic entities that evolve with the needs of their users. The technical aspects of productization, including modularity, microservices, and the integration of XaC and XaaS, enable scalability and adaptability.

Collaboration is equally vital, with various models (cross-functional teams, pod-based models, and others) promoting effective teamwork and innovation. Addressing challenges such as misalignment, resistance to change, and technical integration issues is essential for fostering a culture of ownership, continuous improvement, and shared responsibility across teams. The success of platform engineering rests on its ability to deliver value to its users. By embracing a product-centric mindset, fostering a culture of collaboration, and continuously iterating based on data-driven insights and user feedback, organizations can create platforms that not only meet but exceed expectations, driving developer satisfaction and accelerating software delivery.

In the next chapter, we are going to explain data lakes and observability, which are the core components of system reliability and engineering. Data lakes play a crucial role in system engineering by providing a centralized, scalable repository for diverse data. Integrating data lakes within a platform engineering framework allows for efficient data storage, processing, and analysis while adhering to key principles like automation and standardization. Observability is essential in platform engineering, enabling teams to gain deep insights into system behavior through logs, metrics, and traces. Observability is the most important for all organizations from the perspective of reliability and scalability of the production system.

Exercises

1. What is the significance of treating platforms as products in platform engineering?

2. What are the key benefits of adopting modular and microservices architecture in platform engineering?

3. What challenges might arise from resistance to change during platform engineering, and how can they be addressed?

4. What is the core difference between treating a platform as a tool versus a product, and why is this distinction important in platform engineering?

5. How does the XaC principle contribute to the efficiency and reliability of a platform, and what are some practical examples of its implementation?

6. What are some common collaboration challenges in platform engineering, and what strategies can organizations employ to overcome them?

7. How do PaaS and GitOps complement each other in building scalable and secure platforms, and what specific benefits do they provide?

8. What are some key metrics (KPIs) that platform engineering teams should track to measure the success of their platforms, and how can these metrics be used to drive continuous improvement?

Answers

1. Treating platforms as products shifts the focus from one-time tool deployment to continuous development, user-centric design, and long-term scalability. This approach ensures that platforms evolve in line with user needs, driving greater adoption, satisfaction, and alignment with organizational goals.

2. A modular and microservices architecture enables greater adaptability and scalability. By breaking down platforms into smaller, independent components, teams can develop, test, and maintain each module separately, allowing for faster

iteration and easier integration of new features or technologies as organizational needs change.

3. Resistance to change can hinder collaboration and the adoption of new processes, tools, or structures. To address this, organizations should implement structured change management processes that include communication, training, and support. Involving team members in the change process and clearly articulating the benefits can help mitigate resistance and align the team with organizational objectives.

4. Treating a platform as a tool typically involves a reactive approach, where it is built to solve immediate problems and receives minimal maintenance afterward. Treating it as a product means adopting a proactive, user-centric approach with continuous development, iteration, and a clear roadmap, just like any consumer product. This distinction is crucial because it ensures the platform evolves with user needs, enhances user satisfaction, and drives long-term value and scalability.

5. XaC promotes automation, consistency, and version control by managing all platform components (infrastructure, security, configurations) through code. This reduces manual errors, enables reproducible environments, and facilitates rollbacks. Practical examples include using Terraform for infrastructure provisioning, defining CI/CD pipelines with GitHub Action, and implementing security policies with OPA.

6. Common challenges include misalignment, resistance to change, conflicting priorities, and technical integration issues. Strategies to overcome these include establishing clear communication channels, fostering a culture of inclusivity, using centralized roadmaps, and implementing standardized APIs. Additionally, a strong change management process, including training and support, is essential.

7. PaaS provides the underlying infrastructure and services, while GitOps provides the governance and automation layer. PaaS simplifies infrastructure management with services like Kubernetes and serverless computing. GitOps ensures consistency and compliance through declarative configurations in Git and automated deployments with tools like Argo CD. Together, they enable scalable, secure, and self-service platforms by automating deployments, enforcing policies, and providing an audit trail.

8. KPIs include developer satisfaction (measured through NPS and surveys), platform adoption (tracked via active users and service onboarding), and deployment frequency (monitored through CI/CD pipeline metrics). These metrics help identify areas for improvement, prioritize changes, and assess the impact of implemented enhancements. By establishing baseline metrics, setting goals, and iterating based on data, teams can drive continuous improvement and ensure the platform meets user needs.

Join our Discord space

Join our Discord workspace for latest updates, offers, tech happenings around the world, new releases, and sessions with the authors:

https://discord.bpbonline.com

CHAPTER 10

Data Lake and Observability

Introduction

In the context of platform engineering, a **data lake** serves as a foundational component that enables efficient storage, processing, and management of large-scale, diverse datasets. Platform engineering focuses on building and managing infrastructure that serves development teams in a scalable, consistent, and self-service manner. Integrating data lakes into this ecosystem helps companies manage the complexities of data storage and analytics in a way that aligns with the principles of platform engineering, like automation, standardization, and scalability. **Observability** in platform engineering refers to the practice of making systems and infrastructure more transparent, providing deep insights into their internal states by collecting and analyzing data such as logs, metrics, and traces. Observability enables platform engineers to monitor, debug, and optimize complex systems, ensuring reliability, performance, and scalability.

Structure

The chapter covers the following topics:

- Observability in platform engineering
- Core pillars of observability
- Challenges in implementing observability

- Data lake in platform engineering

- Data lake architecture in platform engineering

- Platform data lake challenges

Objectives

By the end of this chapter, you will gain a comprehensive understanding of observability and data lakes in the context of platform engineering. You will learn how to design, build, and leverage observability principles to create robust, scalable, and efficient platforms. Moreover, you will be equipped to implement best practices for monitoring, troubleshooting, and optimizing your platform's performance, ensuring a seamless experience for developers and end users alike. By mastering these concepts, you will be empowered to build and manage modern, data-driven platforms that meet the evolving needs of your organization.

Observability in platform engineering

Observability empowers us to understand and improve our systems by continuously gathering data, analyzing it for meaningful patterns, and using those insights to make informed decisions and adjustments. Platform engineering focuses on building self-service platforms for development and operations teams, abstracting infrastructure complexity while maintaining high availability and efficiency. Observability plays a crucial role in achieving these goals by providing a comprehensive view of how systems behave in real-time, allowing engineers to proactively detect and resolve issues. With the continuous growth of system complexities and the data we process every second, we need better observability to understand the state of our workloads.

Observability vs. monitoring

Observability and monitoring are related but distinct concepts. While monitoring focuses on tracking the health and performance of a system, observability takes a broader approach. Think of monitoring as checking your car's dashboard. It tells you essential information like speed, fuel level, and engine temperature, alerting you to potential issues like low oil pressure.

Observability, on the other hand, is like having a mechanic inspect your car. They not only check the dashboard but also use specialized tools and knowledge to diagnose underlying problems, understand the impact of wear and tear, and predict potential failures.

Observability goes beyond basic health checks to consider the following:

- **Impact of changes**: The effect of code updates, configuration adjustments, or new deployments on the system's behavior.

- **External dependencies**: The influence of third-party services, **application programming interfaces (APIs)**, or infrastructure components on an application's performance.

- **Root cause analysis**: The reason for the occurrence of a particular issue, and future prevention.

Challenges for modern applications

Modern-day applications are built using microservice-based architecture and are inherently distributed, meaning they often communicate over a network rather than within the same process or even the same machine. This distribution adds complexity because you need to understand not just what is happening but also where it is happening across your system.

Imagine a user request flowing through multiple microservices. To troubleshoot issues or analyze performance, you need end-to-end visibility and the ability to drill down into each service involved.

Furthermore, microservices are more volatile than traditional monolithic applications. Containers and serverless functions can be created and destroyed frequently, with their IP addresses changing constantly. This dynamic environment demands robust monitoring and tracking solutions. So, observability solutions are designed to help you with this.

Observability use cases

Assessing code changes requires careful analysis of performance, resource consumption, and potential regressions using metrics like response time and tools like profiling and automated testing. Monitoring external dependencies, optimizing service performance through techniques like caching and database optimization, and fostering developer productivity through clear goals and effective communication are all crucial for maintaining a healthy and efficient software development lifecycle. The following is the list of questions for different personas:

- **For developers**:
    - **Impact of code changes**: When you modify code, how can you assess its effect on performance, resource consumption, and potential regressions? What metrics and tools are essential for this analysis?

    - **Third-party dependencies**: How can you monitor the availability, health, and performance of external APIs and services that your application relies on?

    - **Optimizing services**: What techniques and data points can you use to improve your service's performance, resource utilization, cost-efficiency, and response times?

    - **Increasing developer productivity**: Beyond perks and flexible schedules, how can you measure and enhance developer productivity, especially concerning long-term code maintainability?

- **For site reliability engineers (SREs) and operators**:

  o **Measuring user experience**: How can you effectively measure and track the responsiveness and reliability of your application or service from the user's perspective?

  o **Tracking health and performance**: What methods and metrics are crucial for monitoring the overall health of your service, including uptime, response time distribution, and the impact of outages on different user groups?

  o **Blast radius exploration**: How can you determine the scope and root cause of errors, distinguishing between issues within your application, the underlying infrastructure (for example, Kubernetes), or the virtual machines?

  o **Auditing access and compliance**: How can you monitor and record access to sensitive services and data, ensuring compliance with regulations and security policies? How can you automate alerts for unauthorized access and maintain an audit trail for inspections?

Core pillars of observability

Observability is typically built on four core pillars:

- **Metrics**: Quantitative measurements that provide insight into the performance and behavior of system components (for example, CPU usage, memory consumption, request latency). Metrics help in the following:

  o Baseline the signals based on metrics.

  o Tracking metrics over time, which can help in capacity planning and scalability.

  o Define **service level objectives** (**SLO**) and **service level indicators** (**SLI**) to track operational and tactical goals.

- **Logs**: Time-stamped records of discrete events that help engineers understand what is happening at different layers of the system (for example, error messages, system events, state changes). The following is a list of events and behaviors for logs:

  o Fine-grained log events that are required for developing or fixing a bug.

  o Expected behavior, such as informational logs.

  o Unexpected behavior, such as a warning or error.

- **Traces**: Records that capture the flow of requests through distributed systems, enabling engineers to pinpoint the source of performance bottlenecks and failures by tracing the path of a request through multiple services. Traces help in following:

  o Traces help in capturing certain characteristics of the execution of processes in a microservices-based architecture.

      o   Traces also help in profiling the processes.

- **Events**: Events provide a rich set of information that offers greater insights about the posture of the system. By combining events with metrics, logs, and traces, one can build a self-healing system that can leverage event-driven remediations.

These pillars provide the foundation for understanding and maintaining the health and performance of the entire platform:

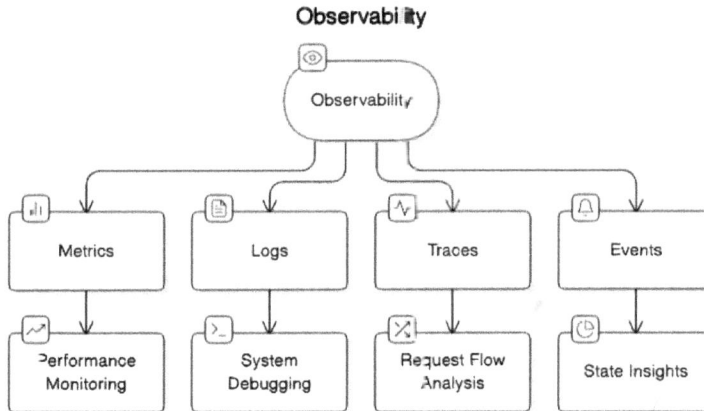

Observability

Observability

| Metrics | Logs | Traces | Events |

| Performance Monitoring | System Debugging | Request Flow Analysis | State Insights |

Figure 10.1: Foundation for understanding and maintaining the health and performance of the entire platform

Importance of observability in platform engineering

In the dynamic world of platform engineering, where change is constant and complexity is inevitable, proactive monitoring through observability has become essential for maintaining a healthy and reliable platform. It is important to shift the priority from reactive to proactive optimization, empowering platform engineers to anticipate and address issues before they impact developers or end users. By providing deep insights into the platform's behavior, observability enables teams to ensure optimal performance, minimize downtime, and foster a seamless developer experience.

Proactive monitoring

Observability enables platform engineers to monitor the platform's health in real-time, tracking **key performance indicators (KPIs)** and detecting anomalies before they cause major outages or performance degradation. Instead of waiting for failures to occur, observability tools provide insights that enable teams to take preventive action.

Faster incident response and resolution

With deep visibility into the internal workings of a platform, observability shortens **mean time to detect (MTTD)** and **mean time to resolution (MTTR)**. Engineers can quickly pinpoint the root cause of issues (for example, a failed service or increased latency in a data pipeline) and respond with minimal downtime or service interruptions.

Optimization of platform performance

Observability provides insights into how systems behave under different loads and configurations. Platform engineers use this data to fine-tune system performance, scale resources efficiently, and ensure cost optimization by right-sizing infrastructure.

Improved developer experience

A well-observed platform allows developers to interact with the platform without worrying about operational issues. Self-service observability tools enable developers to debug their applications and services independently, reducing the need for manual intervention from platform teams.

Observability stack and tools in platform engineering

The observability stack comprises various tools and frameworks that allow platform engineers to collect, analyze, and act on system data. These tools often integrate with the platform's infrastructure, providing a seamless way to observe and monitor distributed systems.

Metrics collection and monitoring

The following are the best open-source tools used for metrics collection and monitoring:

- **Prometheus**: A widely used open-source system for monitoring and alerting based on time-series data. It is highly scalable and integrates with Kubernetes and other platforms for automatic metrics collection.

  o It offers a complete package for working with metrics, such as gathering, storing, querying, and sharing them across different systems. Prometheus also has a built-in alert system and an easy-to-use interface.

  o As it is a time-series database, each data point is identified by a name and optional labels in Prometheus. The name describes what you are measuring, like the total number of API requests (`api_requests_total`). Labels add context to this measurement, allowing you to filter and analyze your data based on different dimensions, such as the HTTP method used or the specific API endpoint.

- **Grafana**: A powerful visualization tool that works with Prometheus and other data sources to create real-time dashboards, helping engineers monitor system performance and trends. Grafana helps in the following stages of observability:

o **Connect to any data**: Grafana seamlessly integrates with a wide range of data sources, from popular platforms like Prometheus, Graphite, InfluxDB, and Elasticsearch to many others.

o **Visualize your way**: Explore a comprehensive library of visualization options and craft bespoke dashboards tailored precisely to your needs.

o **Stay informed with alerts**: Configure Grafana to send alerts based on specific conditions, empowering you to proactively identify and resolve issues before they escalate.

o **Expand and enhance**: Tap into Grafana's vibrant community and extensive ecosystem of plugins and integrations to unlock even greater functionality and customization.

Logging

In the world of platform engineering, observability is the most important aspect of managing production systems. To gain deep insights into the health and performance of your platform, robust logging and monitoring tools are essential. The following are the tools that provide powerful mechanisms for collecting, processing, and analyzing log data, enabling proactive monitoring and efficient troubleshooting:

- **Elasticsearch, Logstash, and Kibana (ELK) stack**: This stack enables centralized logging, where logs from various services and infrastructure components are collected and analyzed. Kibana provides dashboards and search capabilities, helping engineers investigate issues through logs. The ELK stack works as follows:

  o **Elasticsearch is the brain**: It is a powerful database that stores and organizes all your data. It is incredibly fast and scalable, capable of handling massive amounts of information and finding what you need in an instant. Think of it as a super-organized library where every piece of information is indexed and easily retrievable.

  o **Logstash is the gatherer**: It acts like a data pipeline, collecting information from different sources (like apps, servers, and websites). It then cleans and prepares this data, making sure it is in a consistent format that Elasticsearch can understand. It is like a librarian who carefully sorts and categorizes books before putting them on the shelves.

  o **Kibana is the storyteller**: It takes the data stored in Elasticsearch and turns it into visual stories. With Kibana, you can create interactive dashboards, charts, and graphs that help you understand your data and uncover hidden insights. It is like a museum curator who designs engaging exhibits to showcase the library's collection in a meaningful way.

- **Fluentd**: An open-source data collector that unifies logging infrastructure and is used for collecting, filtering, and forwarding logs to systems like Elasticsearch. Imagine you have several applications running in containers, each generating logs.

Fluent Bit acts like a tiny courier that picks up these logs from each container. It can then process the logs, for example, by filtering out unnecessary information or adding timestamps, and deliver them to a central location for storage and analysis. It helps with the following:

- o **Centralized logging**: Instead of having logs scattered across different containers, you have a single, unified view of your application's activity. This makes it much easier to search, analyze, and troubleshoot issues.

- o **Reduced overhead**: Fluent Bit is designed to be lightweight and efficient, so it consumes minimal resources on your containers.

- o **Flexibility**: It supports a wide range of input and output plugins, allowing you to collect logs from various sources and send them to different destinations.

- o **Real-time monitoring**: Fluent Bit can forward logs in real-time, enabling you to monitor your applications and identify problems as they occur.

Fluent Bit simplifies log management in containerized environments, making it easier to collect, process, and analyze log data.

Distributed tracing

As platforms grow in complexity, especially with the adoption of microservices architectures, understanding the flow of requests and identifying performance bottlenecks becomes crucial. Distributed tracing tools like Jaeger and frameworks like OpenTelemetry provide the necessary insights to effectively monitor and optimize these intricate systems:

- **Jaeger**: A distributed tracing tool that helps engineers trace requests across complex microservices architectures, providing insight into latencies and performance bottlenecks.

  Jaeger, a distributed tracing system created by *Uber*, helps you understand how requests travel through your complex applications. Imagine it as a detective who follows the trail of a request as it jumps between different microservices. It has built-in support for various backends, including Apache Cassandra, Elasticsearch, or OpenSearch, and custom ones, like ClickHouse, via the third-party storage plug-in framework. Jaeger's overall architecture is a collection of microservices, written in Go, that work together.

  The core Jaeger components are the following:

  - o **Agent (optional)**: This is like a local informant, which gathers clues (trace data) from your application and sends them to the detective (collector). It is becoming less important as OpenTelemetry takes over this role.

  - o **Collector**: The detective receives clues from various sources, organizes them, and stores them securely in a database.

o **Query service**: This acts like the detective's assistant, who retrieves the relevant clues (traces) from the database when needed.

o **UI**: Think of this as the detective's case board, where you can visually analyze the clues (traces) and see the bigger picture of how your application is performing.

o **Ingester**: This is a specialized assistant who handles clues (traces) coming from a specific source (Apache Kafka).

• **OpenTelemetry**: A framework that offers standardized APIs and libraries for generating, collecting, and exporting telemetry data (traces, metrics, logs), making it easier to implement observability across diverse systems.

It provides a vendor-agnostic model for emitting traces, metrics, logs (and, going forward, also profiles with both backward compatibility (via receivers and exporters) and native functions via a dedicated protocol. OpenTelemetry includes auto-instrumentation support for some popular program languages and runtimes, such as Java or **Java Virtual Machine (JVM)**, .NET, JavaScript or Node.js, and Python. The following figure describes the OpenTelemetry model:

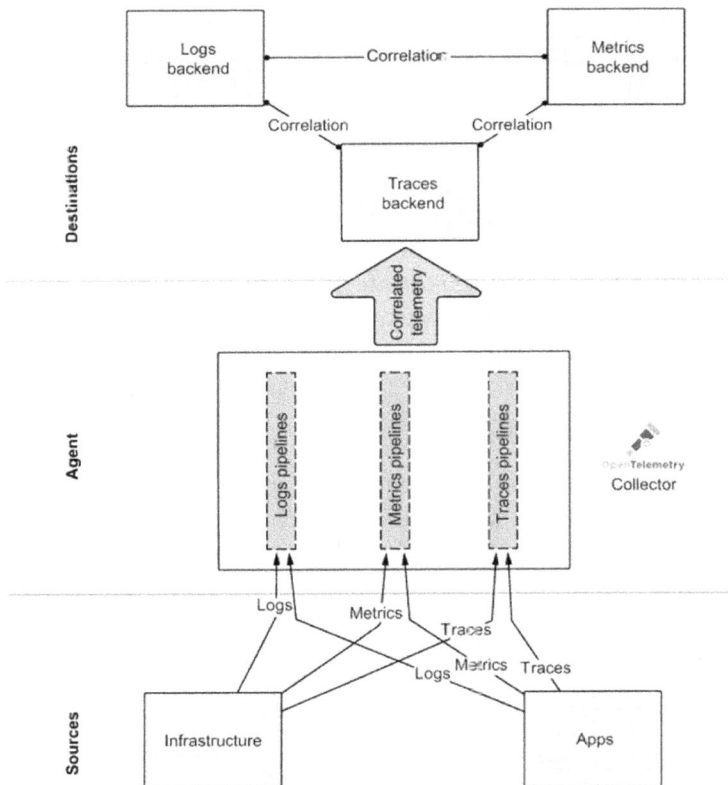

Figure 10.2: *OpenTelemetry model*

Source: *https://opentelemetry.io/docs/reference/specification/logs/overview/*

Alerting and incident management

A developed application or system can sometimes exhibit unexpected behavior that throws a wrench in its smooth operation. These hiccups can range from minor performance glitches to major disruptions that impact functionality. When these unexpected behaviors occur, it is crucial to address them promptly and learn from the experience to prevent recurrence. However, sometimes, these issues resurface before those lessons can be fully implemented. In these cases, having a runbook, which is a collection of documented procedures and solutions from past incidents, can be invaluable. This runbook acts as a guide for navigating familiar territory, allowing for faster resolution and minimizing downtime. This is where alerting and incident management solutions like Alertmanager and PagerDuty come into play:

- **Alertmanager**: Works with Prometheus to handle alerts based on threshold breaches in monitored metrics. It enables engineers to setup rules for sending notifications when issues arise.

- **PagerDuty**: An incident management platform that integrates with observability tools to alert on-call engineers about critical incidents in real-time.

Implementing observability in platform engineering

Observability is paramount to ensure the smooth operation and optimal performance of an **internal developer platform** (IDP). It provides crucial insights into the platform's health, performance, and usage patterns, empowering developers to effectively troubleshoot issues, fine-tune performance, and make informed decisions based on data to enhance the platform. The following sub-sections explore the key aspects that make observability indispensable for platform engineers.

Designing for observability

Implementing effective observability requires careful planning and consideration. Platform engineers must adopt a strategic approach that encompasses instrumentation, standardization, scalability, and tool selection to maximize the benefits of observability:

- **Instrumentation by default**: Platform engineers should build observability into systems from the start, ensuring that every service, application, and component emits metrics, logs, and traces. This allows for a granular view of the platform's internal workings and simplifies root cause analysis.

- **Standardization across the platform**: Engineers should establish standardized observability practices, tools, and conventions across all services and infrastructure layers. For example, standardizing the format of logs and the types of metrics collected makes it easier to correlate data across services.

- **Design for scalability and performance**: Engineers should ensure that integrated tools minimize the overhead of observability tools. Another important factor is to handle the growing data volumes as per the scale of the organization.

- **Choose the right tools**: Use the right toolset while designing your observability solution. There are lots of open-source tools, such as Prometheus, Grafana, Jaeger, ELK, that are available with professional support.

End-to-end visibility

To achieve comprehensive observability, platform engineers must ensure visibility across all layers of the platform, from the underlying infrastructure to the application layer. This holistic view enables effective monitoring and troubleshooting of complex systems in the following ways:

- Observability must provide visibility across the entire platform stack, from the underlying infrastructure (for example, cloud resources and network components) to application-level operations (for example, API performance and database queries).

- Tools like OpenTelemetry and Jaeger allow platform engineers to trace requests across distributed microservices, helping identify where latencies or failures occur in the system.

This end-to-end visibility provides the following benefits to the engineering teams:

- **Improved troubleshooting**: Quickly identify and resolve issues by understanding the complete request flow.

- **Enhanced performance**: Optimize system performance by identifying and addressing bottlenecks across the entire system.

- **Increased reliability**: Proactively identify potential issues and prevent outages by monitoring the health of all components.

- **Better collaboration**: Provide a shared understanding of the system's behavior, facilitating communication and collaboration between different teams.

Automation and resilience

Observability, automation, and self-healing are essential ingredients for building and managing robust and efficient systems, especially in the context of dynamic and complex environments like cloud-native applications and IDPs. Observability not only provides insights but also enables powerful automation:

- Observability can drive automation through integration with orchestration tools like Kubernetes. For example, when certain thresholds are breached (such as high CPU usage), the platform can automatically scale resources or restart problematic services, improving resilience without manual intervention.

- Engineers can implement automated remediation strategies using alerting tools and scripts that act on observability data to trigger predefined actions in case of anomalies.

Collaboration and autonomy

By fostering a culture of observability, collaboration, and self-service, you can empower developers, improve efficiency, and drive innovation.

Platform engineering teams should enable self-service observability for development teams. This means providing easy access to dashboards, logs, and metrics so developers can monitor the health of their own applications and troubleshoot issues independently. Observability empowers teams to collaborate effectively, leading to faster problem-solving and improved system health as follows:

- **Breaking down silos**: Observability promotes collaboration by breaking down silos between development, operations, and security teams. Shared access to data and insights encourages communication and joint problem-solving.

- **Shared responsibility**: Observability promotes a sense of shared responsibility for the platform's health. When everyone has access to the same information, it is easier to identify and address issues collaboratively.

- **Faster resolution**: Collaboration enabled by observability leads to faster resolution of incidents. Teams can work together to identify the root cause of problems and implement solutions quickly.

By democratizing observability, platform engineers allow developers to take more responsibility for the operational aspects of their applications, reducing the bottleneck on centralized Ops teams.

Distributed systems observability

In distributed systems and microservices architectures, observability becomes even more critical because of the complexity and interdependencies between services. Key challenges and strategies include the following:

- **Service dependencies and traceability**: Observability tools must be able to trace the flow of requests across multiple services to understand how they interact and where bottlenecks or failures occur. This is achieved through distributed tracing.

  o **Tracking requests**: Distributed tracing is a technique used to monitor and profile requests as they flow through a distributed system. It provides a way to track a request across multiple services, capturing timing information and identifying performance bottlenecks or errors along the way.

  o **Live monitoring**: Distributed tracing gives you a live, dynamic x-ray of your application's architecture. You see exactly how your microservices interact, pinpoint which ones are causing errors, and identify performance bottlenecks at a glance.

o **Boost application performance**: Distributed tracing reveals exactly where your application is spending the most time, allowing you to laser-focus your efforts on the slowest services for maximum impact.

o **Eliminating bottlenecks**: Distributed tracing helps you quickly identify the culprit services. You can then roll them back to a stable version to minimize downtime and disruption.

- **Real-life examples are as follows**:

  o **E-commerce order fulfillment**: Imagine a customer placing an order on an e-commerce website. This seemingly simple action might involve several microservices:

    - **Order service**: Receives the order request and creates an order record.

    - **Inventory service**: Checks product availability and reserves items.

    - **Payment service**: Processes the payment.

    - **Shipping service**: Calculates shipping costs and generates a shipping label.

    - **Notification service**: Sends order confirmation emails.

  Distributed tracing can track the order request as it flows through these services, capturing timing information and potential errors. This helps identify bottlenecks, such as a slow payment processing step or an issue with the inventory service. It also allows developers to understand the overall performance of the order fulfillment process and optimize each step for a smoother customer experience.

  o **Ride-hailing service**: In a ride-hailing app like *Uber* or *OLA*, a single ride request can trigger the following complex chain of events:

    - **Rider app**: Sends the ride request.

    - **Matching service**: Finds a suitable driver.

    - **Driver app**: Notifies the driver and provides ride details.

    - **Mapping service**: Provides real-time location data and navigation.

    - **Payment service**: Handles payment processing.

    - **Rating service**: Allows riders and drivers to rate each other.

  Distributed tracing can help monitor the performance of each service involved in the ride request, identify potential issues like delays in matching riders with drivers, and ensure a seamless experience for both riders and drivers.

Engineers should instrument every microservice to emit traces that capture how requests propagate across the system. These traces can be visualized to detect performance issues in specific services or external dependencies (for example, databases and third-party APIs).

- **Latency and bottleneck detection**: In distributed environments, performance issues may not always be localized to a single service but could result from how services communicate (for example, network latency or overloaded message queues). Observability tools must detect these cross-service latencies and provide insights into where the bottlenecks occur.

- **Fault isolation and reliability**: Observability helps in isolating faults in distributed systems by providing granular insights into the health of individual services and their interactions with others. Engineers can use these insights to design more resilient systems, implementing techniques like circuit breakers and retries.

Challenges in implementing observability

Observability offers incredible insights, but it also comes with challenges. Here is how to address observability challenges of data overload, tool complexity, and cost:

- **Data volume and noise**: As platforms grow, the sheer volume of observability data can become overwhelming, leading to alert fatigue and difficulty in distinguishing important signals from noise. Engineers must design systems that intelligently filter and prioritize critical alerts.

- **Tooling complexity**: While there are numerous observability tools available, integrating them into a cohesive stack can be challenging. Engineers must ensure that tools work seamlessly together and provide unified views of logs, metrics, and traces.

- **Cost of observability**: Collecting, storing, and processing observability data at scale can incur significant costs, especially in cloud environments. Engineers must balance the need for visibility with the cost of storing and analyzing data and implementing strategies like data retention policies and sampling.

The future of platform observability

Observability is evolving rapidly. The following are the emerging trends shaping the future of platform engineering:

- **AI/ML-driven observability**: ML is increasingly being applied to observability, where models can predict anomalies, detect patterns, and even suggest root causes of issues. AI-driven observability platforms can provide proactive insights into potential failures before they happen.

- **Unified observability platforms**: The trend towards unified observability platforms combines metrics, logs, and traces into a single system, reducing the need for fragmented tools. This creates a holistic view of platform health and simplifies monitoring, debugging, and optimization.

- **Security and observability convergence**: As security becomes a growing concern in platform engineering, observability is converging with security practices (often termed **SecOps**). Integrating security monitoring and observability allows platform engineers to detect suspicious behavior or breaches through system-level insights.

Data lake in platform engineering

A data lake is a centralized repository designed to store vast amounts of structured, semi-structured, and unstructured data at scale. Within the context of platform engineering, a data lake plays a critical role in managing and organizing data infrastructure, ensuring the availability and accessibility of data across an organization's platforms. Platform engineering emphasizes building scalable, standardized, and efficient infrastructure that supports the full lifecycle of software and data, making data lakes a key component of this ecosystem.

Role of platform engineering in data infrastructure

Platform engineering focuses on providing self-service platforms that enable development teams to deliver and manage applications and data more efficiently. By integrating data lakes into the broader platform, platform engineers create a foundation that allows teams to work with data at scale without needing to manage the underlying infrastructure.

Key responsibilities of platform engineering related to data lakes include the following:

- **Standardization**: Defining common tools, APIs, and frameworks to interact with the data lake, ensuring consistent access and data handling practices across teams.

- **Automation**: Automating data ingestion, transformation, and governance tasks to reduce manual overhead and improve data reliability.

- **Scalability**: Building systems that can grow with increasing data volumes and user demands while maintaining performance.

- **Security and governance**: Enforcing security policies, access controls, and data governance mechanisms to protect sensitive data and ensure compliance.

Data lake architecture in platform engineering

In a platform engineering context, the architecture of a data lake consists of multiple layers, each providing the following specific functions to handle the large volumes and diversity of data:

- **Storage layer**: To effectively manage the flood of observability data, we need a scalable and flexible storage solution. The following are the characteristics of a data lake built for this purpose:

  o Built on distributed storage systems such as Amazon S3, **Hadoop Distributed File System** (**HDFS**), or Azure Data Lake Storage.

  o Stores raw data in its native format, whether structured (tables), semi-structured (JSON, XML), or unstructured (images, audio).

  o Provides elasticity to handle petabytes of data and ensures cost-efficiency.

- **Ingestion layer**: The following are characteristics and tools for building robust data ingestion pipelines:

  o Handles the movement of data from various sources (databases, IoT devices, applications) into the data lake.

  o Tools like Apache Kafka, Apache NiFi, or AWS Glue automate the ingestion of streaming and batch data.

  o Ensures the scalability and reliability of data ingestion pipelines, making sure that data flows uninterrupted.

- **Processing layer**: The following are characteristics and tools for processing layers to support on-demand data processing and transformation:

  o Data engineers and scientists process the data stored in the lake using frameworks like Apache Spark, Presto, or Databricks.

  o The platform engineering team ensures that this layer is integrated into the platform's compute infrastructure, supporting on-demand data processing and transformation.

- **Metadata and governance layer**: The following are characteristics and tools for the metadata and governance layer:

  o Tools like Apache Atlas or AWS Glue catalog and track data lineage, making it easier for teams to find, understand, and trust the data they use.

  o This layer is critical for managing security, auditing, and compliance requirements, which platform engineers implement at scale.

- **Consumption layer**: The following are characteristics and tools for the consumption layer:

  o Supports data query and analytics tools like AWS Athena, BigQuery, and Elasticsearch that allow end users to access and analyze data directly.

  o Platform engineers ensure the integration of BI tools (for example, Tableau and Power BI) with the data lake for business analytics.

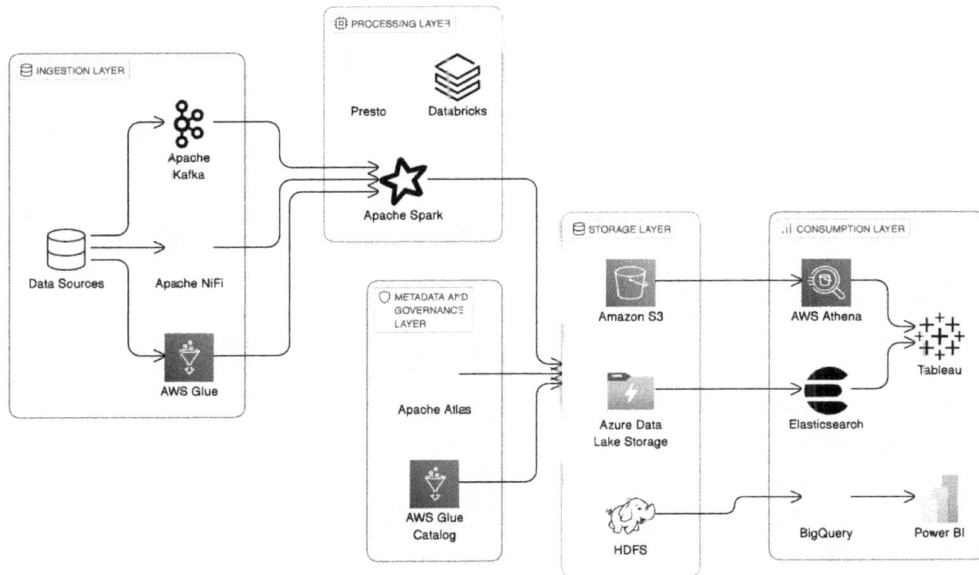

Figure 10.3: Characteristics and tools for the consumption layer

Data lake as part of a unified platform

In platform engineering, the data lake is part of a broader unified platform that connects infrastructure, tools, and services used by development teams, data scientists, and other stakeholders. This platform may integrate into the following:

- CI/CD pipelines to automate the deployment and scaling of data processing applications.

- APIs and services that enable developers to easily interact with data in the lake without needing to know the intricacies of the underlying infrastructure.

- Orchestration tools (for example, Apache Airflow) that manage complex data workflows, ensuring smooth and efficient data movement across the platform.

By integrating the data lake into the platform, platform engineering allows teams to focus on innovation and data-driven projects without worrying about operational complexity. Teams can build applications, analytics models, and AI/ML pipelines directly on top of the data lake.

Observability and monitoring in data lakes

Observability is essential to maintain the reliability and performance of data lakes. It ensures that platform engineers can monitor, debug, and optimize the data lake infrastructure as it scales. Key areas to observe include the following:

- **Ingestion pipeline performance**: Track throughput, latency, and error rates of data flowing into the lake.

- **Storage and processing health**: Monitor storage usage, access patterns, and the health of processing clusters.

- **Data quality and freshness**: Ensure that data entering the lake is accurate, consistent, and updated in a timely manner.

- **End-to-end traceability**: Observability tools (for example, Prometheus, Datadog, or ELK stack) track data workflows from source to consumption, helping teams troubleshoot failures and bottlenecks.

Benefits of data lakes in platform engineering

Data lakes can quickly become unmanageable and expensive if not handled properly. Platform engineering provides the solutions to ensure scalability, cost-efficiency, and flexibility:

- **Scalability**: Platform engineering ensures that the data lake can handle growing data volumes and user demands without compromising performance.

- **Cost efficiency**: By utilizing distributed storage and compute resources, platform engineers manage infrastructure costs effectively, enabling large-scale data storage at lower costs than traditional systems.

- **Flexibility**: A well-engineered data lake supports multiple data formats and use cases (real-time analytics, AI/ML workloads, BI reporting) from a single repository, making it a versatile tool for organizations.

- **Collaboration**: Platform engineering fosters collaboration between development teams, data engineers, and data scientists by providing self-service tools and platforms to work with data from the lake.

Platform data lake challenges

Successfully managing a data lake requires a proactive approach. Platform engineering addresses challenges related to data governance, performance, and the complexities of distributed systems using the following practices:

- **Data governance**: As data lakes grow, maintaining data quality, lineage, and governance can become complex. Platform engineering needs to implement policies and tools to manage access, security, and compliance.

- **Performance optimization**: Large-scale data lakes can suffer from performance issues, especially when handling diverse workloads. Engineers need to balance cost, performance, and availability when designing data lake solutions.

- **Complexity of distributed systems**: Ensuring observability, monitoring, and debugging for distributed data systems can be challenging, especially in hybrid and multi-cloud environments.

Future of data lakes in platform engineering

As platform engineering evolves, data lakes are becoming more sophisticated and integrated into a variety of data architectures.

- **Data lakehouse**: A hybrid model combining the flexibility of a data lake with the performance and structure of a data warehouse. This approach is gaining popularity as it enables both high-performance analytics and large-scale, unstructured data storage.

- **Serverless data lakes**: Serverless architectures are simplifying the management of data lakes by abstracting infrastructure concerns, allowing platform engineers to focus on data processing and application development.

- **Multi-cloud data lakes**: Organizations are adopting multi-cloud strategies for data lakes to avoid vendor lock-in and improve resilience. Platform engineers play a key role in integrating these environments while ensuring consistent performance and observability.

Revisiting our platform

Figure 10.4 illustrates a comprehensive platform engineering ecosystem that integrates various essential components, from developer tools to infrastructure management. At the core is the developer portal, which serves as a one-stop shop for self-service, empowering developers to efficiently manage their workflows. The self-service **Backend For Frontend** (**BFF**) acts as an orchestrator for backend services, enabling seamless self-service functionality. Surrounding these core elements are key capabilities such as AI/ML-driven insights, **continuous integration** (**CI**) with guardrails, and **continuous delivery** (**CD**) systems that facilitate automated deployments with zero downtime. The infrastructure layers include **infrastructure as code** (**IaC**) for automating environments, **Kubernetes as a service** (**KaaS**), **database as a service** (**DBaaS**), and a cloud infrastructure optimized for scalability and resilience. Together, these components ensure a robust, scalable, and self-service-oriented platform that is highly adaptable to diverse development and operational needs.

Figure 10.4 is the data lake, which aggregates data across the platform to provide actionable insights and metrics. The observability platform, positioned at the side, enables the monitoring and analysis of system health, detecting anomalies, and supporting faster incident response times. Various elements, such as **secrets management (SM)**, **certificate management (CM)**, and managed Kubernetes, ensure secure and compliant operations, while tools like universal artifact registry and **centralized access management (CAM)** enforce governance and standardization. This holistic approach to platform engineering enables organizations to deliver software efficiently, optimize resource usage, and ensure continuous improvement through insights gained from both the observability layer and AI/ ML feedback loops. The following figure explains the self-service and observability for platform engineering:

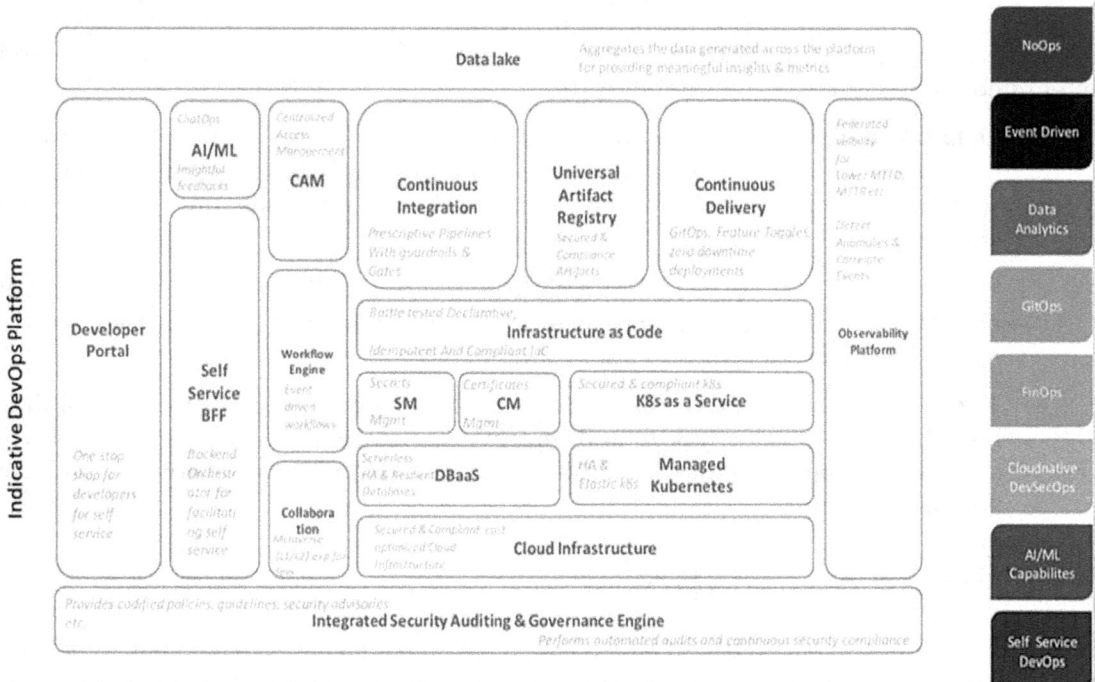

Figure 10.4: Platform engineering, self-service platform and observability

In the context of the figure, Observability is presented as a crucial platform capability that underpins the entire system's health, reliability, and performance. Positioned on the right, the Observability Platform provides insights across all the interconnected services, enabling platform engineers to monitor, debug, and optimize complex infrastructure and applications. Observability integrates key metrics, logs, traces, and events, ensuring that any anomalies, performance bottlenecks, or failures within the infrastructure are detected early. This approach lowers critical metrics like MTTD and MTTR, allowing teams to quickly identify and address issues before they impact the broader system. By proactively monitoring the platform, engineers can ensure high availability, stability, and scalability, especially in environments with distributed services and microservice architectures like KaaS and DBaaS. Additionally, Observability data can inform AI/ML-driven feedback mechanisms, continuously improving platform operations through insights.

The data lake in *Figure 10.5* serves as a centralized data repository that aggregates and stores massive amounts of structured, semi-structured, and unstructured data from across the platform. In the context of platform engineering, the data lake acts as a critical component, supporting the collection and processing of telemetry, operational data, logs, and other system-generated information. This data feeds into the observability platform, allowing for meaningful insights that can help optimize infrastructure management and improve system resilience. By storing vast amounts of data in its raw form, the data lake provides scalability and flexibility, making it easier for teams to perform analytics, generate reports, and create models for predictive maintenance or optimization. Additionally, it facilitates data-driven decision-making across the platform, enhancing the overall efficiency and effectiveness of infrastructure management and operations. In combination with observability, the data lake supports both real-time monitoring and long-term analysis of system behavior. The following figure explains the different self-service and observability components, such as the data lake and observability platform:

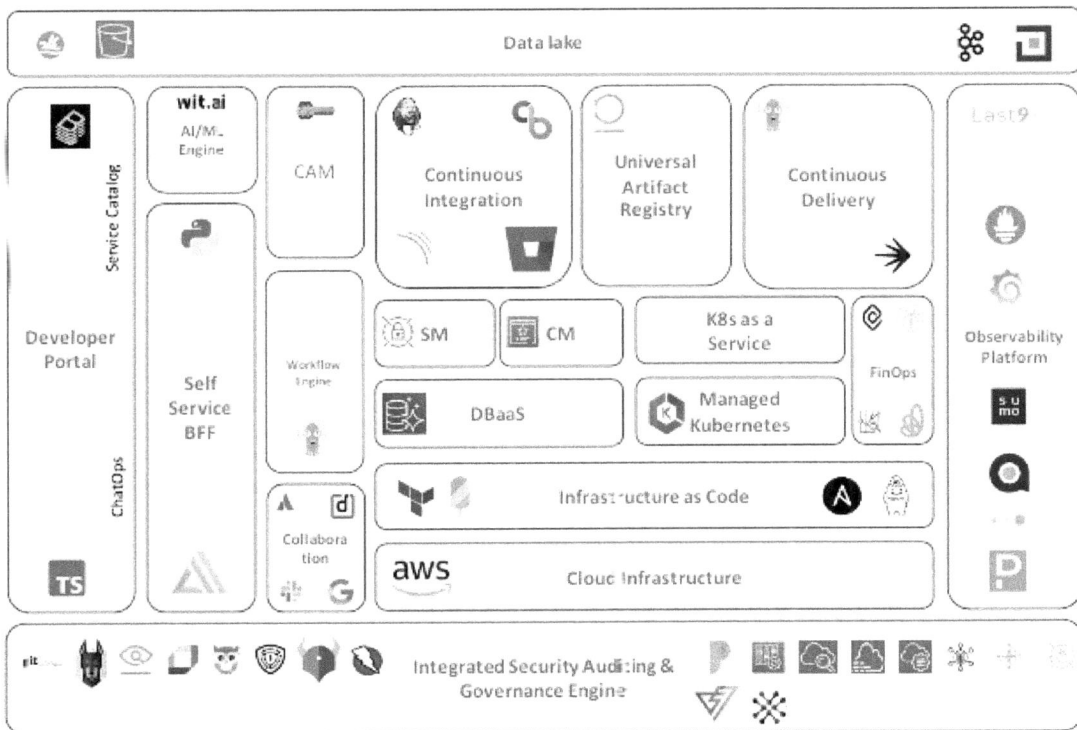

Figure 10.5: Platform engineering a PHY model

In the preceding figure of the PHY platform, the data lake was built using Apache DevLake, S3, Kafka, and DefectDojo. The observability stack was built using PagerDuty, Anodot, Sumo Logic, Grafana, Prometheus, and Last9.

Conclusion

This chapter emphasized the pivotal role of observability in platform engineering, helping teams monitor, debug, and optimize their platforms. Observability, with its pillars of metrics, logs, traces, and events, ensures system reliability and performance in platform engineering. Data lakes complement platform engineering by providing a scalable and flexible repository for vast amounts of diverse data. As observability and data lake management evolve, trends like AI-driven insights, unified platforms, and SecOps integration will shape future platform strategies, making observability and data infrastructure more intelligent, automated, and secure.

The next chapter will cover the latest trends in platform engineering, the transformative power of AI/ML, and the emergence of PAI-Ops, a new paradigm for platform and AI operations.

Exercises

1. What are the core pillars of observability in platform engineering?

2. Why is observability important for platform engineering?

3. What are some common observability tools used in platform engineering?

4. What role does a data lake play in platform engineering?

5. What are the future trends in observability for platform engineering?

Answers

1. The four core pillars of observability in platform engineering are metrics, logs, traces, and events. Metrics provide quantitative insights into system performance, logs capture time-stamped events, traces follow request flows across distributed systems, and events offer detailed insights, aiding in proactive system maintenance.

2. Observability is crucial because it enables proactive monitoring of system health, faster incident response, and resolution, optimization of platform performance, and an improved developer experience. It helps engineers detect and resolve issues before they impact users, leading to more reliable and efficient platforms.

3. Key tools include Prometheus (metrics collection), Grafana (visualization), the ELK stack (centralized logging), Fluentd (log collection), Jaeger (distributed tracing), and OpenTelemetry (standardized telemetry data collection). These tools collectively enable deep monitoring and debugging of complex systems.

4. In platform engineering, a data lake acts as a centralized repository for large volumes of structured, semi-structured, and unstructured data. It supports

scalability, flexibility, and efficient data management, enabling teams to store, process, and analyze data without managing the underlying infrastructure.

5. Future trends include AI/ML-driven observability for predictive insights, unified observability platforms that combine metrics, logs, and traces into a single view, and the convergence of SecOps, enabling better detection of system-level threats.

References

1. *Kreps, J. (2014). Kafka: A Distributed Messaging System for Log Processing. LinkedIn Engineering Blog.*

2. *Chandramouli, R., & Benson, A. (2022). AI for Observability and Monitoring. Proceedings of the IEEE.*

3. *Chin, C., Puttaswamy, A., & Seneviratne, S. (2017). The ELK Stack: Elasticsearch, Logstash, and Kibana for Distributed Systems Monitoring. InfoQ.*

4. *AWS Whitepapers. (2020). Data Lakes and Analytics on AWS.*

5. *Cunningham, T. (2021). Distributed Tracing for Microservices with OpenTelemetry. DZone.*

6. *Fowler, M. (2019). Observability: A Guide for Microservices. Thoughtworks Tech Radar.*

7. *Lakehouse Paper. (2020). The Rise of the Data Lakehouse. Databricks Blog.*

Join our Discord space

Join our Discord workspace for latest updates, offers, tech happenings around the world, new releases, and sessions with the authors:

https://discord.bpbonline.com

## CHAPTER 11

Future Trends of Platform Engineering

Introduction

Platform engineering is an ever-evolving field. Emerging technologies and trends, such as **artificial intelligence and machine learning (AI/ML)** and blockchain, will continue to shape the future of platform engineering.

AI/ML are going to transform platform engineering by helping teams automate and optimize many aspects of software development, including testing and monitoring. Platform engineering is poised to revolutionize software development by streamlining operations and boosting efficiency through the creation of self-service developer platforms. This approach empowers developers to work autonomously and with greater speed. Looking ahead, the integration of AI/ML into platform engineering promises even greater advancements. As companies increasingly embrace digital transformation, platform engineering will be essential for achieving their goals.

Structure

The chapter covers the following topics:

- Emerging technologies and future trends
- AI/ML with platform engineering
- Platform and AI operations

- Platform engineering and AI case studies

Objectives

By the end of this chapter, you will gain a very good understanding of emerging trends and the role to be played by AI/ML and GenAI in platform engineering. From the perspective of dev experience, **generative AI (GenAI)** is going to play a major role in the future version of the platform. There is a lot of work that has been started where GenAI will empower developers with automated code generation for **infrastructure as code (IaC)**, intelligent code completion, and even natural language interfaces for interacting with the platform. This will lead to faster development cycles, reduced errors, and a more intuitive and efficient platform experience.

Emerging technologies and future trends

Platform engineering is a self-service portal with all the tools and resources required by developers to build, deploy, and run applications smoothly.

Platform engineering is constantly evolving, with new technologies emerging to enhance its capabilities and address the growing complexities of software development. Here are some of the most exciting emerging technologies shaping the future of platform engineering:

- **AI/ML**: GenAI and **large language models (LLMs)** are emerging technologies which has disrupted the way of working and laid the foundation for future innovations. Platform engineering will also be helped by GenAI and LLM:

  o **AI-powered automation**: Think of AI as your tireless assistant. It takes over the tedious, repetitive tasks, like provisioning resources or running tests, and even anticipates and prevents problems before they happen. This frees up your platform engineers to focus on more strategic and creative work.

  o **Intelligent recommendations**: AI acts like a personalized guide for your developers. It learns their preferences and habits, and then suggests the right tools, services, and best practices for their specific needs. This boosts productivity and helps them make informed decisions.

  o **Enhanced observability**: AI gives you x-ray vision into your platform. It sifts through mountains of data to uncover hidden patterns and potential issues you might otherwise miss. This allows for proactive problem-solving and continuous optimization of your platform's performance.

- **Edge computing**: Platform engineering is not just about speed; it is about building an unbreakable foundation for your applications. We aim for near-zero downtime, ensuring your services are always available to your users. To do this, we prioritize both the developer experience (smooth workflows for your team) and the user experience (seamless performance for your customers).

The following are the advantages of edge computing:

o **Lightning-fast responses**: By processing data closer to the source, we eliminate lag and deliver real-time performance. Imagine the difference for your users in applications like online gaming or high-frequency trading.

o **Increased resilience**: Distributing your platform across multiple edge locations creates a safety net. If one location falters, others seamlessly take over, preventing disruptions and downtime. Distributing workloads across edge locations improves resilience and reduces the impact of outages.

o **Unlocking new potential**: Edge computing opens exciting possibilities. We can bring your platform closer to your users, wherever they are, for unparalleled responsiveness and performance.

• **Blockchain technology**: In today's digital world, user trust is paramount. Blockchain technology provides the bedrock for building that trust by ensuring the integrity and security of your platform.

The following are the benefits of blockchains:

o **Unbreakable security**: Blockchain acts like an unalterable digital ledger, securing your platform's components and data. This transparency and immutability foster trust among your users.

o **Decentralized power**: By distributing your platform across a blockchain network, you eliminate single points of failure and reduce reliance on centralized infrastructure. This creates a more resilient and trustworthy system.

o **Engaging incentives**: Blockchain allows you to create tokenized reward systems, encouraging user participation and contributions to your platform's ecosystem. This fosters a sense of community and shared ownership.

• **Extended reality**: Imagine a platform that is not just used, but experienced. **Extended reality** (**XR**) technologies like VR and AR unlock a world of immersive possibilities, transforming how users interact with your platform and each other.

The following are the XR's potential:

o **Deeper engagement**: XR creates captivating experiences, drawing users into your platform and fostering a sense of presence and connection. Imagine collaborating with colleagues in a shared virtual space or visualizing complex data in a 3D environment.

o **Intuitive interaction**: XR reimagines how users interact with your platform. Instead of menus and buttons, they can navigate complex environments with VR headsets or use AR overlays to interact with data in their physical surroundings.

o **Accelerated learning**: Onboarding and training become engaging adventures with XR. Users can learn by doing in interactive simulations, speeding up adoption and mastery of your platform.

By keeping an eye on these emerging technologies, platform engineering teams can stay ahead of the curve and build innovative platforms that meet the evolving needs of developers and businesses.

Stages of platform engineering evolution

The following figure illustrates the evolution of platform engineering through different stages, highlighting the increasing influence of cloud technologies and AI:

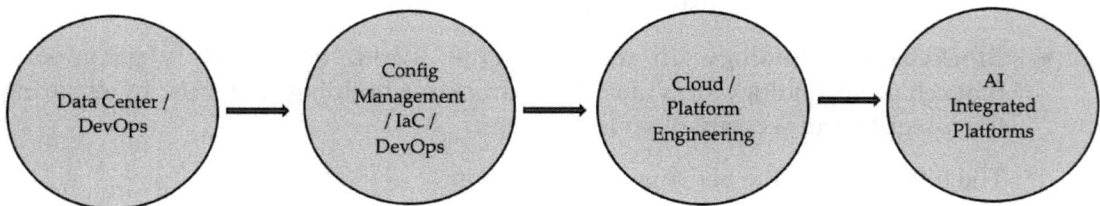

Figure 11.1: *Platform engineering evolution*

Journey of platform engineering

Think of platform engineering as having gone through these key stages:

- **The early days (data center or DevOps)**: Back then, it was all about managing physical servers and introducing basic automation. Platform engineering was just starting out, with limited self-service for developers.

- **Automation takes hold (configuration management, infra, DevOps platform engineering)**: This is where things get interesting. Teams started using tools to automate infrastructure setup and management. Platform engineering began to offer developers self-service access to key resources.

- **The cloud revolution (cloud or platform engineering)**: The cloud changed everything. Organizations moved their focus to cloud platforms, and platform engineering matured. Developers gained access to a wider range of cloud services with greater ease.

- **The intelligent future (hybrid cloud, AI-led and AI-infused platforms)**: This is where we are headed. Organizations are embracing a mix of cloud environments and infusing them with AI. This means smarter automation, optimized resources, enhanced security, and AI-powered insights for developers.

The preceding key milestones and trends have shaped the field of platform engineering.

Here is what is driving the evolution of platform engineering:

- **Automation is king**: Every step of the way, we have seen a relentless push for automation. This means less manual work, greater efficiency, and faster results.

- **The cloud is essential**: Cloud computing has become the backbone of modern platforms. It provides the scalability, flexibility, and cost-effectiveness that today's applications demand.

- **AI is the future**: AI is transforming platforms. It is being used to optimize performance, strengthen security, and provide intelligent assistance to developers.

- **Developers are at the heart**: Throughout this evolution, the focus has always been on making life easier for developers. This means giving them self-service capabilities, automated workflows, and a seamless development environment so they can focus on what they do best: building great software.

Staying ahead in platform engineering

To excel in the rapidly evolving world of platform engineering, organizations need to:

- **Embrace the cloud and AI**: Cloud technologies and AI/ML are no longer optional. They are essential for building and managing modern, competitive platforms.

- **Upskill your teams**: Platform engineering teams need to master cloud-native technologies, AI/ML, and automation to stay ahead of the curve.

- **Empower developers with AI**: AI-powered platforms are the key to unlocking developer productivity, accelerating software delivery, and driving innovation.

This can be used as a valuable roadmap for organizations looking to embrace modern platform engineering practices and leverage the power of cloud and AI.

AI/ML with platform engineering

Platform engineering with AI is to help organizations. It helps make developers' lives easier and makes them more productive:

- **Improve developer experience**: Augmenting platform engineering practice with AI will help the developer community to easily adopt the self-service developer platform and make better software. Platform engineering with AI will help:

  o **Generate, explain, debug, and review code**: AI assists in generating code snippets, completing repetitive code blocks, and even suggesting entire functions based on natural language or comments. This helps developers do mundane tasks and allows them to focus on more complex and creative problem-solving.

o **AI integration with platform engineering**: It helps build operational data analysis capabilities. AI can help analyze complex operational data and provide insights for developers that are easy to understand. Developers do not need to know the complex query language to pull data.

o **Help code completion and suggestions**: AI-powered IDE or command line tools to context-aware code completion, suggest relevant APIs, and even predict potential errors, helping developers write code faster and with fewer errors.

o **Fix errors**: AI can help in suggesting fixes to errors or automatically resolve common errors in build pipelines, reducing friction and interruptions and speeding up development.

- **Enhance software delivery efficiency**: The objective of AI integration with platform engineering is to streamline and optimize the software delivery process as follows:

o **Test impact analysis**: AI can help in quick test impact analysis. AI can identify the test cases that need to be executed on code changes, reducing build time and getting quick feedback.

o **Change impact analysis**: AI can help in predicting the potential impact of code changes, help in the identification of risks, and prevent regressions.

o **Correlation**: AI can help in event correlation across the software delivery pipeline to identify the patterns and root causes of issues, enabling faster resolution.

- **Optimize software delivery infrastructure**: Platform engineering with AI integration ensures the infrastructure supporting software delivery is optimal and scalable. There are many companies that have moved to the public cloud due to digital transformation or have started their journey on this. The infrastructure team cannot manually scale up or down the infrastructure without automation and intelligence. Optimization involves:

o **Anticipate demand**: AI can forecast your infrastructure needs, automatically scaling resources up or down to ensure optimal performance and cost-efficiency. This means your self-service platform is always ready to handle any workload.

o **Optimize configurations**: AI analyzes how resources are being used and recommends the best configurations to avoid overspending and waste.

o **Streamline setup**: AI can automatically configure your infrastructure based on real-time traffic patterns. This is especially valuable for container-based platforms, where AI can significantly reduce manual effort for developers and boost overall efficiency.

A quick summary of AI integration with platform engineering for the **software development lifecycle (SDLC)** and boosting developer productivity is as follows:

AI capability	Improve developer experience	Enhance software delivery efficiency	Optimize software delivery infrastructure
Automation	• Auto-generate code, tests, and documentation • Automate repetitive tasks	• Automate CI/CD pipelines • Automate deployments	• Auto-scale resources • Automate infrastructure provisioning
Intelligent assistance	• Provide intelligent code suggestions • Answer developer questions • Offer personalized recommendations	• Analyze code changes • Predict the impact of changes	• Monitor performance • Recommend optimizations
Analysis and insights	• Facilitate knowledge sharing	• Identify bottlenecks • Optimize workflows	• Predict potential issues • Optimize resource allocation

Table 11.1: Platform engineering with AI capabilities

AI integration challenges in platform engineering

While the potential of AI in platform engineering is immense, it is crucial to approach its integration strategically. Here is how platform engineering teams can effectively navigate the challenges:

- **Pinpoint the bottlenecks**: Start by identifying the biggest pain points and inefficiencies in your existing platform engineering processes. This will help you determine where AI can make the most significant impact.

- **Prioritize for maximum impact**: Focus on addressing the most critical constraints first. This ensures that you reap the maximum benefits from your AI investments and avoid getting sidetracked by less important issues.

Key areas for AI augmentation in platform engineering

Platform engineering has evolved significantly, driven by automation, cloud adoption, and the rise of AI/ML. Organizations must embrace these technologies and upskill their teams to stay competitive. AI can optimize key areas like CI/CD pipelines, testing, infrastructure management, and security, leading to increased efficiency, scalability, and developer empowerment.

Here is how AI can revolutionize key areas of platform engineering:

- **CI/CD pipelines**: AI can streamline your pipelines, automate testing, and make deployments smoother and faster.

- **Testing and quality assurance**: Manual testing bottlenecks can be removed as AI can automate test creation, execution, and analysis, leading to better test coverage and quicker releases.

- **Infrastructure management**: AI takes the heavy lifting out of managing your infrastructure. It can automate provisioning, scaling, and configuration, freeing up your team and boosting efficiency.

- **Security and compliance**: AI acts as your vigilant security guard, constantly monitoring for threats, automating responses, and ensuring you meet all compliance requirements.

AI integration in SDLC processing of platform engineering

AI is rapidly changing how we build and deliver software, and platform engineering is no exception. Here is how AI can be embedded into the SDLC processes of platform engineering, supercharging its capabilities:

- **AI-powered automation for streamlined development**: Imagine a development process where AI handles the heavy lifting, allowing your team to focus on innovation. Here is how AI can revolutionize development and build processes:

  o **Automated code generation**: AI becomes your coding assistant, analyzing requirements and generating code snippets, saving developers time and effort.

  o **Self-service infrastructure**: If you need a server or database, AI automatically provisions the necessary resources based on developer requests and predicted needs, eliminating delays and optimizing resource allocation.

  o **Smart CI/CD pipelines**: AI supercharges your CI/CD pipelines, dynamically adjusting parameters, predicting bottlenecks, and automatically triggering builds and deployments based on code changes and performance data.

- **Enhanced code quality and security**: Building secure and reliable platforms is paramount. AI can be a powerful ally with platform engineering in enhancing code quality and security, automated code reviews, proactive vulnerability detection, and predictive maintenance for increased platform stability and reliability.

  o **AI-powered code reviews**: AI acts as your tireless code reviewer, catching bugs, security vulnerabilities, and style inconsistencies in real-time. This provides developers with immediate feedback, leading to higher-quality code.

- o **Automated security testing**: AI automatically performs security scans and penetration tests, identifying vulnerabilities early in the development process and reducing the risk of security breaches.

- o **Predictive maintenance**: AI analyzes system logs and performance data to predict potential failures and proactively recommend maintenance tasks. This ensures your platform remains stable and reliable.

- **Optimized resource management**: AI is revolutionizing how we build and manage platforms. Efficient resource management is crucial for any platform. AI can help optimize resource utilization and reduce costs:

  - o **Intelligent resource allocation**: AI acts as a resource orchestrator, analyzing usage patterns and predicting future demand to ensure your platform has the right resources available at the right time.

  - o **Cost optimization**: AI helps you save money by analyzing resource usage and recommending more efficient configurations or alternative services.

- **Improved developer experience**: Happy developers are productive developers. AI can help create a more satisfying and efficient developer experience in a self-service portal through:

  - o **Personalized recommendations**: AI acts as a personal assistant for developers, offering tailored recommendations for tools, services, and best practices based on their individual needs and preferences.

  - o **Intelligent chatbots**: AI-powered chatbots provide instant support, answering questions, troubleshooting issues, and guiding developers through platform features. This means less time searching for answers and more time building great software.

- **Continuous learning and improvement**: Platforms should never stop improving. AI can help the team to learn and adapt continuously:

  - o **Performance analysis and optimization**: AI acts as a platform analyst, identifying bottlenecks, inefficiencies, and underutilized resources. This data-driven insight helps you optimize performance and streamline workflows.

  - o **Automated feedback loops**: AI gathers feedback from developers, providing valuable insights into platform usability and areas for improvement. This ensures your platform evolves to meet the needs of your users.

- **AI in action (real-world examples in platform engineering)**: Here are a few examples of how AI is already transforming platform engineering:

o **GitHub Copilot**: This AI-powered tool acts like a coding partner, suggesting code completions and generating code snippets in real-time, boosting developer productivity.

o **Harness**: Harness uses AI to make continuous delivery smarter and safer, automating deployments and rollbacks based on real-time performance and risk analysis.

o **Dynatrace**: Dynatrace leverages AI to monitor your applications, detect anomalies, and pinpoint the root cause of performance issues, ensuring smooth and reliable operations.

By embedding AI into the SDLC processes of platform engineering, organizations can create more efficient, reliable, and developer-friendly platforms that accelerate software delivery and drive innovation.

A good reference on how AI is changing the future of platform engineering is as follows:

https://platformengineering.org/blog/ai-is-changing-the-future-of-platform-engineering-are-you-ready

The following figure illustrates how LLMs can be leveraged to enhance various aspects of platform engineering, categorized by user persona (developer, platform engineer, economic buyer/manager) and use case complexity:

☐ Easy to implement   ☐ Medium   ▨ Hard   ▨ Very complex, will take expertise in LLMs

PERSONA \ USE CASE	Creating configurations	Usage of an IDP	Enablement / Documentation	Support
Developer	Create config files from natural language description. Describe what config file does in plain English (reverse). Fix errors in config files. Co-pilot supporting real time creation of configs.	Query for deployment context and get a verbose response. Commands and deployments through natural language interface.	Answer queries around products in general, features, application examples / sample code, command syntax, etc. with a 3rd party solution. Answers queries around training content, training videos, tutorials, use case samples, etc. with a 3rd party solution.	Answer queries to general topics and get a verbose response. Answer specific support queries around errors, issues, potential bugs, requests for samples code, use cases, also see Enablement/ Documentation.
Platform engineer	Co-pilot supporting real time creating of configs.	Query for deployment context or issues and get a verbose response. Query for infra stats (change dates, list of resources, cost information, etc.). Commands and deployments through natural language interface.	Answer queries around products in general, features, application examples / sample code, command syntax, etc. with a DIY solution. Answer queries around training content, training videos, tutorials, use case samples, etc. with a DIY solution.	Answers questions to problem sets around specific infrastructure configurations, security and compliance, etc.
Economic buyer / manager	n/a	Query for usage reports (usage statistics, list of resources and services, time saved through the IDP, cost information, ROI, etc.) as verbose response.	Verbose answers to value proposition, product, fit for pot. use cases, appl. by industry, ROI, etc.	Verbose answers to value proposition, product, fit for pot. use cases, application by industry, ROI, etc. Guided questionnaire for benchmarking current stage of platform engineering journey.

Figure 11.2: AI changing the future of platform engineering

This figure outlines how AI can be integrated into platform engineering, categorized by who is using it (developers, platform engineers, or decision-makers) and what they are using it for (building configurations, using the platform, learning about it, or getting support).

Implementation complexity

The preceding figure also highlights the varying complexity of implementing these AI solutions. Some use cases, like creating configurations from natural language, are relatively easy to implement. Others, like providing verbose answers to complex economic questions, require more advanced AI capabilities and expertise in LLMs.

AI integration in SDLC stages in self-service portal

AI can be used to enhance different stages of the SDLC, from planning and coding to testing, release, and monitoring. AI can automate tasks, improve efficiency, and provide intelligent assistance throughout the entire process. Imagine a self-service portal powered by AI that acts as your assistant, streamlining your workflow and boosting your productivity. From planning and coding to release management and monitoring, AI transforms how you work, allowing you to focus on what matters most: innovation and delivering exceptional results. The following are the different stages of SDLC where AI can help you:

- **AI for smarter planning**: Imagine AI as your planning assistant, helping you streamline and organize your projects in the self-service portal.

  o **Meeting summaries**: AI automatically generates concise summaries of meetings, highlighting key decisions and action items, so you do not have to sift through lengthy notes.

  o **Issue tracking and prioritization**: AI analyzes and summarizes comments on issue tracking systems, making it easier to understand the context and progress of each issue. It also automatically prioritizes issues and categorizes them, streamlining workflows and ensuring that the most important issues are addressed first.

  o **Test generation**: AI translates user stories into formal acceptance tests, ensuring that the software meets user requirements.

  o **Threat modeling**: AI helps identify potential security risks and vulnerabilities, assisting in the creation of threat models.

  o **Jargon buster**: AI provides clear definitions and explanations for technical terms and company-specific jargon, improving communication and understanding.

- **AI-powered code creation and enhancement**: AI can help developers as a coding companion, write better code, write test cases, and do documentation.

  o **Code generation and improvement**: AI tools assist in writing, understanding, and improving code by providing suggestions, identifying errors, and even generating code snippets.

  o **Automated unit tests**: AI can automatically create unit tests based on your code or natural language descriptions, improving code quality and test coverage.

  o **Design-to-code conversion**: AI can translate your UX designs directly into code, speeding up development and ensuring consistency between design and implementation.

  o **Automated documentation**: AI automatically generates code comments and documentation, making your code easier to understand and maintain.

  o **Vulnerability explanations**: AI provides clear explanations of security vulnerabilities, helping developers understand and fix them effectively.

- **AI-powered verification**: AI can help quality control, meticulously checking developers' code and ensuring it is secure and reliable:

  o **Streamlined code reviews**: AI summarizes code changes and highlights important comments in pull requests, making code reviews faster and more efficient.

  o **Automated vulnerability fixing**: AI automatically identifies and fixes security vulnerabilities in your code, reducing the risk of breaches.

  o **Intelligent test selection**: AI selects the most relevant tests to run, shortening build times and providing faster feedback during continuous integration.

  o **Synthetic test data generation**: AI generates synthetic test data, allowing for more comprehensive testing without relying on sensitive real-world data.

- **AI-powered release management**: AI can help in release management, ensuring your deployments are smooth, reliable, and optimized:

  o **Continuous release verification**: AI continuously monitors and verifies releases, ensuring they meet quality standards and performance requirements.

  o **Experiment analysis**: AI analyzes the results of experiments, helping you understand how different variables affect software performance.

  o **Change impact assessment**: AI assesses the potential impact of code changes, helping you understand the risks and benefits before deploying.

  o **Failure prediction**: AI predicts the likelihood of deployment failures based on factors like code complexity and test results, allowing you to proactively address potential issues.

- o **Automated feature flag management**: AI automatically enables or disables feature flags based on system health and performance, ensuring a smooth user experience.

- **AI-powered configuration management**: The self-service portal manages configuration management and ensures your systems are always setup for optimal performance.

  - o **Automated runbooks**: AI generates automated runbooks for configuring infrastructure and applications, reducing manual effort and ensuring consistency.

  - o **Drift detection and remediation**: AI continuously monitors your systems for configuration drift, automatically correcting any deviations from the desired state.

  - o **Cloud configuration recommendations**: AI recommends optimal cloud configurations based on your application needs and best practices, ensuring you get the most out of your cloud resources.

- **AI-powered monitoring (proactive and intelligent)**: AI in the self-service portal works as a vigilant watchdog, constantly monitoring your systems and proactively addressing issues:

  - o **Anomaly detection and self-healing**: AI analyzes operational data to identify patterns, detect anomalies, and even trigger automated self-healing actions to resolve problems before they impact users.

  - o **Workload optimization**: AI optimizes workload distribution and resource allocation, improving efficiency, reducing costs, and enhancing sustainability.

  - o **Predictive analytics**: AI predicts future system behavior and provides recommendations for proactive intervention to prevent problems and optimize performance.

Platform and AI operations

Platform and AI operations (**PAI-Ops**) represent the evolution of IT operations, driven by the convergence of platform engineering and AI. It signifies a shift towards more intelligent, automated, and efficient management of IT systems and applications.

Key components of a PAI-Ops platform:

- **Application runtime**: This is where your applications live and breathe. PAI-Ops leverages modern technologies like containers and Kubernetes to provide a consistent and reliable environment.

- **Service mesh**: A dedicated layer that manages communication between your applications, ensuring security and reliability.

- **Pipelines**: Automated pipelines that build, test, and deploy your applications quickly and efficiently.

- **Compliance and governance**: Built-in security and compliance measures to protect your data and meet regulatory requirements.

- **IDP orchestration**: A collection of tools that work together to manage and automate your platform.

- **Service catalog**: A curated selection of services and tools that developers can easily access and use.

- **Observability**: Tools and practices that provide deep insights into your applications' performance and health.

- **Data infrastructure**: Ensuring your applications have access to the data they need, including databases and data pipelines.

- **Reporting and dashboards**: Track key metrics related to developer experience and platform performance to continuously improve and optimize your PAI-Ops platform.

Power of PAI-Ops in modern IT

PAI-Ops brings together three key elements to transform IT operations:

- **Platform engineering**:

  o **The foundation**: Platform engineering provides a solid base for PAI-Ops by creating a standardized and robust **internal developer platform** (IDP).

  o **Developer empowerment**: This platform gives developers self-service access to tools and resources, automates workflows, and ensures consistent environments.

  o **Streamlined delivery**: This foundation streamlines software delivery and reduces the burden on IT operations.

- **Artificial intelligence**:

  o **Intelligence boost**: AI supercharges the platform with intelligent automation, predictive analytics, and the ability to automatically fix issues.

  o **AIOps**: AI is used to analyze data, identify patterns, and automate tasks, making IT operations smarter and more efficient.

  o **Continuous improvement**: AI drives continuous improvement by optimizing performance, detecting anomalies, and quickly identifying the root cause of problems.

- **Operations**:

  - o **Day-to-day management**: This focuses on the daily tasks of managing and maintaining IT systems and applications.

  - o **AI-powered efficiency**: By leveraging the AI-powered platform, routine tasks are automated, efficiency is improved, and human error is reduced.

  - o **Proactive operations**: This enables proactive monitoring, faster responses to incidents, and optimal use of resources.

Real-life examples of PAI-Ops in action

Here is how PAI-Ops can be applied to solve common IT challenges:

- **Smart alerts**: AI sifts through system logs and metrics to identify critical alerts and filter out noise, enabling faster incident response.

- **Self-healing systems**: AI automatically resolves common issues and performs routine maintenance, freeing up the operations team for more strategic work.

- **Peak performance**: AI continuously monitors application performance and identifies opportunities for optimization, ensuring a smooth and responsive user experience.

- **Enhanced security**: AI strengthens your security posture by detecting anomalies, identifying vulnerabilities, and automating security tasks.

- **Cost efficiency**: AI analyzes resource usage and recommends cost saving measures, like right-sizing instances and optimizing cloud spending.

Platform engineering and AI case studies

Platform engineering, AI, and **retrieval augmented generation (RAG)** are powerful concepts that, when combined, can significantly enhance the capabilities and efficiency of modern software development and IT operations. Let us explore how these concepts intertwine:

- **Platform engineering**:

  - o **The foundation**: Platform engineering provides the groundwork by creating self-service platforms with automated workflows and standardized environments. This empowers developers to build and manage applications with greater efficiency.

- **Artificial intelligence**:

  - o **The brain**: AI brings intelligence and automation to the platform. It automates tasks, optimizes resources, enhances security, and provides valuable insights to developers.

- **Retrieval augmented generation**:

  o **The knowledge**: RAG gives AI access to a vast library of information, allowing it to generate more accurate, comprehensive, and up-to-date responses.

- **Synergy of platform engineering, AI, and RAG**:

  o **AI-powered IDPs**: AI can be integrated into IDPs to automate tasks, provide intelligent recommendations, and enhance observability. RAG can further enhance these AI capabilities by providing context and access to external knowledge.

  o **Improved developer experience**: AI and RAG can personalize the developer experience by providing tailored recommendations, intelligent assistance, and access to relevant information.

  o **Enhanced platform capabilities**: AI and RAG can enhance platform capabilities by enabling features like intelligent alerting, automated remediation, performance optimization, and security management.

  o **Data-driven decision making**: AI and RAG can analyze platform usage data and provide insights to drive continuous improvement and optimize platform performance.

The combination of platform engineering, AI, and RAG represents a powerful approach to building and managing modern software development and IT operations. By leveraging these technologies, organizations can create more efficient, reliable, and developer-friendly platforms that drive innovation and business success.

RAG case study for the fintech domain

The fintech industry faces increasing pressure to deliver secure, reliable, and high-performing digital financial services. Customers expect seamless online transactions, real-time data access, and robust security measures. Any downtime or performance degradation can erode trust and impact revenue.

The following is the approach to building an AI-integrated IDP for a fintech company:

- **Identify critical fintech services**: Identify the core services and applications crucial for business operations. This includes payment processing systems, trading platforms, customer onboarding portals, fraud detection systems, and regulatory reporting applications.

- **Develop domain-specific RAGs**: Define KPIs and golden signals specific to the fintech domain. This may include:

  o **Transaction latency**: Measure the time taken to process transactions, ensuring quick and efficient service.

- o **Uptime and availability**: Track the availability of critical systems to minimize service disruptions.

- o **Fraud detection rate**: Monitor the accuracy and effectiveness of fraud detection systems.

- o **API response times**: Measure the responsiveness of APIs used for integrations with other financial institutions and services.

- o **Regulatory compliance**: Track adherence to regulatory requirements and reporting obligations.

- **Create a platform abstraction layer**: Build a platform that abstracts the complexity of the underlying infrastructure and provides a standardized interface for developers to access resources and services.

- **Empower developers with self-service**: Create a developer portal with self-service access to tools, documentation, APIs, and sandboxes for testing and deploying fintech applications.

- **Standardize development environments** Standardize development environments and tools to ensure consistency, reduce integration issues, and accelerate development cycles.

- **Implement comprehensive observability** Integrate monitoring and observability tools to track golden signals, analyze performance data, and proactively identify potential issues.

- **Automate CI/CD pipelines**: Automate the build, testing, and deployment of fintech applications to ensure rapid and reliable releases.

- **Prioritize security and compliance**: Implement robust security measures, including encryption, authentication, and authorization, to protect sensitive financial data and comply with industry regulations.

The following are the benefits:

- **Enhanced customer experience**: By focusing on RAGs, the platform aims to deliver a seamless and reliable digital financial experience.

- **Improved operational efficiency**: Self-service tools and standardized environments streamline development and operations.

- **Reduced risk and fraud**: Robust security measures and real-time monitoring minimize the risk of fraud and security breaches.

- **Accelerated innovation**: Automated CI/CD pipelines enable faster delivery of new features and services.

- **Increased agility and scalability**: The platform provides the flexibility to adapt to changing market demands and scale operations efficiently.

This case study illustrates how platform engineering, combined with a focus on fintech-specific RAGs, can help organizations build and deliver secure, reliable, and high-performing financial services that meet the evolving needs of customers and drive business growth.

RAG case study for the gaming domain

The gaming industry faces unique challenges in delivering highly reliable, low-latency, and scalable online gaming experiences to millions of players worldwide. Issues like lag, downtime, and security breaches can significantly impact player satisfaction and revenue.

The following is the approach to building an AI-integrated IDP for a gaming company:

- **Identify critical gaming services**: Pinpoint the core services that are essential for a smooth gaming experience. This includes game servers, matchmaking systems, in-game stores, chat functionality, and authentication services.

- **Develop domain-specific RAGs**: Define KPIs and golden signals specific to gaming. This may include metrics like:

    o **Latency**: Measure network latency to ensure a responsive gaming experience.

    o **Server tick rate**: Track the frequency of server updates to maintain smooth gameplay.

    o **Player connections**: Monitor the number of concurrent players and connection stability.

    o **Matchmaking time**: Measure the time it takes for players to find matches.

    o **Error rates**: Track the frequency of in-game errors and disconnections.

- **Create a platform abstraction layer**: Build a platform that abstracts the underlying infrastructure complexity, providing developers with a standardized interface to interact with game services and resources.

- **Empower developers with self-service**: Create a developer portal with self-service access to tools, documentation, SDKs, and APIs for integrating RAGs into their games and services.

- **Standardize game development environments**: Standardize development environments and tools to ensure consistency and reduce integration issues across game development teams.

- **Implement real-time observability**: Integrate real-time monitoring and observability tools to track golden signals, visualize performance data, and proactively identify potential issues.

- **Automate CI/CD pipelines**: Automate the build, testing, and deployment of game updates and new features to accelerate release cycles and ensure quality.

- **Prioritize security and anti-cheat measures**: Implement robust security measures and anti-cheat systems to protect game integrity and player data.

The benefits are as follows:

- **Improved player experience**: By focusing on RAGs, the platform aims to deliver a smoother, more reliable, and enjoyable gaming experience.

- **Increased developer productivity**. Self-service tools and standardized environments empower developers to work more efficiently.

- **Enhanced scalability and performance**: The platform enables dynamic scaling of game services to handle fluctuations in player demand.

- **Proactive issue resolution:** Real-time observability allows for quick identification and resolution of performance bottlenecks and potential issues.

- **Faster time to market**: Automated CI/CD pipelines accelerate the delivery of game updates and new features.

This case study demonstrates how platform engineering, combined with a focus on gaming-specific RAGs, can help game developers create and maintain high-quality online gaming experiences that delight players and drive business success.

Conclusion

This chapter has explored the future of platform engineering, emphasizing the transformative role of emerging technologies like AI/ML, edge computing, blockchain, and XR. We have seen how these technologies can enhance automation, optimize performance, improve developer experience, and drive innovation. The journey of platform engineering, from its early days in data centers to the intelligent future of AI-infused platforms, highlights the continuous quest for efficiency, scalability, and developer empowerment.

Organizations and platform engineering teams must embrace these advancements, upskill their capabilities, and strategically integrate AI/ML to build and manage modern platforms that meet the evolving needs of businesses and developers alike. The future of platform engineering promises exciting possibilities, and by staying ahead of the curve, organizations can leverage these technologies to accelerate software delivery, drive innovation, and achieve greater business success.

Exercises

1. What is the significance of AI-powered automation in platform engineering?

2. How does edge computing enhance the resilience of a platform?

3. What are the key benefits of integrating blockchain technology into a platform?

4. How can AI be integrated into the SDLC process of platform engineering?

5. What are the key trends shaping the evolution of platform engineering?

6. What are some real-world examples of AI-powered tools used in platform engineering?

7. How can AI be applied within a platform engineering context, considering different user personas and use cases?

8. What are the key components of a PAI-Ops platform?

Answers

1. AI-powered automation plays a crucial role in platform engineering by taking over repetitive tasks, optimizing resource allocation, and even predicting and preventing potential problems. This frees up platform engineers to focus on more strategic and creative work, improving efficiency and innovation.

2. Edge computing increases platform resilience by distributing workloads across multiple edge locations. If one location experiences an outage, the others can seamlessly take over, preventing disruptions and downtime. This ensures that services remain available to users even in the face of localized failures.

3. Blockchain technology offers several benefits for platforms, including enhanced security and trust, decentralization, and tokenized incentive systems. Its immutability and transparency foster trust among users, while decentralization increases resilience and reduces reliance on centralized infrastructure. Tokenization can incentivize user participation and contribution to the platform's ecosystem.

4. AI can be integrated into the SDLC process of platform engineering in various ways, including intelligent automation, enhanced code quality and security, optimized resource management, improved developer experience, and continuous learning and improvement. AI can automate tasks, provide recommendations, enhance observability, and optimize resource allocation throughout the SDLC.

5. The evolution of platform engineering is driven by several key trends, including increasing automation, the shift to cloud computing, AI-driven optimization, and a focus on developer experience. Each stage of platform engineering's development demonstrates a greater emphasis on automation, cloud adoption, and AI/ML integration to improve efficiency, scalability, and developer empowerment.

6. Some examples of AI-powered tools used in platform engineering include GitHub Copilot, Harness, and Dynatrace. GitHub Copilot uses AI to assist with code generation, Harness employs AI for continuous delivery and automated deployments, and Dynatrace leverages AI for application performance monitoring and anomaly detection.

7. AI can be applied in various ways depending on the user persona (developer, platform engineer, economic buyer) and the specific use case (creating

configurations, using the IDP, enablement/documentation, and support). AI can assist in creating configurations, providing personalized recommendations, enhancing the IDP's usability, and offering intelligent support and documentation.

8. A PAI-Ops platform combines platform engineering, AI, and operations to create a more intelligent and automated approach to IT management. Key components include the application runtime, service mesh, pipelines, compliance and governance, IDP orchestration, service catalog, observability, data infrastructure, and reporting and dashboards.

References

1. **https://platformengineering.org/blog/ai-is-changing-the-future-of-platform-engineering-are-you-ready**

Join our Discord space

Join our Discord workspace for latest updates, offers, tech happenings around the world, new releases, and sessions with the authors:

https://discord.bpbonline.com

Index

E